Mao Zedong Thought

Historical Materialism Book Series

The Historical Materialism Book Series is a major publishing initiative of the radical left. The capitalist crisis of the twenty-first century has been met by a resurgence of interest in critical Marxist theory. At the same time, the publishing institutions committed to Marxism have contracted markedly since the high point of the 1970s. The Historical Materialism Book Series is dedicated to addressing this situation by making available important works of Marxist theory. The aim of the series is to publish important theoretical contributions as the basis for vigorous intellectual debate and exchange on the left.

The peer-reviewed series publishes original monographs, translated texts, and reprints of classics across the bounds of academic disciplinary agendas and across the divisions of the left. The series is particularly concerned to encourage the internationalization of Marxist debate and aims to translate significant studies from beyond the English-speaking world.

For a full list of titles in the Historical Materialism Book Series available in paperback from Haymarket Books, visit:
https://www.haymarketbooks.org/series_collections/1-historical-materialism

Mao Zedong Thought

Wang Fanxi

Edited, translated, and with an introduction by
Gregor Benton

Haymarket Books
Chicago, IL

First published in 2020 by Brill Academic Publishers, The Netherlands
© 2020 Koninklijke Brill NV, Leiden, The Netherlands

Published in paperback in 2021 by
Haymarket Books
P.O. Box 180165
Chicago, IL 60618
773-583-7884
www.haymarketbooks.org

ISBN: 978-1-64259-422-5

Distributed to the trade in the US through Consortium Book Sales and Distribution (www.cbsd.com) and internationally through Ingram Publisher Services International (www.ingramcontent.com).

This book was published with the generous support of Lannan Foundation and Wallace Action Fund.

Special discounts are available for bulk purchases by organizations and institutions. Please call 773-583-7884 or email info@haymarketbooks.org for more information.

Cover design and art by David Mabb. Cover art is a detail of Rhythm 69 no.65, (William Morris Block Printed Pattern Book, with Hans Richter Storyboard, developed from Hans Richter's 'Rhythmus 25' and Kazimir Malevich's film script 'Artistic and Scientific Film – Painting and Architectural Concerns – Approaching the New Plastic Architectural System'), paint and wallpaper on canvas (2007).

Printed in the United States.

10 9 8 7 6 5 4 3 2 1

Library of Congress Cataloging-in-Publication data is available.

Contents

Notes on the Translation   VII
Abbreviated Source Designations   IX

Introduction   1
   Gregor Benton

Mao Zedong Thought

   Preface   43

   Foreword   46

1   The Personality Cult   49

2   The Sources and Components of Mao Zedong Thought   66

3   Mao Zedong Thought and 'Mao Zedong Thought'   86

4   A Brilliant Tactician   101

5   A Middling Strategist (Part 1)
   New Democracy and Permanent Revolution   129

6   A Middling Strategist (Part 2)
   Armed Revolution and Revolutionary Strategy   150

7   Theory and Practice   172

8   Literature and Art   194

9   Self-Reliance and Communism in One Country   231

10   Mao in History   266

   Appendix 1: Seven Theses on Socialism and Democracy (1957)   275

Appendix 2: Thinking in Solitude (1957)   277

Appendix 3: On the 'Great Proletarian Cultural Revolution'   293

Appendix 4: The 'Criticize Lin Biao, Criticize Confucius' Campaign (1974)   300

Bibliography   305
Index   308

Notes on the Translation

This translation is shorter than the original Chinese by around one third. Wang often talked with me about translating this book into English to 'present our experience to foreigners.'[1] While he was alive, other priorities prevented me from doing so, but now that I am retired and my desk is almost cleared, I finally have the time to realise his wish. Would he have been prepared to suffer such a heavy cut to this his favourite book? I imagine that he would, if cutting it was the only way to convince a foreign publisher to bring out a volume that was, after all, written more than half a century ago. The principles by which I pruned the text were to cut or shorten bits that seemed ephemeral or relevant only to debates current at the time the book was written (the early 1960s); remove some references of interest only to a Chinese readership; and tighten up the writing, by abridging bits that struck me as repetitious or argued in unnecessary detail and to excessive length. (Wang himself concedes in the Preface that the book is marred in some places by repetition and other imperfections, mainly because its writing was interrupted by frequent illness.) Have I preserved the essentials of his argument intact? Most readers will have to take my word for it that I have, but specialists in Chinese history and politics who would like to know what the book looked like before revising can refer to the original Chinese work, which has been published repeatedly in Taiwan and Hong Kong and has long circulated on the Chinese Mainland.

The Italian saying *traduttore, traditore* (translator, traitor) is often used to intimate the conflict a translator faces between being true to an original text and accommodating it to the needs of a target audience. Peter Ives, in his discussion of Gramsci's concept of translation, reminds us that translation 'is not a technical activity [but] requires normative judgment.'[2] Does my judgment qualify me not just to translate but to shorten and condense Wang's work, in the interests of communicability, while staying faithful to its core arguments? I was Wang's friend and associate for many years, and I am closely familiar with his political opinions and his attitudes. Where necessary, I consulted friends about the meaning of particular words and phrases, and they generously took the time to propose solutions to my difficulties. Wang is, perhaps fortunately for me, no longer here to say yes or no to what I've done. However, had he been, I like to think he would have accepted my excisions in the spirit in which I made

---

1 Lenin at the Third Congress of the Comintern in 1921. Gramsci translated Lenin's 'present' as 'translate,' implying that 'presentation' is more than lateral transmission.
2 Ives 2004, pp. 101–3.

them – to preserve the integrity of his thoughts while spreading them to a new generation of readers, in the belief that it would be intolerable to deprive non-Chinese speakers interested in revolution in general and the Chinese Revolution in particular of access to a work so rich in painfully acquired insight.

Abbreviated Source Designations

Editions of works regularly cited by Wang are given in the footnotes using the abbreviations below. Other citations are presented wherever possible using the standard author-date system.

CW   V.I. Lenin, *Collected Works*, Moscow: Progress Publishers, various dates.
MECW Karl Marx and Frederick Engels, *Collected Works*, London: Lawrence and Wishart, various dates.
W   Joseph Stalin, *Works*, Moscow: Foreign Languages Publishing House, various dates.
SW   Mao Zedong, *Selected Works*, Beijing: Foreign Languages Press, 1961–5.

Editor's Introduction

Gregor Benton

Wang Fanxi, a leader of the Chinese Trotskyists, wrote this book on Mao more than fifty years ago, while in exile in the tiny Portuguese colony of Macao across the water from Hong Kong. The sources at his disposal were limited and not necessarily reliable, for Mao texts published in Beijing at the time were highly selective and doctored to make Mao seem infallible, and their originals were not generally available. *Mao* is an analytical history that does not try to compete in coverage and detail with narrative studies by historians. Its strength lies less in describing events in Mao's life than in explaining Maoism and setting out Wang's view on it as a political movement and a current of thought within the Marxist tradition to which both Wang and Mao belonged. An extended argumentative essay with a clear and provoking thesis, the book has stood the test of time since its writing, while more descriptive studies of a similar age have been made redundant by new findings.

Wang was not just an observer of the Chinese Revolution but an active (though ill-starred) participant in it. Like Mao, he was a veteran member of the Chinese Communist party (CCP), and therefore well qualified to comment on Mao's political career. In 1949, his Trotskyist party sent him away from Shanghai to coordinate its work from Hong Kong, a place of supposed safety, but in Hong Kong he was arrested almost immediately by the colonial authorities and deported to Macao, even before the Maoists had netted up his comrades back in China. He spent much of his early exile in Macao pondering on where he and his fellow-Trotskyists had gone wrong after founding their movement in 1931, as well as exploring Maoism's strengths and weaknesses. His account is fair and even-handed, despite his political differences with Mao and Mao's persecution of the Trotskyists, both before and after 1949. This balance was unusual at the time. Where Wang saw both good and bad in Mao, most studies on him in the early 1960s, an age of extremes, were more polarised.

Mao's story is already familiar to historians and even general readers, but Wang is, by comparison, unknown outside the narrowest circles. In this introduction I therefore look at the unknown Wang rather than at the well-known Mao, to provide a setting within which to understand Wang's thinking and to unveil something of his character, before going on to discuss his *Mao*.

1   Wang's Life: A Brief Sketch

Wang was born in Xiashi in Haining county, Zhejiang province, on March 16, 1907, four years before the overthrow of the Qing dynasty (1644–1911) and the birth of the Republic in 1911 and twenty years before the end of warlordism and the establishment by Chiang Kai-shek of a new Nationalist government in Nanjing. His original name was Wang Wenyuan, but he went under many aliases, pennames, and party names. To his friends, he was Uncle Gen, an abbreviation of one of his political names, Lian*gen*.

He described his birthplace as 'a strange mixture of backwardness and enlightenment' – culturally backward but politically enlightened and generally economically buoyant, because of the local dominance of commercial capital and the town's role as a regional rice market.

Wang's early schooling was mainly in Confucianism, and his teachers at the time were respected members of the local gentry. However, a coup happened in the local educational inspectorate under the Republic in 1919, and new teachers were brought in to replace the recalcitrant Confucians. These newcomers had been trained in the spirit of the New Cultural Movement led, in Beijing, by Chen Duxiu, Wang's future mentor and comrade. They removed the tablet to Confucius from the assembly room and Confucian texts from the curriculum, and imported a new teaching style, modern subjects, a new relationship between teachers and students, and new democratic politics.

Wang's father was a minor member of the scholar-gentry class and a merchant. He sent Wang to study commerce after his son's graduating from primary school. However, the new outlook Wang had acquired in his later schooling after 1919 emboldened him to resist his father. He was eventually expelled from Hangzhou Commercial Middle School, a place of mental torture for him, after going on strike against the Principal. Unexpectedly, his father allowed him to transfer to an ordinary middle school. The father then died, leaving Wang free to follow his own lights.

At the new school, some students embraced the radical politics that spread across China after the May Fourth Movement of 1919 (an outcome of the radical New Culture Movement that arose around 1915), but they did not at first include Wang, whose interests were literary rather than political. He believed in 'study for study's sake,' and was more a nationalist than a socialist. However, all this changed as a result of the May Thirtieth Movement of 1925, when workers emerged as a major factor in Chinese politics. May Thirtieth was also a watershed in the development of the CCP, which had previously struggled to assert itself. Wang forgot his attachment to the 'cause of learning' and threw himself into political activity. Harassed by conservative local authorities, he left

Hangzhou for Beijing, already committed to supporting Chen Duxiu's left-wing positions. In Beijing, he gained entry to Peking University, a radical hotbed at the time.

At first he lived a Bohemian life in Beijing, contributing to famous literary journals like Lu Xun and Zhou Zuoren's *Yusi* ('Threads of talk'). However, within weeks he had made the passage from 'Bohemian scribbler' to soldier of the revolution by joining the communist party, along with other students. Though nominally enrolled in the Department of Letters, from then on he wrote next to nothing of a literary kind, an abstention he maintained right up until the 1950s. Other writers in his class also joined the revolution. Among them were Wang Shiwei and Zhang Guangren (better known as Hu Feng). So, by coincidence, Wang's class contained three of the CCP's later dissidents and its two best-known literary martyrs.

Wang's greatest concern, which he shared with other student Communists, was his lack of 'even a rudimentary grasp of theory'.[1] This was due to the suppression of Marxist writings in Chinese – in any case few in number at the time – by the then warlord regime in Beijing, but also to the activist orientation of the party top, which saw 'too much study' as 'good only for spouting hot air'.[2] Thirsty for action and too poor to buy a winter gown, Wang gave up his studies and went south to subtropical Guangzhou, where the revolution against imperialism and warlordism was in full spate, and where simple Marxist texts were available in heaps. Wang was repelled by the pleasure-seeking and job-seeking of many of the Communists he met in Guangzhou. Although dazzled by the workers' movement and the Guangzhou-Hong Kong general strike of 1925–6, which paralysed local trade and industry, he returned on party orders to Beijing, hardened and even more determined to make revolution.

Wang was immediately pitched into the thick of revolutionary work in Beijing, and no longer had time to study Marxism. Only two books of a theoretical character circulated in the party at the time – the first part of Bukharin's *ABC of Communism* and Julian Borchardt's *The People's Marx*. The first was relatively easy to grasp but the latter was beyond most members' comprehension. Wang and his comrades were 'working away in an almost light-heartedly optimistic frame of mind, under a regime [in Beijing] of intensifying terror',[3] inspired by an ideology they barely understood. They were unequipped, 'either emo-

---

1 Wang Fan-hsi 1980, p. 20.
2 Wang Fan-hsi 1980, p. 18.
3 Wang Fan-hsi 1980, p. 31.

tionally or ideologically,' for the events of April 1927, when the execution of the Communist leader Li Dazhao in Beijing coincided with an even greater bloodbath in Shanghai, where Chiang Kai-shek started to slaughter tens of thousands of the Communists who up to then had been his allies against the warlords. Wang and his comrades sought an explanation for the collapse of the alliance, which had endured mainly at the insistence of the Stalinists in Moscow, but they received none, other than an assurance that the revolutionary tide was still high but under a new Guomindang leader (Wang Jingwei) and in a new place (Wuhan).

Wang Fanxi and other endangered cadres were sent to Wuhan, where they resumed work, but Wang Jingwei soon turned against the Communists. Wang Fanxi was arrested for writing an article criticising Wang Jingwei and was sent to gaol, probably the first Communist gaoled in Wuhan. Released after the intercession of well-connected friends, he was then ordered to join an exodus to Moscow. Like many other young Communists, he would have preferred to take up arms in China, the path followed by Mao.

In Moscow, Wang and scores of other exiles went to study at the Communist University for the Toilers of the East. Many were disappointed to end up in a political rather than a military school, where they could have learned to bear arms. Hungry for knowledge, they threw themselves on the available political literature. Hundreds of those in Moscow, including Wang, secretly joined the Trotskyists, who they felt best understood the 1927 defeat. They were in any case 'upset by the arbitrary and bureaucratic way in which the Stalinists conducted the inner-party struggle',[4] and instinctively sympathised with the Soviet Opposition. The rebel faction of Chinese students waged its own struggle against the leadership of the 'Moscow branch of the CCP,' which had by then been put by the Russians in the hands of Wang Ming, seen by the Chinese Trotskyists (and, in time, by Mao in China) as a tool of Stalin and a 'red comprador.'

In late 1927 and 1928, a purge of the Chinese Trotskyists in Russia ended in some being expelled from the party and sent back to China. The student body as a whole came under Wang Ming's dictatorship, which policed them by strong-arm methods and bureaucratic tricks. Many of the Trotskyists kept in Russia were liquidated or sent to labour-camps. Some of those sent back remained Trotskyists and began to ally with an incipient China-based Opposition. Those Oppositionists still undercover in Moscow, including Wang, itched to get back

---

4 Wang Fan-hsi 1980, p. 59.

to China to set up a united Trotskyist organisation. Late in 1929, Wang and a score of others, disguised as overseas Chinese merchants, slipped into Shanghai by way of Korea.

Even though Wang and the other returning Trotskyists kept their membership of the Opposition secret, the secret soon got out. However, the party centre was noticeably less interested than the Russians in Soviet factionalism, so for a while it tolerated the presence of Oppositionists among its members. Wang was appointed to serve as Zhou Enlai's aide on the Central Committee. By the time he and the other returners were expelled, they had met up with Communist dissidents in China, including supporters of Chen Duxiu, the recently ousted and now vilified party leader. Chen's view of the situation in China mirrored Trotsky's, and Chen's supporters were already drifting towards Trotskyism. After several months of factional squabbling, caused partly by differences of principle but also by power play and personal ambition, the Chinese Oppositionists put aside their disputes and united under Chen Duxiu, but only after Trotsky's urgent intervention from his place of exile in Turkey. A Unification Conference of the Oppositionists in May 1931 made the fight for a Constituent Assembly – a strategy launched by Trotsky but compatible with Chen Duxiu's view of what needed to be done in the wake of the defeat of the revolution – its central focus.

Within weeks, however, Wang and most of the Oppositionists were behind bars, in some cases extradited by the British from Shanghai's International Settlement into the hands of Chiang Kai-shek's political police. In 1934, Wang was temporarily released and tried to restore the Opposition, but in May 1937 he was rearrested. Wang's 'darkest days' began, and lasted until the autumn of 1937, when Chiang emptied his gaols of political prisoners after the Japanese invasion (Wang was among the last to be freed).

At the start of the war, Chen Duxiu refused to cling to what he called 'Trotsky's old articles.' Inspired by Chen's thinking, Wang tried to infiltrate existing armed forces in order to create a new radical focus for the anti-Japanese resistance. (He rejected Chen's other suggestion, to fight to unite all democratic factions independent of the Guomindang and the CCP.) Wang's way into the army was through Chen's old friends General He Jifeng and Commander Ji Xingwen, heroes of the resistance who had fallen out with Chiang Kai-shek but were still under his general command. Wang's plan was to strengthen He and Ji's efforts by promoting agrarian reform in the areas they garrisoned and revolutionising their troops, but He was relieved of his command (perhaps because of his dealings with Chen Duxiu) and the plan fell through. A few Trotskyists led guerrilla columns in Shandong and Guangdong, but other Trotskyists denounced such ventures as 'military opportunism.'

After the bursting of Chen and Wang's military bubble in Wuhan, Wang returned to Shanghai, where he restored ties to other old comrades, resumed his propaganda work, and translated books by Malraux, Victor Serge, and others. The proudest achievement at this time of Wang and Zheng Chaolin, his close friend and ally in the Trotskyist movement, was to translate Trotsky's *History of the Russian Revolution*, a task that took around one year. But most of the two thousand sets published but not yet sold were burned at the start of the Pacific War in late 1941, to stop the Japanese finding them and taking reprisals against the publisher.

On the eve of the Pacific War, the Chinese Trotskyists, who had united only on Trotsky's insistence, split on how to characterise China's resistance to Japan and on the role of democracy in revolutionary parties. Wang and Zheng argued that China's resistance would remain progressive only as long as it was waged independently of the imperialist powers – once enmeshed in the World War, its progressive aspect would 'dwindle away' and the Trotskyists would have to 'lay more stress on the victory of the revolution than of the war' (234). Wang called this strategy 'victoryism,' a play on Lenin's idea of defeatism in the First World War. The group under Peng Shuzhi, on the other hand, argued that the resistance would remain progressive even if it became caught up in the wider war. This difference was paralleled by another on the role of factions and minorities in the party. Wang and Zheng argued for their right to exist and speak out: Peng said that such activity would violate Leninist norms of organisation. The opposing factions split, never to reunite.

Another major difference between the two groups concerned their attitude to Chen Duxiu, who died in May 1942. In the years leading up to his death, Chen had begun to rethink his attitude to democracy and to equate Stalinism and fascism, unlike Trotsky, who continued until his assassination in 1940 to view the Soviet Union as a 'deformed workers' state.' Chen's switch led Peng to denounce him for 'failing to maintain his integrity in later life.' Wang, however, mourned Chen's death as a blow to the revolution, and fought to restore him to his rightful place in the history of modern China and the Opposition. Wang's toleration of Chen's views on democracy and Stalin and his pledge to learn from them cannot be seen aside from his enduring fight for democracy within the Chinese Opposition.

In the war, the Trotskyists fought to revive the workers' movement in Shanghai, Hong Kong, and elsewhere, but the odds against them were insurmountable. Wang later concluded that they would have done better to devote some forces to the villages and build guerrilla bases like the Maoists. Instead, they suffered blow after blow, at the hands of the Guomindang, the Japanese, and the Maoists.

After the Japanese surrender, the two parts of Chinese Trotskyism carried on down separate paths. Each tried to give shape and direction to the workers' movement that briefly emerged in the immediate post-war years, and each published pamphlets, books, and journals. In 1948, Peng's group set up the Revolutionary Communist Party of China (RCP), and in 1948 Wang and Zheng's group founded the Internationalist Workers Party of China (IWP), both tiny. Meanwhile, in the countryside, Mao's army was approaching a definitive victory over Chiang Kai-shek. The RCP was founded just as the Maoist People's Liberation Army was about to take Nanjing, Wang and Zheng's while it was marching on Shanghai. Both Trotskyist parties took last-minute measures to meet the challenges ahead – the IWP by staying in China, splitting into discrete units, and going underground as far as possible, the RCP by transferring its central committee and other leaders to Hong Kong. In the IWP, only Wang Fanxi was sent into exile.[5] Although no less moved than Zheng by 'the spirit of St Peter' (who had stayed in Rome to be crucified), in May 1949 Wang was sent by his comrades to Hong Kong, beyond the CCP's reach, where it was hoped he would be able to establish a co-ordinating point from which to collaborate with Zheng in Shanghai. But the plan failed, for Wang was arrested by colonial officials in his supposedly 'safe' place and deported to Macao, even before the Trotskyists in Shanghai were swept up by the Maoist authorities (in December 1952) and sent to prison for the next few decades.

In Hong Kong, across the Pearl River Delta from Macao, Trotskyist remnants found it difficult to survive harassment by the colonial government. After Wang's deportation, Peng Shuzhi and others fled to Vietnam, whence to France and, later, the United States. In the early 1950s, some Trotskyists helped lead workers' strikes in the colony, but this led to further crackdowns on them.

In the 1950s, Wang in Macao, Peng Shuzhi in various places, and the Trotskyists left behind in China (before their arrest) and in Hong Kong wrote articles and pamphlets trying to explain the Maoist victory and the nature of the Maoist state – was it bourgeois, petty-bourgeois, or proletarian? But their political fragmentation and geographic dispersal made it hard for them to engage in productive debate.

In time, the movement in Hong Kong became inactive. However, in the late 1960s youngsters in Hong Kong caught up in the worldwide youth revolt came under the influence of China's Cultural Revolution. Anarchists and Maoists led the Hong Kong movement, but in the early 1970s exiled Trotskyist leaders,

---

5 Eventually, other IWP members, including Lou Guohua, Wang Guoquan, and Sun Liangsi, also ended up in exile.

including Wang and Peng, began influencing it from outside. Trotskyist publications reappeared in the colony, calling for class struggle, internationalism, the overthrow of the Maoist dictatorship on the Mainland, and true democracy and an end to colonialism in Hong Kong. This Trotskyist resurgence alarmed pro-Beijing forces in the colony, whose leaders denounced the Trotskyists as national traitors, an echo of the campaigns of the 1930s and 1940s. The movement met with new crackdowns by the colonial state. Wang repeatedly intervened in it from across the water in Macao, and gained a small following.

Wang paid occasional furtive and illegal visits to Hong Kong, but he continued to live and work in Macao, where he was eventually threatened by grave danger. After his deportation from Hong Kong in 1950, he had spent most of his free time writing and receiving visits from his comrades in Hong Kong and overseas. His writings included memoirs, pamphlets, plays, film-scripts – and this book on Mao. He also translated books on revolutionary themes from various languages, to make money – some of his invariably elegant translations appeared under self-disparaging pseudonyms such as Hui Qian (pronounced *wei qian*, 'for money,' in his native dialect), at a time when translation was still highly prized in China as a literary form. However, he earned his livelihood principally by teaching in a Macao school. In the Cultural Revolution of 1966–9, local Maoists became increasingly powerful in the colony, although it remained nominally under Portuguese rule. From behind the scenes, the Maoists threatened measures against Chinese dissidents who criticised Beijing. Wang lost his teaching job because of Maoist pressure, and was in danger of being whisked across the border into the hands of the Chinese authorities. To save him from that possible fate, in 1975, with the help of Tariq Ali, Ralph Miliband, and others, I brought him to Leeds, where I was then teaching. For the next quarter of a century, Wang and I collaborated on a series of translations of books and articles by him, Zheng Chaolin, Chen Duxiu, and others. In Leeds, Wang kept up a constant commentary, latterly in diary form (published posthumously in Hong Kong), on current affairs, the Fourth International, his daily life, and his friendships.[6]

In Leeds, Wang befriended some radical students from Taiwan, principally Cheng Lingfang and Qian Yongxiang, and produced a pamphlet with them on the Taiwan question. He also won a following among young British Chinese and became a close friend of the Chinatown activist Jabez Lam. A constant stream of young men and women visited him, and they set up a series of radical journals to shake up Chinatown. Wang continued to correspond with his comrades

---

6 Wang Fanxi 2004.

in Hong Kong, who also visited him in Leeds. Old and new comrades associated with the Fourth International in the United States and Paris, like Pierre Rousset, Pierre Frank, and others, visited him and corresponded with him. From the point of view of writing and publishing, his years in Leeds were highly productive, although his advancing age (he was 68 when he arrived in England) gradually slowed him down.

The crowning moment of Wang's British exile came in June 1979, when news arrived out of the blue of the release of Zheng Chaolin, unrepentant and unbowed after 27 years in gaol under Mao (on top of the seven he had earlier served under Chiang Kai-shek), together with eleven other Trotskyist survivors. The two old men resumed a lively correspondence, finally implementing the strategy of *liying waihe* (coordinating from inside and outside) they had planned in 1949. The correspondence continued until Zheng's death in 1998, although Zheng's increasing blindness made his handwriting ever harder to decipher. At some point, I and the Danish Trotskyist Finn Jensen smuggled a tape-recording by Wang into China and recorded Zheng's reply, enabling them to speak together for the first time in forty years. Both Wang and Zheng liked wearing berets, a fashion they had probably adopted as young men in France and Russia, where – decades before the Che Guevara phenomenon – the beret had revolutionary and bohemian connotations. After Zheng's release in 1979, Wang mailed him a French beret, which he proudly wore in photographs as a declaration of his politics and a sign of his continuing tie to Wang

Neither of the two main sections of the Fourth International, in New York and especially in Paris, paid much attention to the plight of the Trotskyists in Mao's gaols. This was partly because many radicals in the 1960s and the 1970s sympathised with guerrilla war. Orthodox Trotskyists rejected guerrillaism as Maoist, but others, less orthodox, saw it as the way forward for revolutionaries in poor countries. Some non-Chinese Trotskyists in the late 1960s and the early 1970s even had illusions in Mao's Cultural Revolution. Given their focus on China, Vietnam, and Cuba, what sense would it make to draw attention to their gaoled comrades in China, who seemed to many of their European and American comrades to have followed the wrong path? Some questioned whether the Trotskyists in China were still alive. Only the North American Trotskyists mounted a small campaign calling for their release and published a small pamphlet, written by Frank Glass (a British Trotskyist who had lived in Shanghai in the 1930s and was by then living in the United States) and Peng Shuzhi (also by that time resident in the United States).[7] The Trotskyists' eventual release was mainly due to changing political circumstances in

---

7 Li Fu-jen [Frank Glass] and Peng Shu-tse [Peng Shuzhi] 1974.

China. However, a campaign launched in 1977 in Leeds by Wang and me may have helped jog the memory of some CCP leaders regarding the Trotskyists' continuing imprisonment, especially that of Zheng Chaolin, who had been a fellow student in France in the early 1920s of China's newly rehabilitated leader Deng Xiaoping. Our campaign led to Zheng's naming as political prisoner of the month by Amnesty International. His imprisonment was taken up by the mainstream press in several countries.[8]

A small group of veteran Trotskyists continued their activities in Hong Kong in Wang's final years. Lou Guohua was part of the correspondence between Wang and Zheng and acted as their go-between. Other Chinese Trotskyists who had become politically inactive and started businesses continued to support Wang and Zheng financially when necessary. But Wang's needs were few, and after he began to receive social benefits in England (having long exceeded pensionable age), he was even able because of his own extreme frugality to send money to his family in Shanghai.

2 Wang's Family

Wang's father was a minor gentry man and a failing merchant, disparaged by the established gentry. To spare his sons the same ignominy, he decided to give them an education in commerce. Wang, the younger son by six years, did not share his father's aspirations. 'I was very unlike my father,' he wrote. 'I think I must have been born an idealist. As a child, I had loved novels of heroism, and I adored a great-uncle who had been in the army and had told me about his father's adventures fighting for the Taipings' (nineteenth-century peasant rebels against the Qing).[9]

Wang's elder brother took responsibility for supporting the family and vowed to restore its fortunes after the father's death in 1924. When Wang said he intended to sit the university examinations in Beijing, his brother approved, seeing his younger brother's graduation as part of his own grand plan for the family. When Wang abandoned books for party organising, the brothers' relations cooled for years. However, they were later reconciled, and the elder brother bought a house for Wang's family in Shanghai, where his dependants lived for nearly sixty years.

---

8 Gregor Benton, 'Teng's [Deng's] Comrade Still Behind Bars,' in the International Edition of *The Guardian, Le Monde*, and *The Washington Post*, November 9, 1977.
9 Wang Fan-hsi 1980, p. 4.

After Wang's transfer to Moscow in 1927, following the defeat of the revolution in China, he met and married his first wife, Ye Nairen, also called Ye Ying. Women made up a small fraction of the Chinese students in Moscow, and the male students competed for their affections. One of Wang's rivals for Ye Ying was the Stalinist leader Wang Ming, her fellow provincial, who controlled the CCP's Moscow branch. After Wang Fanxi's return to Shanghai and during his imprisonment in Suzhou in 1931–4, Ye Ying left him for a Guomindang officer. The couple had two sons before their break-up, one (Ye Sen) brought up by Ye Ying herself and one (Wang Yuping) brought up by Wang's mother in his hometown. Wang never met Ye Sen again and lost touch with Wang Yuping for decades.[10]

Wang's second wife, Ma Yusheng, was a non-political woman who bore him two daughters, Wang Fenggang and Wang Yanqi. Ma Yusheng was forced to 'divorce' Wang in 1957 (when he was in exile in Macao), after the start of an anti-rightist campaign in China. The authorities sent her to Macao to get Wang back to China, but he refused to go. (Subsequently, for whatever reason, the order to divorce was not enforced.) Ms Ma took care of the family alone, for more than fifty years. The couple's link was renewed in 1978, with the help of Lou Guohua, who had been similarly abandoned by his first wife while in prison and had also subsequently married a non-political woman. Starting in 1978, Wang, in Leeds, did his best to support his wife and family materially. His wife died in 2005, and a joint burial with Wang in Shanghai was arranged by Wang's daughter in 2007.

The disruption of Wang's second marriage, his loss of contact until late in the century with his children, and the continuing imprisonment or dispersal under surveillance of his comrades in China severed his most important relationships. However, he stayed in touch by letter with his comrades in Hong Kong – for a while, a dwindling band, but later, starting in the 1960s, revived by newcomers from a younger generation of radicals. He also had many non-political friends in Hong Kong and Macao, with whom he continued to correspond after his move to England. Most of the new friends he made in Leeds starting in 1975 were young people from Hong Kong, Taiwan, and China and young British Chinese, but he also made many new non-Chinese friends.

In the 1990s, Wang was contacted privately by Mainland officials, who urged him to return to China and live out his final years together with his family and friends. During his fifty years of separation from his family, he had long

---

10   Wang Yuping visited his father in Leeds in 1988 (see Pan Huilian, 'Zhejiang Haining fang Wang Fanxi zhi zi' ['A visit to Wang Fanxi's son in Haining in Zhejiang'], http://octrev.mysrvnet.com/238/238_c66.htm, downloaded March 10, 2017; also published in *Qianshao yuekan*, May 2015, pp. 94–5).

dreamed of a reunion, but he set as a precondition the full political rehabilitation (they had already received a civic rehabilitation) of Chen Duxiu and the Trotskyists, thus chiming with Zheng Chaolin's letters of appeal to Party Congresses after 1979. Neither he nor Zheng received an answer.

3 A Communist of a Different Sort

Apart from a brief spell of liberal approbation during the Japanese War, when they were widely portrayed as mild agrarian reformers, the Chinese Communists were reviled for years (especially after the start of the Cold War) in the mainstream Western media, as monsters, as bad as if not worse than Stalin and the Bolsheviks. Trotsky and his followers have been similarly vilified, particularly because of their promotion of violent revolution and their rejection of alliances with bourgeois parties of the sort that Stalinist parties sometimes practised after 1934 and in the anti-fascist war. The vilification of the Trotskyists extended to China, where it was fuelled by the lies and slanders of the CCP, even though the Chinese Trotskyists have never been in a position to demonstrate their supposed enormity, having been for much of the time behind bars, first under Chiang and then under Mao. But the demonising of the Chinese Trotskyists is belied by their politics and personalities.

As a political force, in practical terms most Chinese Trotskyists were associated from start to finish with socialist revolution allied to democracy. Although Wang did not rule out violence in revolutions, he never gloried in it, and he points out in this book that the need for violence in revolutions is no foregone conclusion. Chen Duxiu began and ended his political life as a revolutionary democrat. The Chinese Trotskyists stood, in the 1930s and the 1940s, on a platform of democratic renewal as the way forward for the revolution. They broke with the CCP not only because of its politics but also because of its suppression of inner-party discussion and – and, especially after October 1949, its despotic rule. Within Chinese Trotskyism, Peng Shuzhi did try to assert the need for 'iron discipline' and 'Lenin-style Bolshevisation' (tenets he had been associated with ever since his leadership of the CCP's Moscow branch in the early 1920s), but Peng's authoritarian view failed to convince the majority, who stood by the old formula.[11]

---

11 According to Kevin Yang (Yang Yang), who has interviewed veteran Trotskyists in Hong Kong, Peng's authoritarian style triggered internal conflicts in the Trotskyist movement in Hong Kong in the early 1950s, between members of the Tsuen Wan branch (dominated by members of Peng's group from Shanghai) and local Trotskyists in the Shao Kei Wan branch.

Most people who met Wang knew him as gentle, serene, and approachable, with none of the brashness and fanaticism often ascribed to leaders of revolutionary movements. He made friends while in England with people of all political persuasions and none. He was careful and polite with acquaintances, spontaneous and unguarded with friends, and a sensitive, receptive listener. He had a rich inner and intellectual life, and was fluent in several languages and widely read in world literature. In another age and place, he would have excelled as a writer or a scholar (just as Zheng Chaolin would have excelled as a philosopher and poet). However, he had none of the academic world's obsession with publication and esteem, and all his writings were published under pseudonyms.

In my introduction to the English translation of his memoir, I described the memoir as follows:

> [I]f self-effacement is a distinguishing feature of the memoir [as opposed to autobiography], then Wang's book has it almost to a fault, since it passes over in complete silence the several deep personal tragedies suffered by its author. To some this may convey the rather forbidding impression of a man of unbending will and single-minded devotion to a cause. Only a closer reading of the text – the generosity of its characterization, the scrupulous balance of its judgment, the complete absence of bitterness, even in the depths of defeat – reveals a person of warmth and compassion, to whom 'nothing human is alien'.[12]

The trials he underwent included months of torture by Chiang Kai-shek's political police, using 'scientific' techniques borrowed from Hitler and Stalin's armoury of repressive means, during his third stay in prison – his 'darkest days.' The tragedies included the joint suicide of his two nephews after their arrest in the early years of the People's Republic of China (PRC).[13]

His friends saw him as saintly (though the antithesis of sanctimonious). This saintliness was a characteristic he shared with Zheng Chaolin, who emerged from decades of imprisonment in 1979 smiling beatifically. Wang more than once used religious symbolism to describe Zheng. While awaiting a probable death sentence in 1931, Zheng was 'like a Buddhist priest who had attained the Way, and who knew beforehand the date of his achievement of nirvana.' When, in 1949, Zheng accepted his comrades' decision that he stay in China rather than go abroad, Wang likened him to St Peter:

---

12 Wang Fan-hsi 1980, pp. ix–x.
13 Personal communication from Xue Feng, February 28, 2017.

Even if we leave aside Zheng Chaolin's other strengths, his Peter-like spirit of martyrdom alone will ensure him a lasting place in the history of the Revolution. Our dilemma was similar in many ways to that of the early Christians under Nero – should we stay in the capital or flee to a safe place? Some approached the question from the point of view of their own fate, others from the point of view of the future of the organization as a whole; but Zheng Chaolin did not wait for a voice from the heavens to ask '*Quo vadis?*': his mind was made up from the very outset.[14]

The truest tribute to Wang's goodness and compassion was by the writer and translator Wang Shiwei, the CCP's first literary martyr, hacked to death in 1947 on a river bank near Yan'an. Wang Shiwei's crime was to criticise the 'dark side' of the CCP's regime in Yan'an (its capital in the Anti-Japanese War) and to have declared that literature must allow dissent and embrace love and 'human feeling.' At his show trial in 1942, fighting for his life before a rabid mob, he said that Wang Fanxi was a 'Communist of humanity'[15] and a person of 'good human nature.'[16]

4   The Production and Publication of Wang's *Mao*

Wang wrote this book between 1961 and 1964. His work was interrupted by bouts of illness, including recurrent tuberculosis, which greatly slowed him. After finishing it, he left the manuscript lying around for years, before finally publishing it in 1973, under circumstances he explains in the Preface.[17] The title calls it a *lungao*, a discursive or interpretive study in draft form rather than a finished study. Readers might disagree with that self-deprecating judgment.

The book appeared at Xinda chuban she ('Sincere Press'), which had been set up in Hong Kong by the Trotskyist Lou Guohua. It has never been published commercially on the Mainland, although it has probably been available there

---

14   Wang Fan-hsi 1980, pp. 167 and 251.
15   Fan Wenlan 1944, pp. 61–9.
16   Huang Changyong 2000, p. 207.
17   A new edition was published in Hong Kong by Xinmiao chuban she and in Taiwan by Lianjie zazhi she, both in 2003. The City University of Hong Kong is currently preparing to bring out yet another edition (together with Wang's 1957 memoir), with a Preface by the Mainland historian Zhu Zheng.

since the 1980s as a 'grey' or 'yellow' book.[18] Grey-yellow books, usually on controversial subjects, were for restricted circulation among high officials, but they reached a broader readership through informal spreading. Copies of Wang's writings, including his book on Mao, were smuggled into China by Hong Kong radicals in the 1970s and 1980s and had an impact on left-wing dissidents in the country, particularly in the South, near Hong Kong. Wang Xizhe, a leading activist in the democracy movement in the 1970s and 1980s, secretly received writings by Wang Fanxi from Hong Kong visitors.[19] Others probably published Wang's book privately, in samizdat form, or copied out excerpts from it and handed them round.[20]

As committed internationalists, Wang Fanxi and other Chinese Trotskyist leaders hoped to influence the Fourth International's debates, to which they believed they could introduce the unique perspective of a Trotskyist movement in a country in which Mao-inflected Stalinists had carried out a revolution – a theoretical impossibility, according to the old Trotskyist definition of Stalinism. Peng Shuzhi, who ended up in Los Angeles and joined the International Secretariat of the Fourth International, was geographically well placed to intervene in international discussions and to disseminate his own view (different from Wang's) across world Trotskyism on the lessons of the Chinese Revolution. He was able to publish a wide range of writings on China and other subjects, both in Chinese and in English, although his output did not include an extended theoretical study of Maoism of the sort Wang aimed for in this book.

However, Wang's book on Mao, despite its intellectual weight, was never read by foreign Trotskyists. Wang was cut off from the outside world in Macao, and had little face-to-face contact with non-Chinese Trotskyists other than the occasional seafarer or British soldier stationed in Hong Kong.[21] The Fourth International was short of translators from Chinese, so although Wang found time to render some of his own articles and statements into English, it was not until the second half of the 1970s, when he reached Leeds, that translations began to flow more freely. Another explanation for Wang's invisibility to his

---

18   See the discussion, below, of Lou Shiyi's role in bringing Wang's book to the attention of other party leaders.
19   Wang Xizhe 1996, ch. 20. Kevin Yang, in a private communication (February 20, 2017), confirms that Lau San-ching (Liu Shanqing) told him that Wang Xizhe received a copy of Wang Fanxi's book on Mao.
20   Lam Chi Leung, private communication, February 20, 2017.
21   In the early 1970s he received visits by Japanese Trotskyists and the British then Trotskyist Tariq Ali, who interviewed him.

comrades overseas was an apparent lack of interest in him on the part of non-Chinese Trotskyist leaders in Europe. They paid him far less attention than Peng received in the United States, especially in the years in which their main focus was on the guerrilla struggle in Latin America and Asia and support for the regimes that emanated from it. They did not offer to support him materially in his old age.

5   Wang and Mao

Wang Fanxi never met or even saw Mao, but he and other Trotskyist leaders naturally followed Mao's political career closely after his rise to power in the CCP in the mid-to-late 1930s. Wang's book on Mao is a study in the roots and meaning of Mao's *sixiang*, a word that means thought in the sense of general intellectual inquiry but is also used to translate the notion of system of thought or (party) ideology. Wang distinguishes between two sorts of Mao Zedong thought, 'actual Mao thought' and Mao Zedong thought as 'a system of thought artificially confected to raise Mao's status in the party and the country to godlike heights, always perfect, always right, and on a par with, or even higher than, Marxism.' It is not always easy to distinguish the one from the other, but where Wang is clearly referring to the latter rather than the former, in the translation I capitalise the word 'thought.'

Wang wrote *Mao* in Macao in the early 1960s, at a time when few primary sources on Mao were freely available anywhere, including China, and even fewer were available to Wang, in exile in a place with few libraries and little scholarly or intellectual life. (For want of alternatives, Wang took most of his Mao citations from the bowdlerised four-volume *Selected Works* published in Beijing.) At the time, there was little in any language, Western or Chinese, on the making of Mao thought, apart from a couple of passages in Edgar Snow's biography[22] and one or two Mainland hagiographies.[23] Today studies abound, in many languages, and some of the themes Wang raised have since been researched more thoroughly and written from far richer sources than were available to him. However, his book remains valuable and effective, not just as part of the historical record in its own right but as the 'comprehensive, objective historical account' he intended it to be and as good analytic and interpretive

---

22   Snow 1968 [1936].
23   Outside China, a notable exception to the early trend of sketchy and biased general studies was Schwartz 1951, rightly hailed as seminal and masterly – but Wang was not able to read it at the time.

history. Despite Wang's own dissatisfaction with it and his concern that it is digressive and unorganised, the study is in fact remarkably coherent and consistent.

Why did Wang write this book at that time? His aim was to explain Mao's victory and thus shed light on the Chinese Trotskyists' own defeat. *Mao* was part of an enterprise he had already begun in privately circulated tracts and in the final chapter, 'Thinking in Solitude,' of the memoir he published (in mimeograph and under the pseudonym Shuang Shan) in 1957.[24] He was also concerned, at a time when the Mao cult was reaching new heights in China, to put Mao's role in perspective and, where necessary, cut him down to size.

But Wang was not absolutely hostile to Mao's politics, in which he found merits as well as demerits. He gave his view on Mao, comparing him with Liu Shaoqi, Mao's practical antithesis, in an essay written during the Cultural Revolution in 1967 (and republished in 1974). The following excerpt helpfully summarises many of the arguments of Wang's book on Mao:

> In many respects, Mao and Liu represent two opposing types. Mao tends towards revolutionary 'romanticism,' Liu towards revolutionary 'realism.' Mao has the air of both a Chinese peasant and an old-style Chinese scholar, while Liu represents the new-style intellectuals, who are closer to the modern workers. Mao's learning is mainly Chinese, while Liu's knowledge of Chinese classical scholarship is quite shallow. Mao began delving into Marxism-Leninism only after establishing a political presence, whereas Liu had received an education in Marxism overseas, before joining the revolution. Mao has great talent and a bold vision, worships heroes, and is deeply imbued with kingly and imperial attitudes, while Liu is cautious and meticulous, close to the common people, and more in tune with democracy. Mao is bold and decisive in action and a brave innovator who emphasises subjective initiative, while Liu is sober, conforms to conventions, and keeps an eye on objective circumstances. Mao has little patience, and considers that the end justifies the means. 'Dogmas' cannot constrain him. Liu advances steadily towards his goal and sees the connection between ends and tactics – principles have a certain hold on him. Mao has all along worked among students, peasants, and soldiers and followed a martial path, while Liu has focused on the workers' movement, party affairs, and planning and organising the party

---

24 See Appx 1. Wang's memoir has been republished several times in Chinese, twice in English (by Oxford University Press and, in a revised and extended edition, by Columbia University Press), and in French, German, and Japanese.

machine. In a word, the two differ greatly in their strengths and weaknesses. They are not of the same type but of opposite types. [...] Compared to Mao's nationalist perspective, Liu is an internationalist. [...] [However,] without Mao's 'nationalism,' Liu's 'internationalism' could never take root in China's backward soil. [...] Mao manifests the naïve egalitarianism of the peasantry; the wild imagination and impractical ideals of the old scholar-gentry; *datong*, 'a world for all,' an idea subscribed to by many, from Confucius to Sun Yat-sen; the belief in 'Communism in one country,' an idea borrowed from Stalin but further refined by Mao. Practising and implementing such policies reveals Mao's courage, his great talent, and his innovative will. [...] Mao has been an outstanding tactician, an artful and cunning manipulator who is prepared to give up principles for temporary tactical gain.[25]

In Wang's view, however, despite their differences and their confrontation starting with the Great Leap Forward in the late 1950s and culminating in Liu's cruel death in the Cultural Revolution, Mao and Liu complemented one another in numerous ways. Did Wang express a preference? He leant more towards the romantic Mao than to the bureaucratic Liu, but he did not see the difference as fundamental – Mao stood for the radical, Liu for the conservative wing of the bureaucracy.[26] Wang admired Mao's fighting spirit and welcomed his mobilisation of youthful energy against bureaucratic privilege in the late 1960s, and hoped that it might – unintentionally rather than by design – whip up a great wind to spread the seeds of revolt more widely and blow together materials to pave the way to a 'true anti-bureaucratic, democratic revolution.' Yet he also recommended supporting parts of Liu's programme and engaging in united actions with Liu's faction should the chance arise, for although Liu and Deng Xiaoping were too timid to spark a revolution, stood for the status quo in China, and were more obviously Stalinist than Mao, Wang felt that on some issues (par-

---

25 Shuang Shan (Wang Fanxi), 'Lun wuchan jieji wenhua da geming' ('On the Great Proletarian Cultural Revolution'), 1967, reproduced in Shuang Shan 1974, pp. 1–43 (second pagination), at 4–9. For a rough English translation of this essay, see W.F.H. (Wang Fanxi), 'On the Great Proletarian Cultural Revolution,' 1967, in The 70s (eds) 1976, pp. 70–106, at 76–80.

26 Peng Shuzhi, in the United States, backed Liu Shaoqi, and argued that 'Liu's victory [over Mao in the early 1960s] could be a first phase in the development of a real revolutionary struggle for socialist democracy' (Peng Shuzhi, 'Mao Zedong yu Liu Shaoqi de guanxi he fenqi' ['The relationship and differences between Mao Zedong and Liu Shaoqi'], in Peng Shuzhi 1982, vol. 3, pp. 267–86, at 284); for an English translation, see Peng Shuzhi, 'The Relationship and Differences Between Mao Tse-tung and Liu Shao-ch'i,' *International Information Bulletin*, no. 2, 1968.

ticularly democracy) their programme was closer than Mao's to the Trotskyists'. But his strategy of turning a fake revolution into a real one got nowhere.²⁷

Wang's *Mao* is an intellectual and political biography that analyses Mao thought and its significance and legacy against the background of a sketch of his childhood and youth and the intellectual and cultural context of the time. The passage in China from biographical history to historical biography, from biography as 'a storehouse of precedent and as a record of exemplary lives' or as mere genealogy to biography as an independent genre, free from Confucian strictures and a 'sub-genre of modern historical writing,' started in the early twentieth century. The new-style history had not just to record events but, in the words of the radical intellectual Liang Qichao, to 'explain the association of causes and consequences to events [...] and to relate this to the total experience of the nation'; and biography too needed to set lives in the context of their society and times. In the 1920s and the early 1930s, the new emphasis in Chinese historiography on society and economy (encouraged by the spread of Marxism, even under the Nationalist dictatorship, and of Western scholarship) led to a temporary turn away from biography. However, biography shot back to prominence in the late 1930s and the early 1940s, after the Japanese invasion of China, in the form of *pingzhuan* or critical biography and new forms of biographical monograph that combined critical commentary with a narrative account of individual lives in their broader setting.²⁸ So Wang's *Mao* had a remarkably short pedigree, though the magnitude of his achievement in writing it will not strike readers unfamiliar with Chinese literary history.

The relative novelty of Wang's approach is even more evident in the context of general Marxist commentary in China, before and especially after 1949. Shortly before writing *Mao*, in the mid-1950s, Wang had written a memoir, based on his own experiences, about which I said the following in introducing its English translation:

> Wang's book is the only full-length autobiography to be published by a veteran of the Chinese Revolution, if one leaves aside the writings of [those like Zhang Guotao] who deserted the revolutionary cause. The main reason for this singularly poor crop of biographical writing is that the CCP, once established in power, immediately set about press-ganging history into the services of the state, so that none dared to write as individuals about the past. Although 'autobiographical' materials have

---

27   Shuang Shan 1974, pp. 29, 34, and 37; W.F.H., 'On the Great Proletarian Cultural Revolution,' pp. 94, 98, and 100.
28   Moloughney 1992, pp. 1–30, at 1–2, 16, and 20–1.

been published by Party Committees in multi-volume collections, they have invariably taken the form of short articles on specific topics, written to meet the orthodox political requirements of the day, and have little in common with what is usually understood by the term 'autobiography.'[29]

The comment about Wang's memoir and its greater truthfulness, fullness, and integrity than comparable writings, especially at the time of its writing but even after Mao's death in 1976, by leaders of the official Party applies almost word for word to *Mao*. The CCP leaders who sided with Mao after the expulsion or demotion of its early leaders, starting with Chen Duxiu in 1927, lived constantly in Mao's shadow after 1935. None dared to publish frank and truthful memoirs of or studies on CCP history, let alone on Mao.[30] Officially approved biographies of Communist leaders were *ipso facto* hagiographic,[31] and even after the relative freeing of thought and scholarship in the 1980s, most biography was for many years mainly in the form of *renwu zhuan* (short, officially approved biographical essays) or *nianpu* (chronological or sequential biographies, with their origin in traditional biography), 'not so much a biography as a collection of notes for a biography.'[32]

So Wang's *Mao*, at the time of its publication, was one of a kind in the field of Chinese Marxist historiography. Narratively coherent, it wove together insights into Mao's individuality and personality while remaining steadfastly focused on its own particular, original view of him. Wang approached his subject from several angles, including critical Marxism, political and intellectual biography, and cultural and sociological biography, integrated into a multi-faceted but generally seamless vision of Mao's life and times.

That is not say that Wang's study of Mao is a balanced biography in which equal weight and attention is given to all parts and stages of his life, includ-

---

29 Gregor Benton, 'Translator's Introduction,' in Wang Fan-hsi 1980, pp. ix–xxi, at xi.
30 The exception was Zhang Guotao, a founding member of the CCP, who left the party in 1938 and later wrote a memoir about his time in it. The prohibition on critical biography endures: it has even been enshrined in law, on March 15, 2017, when China's National People's Congress passed legislation that made 'defaming' Communist 'heroes and martyrs' a civil offence.
31 Inner-party memoirs, including *wenshi ziliao* ('Historical materials'), sometimes collectively authored, invariably edited, and written for restricted circulation, are more likely to yield useful information, although they too are winners' history that usually cleaves to a party line.
32 D.C. Twitchett, 'Chinese Biographical Writing,' in W.G. Beasley and E.G. Pulleyblank (eds.) 1961, pp. 95–114, at 113, cited in Moloughney 1992, p. 11.

ing his childhood, family, friendships, goals, and inner and emotional development. Instead, it focuses on the intellectual influences that shaped Mao's entry into public and political life. It is an analytic history rather than a narrative, and takes a selective approach determined not only by its author's focus and concern but by the nature of the materials available to anyone embarking on such an enterprise in the early 1960s, when Mao's biography in the sense in which the word is usually understood, as a full and accurate picture of the interconnections between a person's inner life and outer life and times, was largely unknown.

As Wang explains in the Preface, four chapters of the book dealing with Sino-Soviet relations were chopped off and published, in 1972, as a separate study, under the pseudonym San Yuan.[33] In the four cut chapters, Wang explains the 'objective reasons' for the CCP's transition from 'leaning on and learning from' the Soviet Union, in the belief that communists have no fatherland, to a state of enmity and war. He locates the fundamental reason for the Sino-Soviet split in a clash of national interests between revolutionary regimes at different stages of development. The CCP came to power in Beijing 32 years after the October Revolution, years of 'reactionary development' in which the Soviet Union completed the process of 'primitive accumulation' upon which the CCP had only just embarked, thus pitting 'poor, blank' China[34] against 'well-fed, well-clothed' Russia. Wang's view, confirmed by several later studies,[35] was that Mao's rise to power had been severely hampered by the Comintern and its Soviet masters, and his eventual achievement of mastery over the CCP represented a victory by him over Moscow and its Chinese surrogate, Wang Ming. Mao therefore had to drive the confrontation with Moscow to extremes in the 1960s, for 'his personal fate was so closely bound up with the Sino-Soviet conflict that any major compromise, even tactical, would impinge on his authority and position.'[36] Mao's complex relations with Stalin and Moscow repeatedly crop up in *Mao*, where they are analysed according to the theses set out in the missing chapters.

---

33 San Yuan (Wang Fanxi) 1972.
34 Mao said in 1958 that the outstanding thing about the Chinese people was that they were 'poor and blank,' and that '[o]n a blank sheet of paper free from any mark, the freshest and most beautiful characters can be written; the freshest and most beautiful pictures can be painted.'
35 Exceptions include Pantsov and Levine 2012.
36 Shuang Shan 1974, p. 9; W.F.H. Wang, 'On the Great Proletarian Cultural Revolution,' p. 80.

6 The Contents of *Mao*

Chapter 1 starts by asking whether Heaven rules humans or vice versa, as a prelude to a discussion of the relationship between 'the hero and the times' and the Mao cult. Wang concludes that too much emphasis on circumstance can lead to fatalism and too much on the power of subjectivity to solipsism and idealism, but that the primary focus must be on circumstance. Tracing the origins of Mao's cult to Russia in the 1920s, when the Stalinists invented 'Leninism' and started the Lenin cult in order to 'set the dead Lenin against the living Lenin and Trotsky,' he shows how it was later redirected onto Stalin. He argues against the view that the cult of the leader is rooted in human nature, and finds its origins instead in social, economic, political, and cultural relations. He rejects the theory that violent revolutions necessarily end in personality cults.

Wang explains Mao's cult as an emanation of orthodox Confucianism, but also as a result of the tininess of the Chinese working class and the party's immersion in the peasantry and its dependence after 1927 on the gun, for war needs personal authority, which can easily generate a cult. Its modern roots were in Soviet practice, which it largely copied, for Mao thought is essentially Stalinism, particularly in the case of the cult of the individual. The Soviet connection is apparent in the fact that the Mao cult dipped in and out of sight in the 1950s in step with Stalin's cult, until the Sino-Soviet split of 1959 broke the synchrony. In time, the Mao cult even outshone Stalin's, by putting Mao not on a par with but higher than Lenin, something Stalin would never have dared do.

Wang's study adds a new dimension to the usual Trotskyist treatment of the personality cult in China, which was to equate it with Stalin's cult and denounce it out of hand. In Wang's opinion, the Mao cult was, in many respects, 'more revolutionary than reactionary,' and had material roots in the needs of the armed struggle. It attached, initially, to Mao's hard-won prestige, whereas Stalin's was by any yardstick undeserved, and was concocted to support his personal ambition. But even though Mao's cult differed from Stalin's, 'both had the same point of origin, in underdevelopment, the lack of a democratic tradition, and a low educational level.' Both were, ultimately, noxious, and Mao's would in time achieve the same level of toxicity as Stalin's. Peng Shuzhi, in contrast, saw the Mao cult in unremittingly negative terms, forged as a weapon for use in the inner-party struggle and entirely reactionary.[37]

---

37 Peng Shuzhi never, as far as I know, analysed the Mao cult in detail, but negative references to it are scattered throughout his talks and writings. As for Wang's distinction between

Chapter 2, on the sources and components of Mao thought, looks at Mao's intellectual maturation, starting in his boyhood. Compared with Lenin, Trotsky, and the Russian leaders, Mao came late to Marxism. Russian revolutionaries responded swiftly to the emergence of Marxism in Russia, which had been exposed for a century to elements of modern thinking, whereas in China the shock of new ideas was sudden and exogenous. Old and new ideas clashed chaotically and were harder to tell apart than in Russia, where decades of events and debates had clarified the distinctions. In China, the collective passage from old to new was telescoped, but in the thinking of individuals it was lengthened by the confusion. This was also true of Mao, whose progression from old-style republicanism to Marxism took thirteen years. Because of this, the ideas and attitudes Mao imbibed in his pre-Marxist period had sturdy roots that strongly shaped his Marxism. The deepest and sturdiest root was Confucianism, to which Mao subscribed for sixteen years before his Marxist conversion, and which (according to Wang) he never truly cut. It endured all the more because Mao, like others of his generation, started making revolution well before he studied Marxism, the opposite order from that in Russia.

Prime among the Confucian elements Mao retained was an uncritical acceptance of the practice of fixed hierarchy and absolute authority, which predisposed him to pursue a bureaucratic and Stalinist approach to power. However, Confucius advocated a practical, pragmatic, scheming, compromising, versatile, and dialectical approach to statecraft, which Mao closely copied at all stages of his career. By opting for the Master's golden mean, he gained the upper hand over his doctrinaire opponents in the CCP, most notably Wang Ming.

The Chinese *youxia* tradition, which even some orthodox Confucians prized and followed, was another corner-stone of Mao's idea of revolution. The *youxia*, or wandering swordsman, was a Robin Hood-type character who went round righting wrongs and robbing the rich to aid the poor. Wang Fanxi (like Zheng Chaolin) had been an avid reader of *youxia* classics as a young boy, and subscribed no less than Mao to their ethos at the time, although unlike Mao he did not later try to put it into practice. (Wang generally stuck by an orthodox approach to revolution, but at the start of the Japanese invasion, against the protests of Peng Shuzhi and others but urged on by Chen Duxiu, he tried to join the military resistance. However, the scheme collapsed.)

Marxism is the third component of Mao thought, but Mao never achieved much depth in it. Few Marxist works were available in Chinese until the late

---

the Stalin cult and the Mao cult, Wang seems to forget that the Stalin cult (as opposed to Stalin's cult of Lenin) was massively amplified in the run-up to and during the Second World War.

1930s, and Mao was anyway busy fighting to survive. It was not until 1937, when the Chinese Red Army settled in Yan'an at the end of the Long March, that he started to come to grips with Marxist thought, but in Stalinist garb. 'At the subconscious and relatively abstract level,' Wang wrote, 'indigenous Confucian and *youxia* thinking have the upper hand, whereas at the conscious and relatively specific level, the foreign component, chiefly derived from Stalinism, holds sway – increasingly so as the years go by.'

Chapter 3 starts by explaining Mao Zedong Thought, the ideology manufactured to serve Mao in the inner-party struggle (chiefly between Wang Ming and Mao) rather than to represent his actual thinking. In that struggle, Mao and his supporters in the leadership tried to ascribe papal-style infallibility to Mao. At the time, Mao's grounding in indigenous thinking, normally his strength after the CCP's retreat into the countryside after 1927, became his weakness, for Wang Ming and his supporters had a far more fluent mastery than Mao of Soviet jargon and Stalinist theory. In the early Yan'an years after 1936, Mao steeped himself in Stalin's writings in order to acquire the veneer of a philosopher and a theoretician and thus to outshine Wang Ming. He quickly succeeded, for although Wang had read more widely than Mao and had good connections in the Kremlin, he had precious few military effectives (except, so it was said, in the party's New Fourth Army in the south) and was, in the end, unable to prevent the proclamation of Mao Zedong Thought and Mao's elevation to supreme leader.

Chapters 4 and 5 arrive at the nub of Wang's view of Mao thought, which is that Mao was a tactician rather than a strategist or theorist (except in the narrow military sense, where he was outstanding as both a tactician and a strategist). Even his greatest contribution to the victory of the revolution, the switch to guerrilla war waged from the villages, was tactical rather than strategic (again, except in the military sense), for it was a method rather than a principle. As such, it was designed to realise Stalin's strategic line in the late 1920s and the early 1930s. It was not derived from principle but was a pragmatic and involuntary adjustment to circumstance – to the defeat of the revolution in 1927. It did not, for a long time (at least in theory), entail the temporary abandoning of the party's focus on the urban proletariat, and the role of peasants continued to be described, for the while, as ancillary. True, over time Mao elaborated practice into strategy, but resort to the tactics underlying that strategy was forced on him and he sought, initially, to disguise or underplay their novelty. He showed no interest in the strategic debates in the late 1920s in the Soviet Union, even those about China, and throughout the 1930s and the 1940s he blindly followed Stalin's twists and turns, even when he doubted or disagreed with them on practical grounds. By elevating warcraft to strategy and subordinating non-military to military activity (and thus to violence), he demoted the urban social movement to a rear support for the army and promoted manipulation and deception, which are at the heart of war. His supporters disparaged revolutionary theory as 'academic' chatter and preferred instead to knuckle down to hard work coupled with a mindless recitation of a handful of abstract programmatic goals. In the 1950s, Mao was forced (again by events) to adopt the idea of permanent revolution, which was actually the Trotskyist strategy for revolution in economically backward countries. But again he did so blindly, having never independently reflected on the relationship between state power and revolution, and was seemingly unaware of or reluctant to acknowledge the truth that he had thus brought to naught all his previous attempts at theory.

In Chapter 6, Wang returns to the interaction of deeds and theories, summing up the issues concisely and elegantly in a passage that goes to the heart of his assessment of Mao. Mao, he says, was never a great revolutionary strategist, and the path he took 'was an extension of the Chinese tradition of peasant revolt, a pragmatic and largely unintended choice forced on him by circumstance.' Such choices, he says elsewhere in the book, took the form of abrupt and violent swings, often generated from the outside. Wang goes on to explain his own understanding of the relationship between action and knowledge:

> In war and revolution, things change constantly and rules are unreliable, which is why Napoleon said *on s'engage et puis on voit* (you commit yourself, and then you see). But this does not negate the value of knowing before doing, and even less so of systematic induction from the facts as a guide to doing. The genius of generals or revolutionary leaders, and whether they succeed or fail, depends on their mastery of the fruits of the knowledge of people in the past and present and the extent to which it informs their planning and strategic thinking. 'Commit yourself and then see' does not contradict the idea of 'plan first and then move.' They are not different things but sides of the same thing, in mutual complement, each indispensable to the other. To throw out the former is like drawing a circle on the ground to serve as one's own gaol, clinging stubbornly to outworn rules and routines; to throw out the latter is to drift aimlessly and rush blindly into battle. It is hard to say which plays the greater role in success or failure, but in determining the quality of a general or a revolutionary, the former does. Only the master calculating in the temple,[38] the presiding genius, can be commander-in-chief and adapt

---

38   The general's temple headquarters (Sunzi).

to changing circumstances, thus deploying the necessary executant talent. But again, the two qualities cannot be separated or counterposed. Decision makers must be good at meeting contingencies and executors must have a lofty view, or they will fail to lay overall plans that are good in all respects and never overtaken by events, plans that, while changing ten thousand times, never depart from the original aim or stand. To rank 'planning first and then moving' above 'committing yourself and then seeing' is simply to say that great strategists, military or political, need to 'think first, then do' more than they need to 'do first, then think.' The distinction is not just between before and after the event. The knowing of those who first know and then do is higher and fuller and can therefore expedite the next doing. The knowing of those who first do and then know might not be true knowing. It is, for the most part, a superficial summary, teeming with errors, of past doing, unable to guide the next step and even a hindrance to it. The thinking of a person mature in all respects is fixed. A person who knows before doing may eventually shrivel into one who does first and then knows, or even one who neither knows nor does. Usually, however, only a tiny number of those who do before knowing can, through study or tempering, turn into people who first know and then do. Mao's road to a strategy of armed revolution was one of doing before knowing.

Chapter 6 also discusses the strategy of armed struggle in China, and what the Trotskyist attitude towards it should have been. He starts by showing that Stalin had never (*pace* Mao) told the Chinese Communists to take the road of an explicitly independent armed revolution. On the contrary, he had instructed them – even at the height of their military adventures in the late 1920s – to hoist the flag of the Guomindang (though not, by then, of Chiang Kai-shek). Mao generally followed Stalin's instructions, but in 1938 he finally adopted a strategy of revolutionary war. However, he did so without considering all its implications, chiefly whether a party divorced from its base in the industrial proletariat can avoid degeneration, remain a workers' party, and complete the revolution. Until the late 1960s, most Trotskyists thought that it could not, but Wang had already concluded otherwise, after years of reflection. In this chapter, he argues that workers' parties are a product of the international setting and can arise even in poor and (semi-)colonial countries, as part of a world revolution. Moreover, socialist parties require illumination by socialist theory, which is brought to them by intellectuals. Such parties usually live cheek by jowl with the workers, but where they are driven from the cities, as the CCP was, or put in gaol, as the Chinese Trotskyists were, they do not necessarily stop representing the workers. Mao's party was physically separated from the workers for more than twenty years (and Wang's for nearly ten). But although it remained committed to socialism and eventually carried trough a socialist revolution, it did change in nature as a result of its immersion in the villages and became haughty and aloof, a development to which Mao paid next to no attention, either from a practical or a theoretical point of view.

Can a workers' party driven into the countryside and waging armed struggle retain its political principles and bearings? Wang himself had set out, in 1938, to make revolution by joining in the war against Japan, under the auspices of Chen Duxiu. At the time, neither Wang nor Chen appear to have explored the implications for Marxist theory of their initiative, which they adopted as a makeshift expedient immediately after the start of the war and their own release from prison, and which most of their comrades at the time deplored. In *Mao*, Wang seeks to formulate the theoretical basis for armed revolution made from the villages – a task that he had skipped over in 1938, in his rush to join the fighting. Armed revolution differs from armed resistance to a foreign invader, but the distinction is blurred, especially in a colonial or semi-colonial country. After 1949, Wang came to view Mao-style social revolution more positively, and tried to reconcile it with the urban strategy the Chinese Trotskyists had recommended in the 1930s and the 1940s. In those years, the Trotskyists had called for a struggle for a Constituent Assembly as a focus around which to unite China's disparate social struggles, including the peasant movement and the Chinese Red Army. After 1935, this was in a sense the path Mao took, though as an accommodation to Stalin's popular-front campaign rather than as a deliberate strategic venture. Mao's united front with democratic parties and democratic elements within the Guomindang, starting in 1935, helped the CCP break from its political isolation, while the Japanese occupation of most of China's big cities and industrial regions went some way towards equalising the territory and the human and material resources available to the CCP and the Guomindang after 1936. In that sense, wartime developments in China seemed, at least in principle, to confirm Wang's view that had the CCP combined armed struggle in the countryside with a fight for democracy and social revolution in the towns starting in 1927, it might have come to power sooner.

Chapter 7 analyses the relationship of theory to practice, as expounded by Mao in 1937 in *On Practice* and *On Contradiction*. Mao's purpose in writing these two pamphlets was to consolidate his earlier military and political victories by winning a philosophical battle against Wang Ming; to expose Wang Ming as a 'dogmatist'; and to parry the charge of 'empiricism' levelled at Mao by Wang Ming. Whereas Wang Fanxi found Stalin's Marxism 'worthless,' he acknowledged that Mao's philosophy had a positive purpose – that of providing a systematic foundation for Mao's work. As a man of action, Mao had little real interest in philosophy, which he studied with a political aim – to establish his credentials as a Marxist. His argument in *On Practice* was that knowledge proceeds from the perceptual to the rational, whence to revolutionary practice. This was, said Wang, a simplistic and mechanical notion, for it suggested that thinking always starts from perception rather than by 'digesting the rationality of one's predecessors and contemporaries' – in Mao's case, Marxist theory. It was therefore a support for Mao's belief in the primacy of practice. *On Contradiction* is a richer study, and illustrates Mao's understanding of the dialectic. His view was, in part, a product of his training in Confucianism and Taoism, which are both eminently dialectical. However, his steeping in China's ancient ways of thought as a youngster predisposed him, in Wang's view, to an abstract, algebraic, and mechanical understanding of the dialectic.

Chapter 8, on literature and art, is the longest, evidence of Wang's strong literary bent. It starts by subjecting the word 'literature' and its Chinese equivalents to comparative semantic analysis. In an article written in 1905, Lenin had described literature (*литература*) as 'a cog and a screw' in one 'single great Social-Democratic mechanism.' But, as Wang points out, *литература* in this context meant the party press (or publications) and 'writing' in general. The term as Lenin used it in his essay was rendered by Lenin's Chinese translators as *wenxue*, implying creative literature. However, Lenin required only party writers to act as 'cogs and screws' in the revolutionary machine, and did not expect the same of non-party ones. After Lenin's death, Stalin seized control of Soviet literature and applied the cog-and-screw precept to writing of all sorts, including creative writing. At the Yan'an Forum on Literature and Art in 1942, Mao followed suit. Using a then standard Chinese translation of Lenin's article, he too applied Lenin's idea of 'cogs and wheels' to creative literature, thus setting tight parameters for generations of Chinese writers and sealing the fate of the mavericks among them. Meanwhile, the literary establishment became a cockpit of bureaucratic factions, and art and literature turned into a means of singing the party's praises.

The rendering of *литература* as *wenxue* was corrected in the second Chinese edition of Lenin's *Collected Works*, where the term *chuban wu*, 'publications,' was used instead, but this did not happen until the early 1980s. The source of the correction was almost certainly the chapter on literature in Wang's book. The preparation of the second edition of Lenin's *Works* in Chinese translation began in the early 1980s, under the direction of Hu Qiaomu, the Marxist philosopher and political thinker. At the time, Hu Qiaomu pointed out that *wenxue* did not properly convey Lenin's meaning, and instructed his team to use other words instead. However, this was easier said than done, given that Mao had copied the earlier mistranslation in his Yan'an Talks, citing Lenin as his authority. Were the error to be publicly exposed, Mao would posthumously lose face. So would the living Hu, who had served as Mao's secretary in 1942, edited Mao's Talks for publication in 1943, and served on the team that published Mao's *Selected Works* between 1951 and 1960. So although Hu Qiaomu publicly conceded that *wenxue* did not correctly translate *литература* in Lenin's sense, the annotation in late 1986 to Mao's works (referring to the Yan'an Talks) simply noted the correction, without explaining its significance. If Hu Qiaomu was copying Wang's argument, how did he come to know about it? Through the intermediacy of Lou Shiyi, a poet and senior literary editor in Beijing and the elder cousin of the Trotskyist Lou Guohua, who published Wang's book in Hong Kong. Lou Guohua sent the book to his cousin, who made it available to the relevant authorities.[39]

Most of the 'universal truths' that Mao copied from Stalin had a disastrous effect on the Chinese Revolution, but Wang argues that Mao's 'national truths' fared better. This went for all Mao's policies and tactics but especially for his innovations in literature and art, which in the early years of the rural revolution spoke to the common people and kindled their creative powers. His promotion of 'national forms' and folk art was a necessary counter to the 'wholesale Westernisation' that mired down and isolated the New Culture Movement that had started up in the 1910s, and stamped the revolution for many Chinese observers as a foreign import. Even speech and writing was corrupted during the movement by foreign words and syntax, and was often comprehensible only to members of the book-trained Chinese elite. Wang declared the results of Mao's counter-reform 'impressive.' However, after 1949 the gains were partly reversed by the import of Soviet literary theories and the rise of the Mao cult.

Wang also comments, though at no great length and without touching on literary issues, on Mao's own poetry, which is classical in structure – ironically so, given his insistence that literature must serve the masses and be popular in form. Mao's poetry was strikingly out of place in China's increasingly uniform literary landscape. Wang uses it to peer into Mao's soul, where he finds not a modern-day revolutionary but an imperious leader in the 'great man' style – self-aggrandising, void even of the compassion displayed by poetry-writing rebels in dynastic times, and moved not by altruism and the desire to end human suffering and bring about universal enlightenment but by personal ambition.

---

39 Nagahori Yūzō 2011, p. 263.

Chapter 9 looks at Mao's economic theories, particularly regarding self-reliance and the 'surreal fantasy' of Communism in a single country. Wang traces these theories to Mao's economic practice in the late 1920s and the early 1930s, which left a deep stamp on his thinking. At the start of his economic work in the small Red regimes that sprang up along the mountainous provincial borders in many parts of China after 1927, Mao pioneered approaches to economic management that continued to shape his economic thinking for the rest of his life. He acted boldly and in the spirit of primitive communism, promoting equality and democracy, especially in the army. Here, he followed the example of Chinese rebel bands in times past. In the early 1930s, he called for 'economic construction' in the base areas and began experimenting with the idea of 'regional socialism,' a miniature version of socialism (or communism) in one country, which he started pushing in the 1960s. This idea was borrowed from Stalin but was domestically inspired by Mao's nationalism and his experience in the civil war and the War against Japan, when self-reliance (a traditional value) was elevated to a patriotic virtue. In the early 1940s, when the Communists were besieged on all sides in their wartime strongholds, by both Japanese and Nationalists, self-sufficiency became the central plank in Mao's economic platform. For the time being it was only a temporary expedient, to be practised while awaiting the Soviet help that began arriving in 1949. During the Sino-Soviet split, however, Mao reverted to a policy of national self-reliance, culminating in the tragedy of the Great Leap Forward.

Chapter 10 considers Mao's position in history, by weighing him against both revolutionaries like Marx and Lenin and rulers in the Chinese past. What mattered most to Mao was China's indigenous storehouse of knowledge, particularly in the fields of statecraft and warcraft. Foreign theories mattered less, except to magnify his status in the world Communist movement and consolidate his hegemony in the CCP. As a man of action, Wang ranks him far higher than as a theorist or thinker, but even as a man of action his constant surrender of principle to expediency ruled him out as truly great. He was a narrow nationalist rather than an internationalist. He incited a Stalin-style cult of himself, while feigning modesty and frugality. On the scale of Han nationalism, however, he ranked practically supreme: he took China to new heights and outclassed the founders of the Han and Tang (though not perhaps Genghis Khan). He led the Han people to stand up, as equals in the world, and restored their sense of national pride.

7 Wang and the Chinese Trotskyists

It is hard to think of any CCP leader after 1927 and before the mid-to-late 1930s whose mastery of modern critical thought matched that of the party's founding intellectuals, Chen Duxiu and Li Dazhao (executed in 1927), and even Chen and Li had only a superficial acquaintance with Marxism before the establishment of the party in 1921, when they plunged headlong into politics and had scant time left for theory. Plans were laid in 1921 for all Marx and Lenin's works to be translated into Chinese, but the plans stayed on paper – not until the 1930s did translations gradually amass.

Mao himself was (like many of his comrades) more at home in the Confucian classics than in contemporary thought. He was poorly informed about Marxism, even after beginning his study of it in the late 1930s, and when he did learn some, he used it principally as a tool to attack Wang Ming. During his brief spell as a librarian at Peking University in 1918–19, he was excluded from the Marxist study circle set up by Li Dazhao, the head librarian. (Some say resentment at his exclusion accounted for his later prejudice against intellectuals.)

Not long after the Russian revolution of 1917, Marxism in the Soviet Union degenerated into a set of dogmas to be mouthed unthinkingly. It was no longer a theory to be used creatively and revised as conditions changed. Those Chinese Communists who went to the Soviet Union in the 1920s studied only the doctrinaire sort of Marxism, which often barely rose above the level of propaganda. In Moscow, they received military or cadre training in addition to political indoctrination. Even Liu Shaoqi, Mao's second-in-command for years and one of the CCP's main theorists, was only minimally acquainted with classical, unadulterated Marxism, despite a year in Moscow in 1921–2. He was famous for taking a bureaucratic approach to party problems, and excelled above all as an organiser. Where he disagreed with Mao, it was on practical matters – he never took his differences to a higher plane.

The Chinese Trotskyist leaders were relatively well-versed in Marxism, classical and critical philosophy, and the history of the world labour movement. This was especially true of Wang and Zheng, Wang's close ally in the Chinese Opposition. In this book on Mao by Wang, it seems right to round off this introduction with a brief comparison of author and subject. Readers might doubt the relevance of such an exercise or even laugh at it, for Mao led the world's greatest peasant revolution to completion while Wang achieved next to nothing. However, as Wang himself reminds us in his second chapter on strategy, 'the schemes of Western sages cannot be judged by their outcomes, while the Carthaginians punished their generals for poor planning even though they narrowly won victory.' So Mao's taking the CCP to victory did not necessarily prove that his judgment was superior to Wang's. When the Trotskyists formed their Opposition in 1931, they included important leaders of the early CCP, such as Chen Duxiu, its founding father, and several former members and aides to members of its Central Committee.[40] Wang joined the Standing Committee of the new organisation and was given charge of its press. To some Communists in the early 1930s, the Opposition looked a viable alternative to the official party, which was deep in crisis after the 1927 defeat. The CCP's way forward after 1927 was not predestined, and the Oppositionists might have resumed a role in the revolution if things in China and the world had unspooled a little differently, for it was not until later in the 1930s that they began to attract the hatred in the CCP that already attached to the Opposition in the Soviet Union.

Wang's path to revolution, like Mao's and that of many other of the party's early recruits, started with a liking for classical novels about China's greenwood rebels. Both men as boys read the Confucian classics, but Mao's immersion in them lasted a lot longer than Wang's, who only studied the *Analects* and received a basically anti-Confucian schooling from the age of thirteen or fourteen. Older than Wang by fourteen years, Mao was less receptive than him at a formative time in his intellectual development to the new waves of thought that were breaking over China at the turn of the century and in the next two decades. Mao came to Marxism at a later age than Wang – nearly thirty, to Wang's eighteen. Mao plunged into active politics early in the 1920s and put books aside, but the young Wang was already acquainted by the age of fourteen or fifteen with a string of famous Western thinkers, ranging from John Dewey and Bertrand Russell to Socrates and Plato, and soon became a very young devotee of Chen Duxiu. After the defeat of the revolution in 1927, hundreds of Chinese Communists were sent to Moscow, where their Soviet hosts had set up schools to indoctrinate foreign Communists in Marxism in its new Soviet-style interpretation. Wang and other secret Chinese Oppositionists became practised critics of the official teaching, and matured into critical Marxists in the truest sense and by the hardest route. Back in China, for years on end their tie to Trotskyists in other countries was cut by war and state surveillance of the mail. With little guidance from abroad and only an occasional chance to discuss their plans with leaders of the Fourth International, they were forced to

---

40 In 1936, Mao told the journalist Edgar Snow that he had sat at Chen Duxiu's feet in the early 1920s, but he cut this passage from the Chinese translation of Snow's book (see Snow 1968 [1936], p. 154).

find their own way forward – this too accounts for the self-reliance of Trotskyists like Wang in matters of theory and everyday politics.

When the Trotskyists were expelled from the CCP in 1929, those (like Wang) who had previously worked for it as paid officials lost their livelihood and had to seek other work. Most had received a modern education and many knew one or more foreign languages, so to fund their organisation and feed their families, they switched to earning a living by translating Marxist literature and social-science books, for which there was a big market in Shanghai. (Wang's first translation, done in 1929, was of Plekhanov's *From Idealism to Materialism*.) Besides their own writings, their publications included books by Marx, Engels, Lenin, Trotsky, Preobazhensky, Kant, Thomas Mann, Darwin, John Dewey, D. Merezhkovsky, André Gide, and Kropotkin. These were brought out by the left-wing publishing houses that mushroomed in the relative sanctuary of Shanghai's International Settlement in the 1920s and the 1930s. Of the 140 books published between 1929 and 1949 by Wang Mengzou's famous Oriental Book Company in Shanghai, nearly half were written or translated by Trotskyists, who were for many years the true conduit of Marxism and critical theory into China.[41] This is why Wang and his comrades were so much better versed in Marxist theory and modern thinking than Mao and his comrades, who climbed the mountains in the late 1920s and had neither the time nor, in most cases, the ability or inclination to do such work. Added to that, Wang and other Trotskyists' experience as Oppositionists in Moscow in the late 1920s (and, in the case of Trotskyists like Zheng Chaolin, in France in the early 1920s) meant they learned to think against the stream and could make critical arguments in support of unorthodox ideas.

Wang and the Trotskyists spent most of the 1930s in prison, and had little opportunity to put their ideas (chiefly, the struggle for a Constituent Assembly) to the test. Mao, on the other hand, remained at large throughout the revolution and gained rich experience of stirring up the villages and waging guerrilla war. Prisons are notorious for being universities of the revolution, and so they often were for the Chinese Trotskyists, who used their time behind bars to immerse themselves in the study of Marxism, economics, and Western classical philosophy. The Trotskyist Zheng Chaolin, a linguistic virtuoso and better read in Marxist theory than most if not all the early Chinese Communists, gave lectures in prison in Communist theory and history, attended not just by fellow-Trotskyists like Wang but by members of the official party. The Trotskyists took

---

41   Gregor Benton, 'Chinese Trotskyism and the World of Letters,' in Benton (ed.) 2014, pp. 1045–6.

advantage of a relatively liberal prison regime in the early 1930s (that changed later) to prepare long-term study plans and got friends and relatives to bring in books.[42]

Mao was an unconventional thinker and a daring innovator in politics and warfare, but he was not equipped with a theoretical framework for his ideas or, at least until 1937, even interested in discovering one. He found it politically expedient (until the late 1950s) to comply – or feign compliance – with the Moscow line. Wang, in part because of his natural intellectual rigour, acumen, creativity, and courage but also because of his wide reading, saw the value of a coherent body of ideas to help explain facts and establish their laws and interconnections, and he recognised the interdependence of theory and practice and the role of theory as both a guide to and product of practice, which is driven by theory and enriches it. Mao, on the other hand, either paid mere lip service to theory, where necessary reconciling practice to it by 'cutting the foot to fit the shoe,' or ignored it, 'like the sailor who boards ship without a rudder and compass and never knows where he may end up.'

Wang too distrusted set prescriptions and saw theory not as an immutable collection of 'dead facts' but as a mutable product of transient circumstance and the life-process, evergreen like Goethe's tree of life that Lenin claimed to kneel before. Mao had little acquaintance with Marxist theory before the late 1930s, beyond a few barely digested precepts, and either could not be bothered to reconcile his many departures from orthodoxy with Marxism or, where necessary, covered them up. Wang, on the other hand, had to defend his theoretical innovations before the court of his often dubious comrades.

Wang's major differences with the more orthodox strain of Chinese Trotskyism, represented by Peng Shuzhi, started at the practical level but, in time, acquired a theoretical dimension. Peng had arrived at Trotskyism by a different path from nearly all his comrades. He had gone to Moscow in 1921, without any practical experience of revolutionary work in China, and stayed there longer than most Chinese students, until 1924. He was officially appointed to lead the students in Moscow, and picked up Soviet attitudes, habits, and theories, including Stalin's version of democratic centralism and the idea of 'iron discipline,' to which he remained attached even after becoming a Trotskyist. He was, in many ways, a Trotskyist version of Wang Ming, and Zheng Chaolin, one of Peng's Trotskyist critics, called him 'a Wang Ming before Wang Ming.'[43]

---

42   See the prison memoir of Zheng Chaolin by Lou Shiyi, a veteran and orthodox but relatively enlightened member of the CCP elite, translated in Gregor Benton, 'Editor's Introduction,' in Zheng Chaolin 1997, pp. xi–xiv; and Wang 1996, pp. 166–9.
43   Benton 1996, pp. 52–6.

Two of Wang's differences with the Peng group were linked to Wang's relationship with Chen Duxiu. Chen knew more than Mao about theory, but he was often even less bound by it than Mao. After the Japanese invasion in 1937, Chen fell out with the Chinese Trotskyists (Wang and one or two others excepted), citing their 'narrow sectarianism.' He thought a workers' revolution was ruled out, in China and elsewhere, for the duration of the war and called for a new approach. This comprised an alliance with democratic forces independent of the Guomindang and the CCP and an attempt to create a military wing for the alliance by infiltrating friendly armed forces. Wang, who at the time was staying with Chen after both men's release from prison at the outbreak of war, disagreed with his first proposal but accepted the second, no less reluctant than Chen to continue reciting 'old dogmas.' He and other of Chen's supporters took steps to realise the military plan. It started to progress but was soon thwarted, probably by secret agents of the Guomindang, and was never repeated. This was no doubt because of the enormous difficulty of entering a battlefield already contested by powerful armies under Chiang, Mao, regional warlords, local militias, and the Japanese and their puppets. In his later writings, Wang returned to the issue of armed struggle, and concluded that in certain respects Mao had been right and the Trotskyists, by concentrating single-mindedly on the cities, wrong. Peng took the opposite view, denouncing Wang as an adventurist for taking such a view and himself holding firmly to the Bolshevik model of revolution.[44] Wang's implicit concession to Mao on the point of a military road had theoretical implications that he explored in detail only after his exile, in the 1950s.

During the war, Wang and his co-thinkers in the Chinese Trotskyist movement made another policy innovation that added a new twist to the Leninist theory of 'revolutionary defeatism.' Lenin's theory posited that the defeat of one's own country was the 'lesser evil' and would facilitate revolution at home. The Chinese Trotskyists agreed that defeatism was inappropriate in a semi-colony like China, whose resistance war was progressive. This led Peng Shuzhi to support Chiang's war while reserving the right to make constructive criticism of its conduct, i.e., a policy of 'revolutionary defencism,' and to oppose trying to win the war by revolution. Wang, however, argued that the task was to transform 'arms of criticism' into 'criticism of arms,' so that resistance turns into revolution, for without class struggle the war could not be won. Wang found an adumbration of this approach in Trotsky's theory of permanent

---

44   Chen Bilan, 'The Real Lesson of China on Guerrilla Warfare: Reply to a "Letter from a Chinese Trotskyist,"' in Benton (ed.) 2014, pp. 985–1000.

revolution, but he took the theory further and dubbed it 'revolutionary victoryism,' which he thought better suited to an age in which wars and revolutions were so closely intertwined.[45] In reality, Mao can be said to have followed a similar path, though he did not try to develop a Marxist theoretical framework for it.

Another issue on which Wang went out on a limb was also inspired in part by Chen Duxiu, and marked him off from both Mao and Peng. Chen had begun his political career as a radical democrat in the first decade of the twentieth century and, in the early 1920s, ran the CCP along more liberal lines than other communist parties at the time, inspired by early radical thought in China and by the Chinese enlightenment movement of the late 1910s in which he had played such a seminal part. After 1937, and especially after the Hitler-Stalin Pact of September 1939, he returned to his first love, democracy, which he saw as the bedrock of true socialism. Wang argued with him at the time, insisting on the distinction between bourgeois and proletarian democracy, but he respected the Old Man's belief and his later actions showed that it had had a deep effect on him. On its tenth anniversary in May 1941, the Chinese Left Opposition split once and for all on the question of the rights of factions and minorities in the party, with Peng et al. calling for centralism and 'iron discipline' and Wang et al. arguing that Leninism was 'not a crude negation of the traditions of bourgeois democracy, but a critique and further development of them' (236). Chen had gone far further than Lenin, rejecting dictatorship of any sort, left or right. While Wang never went to that extreme, he stated the case for democracy as an indispensable part of socialism with utmost clarity and emphasis. He held fast to this view for the rest of his life (as did Peng to his contrary view), and he strove to incorporate Chen's insights into his political thinking.[46]

Unlike many of the Chinese Trotskyists, who had spent long periods abroad (in Japan, France, or the Soviet Union), Mao never left China until after the proclamation of the People's Republic. He therefore knew far less than the Trotskyists about the Communist movement outside China. He spoke no foreign languages, and he was an internationalist only when it suited him. The Trotskyists, in contrast, were convinced internationalists and dedicated to drawing lessons from events and debates in the history of world Communism and reflecting on what they might mean for China. Mao, of course, as a peasant,

---

45 Wang Fanxi, 'Introduction: Leon Trotsky and Chinese Communism,' in Benton (ed.) 2014, pp. 844–7.
46 See Shuang Shan (Wang Fanxi), 'On Chen Duxiu's Last Views,' in Benton (ed.) 2014, pp. 773–4.

was far more closely acquainted with life in the villages, of which few Trotskyists had much first-hand experience.

Also unlike the Trotskyists, Mao was used to giving orders to his generals and officials, and having them implicitly obeyed. This was never likely to nurture in him subtlety of mind or spirit, and high-handedness became an irradicable part of his political style. Among the Trotskyists, only Peng Shuzhi ever wielded a similar sort of power (though on a vastly miniaturised scale) before his expulsion from the CCP, while ruling over a couple of hundred Chinese students in Moscow in the early 1920s. Probably as a result of this experience, his idea of authority was quite different from that of the relatively free-spirited and easy-going Chen Duxiu. However, Peng's rule was constrained by his masters in the Comintern, whereas Mao's was comparatively untrammelled. Even so, Peng continued for the rest of his political career, even as a Trotskyist, to promote the virtues of authority and 'natural leadership,' which is why he was all along destined to fall out with Chen Duxiu and with Wang and Zheng.

The Chinese Trotskyists were better read than Mao and better instructed in Marxist theory, but it was Mao who led the revolution to victory, despite or because of his contempt for 'foreign dogmas.' After 1949, Wang concluded that the Trotskyists had been too orthodox, especially on the question of war and the peasantry, at a time when events in China required a radical rethinking of some aspects of Marxist and Leninist theory. Peng, however, continued to think that the Trotskyists had been right and that Mao had won power by accident, because of 'exceptional historical circumstances' (chiefly, the Japanese invasion).

Towards the end of his life, in the prefaces and postscripts to new editions of his memoirs and in his letters and reading notes, Wang continued to assert his allegiance to Trotskyism. He deeply regretted the Fourth International's inability to intervene in the 'general collapse of Stalinism' that started in 1989. He remained hopeful right up to his death, but while he insisted that the Trotskyists' and Marx's 'basic programmatic strategies' would not go out of date 'as long as the construction of our society continues to rest on an opposition of robbers and robbed, repressers and repressed,' he accepted that the exit from the crisis would require new policies to suit the new reality and match the cunning of 'Old Man History.'[47]

---

47 Wang Fanxi, 'Preface to the Morningside Edition of *Memoirs of a Chinese Revolutionary*,' in Benton (ed.) 2014, pp. 1120–3.

8   Conclusions

In Wang's book, Mao appears in complex lights. Wang concedes Mao's superior achievement in the Chinese Revolution and, by implication, concedes the failings – chiefly, an excess of orthodoxy – of the organisation he himself helped lead. The Chinese Trotskyists clung to the cities because they believed that the cycle of Chinese history, leading from one despotism to the next interrupted by brief rebellions, could only be broken by the modern urban classes, the workers and the radical wing of the intelligentsia, supported by the peasants. They stayed put partly, however, because the cities were what they knew, while the villages were *terra ignota* for which they lacked maps. They also lacked the human resources and the guns and funds to force their way into the villages and hold at bay the several national and myriad local armies that controlled them. Wang's own quixotic attempt to rouse the peasants by educating in revolution the rank-and-file soldiers of divisions under He Jifeng and Ji Xingwen fell apart, and the handful of guerrilla columns that sprang up under Trotskyist leadership here and there in the Chinese countryside were gobbled up or ground to pieces by armies of the CCP or the Guomindang. Wang does not talk about these things in his book, but they are essential background to his thoughts on Mao. So although the book is purportedly about Mao's thoughts and actions, it also has, as its invisible complement, the failed project of the Trotskyists.

Mao is a true mirror on its author. Wang's characteristic style of writing and argument, measured but impassioned, unfailingly generous and even-handed, void of invective or polemic, comes unexpectedly in a study by a man of such deep political commitment, whose close friends and relatives had ended up as Mao's victims, dead or behind bars.

Wang's aim in writing *Mao* was to measure Mao's greatness, explore his originality and creativity, and criticise his weaknesses and failings. However, Wang's analysis was not impartial, aimless, or detached. One of his main purposes was to defend and rehabilitate the theory of permanent revolution, Trotskyism's central theoretical postulate – not in order to vindicate Chinese Trotskyism historically, for the issue had in his view already been settled in China and now belonged to the past, but for the sake of revolutionaries in Asia, Africa, and Latin America who might be tempted to try to follow Mao's prescriptions. Wang was also anxious to map out a course for present or future dissidents in China, once the Mao dictatorship began to loosen up or to crumble under economic, demographic, or democratic pressures. Mao never showed any practical interest in the democratic heritage of May Fourth that was among the things that brought the CCP into being, and he accommodated easily to the CCP's 'Bolshevisation' in the mid-1920s and its Stalinisation later in the decade. The armed, rural road to power, of which he was the chief initiator and mastermind, made a democratic outcome even more unlikely, for it substituted peasants for workers and armies for social movements. However, Wang believed that without democracy the new government in Beijing would meet with repeated social and political crises, so he made the call for it the cornerstone of his critique of Maoism.

Acknowledgements

The following people helped solve various problems regarding the translation: Cheng Lingfang, Donald Gasper (who also created the index), Lam Chi Leung, Qian Yongxiang, Vincent Sung, Xue Feng, Kevin Yang, and Parson Yung. My thanks to them all. I am also deeply grateful to Hilde Kugel and Lydia Bax for helping to prepare the text for publication and to Sebastian Budgen, Danny Hayward, and Rebecca Urai Ayan for their encouragement and support of the project.

Mao Zedong Thought

Preface

This is a draft study. As the term suggests, it is not an ordinary book. It does not belong to a standard genre. It is not rigidly divided into distinct chapters and carefully or precisely organised. It does not progress in a fully logical succession, and it is not, in all respects, complete.

A year ago, when I published the four chapters of this book dealing with Sino-Soviet relations as a separate study, under the pseudonym San Yuan,[1] I described the work as a substantial attempt to give a 'comprehensive, objective historical account' of Mao Zedong thought. I was being neither modest nor conceited. It is indeed a serious and open-minded study, but it is still no more than a first attempt. There are two main reasons. First, ill health interrupted my work, often for up to six months at a time. So although it is not a particularly long book, it took a total of three years and seven months, from January 1961 to August 1964, to finish. Writing like that, it is hard to keep up a unified approach, to perfect the text, and to avoid repetition. Second, I was forced to live in a secluded place where materials and reference books were hard to get, so I had to leave some problems unattended, at least for the time being. These constraints made the book less comprehensive and complete than I would have wished.

Because of my dissatisfactions, I set the manuscript aside for nearly ten years. Last autumn, encouraged by a friend, and with the help of Sincere Press, I finally published the four chapters on the Sino-Soviet conflict, so that at least part of the manuscript could be read. The book turned out, judging by the publisher's and readers' reaction, to be not as bad as I'd imagined. My little book received quite a warm welcome. From the preface, readers gleaned that another ten chapters had not yet gone to press, and urged the publisher to bring them out as quickly as possible. Some paid for their copies in advance, to help get it printed.

I was deeply moved. The experience made me realise that a book, as long as it is seriously written and inspired by scholarly intent, as long as it is without ulterior motives and aims simply to speak truth, will find readers and even acclaim despite its faults. My years of profound loneliness were dispelled. I knew that I was not alone in the world, and I was determined to press on with the entire book.

---

1 San Yuan (Wang Fanxi) 1972.

However, the manuscript had gathered dust for more than eight years. Much had happened in the meantime. Would it have to be rewritten? I found that to change it was neither possible nor necessary. Impossible, because one change would lead to another and unsettle the whole; unnecessary, because my initial intention had always been to focus on fundamentals, while the changes of the previous eight years had only confirmed my basic thesis. The book therefore neither permitted nor required rewriting, and will look the same as it did eight years ago.

Between its writing and going to press, much has happened in regard to Mao Zedong and Mao thought, not least the Great Proletarian Cultural Revolution, which Mao himself launched and which was one of his most consummate performances. Logically, the book required a special chapter, or at least some supplementation. But I have already written a separate article on the Cultural Revolution[2] and the book is already long enough, without adding an appendix. Inserting paragraphs or lengthy notes would make the book complex, unwieldy, and unreadable, so I didn't do that either.

But even though I don't discuss the Cultural Revolution as such, much of what I say about Mao thought, particularly in relation to literature and art, the economy, and the People's Communes, will help readers understand its course. You might even say that only when you know the special features of Mao thought can you properly understand this 'great revolution,' why it happened, the form it has taken, its course, and its tendency and meaning.

Here I cannot deal with all aspects of the relationship between Mao thought and the Cultural Revolution. However, I can say this: Mao's strengths and weaknesses, in terms of character and intellect, sometimes complementary and sometimes not, alternate between flickering like a hegemon ghost over the movement and diving deep into it as animating spirit. Were it not for 'communism in one country,' would so many profound contradictions ever have arisen? But for his economic romanticism and aiming for the moon, would there have been three years of disaster? But for these catastrophic errors, would the leadership of the party ever have fallen into the hands of 'capitalist roaders'? After his loss of power, but for the mettle Mao displayed and his bold and decisive challenge to heaven and earth, who but he could have staged such a massive dress rehearsal of revolution? When the dress rehearsal became the play and the rebels acting on imperial decree turned into actual revolutionaries, conjuring an insurgency from the barrel of a gun and seizing control of the army in the name of the party, who but the master of stratagems and the supreme political

---

2   Excerpted in Appendix 2.

trickster could have saved the day? Who but he that turns principle into dogma and theory into shop sign, leaping from left to right and back again in constant self-contradiction, forever retreating on his word ...

To say the Cultural Revolution was caused single-handedly by Mao thought or that Mao thought can explain everything about it would be heroes' history, not Marxism. There are limits to the powers of an individual, no matter how great and important. Clearly, Mao and Mao thought played a role in the Chinese Revolution in general and the Cultural Revolution in particular, and left a deep mark on it. Equally clearly, that role, however grand, was neither decisive nor unique. Ultimately, objective conditions outweigh subjective intent. The historical and social 'situation' trumps the schemes of anyone, however great. So in the entire Chinese Revolution, and even more so in this Cultural Revolution, those who use Mao's personality and ideas to explain things, as either conducive or detrimental to the revolution, must retain perspective. The proposition that being determines consciousness must inform all our analysis, and in seeking to understand where Mao was right and where he went wrong we must start from China's special circumstances and relationship with the world. Only then can we grasp the role of Mao thought in the Chinese Revolution and especially in the Cultural Revolution.

After completing the manuscript, I asked friends to read it, and they offered me invaluable advice. They indicated errors in citations and factual discrepancies, and in some cases they dissented from my opinion. Their comments have contributed to the writing of this book, and I would like to thank them.

December 7, 1972

Foreword

Mao Zedong and Mao thought have played a major role in China's political history over the past three decades, and continue to do so, in China and the world. In future, that will remain the case. Both are worthy of close study.

The CCP has raised the study of Mao thought to a 'major political task.' To coincide with the publication of the fourth volume of Mao's *Selected Works*, a vigorous study movement was launched in the party and among the people. How should we view this movement and these tasks? If Mao's life and thought are worthy of detailed study, should we not support the CCP's study movement?

But studying Mao thought is not the same as the CCP's advocacy of a study movement. The former must be scientific, while the latter is political. A sober scholarly analysis of Mao and Mao thought is one thing, deifying him and establishing his 'infallible' authority on the basis of selective and even falsified evidence to ensure a predetermined outcome, all under party leadership, another. We support the former and oppose the latter. A scholarly analysis of Mao and Mao thought to determine the truth will enable people to understand the causefulness of events and draw the appropriate lessons, also in other countries, especially colonial countries, so that their workers and peasants can win their revolutions. Sober scientific study of Mao and Mao thought will help recover truths hidden by narrow factional interests, so that the views expressed by different groups over the past thirty years about the Chinese Revolution can get a fair hearing. Such a study will raise rather than lower Mao thought's historical status. For the infallible and the divine are lifeless, whereas human beings who are both right and wrong, particularly those who are less wrong and more right than most, live life to the full. Sadly, the study launched by today's CCP (including Mao) seeks not to establish the content and maturation of Mao's becoming but to make him a god, to turn a being of flesh and blood into a dead or incorporeal thing and his ideas into myths.

The CCP leaders make no secret of the fact that the movement to study Mao thought is political, but they do not reveal its actual content. They dare not say that its purpose is to establish and consolidate the Mao cult. We oppose studying Mao thought in order to deify Mao, but we welcome its scholarly and historical analysis. Yet there are insurmountable difficulties in the way of one. The materials needed are many, and I found them hard to come by; and the few that are attainable have undergone cosmetic surgery, making it hard to know what's true and what's false. The primary resource is Mao's own works, but they are available only in four selected volumes that have (according to their editors) been 'technically' amended, supplemented, revised, and modified. Exactly what is a technical revision? We are not told, and the changes are not specified. In reading Mao's writings, we cannot know exactly what he foresaw and what he knew only after the event. So there are many obstacles in the way of a faithful, scientific, and historical analysis, and some of my judgments are therefore provisional and hypothetical.

Why has Mao published selected works rather than complete works? According to the editorial committee, because 'the Guomindang reactionaries had destroyed revolutionary literature,' whose scattering in the long years of revolution meant that Mao's complete writings 'cannot now be found.' That it is perhaps partly true, but it is hardly the whole truth. The main reason Mao has not published his complete works is because he sees practice as more important than theory and puts tactics above principles, so his work brims with contradictions and inconsistencies. Now that the revolution has been won, his cringing before Chiang Kai-shek in the late 1930s, done as a tactic, is too embarrassing, especially in the eyes of the younger generation, who idolise him. To establish the myth of his infallibility, he has no choice but to select.

No doubt this approach is reprehensible. Quite apart from the need for historical truth, it is always wrong to miseducate the young. Yes, they can learn from right decisions, but they can learn even more from wrong ones. Human beings cannot learn from God's miracles, only from human actions. Unfortunately, politicians poisoned by the personality cult and the system geared to it fail to grasp that simple truth.

May a writer, in compiling and publishing work, make choices? Is it all right to supplement and revise? First, which writer are we talking about, and which works? If we are talking about creative or scholarly writers whose work is not directly concerned with living people and is not controversial, they are clearly free to revise their work and even should do, in order to perfect it, for readers' benefit. But political writings are historical documents, often written as polemics, and proof of right and wrong, so they should not be amended after the event. Even technical amendments should be indicated in annotation or appendices providing the unmodified original, because of the duty to be faithful to the past. Every serious political thinker and academic must respect this truth. Stalin committed numerous crimes against the cause of socialism, but among the biggest was to falsify history, forge documents, and distort or fabricate his own and his opponents' writings. I am not saying that Mao is as bad as Stalin, simply that selection and revision is part of Stalinism. If Mao has not yet gone too far along this road, is there still time for him to turn round? (One reason he has not followed Stalin completely in this respect is that he is not without achievements in the Chinese Revolution, unlike Stalin, who had to forge his revolutionary credentials.)

Here are two historical examples from which Mao might learn:

1. Marx and Engels wrote *The Communist Manifesto* in 1847. Twenty-five years later, in 1872, they added a preface saying 'the *Manifesto* has become a historical document which we have no longer any right to alter.'
2. In the second edition of *Anti-Dühring*, a book written by Engels to rebut Dühring but principally to set out Engels and Marx's own insights, Engels wrote:

> With the exception of one chapter, the present new edition is an unaltered reprint of the former edition. For one thing, I had no time for a thoroughgoing revision, although there was much in the presentation that I should have liked to alter. Besides I am under the obligation to prepare for the press the manuscripts which Marx has left, and this is much more important than anything else. Then again, my conscience rebels against making any alterations. The book is a polemic, and I think that I owe it to my adversary not to improve anything in my work when he is unable to improve his.[1]

Mao's writings, save for his poems, are political history, and most are polemical. Does he have the right to revise the original text? How, in all conscience, should he handle the republication of his work? The answer is obvious.

---

1 Engels, Preface to *Anti-Dühring*, MECW, vol. 25, 9.

CHAPTER 1

The Personality Cult

Does Heaven rule humans, or do humans rule Heaven? Chinese thinkers have forever wrestled with these two propositions without reaching a successful resolution. Some tend towards the former, focusing on objectivity, destiny, and fate; others towards the latter, focusing on subjectivity, striving, and human affairs. The one is fatalistic, but not void of objective and material ingredients; the other is positive and dynamic, but mostly lapses into solipsism and idealism.

Moral sayings derived from this confrontation include 'do your best and leave the rest to Heaven,' 'humans propose, God disposes,' and 'Heaven helps those who help themselves.' These approaches, while not fundamentally resolving the relationship between 'the hero and the times,' 'Heaven and the human being,' have at least the merit of pointing out the reciprocal nature of the relationship, that of principal and subordinate. It is not surprising that ancient Chinese thinkers were unable to solve this problem. China was long mired in a peasant economy ruled by commercial capital where productivity stagnated, so that it was hard to gain a clear understanding of what was meant by 'situation' and 'disposing Heaven,' the role of each, and how to create and determine the hero and the human being. Only after the development of industrial capitalism, with its simple and naked class relations, can thinkers identify the relationship, previously hidden, between situation, destiny, and Heaven.

Only with Marx's discovery of the laws of historical materialism was the relationship between hero and situation resolved. Marx's dialectical, non-mechanical materialism made it possible, while focusing primarily on circumstance, to reject passive fatalism and give appropriate weight to effort. Thus the relationship between people and things, subjective and objective, heroes and masses, was settled.

Marx himself applied this approach in his own writings. In 'The Eighteenth Brumaire of Louis Bonaparte,' he opposed both Hugo's representation of Napoleon's coup as 'the violent act of a single individual' and Proudhon's materialist explanation of it as 'the result of an antecedent historical development.' In the preface to the second German edition, he said:

> Victor Hugo confines himself to bitter and witty invective against the responsible producer of the coup d'état. The event itself appears in his

work like a bolt from the blue. He sees in it only the violent act of a single individual. He does not notice that he makes this individual great instead of little by ascribing to him a personal power of initiative unparalleled in world history. Proudhon, for his part, seeks to represent the coup d'état as the result of an antecedent historical development. Inadvertently, however, his historical construction of the coup d'état becomes a historical apologia for its hero. Thus he falls into the error of our so-called objective historians. I, on the contrary, demonstrate how the class struggle in France created circumstances and relationships that made it possible for a grotesque mediocrity to play a hero's part.[1]

In the *Eighteenth Brumaire*, Marx showed how the situation created by the class struggle in France, combined with special circumstances, allowed Napoleon III, this 'grotesque mediocrity,' to become a hero. However, at the same time he pointed out that it was precisely because the character of this petty man accorded with the needs of the reactionary situation at the time that each could complement the other, in reactionary intrigue. Here, Marx depicts the situation as primary and the hero as supplementary, but points up the relationship between the two, thus reconciling cause and effect.

Plekhanov explained this relationship even more clearly in *On the Role of the Individual in History*. He wrote:

> A great man is great not because his personal qualities give individual features to great historical events, but because he possesses qualities which make him most capable of serving the great social needs of his time, needs which arose as a result of general and particular causes. Carlyle, in his well-known book on heroes and hero-worship, calls great men *beginners*. This is a very apt description. A great man is precisely a beginner because he sees *further* than others, and desires things *more strongly* than others. He solves the scientific problems brought up by the preceding process of intellectual development of society; he points to the new social needs created by the preceding development of social relationships; he takes the initiative in satisfying these needs. He is a hero. But he is not a hero in the sense that he can stop, or change, the natural course of things, but in the sense that his activities are the conscious and free expression of this

---

[1] Marx, *The Eighteenth Brumaire of Louis Bonaparte*, Preface to the Second Edition (1869), vol. 21, 56–7.

inevitable and unconscious course. Herein lies all his significance; herein lies his whole power. But this significance is colossal, and the power is terrible.[2]

Plekhanov's definition of the great man or the hero also explains historical figures like Napoleon III, seemingly great but actually small. If no truly great human being or true hero rises to the needs of the day, others who match the requirements of the old society, who consciously serve reactionary goals, will, because of the special circumstances thrown up by class struggle, rise for a while to the top and become great and heroic – but, for Plekhanov, they are neither great nor heroic.

History is full of heroes of both sorts. Many great human beings have both characteristics. Only analysts who adhere to the Marxist view of historical personalities can distinguish between them, so as not to 'mistake the enemy for one's father' or 'charge with villainy a person of virtue'; only such a person can tell heroes apart, so that tyrants and oppressors do not become invisible.

Over the past three decades, the personality cult has taken over in the communist movement, although there is no basis for it in Marxism. It started in the early 1920s and took shape in the late 1920s in the Communist Party of the Soviet Union (AUCP(b)), with Stalin at its centre. At first it seemed to cater to the needs of the inner-party struggle – to weld a generation of old Bolsheviks into one. This happened following Lenin's illness and death. Lenin was the natural leader of the majority of Russian Social Democrats, a position he gained because of his natural talents, his vast learning, and his deep loyalty to the revolution and record of service to it. To adapt Plekhanov's formula, one might say that because Lenin 'saw *further* than others, and desired things *more strongly* than others, he solved the scientific problems brought up by the preceding process of intellectual development of society; he pointed to the new social needs created by the preceding development of social relationships; he took the initiative in satisfying these needs.' So he became a hero, and a leader. This was because in the real struggle, not just on paper, he showed greater mettle than any Marxist revolutionary anywhere, and was the 'most capable of serving the great social needs of his time.' You could say he was a born leader. As long as times did not change, no Bolshevik dared compete with him.

---

2 G.V. Plekhanov 1961.

Lenin was deeply aware of his own strength. Like all true heroes, he despised the personality cult. Like Carlyle's Cromwell, he hated the mediocrities who desperately crave recognition of their talent, the sort of whom Carlyle said:

> I advise you to keep out of his way. He cannot walk on quiet paths; unless you will look at him, wonder at him, write paragraphs about him, he cannot live. [...] Such a man will say: 'Keep your gilt carriages and huzza-ing mobs, keep your red-tape clerks, your influentialities, your important businesses. Leave me alone, leave me alone; there is too much of life in me already!'

Lenin, in whom there was also 'too much of life,' lived spartanly and modestly. This was because he had characteristics of the truly great person, devoid of pomposity, scheming, and false pride. He had no need for petty contrivances. His leadership was beyond dispute. He was not afraid to let his peers compete with him – in ability, learning, and hard work. He welcomed the fight, for truth becomes clearer the more it is contested, and nine times out of ten times truth wins; and if truth is on the other side, then one must say so and adjust. As Confucius said, 'The mistakes of an ethical person [*junzi*] are like eclipses of the sun and moon: everyone sees them. Once the errors are corrected, everyone looks up to the *junzi*.' After the darkness, the light shines even brighter. Debates in the party in Lenin's days, whoever was right and whoever wrong, never impinged on the debaters' position in the leadership, and even less so did they lead to organizational or administrative sanctions. To be convicted of holding an opinion, and paying for it with life or liberty, was beyond people's wildest imagining. So although Lenin enjoyed supreme authority, there was no personality cult in the party before October, and none either at home and abroad in the world communist movement after October. Lenin did not want to be worshipped, and those who wanted to worship him did not dare pollute with shallow vulgarities the esteem in which he was held.

When Lenin died, unimpeachable authority died with him. On grounds of insight and merit, Trotsky was the obvious choice to succeed him. After October, Trotsky showed himself to be wise, capable, meritorious, and a literary talent, a head above the other old Bolsheviks and Lenin's equal. In some fields, especially in the eyes of the people, he surpassed even Lenin. As Lenin's right-hand man, everyone expected Trotsky to take over when Lenin died. When Lenin fell ill, especially when he became concerned about the bureaucratisation of government bodies and Stalin's tyrannical treachery, he wanted Trotsky to be leader. However, he had a second stroke just two months later, and Stalin, Kamenev, and Zinoviev took over as a troika and excluded Trotsky, using as a pretext Trotsky's pre-October conflicts with Lenin and the Bolsheviks. Even so, Stalin could not count on success, for Trotsky had better revolutionary credentials and far greater popular prestige. Stalin needed to destroy Trotsky's popularity. Zinoviev and Stalin's magic wand was the personality cult. First, they transformed Lenin into a god and then they invented 'Leninism,' against which they pitted 'Trotskyism.' When Lenin died, they turned him into a communist Mohammed and laid him in a crystal coffin in a mausoleum, pitting the dead Lenin against the living Lenin and Trotsky. After the start of the personality cult, Lenin became the all-knowing incarnation of infallible truth, with his long-term disputant Trotsky cast as Judas or Satan. Stalin and Zinoviev, who had always followed Lenin and never denied him, became his Peter and Paul. This started in early 1920.

In 1925, especially after the defeat of Trotsky's Left Opposition in 1927, the personality cult changed tack. At first it was aimed at Trotsky, but after Trotsky's exile it was used to deify Stalin and attack the old Bolsheviks (including Zinoviev), together with inner-party democracy and socialist revolution in Russia and around the world. Stalin achieved his aim. However, he was helped by favourable circumstances. Given that he had barely been heard of before 1924, how can one explain his rise? Trotsky said transforming the mediocre Stalin into Stalin the supreme genius could happen because the Soviet Union was building socialism on a backward base, and because the world revolution suffered defeats in the mid 1920s that left the only workers' state isolated and vulnerable to imperialist pressure. You can read in Trotsky's writings about how this happened – there is no need to repeat it. Here, I want to discuss what some people have identified as the personality cult's 'more fundamental' grounds. They say that Stalin's personality cult welled up from the depths of human nature, and that any violent revolution will result in one. Others say that it was an embodiment of Lenin's idea about communist parties and professional revolutionaries, so what Stalin did, for good or ill, was Lenin's fault. Because these statements, though general, touch on Stalin's, and Mao's, personality cult, I want to look at them in detail. If personality cults well up from the depths of human nature, if violent revolutions inevitably lead to them, if Lenin's ideas about the party and the leadership of the revolution are the intellectual roots of the cult of the individual, then what Stalin did was rational and necessary, and so is the cult of Mao. By the same token, Trotsky's opposition to the cult was illusory, ahistorical, and unrealistic. If Stalin's and Mao's personality cults conformed to human nature and the laws of revolutionary history and started with Lenin, to oppose them is to oppose human nature, history, and Lenin.

Worship is said to be intrinsic to human nature. The first humans were in awe of nature and bewildered by society's disasters. Individuals were puny, and subject to a constant terror that drove them to seek protection in Heaven, gods, the emperor, and leaders. There, human beings acquired the reality or illusion of safety, and took to worship. That is the primary (though not the sole) root of the worship of nature. So worship originated in fear. Naturally, human relations are also marked by noble sentiments such as admiration, love, and respect, which are the basis of mutual worship. Fear alone will never triumph over worship born of heartfelt admiration. But love based only on heartfelt admiration cannot in itself lead to worship as a mass-based force. Many things cause people to mesh as a crowd, but the most important is *li* (interest) rather than *yi* (righteousness). Only on the basis of *li* can long-term emotional attachments be established and sustained. A great artist, poet, or thinker can be loved and honoured, but such a person cannot as such become leader of the people, and even less so be served by a system of worship internally coercive and externally exclusive. Religious figures, politicians, and militarists are different. They may well be loved and respected. However, it is not love and respect that joins them to the people but the fact that they represent and can protect the people's (or part of the people's) interests – or, where they are not worshipped, harm the people's interests. 'Submit to me and prosper, oppose me and die' is said to be the voice of the tyrant, but all systems of rule offer the same choice. Leaders are not suspended in a vacuum or ordained by Heaven. They can arise only if they first submit to the interests of a section of the people – whereupon, especially if they become the symbol of an organized mass, the people submit to them or die. Usually they submit, worshipping them willy nilly.

So the cult of the leader is rooted not in human nature but in social, economic, political, and cultural relations. The relationship between ruler and ruled will depend on the nature of the society, economy, politics, and culture; the nature of the leader cult will depend on the relationship between ruler and ruled. In general, where social conflict is less pronounced, where the productive forces of society are more developed, and where people's cultural and educational level is high – in such a society, the status of the leader is less, the leader is less likely to rise above society, and the people are less likely to worship the leader, so the leader cannot establish a personality cult. Plutarch said that 'ingratitude towards great men is the mark of a strong people.' This puts it in a nutshell: people worship leaders in inverse proportion to people's self-awareness. After Churchill led the British to victory in the Second World War, they kicked him out and he is said to have quoted Plutarch's maxim in return. There is no reason to sympathise with Churchill, whose political fortunes were anyway due in large part to British political maturity. His quoting Plutarch is interesting only in that it helps explain that the roots of leader worship are in society and history, not in human nature.

As for whether all violent revolutions necessarily end in personality cults, Carlyle is again helpful:

> May we not say, moreover, while so many of our late Heroes have worked rather as revolutionary men, that nevertheless every Great Man, every genuine man, is by the nature of him a son of Order, not of Disorder? It is a tragical position for a true man to work in revolutions. He seems an anarchist; and indeed a painful element of anarchy does encumber him at every step, – him to whose whole soul anarchy is hostile, hateful. His mission is Order; every man's is. He is here to make what was disorderly, chaotic, into a thing ruled, regular. [...] The carpenter finds rough trees; shapes them, constrains them into square fitness, into purpose and use. Thus too all human things, maddest French Sansculottisms, do and must work towards Order. I say, there is not a man in them, raging in the thickest of the madness, but is impelled withal, at all moments, towards Order. His very life means that; Disorder is dissolution, death. No chaos but it seeks a centre to revolve round. While man is man, some Cromwell or Napoleon is the necessary finish of a Sansculottism.[3]

Carlyle concludes that modern heroes are all revolutionaries. Each 'is by the nature of him a son of Order,' whose mission is 'to make what was disorderly, chaotic, into a thing ruled, regular.' Every revolution leads to disorder, that is, to the destruction of the old order, but no revolution can remain disorderly forever – it cannot destroy endlessly, but must create order. However, the order created out of disorder is not always the same in nature. It may be a new order, or a restoration of the old order. If one evaluates the former and the latter by the standards of human progress, they mean different things; the leaders of the first cannot be equated with the leaders of the second. But Carlyle does not distinguish Cromwell from Napoleon. This is because he does not view history from the standpoint of class struggle but from that of abstract moral principles, from the surface phenomena of order and disorder, employing the vacuous concepts of 'true' and 'false.' So although he knows that Cromwell is a greater hero than Napoleon, his criteria for discriminating between the two lacks force: the former is the more 'honest.' Carlyle does not think from the point of view of the progress of human history. Cromwell was indeed a hero, while Napoleon was not. For Cromwell set up a revolutionary dictatorship, while Napoleon set up a dictatorship that was the high tide of French reaction.

---

3   Carlyle, ch. 6.

'No chaos but it seeks a centre to revolve round.' Any revolution, past or present, in China or abroad, triggered or prepared, must, if it lasts for at least a while and achieves at least a small hold, have a centre to spin round. Mass revolutionary movements must, will, and can seek out a centre, a leading core, and a core within the core, a leader, Carlyle's hero. Otherwise, the revolutionaries will be a disorderly mob unable to move forward or endure, let alone succeed. So when Carlyle said 'some Cromwell or Napoleon is the necessary finish of a Sansculottism,' he drew attention to a historical necessity: that the masses after the revolution are bound to form a dictatorship. Unfortunately, he could not dive from the shallows into the depths, so he could not see that what, on the surface, looked like individual dictatorships were actually different systems: a Puritanism representing the Sansculottes, and the Corsican Emperor's final burial of Sansculottism. He does not distinguish between the social and historical significance of dictatorial heroes but merely points to the inevitability of revolutionary dictatorship.

Nearly all revolutions are about the transfer of state power. Social revolutions use this power to change class and property relations, which cannot happen without a revolutionary dictatorship. So revolutionary dictatorship and revolution are inseparable. A revolution that does not try to set up a dictatorship is a sham, or has been betrayed. All true revolutionaries, and historians, must admit the need for revolutionary dictatorship.

That does not mean that violent revolution always ends in a personality cult. Personality cults and the need for leaders are not the same. True, revolutionary dictatorship is often manifested in a dictatorial leader. But such leaders, as long as they are revolutionaries, and especially if they have emerged from a people's revolution or a workers' revolution, will not normally, knowingly or unknowingly, create a personality cult. One could even tie surrounding revolutionary leaders with cultic rites to the leader's personal qualities as a revolutionary and to periods of advance and retreat of the revolution he or she embodies. The better a leader's personal qualities, the better will that leader represent the people's interests and the less need will there be for a personality cult; and vice versa.

Lenin is sometimes represented as the inventor of the personality cult, but there are no grounds to support this. In *What Is to Be Done?* he wrote:

> Take the Germans. It will not be denied, I hope, that theirs is a mass organisation, that in Germany everything proceeds from the masses, that the working-class movement there has learned to walk. Yet observe how these millions value their 'dozen' tried political leaders, how firmly they cling to them. Members of the hostile parties in parliament have often taunted

the socialists by exclaiming: 'Fine democrats you are indeed! Yours is a working-class movement only in name; in actual fact the same clique of leaders is always in evidence, the same Bebel and the same Liebknecht, year in and year out, and that goes on for decades. Your supposedly elected workers' deputies are more permanent than the officials appointed by the Emperor!' But the Germans only smile with contempt at these demagogic attempts to set the 'masses' against the 'leaders,' to arouse bad and ambitious instincts in the former, and to rob the movement of its solidity and stability by undermining the confidence of the masses in their 'dozen wise men.' Political thinking is sufficiently developed among the Germans, and they have accumulated sufficient political experience to understand that without the 'dozen' tried and talented leaders (and talented men are not born by the hundreds), professionally trained, schooled by long experience, and working in perfect harmony, no class in modern society can wage a determined struggle.[4]

Here, Lenin makes the following points. (1) The party needs professional revolutionaries; (2) without such people, no class can be strong; (3) to be strong and solid, leaders must retain people's confidence; (4) in contemporary society, geniuses are not produced in the hundreds. Corrupt and ambitious politicians proclaiming themselves geniuses can, of course, abuse Lenin's conclusions, but Stalin's bureaucratic dictatorship and personality cult find no support in them. The central question is not corruption and manipulation but whether Lenin's prescriptions are necessary for the struggle. Do they accord with hard facts? Lenin hated people who cajole the public with claptrap and try to confuse and bewitch them, and he always refused to betray his convictions by catering to people's vanity or backwardness. Today, genius is rare; it is not easy for the proletariat to break its shackles. Workers must nurture from their own ranks or from other classes a minority of experts to lead their struggle; if such experts are not trusted, they will be unable to make the movement strong and solid.

Lenin's thinking about organisation is, in today's conditions, indispensable for making proletarian revolution, but that a new bureaucracy can form from it and that ambitious leaders can use it to promote personality cults is true. Lenin believed, rightly, that as long as the revolution keeps moving forward, widening and deepening, corrupt practices can be held at bay and ambitious leaders can be thwarted. At the start of the twentieth century, Lenin favoured a cent-

---

4   Lenin 1973, p. 150.

ralised organization, but in the late 1920s Stalin's personality cult arose, as a consequence of the failure of world revolution and the confinement of socialism to backward Russia. If, after 1919, the October Revolution had ignited the fire of world revolution, the Soviet Union would have escaped the nightmare of Stalinism, and Stalin would never have become sole leader. Lenin's insistence on centralised leadership to ensure the victory of the revolution was not the inevitable premise of the Stalin cult, which was a product of historical circumstance, and Lenin had more to say about party organisation than in the passage cited above.

Lenin never dealt in empty abstractions. When he wrote *What Is To Be Done?*, in 1902, Russia's Marxists were not yet, strictly speaking, organised. (The Russian Social Democratic Labour Party was founded in 1898, but its members were quickly arrested, and it next met in 1903.) Different groups had different ideas about what policy to follow. Lenin spoke of 'the confusion and vacillation that constitute the distinguishing feature of *an entire period* in the history of Russian Social-Democracy,' and declared that 'we can make no progress until we have completely put an end to this period.' *What Is To Be Done?* proposed ending the confusion by centralising the leadership. Lenin never shot without a target, and arrow and target cannot be separated, as Stalin did in attacking Trotsky and others.

If one examines Lenin's view of the party and the state and the relationship between leaders and led on the basis not of fleeting or incidental comments but holistically, it is clear that Lenin did not incline towards centralising leadership. The more the revolution took hold, with the workers establishing their own state, the Bolshevik becoming the ruling party, and Lenin finding new targets for his arrows, the more he favoured mass democracy. The evidence is overwhelming. *State and Revolution* asks how to break the bureaucratic system and prevent its recurrence, how, slowly but surely, to eliminate oppression and to realise true, universal democracy. At the end of the civil war, Russia was forced for the time being to build its new system in just one country. Lenin's entire resolve, throughout his illness, was bent on opposing the bureaucratisation of the party and the state, and his main target was Stalin, who represented the bureaucratic tendency. In neither his thinking nor his actions did he initiate the personality cult that Stalin exemplified. On the contrary, he opposed it.

So the personality cult did not grow out of human nature or violent revolution. Leaders must enjoy the people's esteem if revolution is to succeed, but they must foreswear cults. Cults represent the betrayal of the revolution, or at least its entry into reactionary crisis. As for Lenin, he cannot be held responsible for Stalin's cult. One can therefore uphold the idea of revolution under the leadership of a group of leaders, violent if necessary, but one must oppose worshipping the leader and all forms of bureaucratism, which are most consistently represented by, and gain theoretical support from, Stalinism.

Mao thought is, in most basic respects, Stalinism, particularly so in the case of the cult of the individual. In terms of its extent, there is not much difference between Mao's personality cult and Stalin's. For bourgeois democrats, the explanation is simple: sow melons and you will harvest melons, sow beans and you get beans: the cult of the individual is intrinsic to communism, and if you don't like it, then don't be a communist and don't support violent revolution. I have already criticised these arguments, and there's no need to do so again. In a word, revolution is necessary, but so is opposition to the cult of the individual. On the leader cult, I reached the following conclusions: (1) the more backward an economy and culture or the more intense the class struggle, the greater the importance of political leaders, the higher their status, and the easier it is to build and consolidate a personality cult – and vice versa; (2) when a revolution is on the rise and its leaders closely reflect the interests of the masses, thus winning respect and prestige, it is almost impossible for the leaders to establish a cult, but when the revolution stalls or suffers setbacks, for internal or external reasons, and revolutionary leaders come under attack, the weaker, more conservative, more compromising, or baser leaders can set up a cult of the leader so that they can betray the revolution under the cover of revolutionary authority; (3) a revolutionary leader, or any political leader who has talent and breadth of vision and is loyal to the cause, will despise flattery and resist being buried alive in a *shengci*, a temple to the living.

That is why in the Lenin-Trotsky era there was no leader cult, and why one arose under Stalin. But on what grounds did Mao worship start? While one might disagree with many of the CCP's policies, one cannot deny that the CCP has, until now, pushed the Chinese Revolution forward. And while Mao, in many respects, lacks the stature of Lenin and Trotsky, he is far wiser and more able, in mind and vision, than Stalin. Finally, Mao directly organised the victory of the Chinese Revolution, while Stalin inherited (or rather, usurped and betrayed) the Russian Revolution. So by rights, Mao should take no pleasure in a leader cult and have no need for one.

It's not hard to show that Mao has set up a leader cult. The evidence is everywhere. However, it is also not hard to find passages extolling humility and the need to guard against pride in Mao's talks or writings. He talks a lot about valuing the masses and sticking to the mass line. These warnings should not be denied, and should even be respected, as uttered in good faith. But that does not refute the existence of a Mao cult, and on a grand scale. It is one thing to urge cadres to 'remain modest, prudent and free from arrogance and rashness in style,' but another to do all one can to shore up one's own leadership. Leaders who want to keep power know that officials must be 'modest, prudent, and free from arrogance and rashness,' or they will fail. But leaders who caution their subordinates against arrogance are not necessarily free of it themselves; selfish, immodest leaders who want to succeed, who are not carried away by their successes and keep a clear head, will not tolerate their subordinates acting overbearingly. That does not stop them being arrogant, and deliberately establishing a leader cult to keep their subordinates humble. They want to maintain the effectiveness of the ruling machine but at the same time to nip rivals in the bud. So most leaders and dictators preach modesty. Even the most imperious monarch delivers the same sermon. Today, no one denies that Stalin ran a personality cult, but he was always telling people to be modest. When Lenin died, Stalin borrowed his name to promote humility and belief in the masses. Such words were never out of his mouth. On the positive side, the aim of this sermonising today is to detoxify the bureaucracy dictatorship produces (though in reality this does not work). On the negative side, it is to cover up the regime's ugliness. So Mao's harping on about modesty does not mean that the CCP has not set up a Mao cult.

On March 13, 1949, Mao said:

> Guard against arrogance. For anyone in a leading position, this is a matter of principle and an important condition for maintaining unity. Even those who have made no serious mistakes and have achieved very great success in their work should not be arrogant. Celebration of the birthdays of party leaders is forbidden. Naming places, streets and enterprises after party leaders is likewise forbidden. We must keep to our style of plain living and hard work and put a stop to flattery and exaggerated praise.[5]

This makes obvious sense. After the CPSU's Twentieth Congress, the CCP quoted it everywhere, to prove it had always opposed the personality cult. But these fine precepts are honoured more in the breach than in the observance. So far there are no Chinese cities and streets named after leaders, like Stalingrad, but eulogising leaders and wishing them a long life on their birthdays was

---

5 Mao, 'Methods of Work of Party Committees,' March 13, 1949, SW, vol. 4, pp. 377–82, at 380. It is hard to believe this passage was in the original speech, though I have no way of checking. Would Mao have dared say this while Stalin was alive? In 1956, Khrushchev said: 'It is enough to point out that many towns, factories and industrial enterprises, kolkhozes and sovkhozes, Soviet institutions and cultural institutions have been referred to by us with a title if I may express it so – of private property of the names of these or those Government or party leaders who were still active and in good health.' The two speeches are similar. Was Mao's revised in 1960? (note by Wang).

already in vogue in the Yan'an era. They no longer do it, but that doesn't mean that the CCP has abandoned the cult of the individual, because these are superficial issues. The eulogisation of Mao is easily on a par with that of Stalin, and in some respects has overtaken it. In the Soviet Union, poets wrote poems praising Stalin as 'brighter than the sun,' which Trotsky ridiculed as pig grunts. But the same pig grunts fill the CCP press. 'The East is Red,' supposedly a Shaanbei folk song, also makes a sun of Mao.

Where Mao's cult outdoes even Stalin's is in putting Mao on a par with Lenin. Stalin, even in his wildest excesses, portrayed himself as Lenin's follower and subordinate, or at most as his comrade-in-arms and fellow leader. Mao, however, knows no such bounds. At the CCP's Seventh Congress in 1945, Mao thought was described as the party's guiding principle, integrating Marxism-Leninism with the practice of the Chinese Revolution 'as the guideline for all its work,' an arrogation without precedent even under Stalin. If Mao thought guides the general direction of the theory and practice of the Chinese Revolution, anyone questioning it is opposing absolute truth.

Why did Mao create this personality cult, and how did he create it? In 1956, the CCP adopted a new constitution that revised the 1945 formulation by deleting the reference to 'Mao Zedong Thought': 'The Communist Party of China takes Marxism-Leninism as its guide to action. Only Marxism-Leninism correctly describes the laws of social development.' Had Mao suddenly become modest? Had the party become democratic after the victory of the revolution, so that the cult of the individual was no longer appropriate? No. The real reason was Khrushchev's denunciation, six months earlier, of Stalin's cult. It was a concession to the international Stalinist movement, and had nothing to do with Mao's cult.

In his article 'Rectify the Party's Style of Work,' Mao briefly described his schooling: 'In my childhood I never attended a Marxist-Leninist school and was taught only such things as, "The Master said: How pleasant it is to learn and constantly review what one has learned." Though this teaching material was antiquated, it did me some good because from it I learned to read.'[6] He then studied in Changsha, where he laid the basis for his knowledge and ideas. Under Yang Changji (1871–1920), he studied Confucian ethics, especially Neo-Confucianism. He also randomly devoured writings of eighteenth and nineteenth-century British and French bourgeois scholars in the social and natural sciences, simultaneously cultivating old and new learning. However, his foundation was in the former rather than the latter: in orthodox Confucian-

---

6 Mao, 'Rectify the Party's Style of Work,' February 1, 1942, SW, vol. 3, pp. 36–52, at 41.

ism (from the Song and the Ming through to Wang Chuanshan and Tan Sitong) rather than in Western bourgeois-democratic thinking.

In 'On the People's Democratic Dictatorship,' Mao wrote:

> From the time of China's defeat in the Opium War of 1840, Chinese progressives went through untold hardships in their quest for truth from the Western countries. Hong Xiuquan, Kang Youwei, Yan Fu and Sun Yat-sen[7] were representative of those who had looked to the West for truth before the Communist Party of China was born. Chinese who then sought progress would read any book containing the new knowledge from the West. The number of students sent to Japan, Britain, the United States, France and Germany was amazing. At home, the imperial examinations were abolished and modern schools sprang up like bamboo shoots after a spring rain; every effort was made to learn from the West. In my youth, I too engaged in such studies. They represented the culture of Western bourgeois democracy, including the social theories and natural sciences of that period, and they were called 'the new learning' in contrast to Chinese feudal culture, which was called 'the old learning.'[8]

This is certainly true. However, it did not change Mao's basic attachment to the formula 'Chinese learning for the foundation, Western learning for application.'[9] For Mao, learning these things expanded knowledge and changed thinking, but they did not enter the blood, and certainly not the soul. The soul cannot be transformed by a few books. Knowledge can have an impact, but the main catalysts are a nation's history and culture and the social environment, especially in childhood, and the people and things one meets while one's consciousness is forming, the thoughts, sentiments, and interests that are one's first love.

Changsha was at the time a 'semi-feudal' bureaucratic political centre, a hub of China's central-southern provinces and of the landowning and commercial economy of the southwest and on a major highway between north and south. A cockpit of the struggle between Confucian diehards and reformers, this ancient city, a fortress of Neo-Confucianism since the Song and Ming, was the soil that

---

7   Hong Xiuquan (1814–1864) was a leader of the Taiping Rebellion against the Qing. Kang Youwei (1858–1927) was a scholar, prominent political thinker, and reformer in the late Qing; Yan Fu (1854–1921) was a scholar and translator, famous for introducing Western ideas into China; Sun Yat-sen (1866–1925), also called Sun Zhongshan, was a revolutionary and founding father of the Republic of China in 1912.
8   Mao, 'On The People's Democratic Dictatorship,' June 30, 1949, SW, vol. 4, pp. 411–24, at 413.
9   A formula first used by Zhang Zhidong in his *Exhortation to Study* (1898), and subsequently widely copied by conservative reformers.

fed the roots of the young Mao's spirit. Yang Changji's Neo-Confucianism, infiltrated by Western idealist philosophy, especially his insistence on cultivating the moral self and practising what you preach; Sima Guang's *Zizhi tongjian*; Han Yu's articles; Shi Nai'an; Luo Guanzhong's novels; Su Dongpo's and Xin Qiji's poetry[10] – these literary giants were the life-blood of Mao's spiritual development. They struck deep roots into the psyche of this peasant youth, a foundation to the foundation of his mind and spirit that has nurtured him throughout his life. Since then, he has absorbed new thoughts and knowledge, first from British and French bourgeois democrats and later from Marxists. But these were superficial, a frame nailed to the existing fundament, things attached to the pinnacle of the spirit. They transformed parts of the foundation, but at its margins.

The formula 'Chinese learning for the foundation, Western learning for application' helped Mao win power, so it is not his weakness but his strength (although weaknesses and strengths often turn into each other). This is a question I will consider later. Here, I simply point out that Mao's attachment to the personality cult and his roots in orthodox Confucianism are strongly related. That communist revolutionaries cherish non-communist thoughts can be blamed in part on old ideas about 'imperial virtues and kingly exploits' and 'righting wrongs in accordance with Heaven's decree.'

The CCP formed a cult of the individual because of China's economic underdevelopment and the crushing weight of its political despotism, which excludes the majority from the cultural sphere. Any political party, even a communist party, born in such an environment can become bureaucratised and acquire a personality cult. This is the fundamental reason. Because the economy is backward, there are few industrial workers to bear up the party, measured against the country's huge population. Some people have even doubted that China could ever produce a true communist party, although facts show them to be wrong. However, the tininess of the modern working class as a proportion of the population caused the CCP to turn to the peasants as the main

---

10 Sima Guang (1019–1086) was a Song dynasty scholar who compiled *Zizhi tongjian* ('Comprehensive Mirror for Aid in Government'), which criticized people and institutions from a Confucian standpoint; Han Yu (768–824) was a a neo-Confucian essayist and poet; Shi Nai'an (ca. 1296–1372) is said to have written *Shuihu zhuan* (variously translated as *The Water Margin, All Men Are Brothers, Outlaws of the Marsh*, and *The Marshes of Mount Liang*), a classical Chinese novel about the 108 outlaws of Mount Liang; Luo Guanzhong (ca. 1330–1400) wrote the classical novel *Sanguo yanyi* (translated as *Romance of the Three Kingdoms*), a story of battles and intrigues; Su Dongpo (1037–1101) and Xin Qiji (1140–1207) were famous Song dynasty poets.

force. This is the chief source of its bureaucratic system. Another source is the way it waged the revolution for more than twenty years.

After the defeat of the revolution of 1925–7, the Guomindang colluded with imperialism to set up a fascist military dictatorship and suppress democratic rights. It was almost impossible to wage legal struggles, and attempts to improve the workers' lot were stamped out. At the time, the CCP was following a disastrous putschist line, after which it gradually embarked on a path of setting up revolutionary governments in the villages and carrying out long-term armed struggle. Again, I'll return to these questions later, but here I want to point out that the way the struggle was waged bore heavily on the leader cult and the cult of the individual. In 'Problems of Strategy in China's Revolutionary War,' Mao wrote:

> It is extremely difficult to convince the cadres and the people of the necessity of strategic retreat when they have had no experience of it, and when the prestige of the army leadership is not yet such that it can concentrate the authority for deciding on strategic retreat in the hands of a few persons or of a single person and at the same time enjoy the confidence of the cadres.

This passage is about strategic retreat, but its significance extends to the entire war. Wars, even revolutionary wars, can't be run democratically. They are won more by politics than by fighting, but victory or defeat on the battlefield depends on the command of a handful of generals, and even of a single individual – on their or the individual general's ability and prestige. Mao was talking from experience. The need for personal authority led to the personality cult.

Mao's cult and Stalin's cult were different, but both had the same point of origin, in underdevelopment, the lack of a democratic tradition, and a low educational level. They are backwardness's revenge on revolution. Both cults are toxic, and we must oppose them. On the other hand, the two cults mean different things. Stalin's represented a direct betrayal of the democratic spirit of the October Revolution, so it was profoundly reactionary. Mao's is only indirectly so (in that it is an extension abroad of Stalinism). Directly, and also more largely, Mao's cult embodies revolutionary dictatorship distorted by national backwardness. It is more revolutionary than reactionary. Stalin wiped out all the Old Bolsheviks to make his Thermidor. The most immediate result of Mao's personalisation of power was to defeat Stalin's agent in China (Wang Ming).[11] In

---

11   Wang Ming (1904–1974), originally called Chen Shaoyu, was a Moscow-educated leader of the CCP and Mao's main rival in the 1930s.

its broader sense, it was mostly due to the needs of the revolutionary struggle (particularly the armed struggle), and only in smaller measure in support of Mao's personal ambition. That is not to say that Stalin's cult was aimed at revolutionaries and Mao's mainly at counter-revolutionaries. A personality cult of any sort harms the revolution. Where a decision must be made on the spot or there is a military crisis, intervention by an absolute authority can guarantee speedy victory. But that does not mean that a leader worshipped by the people and the party must be given absolute authority over life and death for the revolution to proceed smoothly. A party or nation under such a saviour is bound to fail, because the presence of the saviour destroys creativity, speeds the bureaucratisation of party and state, and is the surest way to destroy the revolution's true leaders, including the cultified one. So even if the Mao cult has, in some senses, played a positive role in the Chinese Revolution, it has far more often played a negative role, and will do so more and more as time goes by.

It is one thing for leaders of revolutions to be praised for their courage and capacity, and quite another for them to become objects of cults, or for someone without prestige to be artificially made into one. The former is natural, necessary, and in the interests of the revolution; the latter is superficial and arrogant, and against the interests of the revolution. Given this distinction, we can cherish real authority in the revolution and oppose the cult of the individual; and we can see what in any individual leader is revolutionary prestige and what is cult of the individual, and in what periods that leader plays a revolutionary role and at what point he or she becomes reactionary.

In the past, Mao was able to contribute to the revolution in part because the Stalin-style personality cult had not yet completely submerged his deserved prestige. In future, as his prestige is increasingly apotheosised, his role in the revolution will become increasingly negative, increasingly reactionary.

The tragedy of the People's Communes set up in 1958 is a clear demonstration of how the Mao cult has damaged the revolution. So we oppose the cult, not just in the revolution's interests but even, in a sense, in Mao's. My goal in studying Mao, and Mao thought, is mainly to restore the semi-deified Mao to Mao the human being; to recover from the Mao myth real Mao thought, which was sometimes right and sometimes wrong.

CHAPTER 2

The Sources and Components of Mao Zedong Thought

To know a person's thinking, one must first ask how it came about. Before it takes final shape, especially if it is comparatively systematic, it passes through a string of changes, long and short, in an unbroken line of negations and accumulations. After it has settled down, this process is in one sense over. In another sense, however, it is not over. It continues to ferment: the outcomes it accumulates continue to hold within them many elements of past changes seemingly negated but actually retained. These residues – especially those left by the mind's first loves – often, knowingly or unknowingly, shape thinking, acting out of the mind's innermost recesses, as its lowest and therefore sturdiest foundation. In this sense, the transforming of a person's thinking is never over, and the changes are always preserved in the depths of the soul.

So to grasp the essence of Mao thought, one must start by asking how it was born and how it grew. Mao thought took rather a long time to mature. Mao's schooling started when he was eight, and at twenty-seven he became a Marxist. From the time he first started learning to read and write to the initial determination of his thinking took nineteen years. That's much longer than the Russian Marxists. Trotsky, for example, became a Marxist at the age of seventeen, and by the age of twenty-six years, in 1905, he was leader of the Petrograd Soviet. Stalin became a Marxist before the age of twenty. Lenin was nine years older, but he completed the passage from populism to Marxism at around the age of twenty.

There are many reasons why Mao came late to Marxism, but one of the most important was that, in China, the transition from advocacy of constitutional monarchy and advocacy of bourgeois revolution by the democrats to the call for workers and peasants' revolution by the communists took little more than twenty years. The same process took hundreds of years in Britain and France and nearly one hundred years in Russia. In countries that took a long time to develop, not only the party of enlightened monarchical reform but even bourgeois radicals were no longer able to influence the young revolutionaries when Marxism emerged. 'Progressive' ideas had already been exposed as reactionary, so once the conditions for proletarian revolution ripened, steeled revolutionaries (like the leaders of the October Revolution born in the 1870s) threw off their old thinking almost at the outset and became Marxists.

China in the late-nineteenth and early-twentieth centuries was different. After stagnating for hundreds of years, Chinese society suddenly, under strong external shock, underwent intense and rapid change. Because it was intense, it took the form of combined development, meaning that before the old could be cleared away, the new had already appeared. Before the new could win, the even newer made it old. Old and new mixed, and sometimes the newest and the oldest lived side by side. Each changed with the other, pulling and dragging at it, this way and that, amid ever greater chaos.

In the intellectual sphere, combined development shortened the process, while ensuring the presence of old dross in new things. The shortening applied to intellectual life as a whole: for individuals, the time taken seemed to lengthen. The maturation of the thinking of people born in those years (Mao was born in 1893, thirty-six years after Kang Youwei, twenty-eight after Tan Sitong, twenty-two after Sun Yat-sen, and fourteen after Chen Duxiu[1]) had, by and large, to follow or repeat the general intellectual development of the time. Kang Youwei was born twenty-two years before Chen Duxiu, a mere moment in the history of thought; but from the point of view of Mao as an individual, the passage from Kang Youwei-ite (1906–9) to Chen Duxiu-ite (1920) took twelve to thirteen years, a long time.

The speed at which revolutionaries become Marxists says a lot about their ideas. The longer it takes, and the older an individual is at the time, the more complex will be their intellectual trajectory, the less flimsy will be their intellectual foundations, and the more the learning and thinking they absorb while maturing will shape the Marxism they finally embrace.

The relationship between the length of time it takes for a person's thinking to mature and the nature of that thinking is clarified by a look at Mao's pre-Marxist period. The nineteen-year prehistory of Mao thought can be divided into the following periods.

1901–6 (eight to ten years old). Mao attended primary school in his village. 'I knew the Classics, but disliked them. What I enjoyed were the romances of Old China, and especially stories of the rebellions.'[2] He read the historical novel *Yue Fei zhuan* (Biography of Yue Fei), *The Water Margin*, *Revolt Against the Tang*,

---

1 Tan Sitong (1865–1898) was a thinker and reformist in the late Qing, executed aged 33 when the Reform Movement failed; Chen Duxiu (1879–1942) was a leader of the New Culture Movement, founder of the CCP, and its General Secretary until 1927. In 1931, he became a Trotskyist and helped found the Chinese Left Opposition, which he then led. In 1932, he went to prison on charges of seeking to overthrow the government and replace it with a proletarian dictatorship.
2 Mao, interviewed by Snow (Snow 1968).

The Romance of the Three Kingdoms, and *Journey To the West*, the story of Xuanzang's seventh-century semi-legendary pilgrimage to India.³

1906–9 (thirteen to sixteen). Mao helped his parents in the fields, and at the same time continued his studies. 'I read almost all the books I could borrow in the village.'⁴ Among them were issues of *Xinmin congbao* (New Citizen) and Zheng Guanying's *Shengshi weiyan* (Warnings in the Golden Age).⁵ Mao told Edgar Snow he liked this book very much.

1909–19 (sixteen to eighteen). Mao studied minor learning (a branch of classical studies) at the Dongshan Higher Primary School in Xiangxiang. He left home and went to Xiangxiang at the age of sixteen. He stayed less than two years. During this time he began to read some natural science and Western new knowledge, and he got a book from his cousin about Kang and Liang's reform movement. He greatly admired Kang and Liang.

1911–2 (eighteen to nineteen). These were volatile years in Mao's life, in which he embarked on his intellectual explorations. In the early spring of 1911 he arrived in Changsha, where he enrolled in Changsha's Xiangxiang Middle School. Six months later, the 1911 Revolution broke out, and he renounced the pen for the sword and joined the New Army.⁶ Six months after that, he left the army and tried to join various vocational middle schools, but to no avail, until finally he got into Hunan's First Provincial Middle School. He was not happy there either, and stayed just a few months. The only thing he could recall was that a Chinese literature teacher lent him *Yupi zizhi tongjian* ('Comprehensive Mirror for Aid in Government'),⁷ which he read avidly and profited from

---

3 Snow 1968, p. 133. Yue Fei (1103–1127) was a general who in the Southern Song dynasty became a symbol for patriotic loyalty in China. *Journey To the West* is a classical novel published in the sixteenth century and attributed to Wu Cheng'en.

4 Li Rui 1957.

5 *Xinmin congbao* was a reformist journal in the early twentieth century. Zheng Guanying (1842–1921) was a business person associated with theories about 'saving the nation by enriching it.'

6 The New Army was the modernised army corps formed under the Qing dynasty in 1895.

7 The *Zizhi tongjian*, published in 1084 by Sima Guang (1019–1086), is a chronicle of Chinese history from the Warring States period (476–221 BCE) to the Five Dynasties (907–960), designed as a reference book to guide emperors' governance. During and after the revolution, Mao is said to have kept his battered copy of it by his bed and to have read it a dozen times. On the basis of Sima Guang's original, the Southern Song philosopher Zhu Xi (1130–1200) wrote a version of it known as the *Tongjian gangmu* ('Outline of the *Comprehensive Mirror*'). The *Yupi zizhi tongjian* (*yupi* means 'imperially endorsed') was a derivative, condensed, and commented version of Zhu Xi's book produced for the Kangxi Emperor (r. 1662–1722) in the early Qing dynasty. The Jesuit missionary Joseph-Anna-Marie de Moyriac de Mailla produced a twelve-volume translation, *Histoire générale de la Chine, ou Annales de cet Empire; traduit du*

throughout his life. After that he left school and went every day to the Provincial Library to read books on world geography and world history, as well as Adam Smith's *The Wealth of Nations*, Darwin's *Origin of Species*, and Mill's *System of Logic*. He also read Rousseau, Spinoza's *Ethics*, and Montesquieu's *The Spirit of Laws*. He promiscuously mixed poetry, novels, stories of ancient Greece, and works on the history and geography of Russia, America, Britain, France, and other countries.[8]

1913–18 (twenty to twenty-five). In these years, Mao laid the foundations for his thinking. He concluded his self-study in the spring of 1913. To appease his father, and get economic support, he enrolled in Hunan's Fourth Normal School, which six months later merged with First Normal, where he studied for five years. He said his knowledge and learning acquired its foundations at First Normal.[9] The best teacher at First Normal, who deeply influenced the young Mao's life and thought and later became his father-in-law, was Yang Changji, who taught moral cultivation and other subjects. Mao said of him: 'The teacher who made the strongest impression on me was Yang Changji, a returned student from England. [...] He taught ethics. He was an idealist, and a man of high moral character. He believed in his ethics very strongly and tried to imbue his students with the desire to become just, moral, virtuous, and useful in society.'[10]

According to Li Rui, Yang Changji's thinking was as follows:

> Mr Yang Changji, also known as Huaizhong, lived in Bancang in Dongxiang in Changsha, so he was also known as Mr Bancang. From childhood, he liked the Cheng-Zhu school of Confucianism. He studied for nine years in Japan and Britain. [...] While abroad, he concentrated on studying education and philosophy, to explore the way of correct conduct. [...] Mr Yang Changji was trained in China's old culture, especially Neo-Confucianism. He also studied the theories of Wang Chuanshan, Tan Sitong, and Immanuel Kant. He examined the social system and general environment of old European democratism, selected from it, criticised it, fused it, and thus created for himself a view of the world based on progressive ethical thinking and stressing practice. Although, philosophically, he was an idealist who believed in the theory of evolution, exaggerated the role of subjective initiative, and preached an ethics in which

---

Tong-kien-kang-mou par de Mailla, published in Paris in 1777–83. For an English translation of excerpts from *Zizhi tongjian*, see Yap (ed. and tr.) 2009, and Yap (trans.) 2016.

8   Snow 1968, p. 144.
9   Li Rui 1957, p. 18.
10   Li Rui 1957, p. 19.

idealism was an important component, some of his views and ideas, especially his spirit of pursuing new ideas and personally undertaking to practise them, played a very positive role among young people he taught. [...] Progressive youth at the First Normal School naturally united around Mr Yang Changji. Everyone happily submitted to him. In the classroom, they listened to him very carefully; after classes, Comrade Mao Zedong and others often went to Bancang Yang's residence to listen to him, pursue scholarship, study ethics, ask for corrections to their notes, or talk about world affairs. Mr Yang was very fond of this group of young people, especially Comrade Mao Zedong. Teachers and students got on well, showing mutual respect and love. In those circumstances, Mr Yang Changji carefully instructed his students; the students sincerely learned from him in many ways, and even copied him.

Mao and his friends said that they were influenced in the following spheres: (1) Tan Sitong and Wang Chuanshan studies; (2) the modernisation of Confucian ethics and the integration of Confucian thinking and Western European democratic idealist philosophy; (3) the introduction of ideas from the early period of *New Youth*; and (4) discretion in words and deeds: 'Meditate,[11] think silently, do not tell lies, do not indulge in vice, etc., live simply and frugally, and engage in physical exercise; be assiduous, respect labour; [...] take cold baths and long walks, etc.'[12]

1918–20 (twenty-five to twenty-seven). This is when Mao became a materialist. After graduating from Normal School in 1918, he went north to Beijing, the centre of the New Culture Movement. He got a job in Peking University Library under Li Dazhao and met many new people, including Chen Duxiu. He strove to absorb new knowledge, by voracious reading. At one point, he was close to the anarchist Qu Shengbai,[13] and he agreed with the anarchists on many things. But he said that Chen Duxiu influenced him most. In the spring of 1919, he left Beijing for Shanghai, whence he returned to Hunan and joined the radical Xinmin Society. After the May Fourth Movement[14] broke out in Beijing, it imme-

---

11 Mao did not approve of meditation ('quietly sitting' in Chinese). In his essay on physical education he said: 'In my humble opinion, there is only movement in heaven and on earth' (note by Wang, citing Li Rui 1957, p. 33).
12 Li Rui 1957, p. 24.
13 Qu Shengbai (1893–1973) was an anarchist and Esperantist who engaged in political disputes with Chen Duxiu.
14 The May Fourth Movement of May 4, 1919, was an anti-imperialist cultural and political movement that grew out of student protests against the Chinese government's capitulation to the foreign powers at the signing of the Treaty of Versailles.

diately spread to Hunan, and he led the student movement in Changsha. He set up a Student Federation Council, ran *Xiangjiang Review*, and campaigned to drive out the warlord Governor Zhang Jingyao. *Xiangjiang Review* was soon closed down and the Federation was dissolved. After a period of writing and political organising, Mao once again left for Beijing, chased away by the Hunan warlords. This time he stayed in Beijing for only a short while (from the end of 1919 to the summer of 1920), but it was an important period in his intellectual development. He described it as follows:

> During my second visit to Beijing I had read much about the events in Russia, and had eagerly sought out what little communist literature was then available in Chinese. Three books especially deeply carved my mind, and built up in me a faith in Marxism, from which, once I had accepted it as the correct interpretation of history, I did not afterwards waver. These books were the *Communist Manifesto*, translated by Chen Wangdao, and the first Marxist book ever published in Chinese; *Class Struggle*, by Kautsky; and a *History of Socialism*, by Kirkup. By the summer of 1920 I had become, in theory and to some extent in action, a Marxist, and from this time on I considered myself a Marxist.[15]

Using this description as a guide, we can tabulate the maturation of Mao's thinking as follows:

First period (eight to sixteen). Mao gained a good grasp of the Confucian classics, in the traditional manner. He also read some Chinese novels (in the early period) and a small number of writings by the old reformers (in the late period).

Second period (seventeen to twenty). He came into contact with Western scientific thinking and writings by British and French bourgeois democrats, and for the first time he came across the Guomindang's *Minli bao* (People's Independent Daily). But he was most influenced in these years by the *Comprehensive Mirror for Aid in Government*, written in the eleventh century.

Third period (twenty to twenty-five). Mao spent these years being guided and influenced by the Neo-Confucian Yang Changji. In his thinking and everyday activity, he systematically imbibed theories of Confucianism, particularly its radical, modernised wing, which had fused with nationalism and become bourgeoisified (represented by Wang Chuanshan and Tan Sitong, right through until the emergence of Chen Duxiu's new ideas in the early days of *New Youth*).

---

15   Snow 1968, p. 155.

Fourth period (twenty-five to twenty-seven). This is when he found a way out. Initially, his thinking 'was still in chaos. [...] In the winter of 1920, [he] began to be influenced and guided by Marxist theory and the history of the Russian Revolution.'

In this simple enumeration, even numbers say a lot. The four periods cover eighteen years, of which eight were during the reign of old Confucian doctrines, three during the passage from old to new, five during the period of Neo-Confucianism, and two during the transition to Marxism. In the pre-history of Mao thought, old and new Confucian doctrines held sway for nearly sixteen years, but it took just one or two years for him to break from them and embrace Marxism (though the break was not clean). I am not trying to make a mathematical argument that Confucianism represented sixteen eighteenths and Marxism only two eighteenths of Mao thought. Even so, the ratio helps to understand the sources of Mao thought and grasp its essence.

Lenin called Marxism 'the legitimate successor to the best that man produced in the nineteenth century, as represented by German philosophy, English political economy and French socialism.'[16] Mao thought also has its sources and component parts. We already know its sources, but it's harder to determine its components. The three sources of Marxism are obvious, and their roles in its making were more or less equally matched. Mao thought is different. Some of its sources are self-evident. But how did they come to constitute Mao thought? What selection and critique did each undergo in constituting it? What share did each occupy in the resulting whole? What factors organically constituted it? Or were they simply pieced together? It is harder to answer these questions than it was for Lenin in the case of Marx, but I will try.

The sources of Mao thought were: (1) Old and New Confucianism, or rather, the Confucianism of Zhu Xi (1130–1200) and Yang Changji (with the latter representing Confucianism of the Cheng-Zhu school, Wang Chuanshan, and, latterly, Kang Youwei and Tan Sitong);[17] (2) the tradition of wandering swordsmen (*youxia*), who robbed the rich and helped the poor;[18] and (3) Western socialist thought.

---

16 Lenin, 'The Three Sources and Three Component Parts of Marxism,' CW, vol. 19, pp. 23–28, at 23.

17 Old Confucianism is classical Confucianism. Neo-Confucianism refers to the Confucian revival in the Tang dynasty (618–907), when the doctrine was reformulated and reinvigorated. The Cheng-Zhu school was one of its main schools, based on the thinking of Cheng Yi, Cheng Hao, and Zhu Xi. Wang Chuanshan (1619–1692) was a neo-Confucian philosopher of the late Ming dynasty. Tan Sitong (1865–1898) was a thinker and reformist in the late Qing dynasty (1636–1911); he was executed aged 33, when the Reform Movement failed.

18 See below.

It is hard to say what visage these three sources assume when they meet in Mao. It is not like in the case of Marxism. When Marx drew on the sources of his ideas, he subjected each to rigorous selection and critique, so that each – whether philosophical, socialist, or economic – reached new heights, unprecedentedly accurate and scientific. The difference between Marxism and its sources is clear at a glance. There is no mistaking what Marx negated, took over, and further developed. The relationship between Mao thought and its sources is not the same. There are few clear boundaries, so it is not easy to see where old ends and new begins. The main reason is, of course, that Mao thought cannot compare with Marx's; one could even say that Mao is not a thinker but a political pragmatist. He did not first create a set of theories (a world view, a view of life, a view of history, an analysis of objectives, a mapping out of strategy) and then engage in revolutionary activity: instead, he first embraced revolutionary goals and then, during long years of revolution, 'investigated and discussed' and learned through struggle, forming his thought thus. Thinking of that sort has its merits, but it lacks system, it cannot be consistent, it puts expediency above principle, and tactics dictate strategy – these are its inevitable characteristics. We first came across this special feature of Mao thought when looking for its sources. When we study the practical application of Mao thought, we will come across it again and again.

Old and New Confucianism is a major source of Mao thought, that much is indisputable. But if I say that Confucianism is not just a source but an enduring component of it, many will object. How could an idealist, 'feudal,' class-bound Confucianism be an integral part of Mao's communist ideology? Yet if I put it another way and say that Mao thought inherited important elements of traditional Chinese thinking, people might agree. But is Confucianism not a major constituent of Chinese tradition, and therefore part of Mao thought? Are people and their ideas not a product of their environment, and of tradition? Yes, great men and women change their environment and make history, but first they must be part of that environment and history if they are to understand them, let alone reshape them.

Confucian thinking is to China what Islamic thinking is to Arab and other countries and Christianity to Europe and the West. For thousands of years, these systems of thought and belief have struck deep into the soul. People of these societies, whether they like it or not, cannot escape their influence, though the extent of it will vary. Revolutionaries, especially communist revolutionaries, must first slough off that which is reactionary in their own nations. Reactionary ideas, even though they might have played a role in the nation's history, must be criticised and overthrown. Those who do not participate in this criticism, e.g., European Christian socialists and the like, are not revolutionaries or socialists but reactionaries' masks and accomplices. The same goes for Confucian communism or Confucian socialism, which naturally has nothing to do with Mao thought. What I mean when I say Mao thought has a residue of, or is integrated by, Confucian components is that Mao, in his childhood and youth, got his first knowledge and ideas from Confucian books, and could not but do so. Up until the age of twenty-five, he was essentially a disciple of Confucius. In those years, he progressed from the orthodox school of Cheng and Zhu towards the 'left wing' of Confucianism (Huang Lizhou, Wang Chuanshan, Kang Youwei, Tan Sitong).[19] After May Fourth, Mao was influenced by the attack on Confucius. He stopped revering Kang and Liang and started revering Chen Duxiu and Hu Shi. But because China's Enlightenment came late, through special international and domestic circumstances, and was unable to constitute itself independently and in the long term, its impact on China's old thinking, especially Confucianism, was shallow and narrow. As class struggle flared up, the New Culture Movement split: some surrendered to the Confucian Family Shop (whose owner, needless to say, wore a Western suit); others put down their books and, after a superficial embrace of Marxism, started making revolution. Hu Shi represented the first group, Chen Duxiu the second. Mao followed Chen. So Mao's Marxism, like Chen's, arose on a Confucian base. That is why I say that Mao thought had Confucian ingredients. As for whether those ingredients have endured until now, and, if so, what they are and what position they occupy in the whole, are questions I will try to answer later.

Generally speaking, China's Marxist revolutionaries first made revolution and then studied Marxism (assuming they had the chance – most never did). So although people joined the CCP, they knew only its fundamental goals, beyond a smattering of general knowledge and acquaintance with its resolutions. On other matters, for example, world views, each had his or her own opinion, but that opinion was generally Confucian. The more they knew and the more systematic their ideas before joining the party, the greater and deeper the accumulation in their minds of non-Marxist thinking. In 1920, Mao decided to become a communist after reading three books. Later, of course, he read dozens or hundreds more, but these could not completely replace the hundreds or thousands of Confucian and Mencian[20] books he had read in the previous eighteen years. In any case, numbers are unimportant here: what matters is that in the development of the human mind first impressions are strongest, and that one's nurturing in the years in which the foundations of one's knowledge and ideas

---

19   Huang Lizhou (1610–1695) was an early Qing reformer.
20   Mencius (372–289 BCE) was the most famous Confucian thinker after Confucius.

are laid continues to play a decisive role, like it or not, throughout one's life. After embracing Marxism, Mao naturally 'opposed today's me to yesterday's me.' But people cannot deny themselves entirely. The deeper the foundations, the harder they are to dig up. Yesterday's conclusions can be discarded, but not the ways in which they were reached. It is the same with languages: the older you are, the harder they are to learn. Vocabulary is relatively easy, followed by syntax, but pitch is hardest, and is rarely mastered. Mao left home at the age of sixteen and started to negate his native Xiangtan dialect and to study Mandarin; but until now, even though he has learned vocabulary and syntax, he still gets his tones wrong. If Mandarin is his Marx, Xiangtan dialect is his Confucius and his Mencius.

Locally accented Mandarin is no less expressive than Beijing dialect. What matters is how sound and language combine. If they combine well, and are spoken fluently and naturally, then the speech of the great majority of Chinese, who do not understand Beijing dialect, is perhaps of greater relevance than the national language. Mao's Xiangtan-accented national language, especially when addressing Hunan's workers and peasants, absolutely trumps the standard language. So Marxism based on local thinking is not only an unavoidable product of the spread of Marxism across the world but, as long as it is properly integrated, more practical and effective than one hundred per cent Marxism in its original packaging. Merely to say Mao thought contains elements of Confucianism does not mean that it is not Marxist, or that it contains reactionary ideas.

Hong Xiuquan, Kang Youwei, and Sun Yat-sen were, at bottom, all Confucians, and all took some truths from the West. They all combined Confucianism and Western truths, and, to varying degrees, all formed their own thinking. Mao was, in this respect, not all that different from his three predecessors. But the ways in which they combined Chinese and Western thought differed greatly, from case to case. Hong Xiuquan's Christianity, Kang Youwei's hotchpotch of utopian idealism and constitutionalism, and Sun Yat-sen's patchwork of Jeffersonianism and Henry George cannot be put on a par with Mao's Marxism. Whether as philosophy or social science, Marxism can hardly be mentioned in the same breath as the ideas adopted by Hong, Kang, and Sun. Important is the extent to which each mastered his Western truths and the facility with which he absorbed them and combined them with Confucianism. On the first count, Mao wins hands down. In the age in which Hong and Kang lived, Western knowledge had not yet been systematically introduced into China, and because they knew only Chinese, they depended on missionaries and others to acquire odd bits of it. Hong Xiuquan, a man of relatively little learning, created his own Christianity, which bore scant resemblance to the original. Kang

Youwei, who was very learned and appeared relatively late on the scene, took Darwin for a utopian socialist and thought Fourier was English. As for Sun Yat-sen, although he had an English-language education and travelled all over the world, he did not value (and even disdained) Western literature and philosophy and was interested only in the rules and regulations that governed American and European democracy. So his Western learning was incomplete, not to say shallow (even shallower than Yan Fu's, and not a patch on Tan Sitong's). Mao knew no foreign languages and wasn't particularly well versed in Western philosophy, but his formative years coincided with China's scramble to catch up with Europe intellectually. The Western learning he achieved was filtered through the Marxism imported into China by the October Revolution and catapulted into fashion there, so although he was never steeped in Marxism, he studied and applied it systematically and in detail. Mao's grasp of Marxism was inhibited by his pragmatism and his Stalinist filiation, but his and his three predecessors' understanding of Western learning are worlds apart. Second, there are the different ways in which each thinker combined Chinese and Western learning. I said earlier that Mao, like Chen Duxiu, and also like Hong, Kang, and Sun, favoured 'Chinese learning for the foundation, Western learning for application.' But that applies only to the constituents of their thinking. If you look at the way in which they are combined, in Mao's case foundation and application cannot be mechanically separated into principal and auxiliary. In Hong, Kang, and Sun's case, however, Chinese learning (i.e., Confucianism, especially the sort infused with a democratic flavour and *datong*-style utopianism) is beyond all doubt the principal, while ornamental appendages picked up from the West are the sundries. The trio, especially Hong and Kang, presented revolution and reform as revitalisation and even as the restoration of ancient ways, and used Western philosophical ideals merely to prove China had long known benevolent government, i.e., government by *ren*. Sun Yat-sen was, of course, more progressive. The new China he wanted to create was a modern Anglo-American democracy, or, even better, a nation based on the principle of People's Livelihood. But what is People's Livelihood? Sun Yat-sen tells us: 'It is the world of great harmony [*datong*] envisaged by Confucius.'[21] Even the soviets were supposedly a realisation of Confucius' idea of *datong*. It is clear what for Sun Yat-sen was principal and what ancillary. Mao, however, never equated the Chinese Revolution and restorationism. He knew that Confucianism and Marxism were opposed, just as idealism and materialism were, and that they

---

21   *Datong* (great harmony or unity) is a utopian vision of the world, founded in Confucian philosophy, in which everything is at peace.

represented different class interests; he knew that the establishment of the former required the destruction of the latter. In short, he realised that it was impossible to graft Marxist tissue onto a Confucian trunk. So he strove to rid himself of Confucian ideas and to replace them with Marxist ones. As a result, the relationship in Mao thought between Chinese and Western learning is not that of principal and ancillary. The two are combined not as patchwork but as compound. Herein lies the difference between Mao on the one hand and Hong and Kang on the other, and the lack of likeness between him and Sun.

But a compound does not cancel its constituents. Even though the elements of Chinese learning in Mao thought were, subsequently, chemically compounded with Western elements, one still cannot deny that they are an integral component of it.

It is worth asking what elements of Confucianism survive in Mao thought. Confucianism is a broad concept, hard to define simply and clearly. For two thousand years, Confucianism dominated Chinese people's thinking, and was the measure of their minds; conversely, Chinese thinking has passed through a great many outstanding minds, each of which reflected the characteristics of its times and bestowed them on Confucianism. Consequently, Confucianism is a name that covers very different views organised in different schools. These schools, in regard to their environments and eras, have played different roles, progressive or reactionary. Here, I am not concerned with the history of Confucianism as such, its sects and schools, so I will limit myself to listing the most important Confucian contributions to Chinese thought. We can then ask whether they are reflected in Mao's words and deeds. Confucius imparted the Six Arts to his disciples, and the influence of his thinking on later generations was deep and wide, particularly through the *Spring and Autumn Annals*, the *Record of Rites*, and the *Book of Changes*. Confucius himself said: 'If someone later understood me, it would be because of the *Spring and Autumn Annals*: if someone criticised me, it would also be because of the *Spring and Autumn Annals*.' This is indeed self-knowledge. The *Spring and Autumn Annals*, whether praising or correcting, are an application to political history and political science of *li*. *Li* is a hierarchical feudal system that serves as a guideline for human relations in all hierarchies. Therefore the basic spirit of the classics is one and the same: a division into upper and lower, a fixed hierarchy. The *Rites* are not absolutely and one-sidedly binding, but rather a relatively progressive contract between different levels. The father is compassionate so the son is filial, the ruler is humane so the minister is loyal: the levels are connected by responsibilities and obligations. The absolutist Qin Shi Huangdi did not like Confucians,[22]

---

22   Qin Shi Huangdi (259–210 BC) founded the Qin dynasty and was the first emperor of a unified China. He was known for his ruthlessness and for burning the Confucian books.

and later some Confucians were able to draw progressive and democratic conclusions from Confucius' teachings. But his *Rites*, and their outcomes in China's society and politics, were far more reactionary than they were progressive. Confucius could become a saint, and was revered above all others for two thousand years by autocrats, mainly because of the 'cardinal principles of righteousness' expounded in the *Spring and Autumn Annals*, the strict hierarchical order set out in the *Rites*. The second main feature of Confucian teaching, one that has played an important role in Chinese history, especially in the thinking of the majority Han ethnic group, is its dialecticity, represented by the *Book of Changes*. 'In his old age, Confucius loved the *Book of Changes*.' He said: 'If some years were added to my life, I would spend five or ten studying the *Changes*.' In fact, Confucius was always a dialectician. Studying and teaching the *Book of Changes* merely gave system to his philosophy of dialectical idealism. Sima Qian (c. 145–86 BCE), author of the *Hereditary Family of Confucius*, made a brief synopsis of Confucian teachings in which he mentions 'frailties from which Confucius was free. [...] Foregone conclusions, arbitrary predeterminations, obstinacy, and egoism.' This is a superior observation by the Great Scribe. These 'four don'ts' are the foundation stone of Confucius' thinking, and he stuck with them throughout his life. Don't surmise, don't be dogmatic, don't be stubborn, don't be subjective. Here, on the one hand, is the spirit of science and dialectical thinking, and, on the other, the golden mean, compromise, and tactful reformism and opportunism, sometimes even to the point of naked cynicism. There have always been a few Confucians who have rallied to the progressive view, but the great majority, to be found everywhere, sided with the reactionaries.

If the cardinal principles of righteousness of the *Spring and Autumn Annals* and the four don'ts are Confucianism's mainstays, it is not hard to see which elements of them Mao thought retains. Mao is a revolutionary. According to the cardinal principles of righteousness, he belongs among the traitors and scoundrels. People will naturally assume that Mao would never, consciously or unconsciously, follow Confucius in honouring the king. But it is not so simple. The *Spring and Autumn Annals* did not specify which king: all kings were to be honoured. So the question is, whether or not you are a king. Once a king, the cardinal principles of righteousness automatically apply to you. Only traitors and scoundrels who fail to elevate themselves remain traitors and scoundrels rather than becoming *shi*, members of the revered scholarly elite. The cardinal principles of righteousness are not so very far apart from vulgar notions like 'losers are always wrong, the winner takes all.' So it makes no difference whether you become a king by 'going against your superiors' or even by invading China from the outside. As long as it's a done job, your kingship can be said to accord with the cardinal principles of righteousness. Mao studied the rites at an early age, though he later shed them. However, in the party, and then in the country, having established his own supreme authority, first over his comrades and then over the whole people, did he not rediscover the cardinal principles of righteousness and apply them? Or, even more to the point, did the Confucian concept of rites, which, on the surface, Mao had long since driven from his mind, not live on in its lower depths, and thus contribute to his bureaucratisation of the party and the political system? Did it not facilitate his acceptance of Stalin's political and organisational line? And did it not expedite the development of the Mao cult? The answer to all these questions, especially the last one, is yes.[23]

The second vestige of Confucianism in Mao thought is even more obvious. Friend or foe, no one would deny that Mao was a great political schemer, or, more precisely, a great tactician. Whether in military, political, or human affairs, Mao was intelligent, flexible, tactful, and cunning – in a word, brilliant. This ability was partly innate and partly, and obviously, learned from Confucius, and above all from the four don'ts. Confucius was less bound than anyone by dogmas. His propositions were never hard and fast. They varied over time and space and by person. The Song dynasty philosopher and educator Zhu Xi called this 'teaching to ability,' just as in philosophy 'the truth is always concrete.' Sometimes he might follow the crowd, while at other times he went against the crowd, depending on circumstance. When his disciples Yan Yuan, Zhong Gong, and Sima Niu asked him about *ren*, he answered each differently. The King of Zhou being a tyrant, 'the Viscount of Wei withdrew from the court, the Viscount of Ji became a slave to Zhou, Bi Gan remonstrated with him and died': three men, three stances, but Confucius called them all *ren*. This is because he could see difference within sameness, and sameness within difference; and he viewed people and things from the appropriate perspective. Confucius said: 'When a man in his own person does evil, a superior man will not associate

---

23   There is an interesting relationship between the development of Mao thought and Confucianism. I mentioned above that the left wing of Confucianism, the democratic and *datong* tendency, which allowed Mao to make the transition to European-style democratism, eventually arrived at socialism and communism. Later, however, when the Chinese communist movement armed itself, Mao became its leader, at the same time as the Soviet Union succumbed to Stalin's totalitarian bureaucracy. These were the years in which Mao mugged up on his Marxism. In them, the orthodox Confucianism he was weaned on, especially the cardinal principles of righteousness, enabled him to accept Stalinism with a clear conscience; on the other hand, Stalinism strengthened the right-wing Confucian-monarchical thinking deep down in him (note by Wang).

with him.' But when Gongshan Furao was holding Bi, 'in an attitude of rebellion,' and invited the Master to visit him, 'the Master wanted to go,' saying: 'If someone employs me, might I not make a Zhou of the East?' 'Am I a bitter gourd to be hung up out of the way rather than eaten?' Some mocked him, as 'roosting about' and with a tongue bordering on 'facile,' but Confucius argued back: 'I hate obstinacy.' He hated invariability, stubbornness. He said: 'I have no absolutely certain approval or disapproval.' When Confucius allied with the Pu, it was not to defend the country; but once he left through the East Gate, he turned his back on the alliance on the grounds that 'if you are forced into an alliance, the spirits will not recognise it.' Confucius was resourceful, practical, experienced, and versatile, qualities present in droves in Mao's words and actions. In thirty years of struggle inside and outside the CCP he has used them to finish off a string of rivals. The first was Wang Ming, sent to China by Stalin. Mao was at a disadvantage in this battle and suffered an early defeat. Had he lacked hidden talents and not thirsted for revenge, he could never have revived his fortunes at Zunyi;[24] and if, having stood up again, he had behaved arrogantly after his small victory over Wang Ming, if he had not paused while ahead, if he had failed to distinguish what is important from what is inessential, if he had not tempered justice with mercy, if he had not stayed at a respectful distance from Stalin, to feign compliance, and to fight judo-style, adjusting to and dodging his opponent, he would never have won victory in the party, let alone in the country. As for the external enemy, Chiang Kai-shek, Mao gave full play to the Confucian spirit of 'no obstinacy, no arbitrary predeterminations.' Catching him and then letting him go at Xi'an[25] and staging a Nationalist-communist reunion in 1937 was a tragicomedy directed by Stalin, but its brilliant enactment was down to Mao. He played the part with great fluency, injecting his entire personality into it. But there was no harm in changing flags and signing an agreement under duress, for 'the spirits will not recognise it.' As for the Guomindang's sneak attacks, they should be met 'on just grounds, to one's advantage, and with restraint,' acting according to circumstance and to the principle, inherited by Confucius from the ancients, of *wuchang*, meaning all things are impermanent. When associating with democratic personalities, look simple and sincere, speak blandly

---

24 The Zunyi Conference was held in January 1935 during the Long March. It paved the way for Mao to assume leadership of the CCP.
25 In the Xi'an Incident of December 1936, Chiang Kai-shek, the Guomindang leader, was arrested by his generals Zhang Xueliang and Yang Hucheng for failing to resist Japan. Zhang and Yang were in secret contact with the CCP. The incident led to the formation of an anti-Japanese united front between the Guomindang and the CCP.

but precisely, bend the body, attend to etiquette, and show goodwill and sympathy. Marx, legs braced, fists flying, and Lenin and Trotsky, with their 'dogmas,' neither would nor could do so; even Stalin the tactician lacked the tact, though not for want of trying. Only Mao, steeped in Confucian thinking, was equipped for it. In this respect, Mao owed more to Confucius than to Marx and Lenin.

That the Chinese tradition of wandering swordsmen (*youxia*, sometimes rendered in English as knights errant) was a major source of Mao thought is less controversial. Mao himself admitted that he didn't like the orthodox classics, but he did like *The Water Margin, Journey to the West*, and other popular classics. These novels have inspired young people in China for centuries, far more so than the canonical works. Lower-class Chinese were hugely influenced by them, and by the operas derived from them. This was true not just of the young Mao but of the overwhelming majority of Chinese children. The only difference was that Mao put ideas from the novels into action. Classical Chinese novels reflected the social chaos in China starting in the Tang and Song. The intellectual brew had a Confucian base and Buddhist and Taoist admixtures. Joining the world and renouncing the world were intertwined. In the entanglement, the radiance of the one cancelled out that of the other and their most corrupt parts shone more brightly in each other's reflection. The positivity of joining the world, the Confucian spirit of doing one's duty, is negated, leaving behind only the vulgar ambition of studying to become an official so as to acquire wealth and emolument; renouncing the world is reduced to a superficiality, like the Buddhist doctrine of karma or the Taoist concoction of pills to achieve immortality. These notions were spun into stories in the novels and spread among the people, endlessly dripping poison. However, there is one idea, especially in the *Water Margin*, that shines across the chaos: that is the *youxia* ethos. Some classical novels particularly attracted young readers, by injecting fresh energy into the tired thinking of Confucianism, Buddhism, and Taoism, turning the novels into art and vessels for the imagination. Without this *youxia* ethos, the old Chinese novel would have stayed buried in the stale world of the Three Teachings.

Mao loved these novels mainly for their ideas, which he absorbed and brought to life. In the Qin and Han Dynasties, Confucianism (*ru*) and knight errantry (*xia*) were said in the same breath. Han Fei (ca. 280–233 BCE) said, 'scholars [*ru*] use their writings to disturb the law, *xia* use martial skills to violate proscriptions.' Which class did *ru* represent? Which class did *xia* represent? When Confucius was alive, *ru* thinking represented the political ideas of the relatively numerous class of small and medium landowners and merchants outside the feudal aristocracy, especially officials of lowly origin. So Confucius' approach was ameliorative, conciliatory, and equivocal, like today's petty bourgeoisie. Later, after Emperor Han Wu started promoting *ru* doctrines as state teaching, Confucianism served the ruling class, as a fig leaf for the tyranny, and stopped being transformational. As for *youxia*, Sima Qian divided them into 'grand *xia*,' '*xia* in simple clothing,' 'village *xia*,' and 'alleyway *xia*,' but usually he meant the latter groups. It is clear that they were commoners. 'Even though their actions do not always conform to the idea of justice, one could take them at their word. Their actions were always effective, promises were always kept. Without a thought for their own safety, they attended to those in danger. If they could conserve someone who had already forfeited his life, they did not vaunt their achievement and would have been ashamed had others made a virtue of it.' The moral excellence of the *youxia*, or their professed moral standards, had much in common with the moral standards of European medieval knights and Japanese samurai. However, they generally came from a lower social class, for whereas European knights belonged to the nobility and samurai were the aristocrats' hangers-on or hired fighters, most *youxia* were commoners – peasants, small landowners, lowly officials – and the overwhelming majority were artisans, peddlers, servants, and jobless vagrants from the big and small towns. In general, the *xia* represented a lower class than the *ru*. They were said to have been pushed aside and abandoned by the Confucians and the Mohists.[26] The *xia* category was very complex, and included both good people and criminals. Many were monsters and despots who bullied the weak and powerless, but there were no few remarkable personalities who genuinely incorporated the above moral values. These people, especially in times of extreme political darkness or war, when ordinary Chinese were being oppressed and exploited, helped stage revolts. They promoted fairness by robbing the rich to help the poor, speaking up for those without a voice, and punishing tyrants. This spirit has endured throughout Chinese history. Without it, there is no 'commoner who values morality and justice, who goes far for justice and dies.' Chinese (especially the *shi* or literati[27]) were reduced under the absolute rule of the spirit of Confucianism to one of two types, identified by Sima Qian as selfish scholar-officials who 'are limited and narrow, and isolated from common customs,' and shameless and vulgar people who 'lower their arguments to conform with common customs and thereby win glory.' In fact, for one or two thousand

---

26 Mohism was a philosophical movement based on the teachings of Mozi (fl. ca. 430 BCE).
27 Scholar-officials or literati (*shi*) formed the gentry class, individuals who, from the Han dynasty to the end of the Qing, had passed the civil-service exams and were appointed by the imperial court to run the central and local government.

years Chinese scholars have belonged to one or the other type. Worse still, the two types are interchangeable. The Song dynasty historian Ouyang Xiu wrote a biography of Feng Dao[28] in which he said, with deep feeling: 'In the entire Five Dynasties I found three virtuous officials and fifteen who died honourably in service. It is perplexing that a great many literati presented themselves as Confucians and claimed to study antiquity, enjoyed people's remuneration, and served the empire. However, inasmuch as those who acted on principles of righteous loyalty hailed solely from the ranks of military leaders and warriors, it only affirms their absence from Confucian ranks.'[29] Ouyang Xiu's insight is not as deep as Sima Qian's. He failed to see that very few orthodox Confucians without the *youxia* spirit of Zhu Jia and Guo Jie did not want to be the Old Man from Changle, as Feng Dao was known. Feng Dao frequently compared himself to Confucius, and people even praised him as Confucius come back to life, which, in a certain sense, he was.

Prominent Confucians have always recognised the importance of 'rectifying *wen* with *wu*.'[30] Tan Sitong valued the *youxia* spirit even higher. Sun Yat-sen sought to win over leaders of the anti-Qing secret societies. No one could ever stage a revolt using *xiucai*,[31] not in thirty or three hundred years, for no *xiucai* would dare contemplate rebelling. Mao learned from the *Water Margin* the importance of climbing Mount Liang[32] and absorbed this *youxia* practice into his thinking, where it meshed with Western learning and formed part of his revolutionary theory of meeting armed force with armed force.

Marxism is the third component of Mao thought, and much easier to deal with than the other two. What sort of Marxism-Leninism did Mao embrace? And what was its specific weight in his thinking? Mao says he turned to Marxism in the winter of 1919, when he read an abbreviated version of the *Communist Manifesto*, Karl Kautsky's *Class Struggle*, and Thomas Kirkup's *History of Socialism*. He never said what Marxist literature he read after that, but the answer is obvious. Mao knew only Chinese, and not many Marxist books were translated into Chinese until after the defeat of the revolution of 1925–7, starting around 1930, so he can't have read much between 1920 and 1930. In any case, people like Mao devoted their time and effort to the revolution, especially

---

28 Feng Dao (882–954) was a government official widely praised as virtuous.
29 Adapted from Richard 2004.
30 *Wen* and *wu* are a binary signifying civility or culture and martial valour or martial arts.
31 A *xiucai* was a member of the gentry class who had passed the imperial examination at county level, and a byword after 1911 for a useless and parasitical old-style intellectual.
32 The stronghold of the heroes of the *Water Margin*.

after 1927, when the switch to armed struggle left even less time for theory. So up to 1930, and even up to 1937, when the Red Army established a relatively stable base in Yan'an, Mao's book knowledge of Marxism was probably not much greater than in 1920. This went not just for Mao, of course, but for all early Chinese communists. Nearly everybody had read Zheng Chaolin's translation of Bukharin and Preobrazhensky's ABC of Communism.[33] Considerably fewer had read Li Ji's translation of Julian Borchardt's popular edition of *Das Kapital*, first published in 1926, and those that had were regarded as advanced theorists.

According to Chen Boda,[34] Mao first got the chance to read Stalin's works extensively after 1937, during the Sino-Japanese War.[35] Chen Boda's testimony is telling. He says that Mao 'broadly read and carefully reflected on' Stalin's writings. So Mao started studying Marxism seriously only in 1937; and the Marxism he studied was Stalin's.[36]

Mao was able to read Stalin's writings in 1937 because the Guomindang relaxed its military pressure on the CCP after the start of the anti-Japanese resistance. He could therefore take time out to study some theory. His immediate reason for doing so was to fight off Wang Ming, who had gone on the offensive. Although he won his fight against the dogmatists, he didn't finish them off at the time. To compete with Wang for the support of Wang's backers in the Kremlin, and to win the trust of the entire party, he had to strengthen his command of theory, especially Stalin's.

I discuss the ideological and political relationship between Mao and Stalin (and Wang Ming, Stalin's agent) in a separate chapter. Two things stand out: although Mao had been a communist for seventeen years, he was forty-four before he began a serious study of Marxism; at the time, and also later, he mainly read Stalin. If we want to know about his Marxism, these two things matter more than most. On that basis, we can say with certainty that Con-

---

33 Written in 1919, during the Russian Civil War, it was regarded as an elementary textbook of communism.
34 Chen Boda (1904–1989) was a secretary to Mao and a party leader in the Cultural Revolution.
35 Chen Boda 1953, p. 25.
36 Chen Boda's testimony is not, by itself, enough to conclude that Mao did not also read writings by Marx, Engels, Lenin, and others. But there are other reasons to think that he did not, save for a couple of things by Lenin. There are almost no direct citations from Marx and Engels in Mao's work, and just a few passages from Lenin's philosophical writings: but Mao widely quoted from Stalin after 1937. Mao despised dead (i.e., mechanical) reading and reading without digesting. What he studied, he applied. Had Mao read deeply in the Marxist classics, it would have shown (note by Wang).

fucianism and *youxia* form the deep structure of his thought and Stalinism its superstructure. At the subconscious and relatively abstract level, indigenous Confucian and *youxia* thinking have the upper hand, whereas at the conscious and relatively specific level, the foreign component, chiefly derived from Stalinism, holds sway – increasingly so as the years go by.

CHAPTER 3

Mao Zedong Thought and 'Mao Zedong Thought'

There are two sorts of Mao thought. One is actual Mao thought, the other is a system of thought artificially confected to raise Mao's status in the party and the country to godlike heights, always perfect, always right, and on a par with, or even higher than, Marxism. I talked about the sources of Mao thought in the previous chapter. Now I want to talk about the production of 'Mao Zedong Thought.'

For a living leader to give an eponym to an ism, to write that ism into a party platform, and to declare it a party's guiding principle is unprecedented in the history of the world labour movement. It is even rarer for a living revolutionary thinker to eponymise a doctrine. It is usually one's enemies that do so, followed later by one's supporters (usually after the eponym has died). Marx only mentioned the word 'Marxism' when laughing at followers of his who made fools of themselves. The word 'Leninism' was invented by the Mensheviks to imply that Lenin was 'not a Marxist.' Lenin never claimed or allowed others to claim that he had departed in any way from Marxism. 'Leninism' was only put forward as Russian Marxism after the start of Lenin's illness, first by Zinoviev and then by Stalin, to attack 'Trotskyism.' Likewise, Trotsky never called himself a 'Trotskyist.' Why did these great thinkers not pin an ism to their names and write it into the party platform? Were they being modest? No, for false modesty is no virtue. The main reason was that they despised the cult of the individual, with its associations of bureaucracy and crassness. Beyond that, they had a strong sense of following in the steps of others and of the need, in future, for constant renewal, so they refused to single out their own names and contributions. Finally, when people know that their thinking is imperfect, they are loath to set their name to it, to turn it into a law of science, and to want the masses to follow it. The methods and stances of great thinkers always matter more than their conclusions, and they know that. They therefore shrink from forcing their conclusions on the party or demanding compliance with them. That's why Marx, Lenin, and Trotsky never countenanced eponymic isms or let others coin them on their behalf, let alone set themselves up as a universal compass.

Mao Zedong Thought is mainly the product of inner-party struggles. Its immediate initial target was the Wang Ming line, i.e., the Stalin (or Russian) line. The CCP has, as I write this, existed for forty years, and has known numerous disputes and wrangles. Apart from the Stalin-Trotsky dispute, which was imported from the Soviet Union, the longest running struggle, and the most extensive and profound in scope, was that between Mao and Wang Ming. In the first revolution, the so-called Chen Duxiu line, the Qu Qiubai line, and the Li Lisan line[1] were not lines at all but labels unfairly stuck on their three eponyms, and were actually the work of Stalin and Bukharin (in the first two cases) and of Stalin alone (in the last case). Chen, Qu, and Li were carrying out the line of the Communist International (Comintern), for whose successive defeats they served as scapegoats.

Wang Ming (originally called Chen Shaoyu) could, in principle, also have ended up a scapegoat, but he survived because of his strong tie to the Kremlin bureaucracy and his many wiles. Wang's record as a revolutionary was the opposite of Mao's. He was sent to Moscow to study at Sun Yat-sen University[2] at the age of fifteen or sixteen. Naturally he hadn't read the Confucian classics, let alone other Chinese literature. He probably wrote better Russian than Chinese, and his intellectual first love was the Stalin school of Marxism-Leninism. Mao accused him of 'knowing only about Greece,'[3] but did he? Apart from a smattering of general knowledge about Western philosophy and political economy gleaned from Soviet textbooks, he knew little about Western culture. About China, he knew next to nothing. He was clever, sly, and good at plotting and scheming, and he was highly ambitious and wanted to be leader. He joined the party in Moscow and studied in Russia during the revolution of 1925–7, so he played no direct part in it. He first revealed his talents after the defeat of 1927, during the struggle between Trotsky and Stalin. Radek was dean of Sun Yat-sen University, where Wang was, and Radek supported Trotsky. The Stalinists at the University led by Mif attacked Radek, the Chinese students split into two factions, and Wang led the Stalin-Mif faction.[4] The Opposition lost, and Radek was dismissed. Mif took over as dean, with Wang as leader of the party branch. After that, Wang and Mif worked closely together and gathered round themselves a big group of activists, including Qin Bangxian,

---

1 The 'Chen Duxiu line' was a 'right-opportunist line' supposedly carried out by Chen in the later part of the first Civil War Period (1924–1927). The Qu Qiubai and the Li Lisan lines were the first and second ''left'-opportunist lines,' between 1927 and 1930.
2 Sun Yat-sen University was a Comintern school in Moscow that trained Chinese revolutionaries between 1925 and 1930.
3 The implication was that Wang Ming could only parrot foreign dogmas.
4 Karl Berngardovich Radek (1885–1939) was active in the Polish and German social democratic movements and a leader in the early Soviet Union. He was part of the Left Opposition in 1923, but later capitulated to Stalin. Imprisoned during Stalin's Great Purge, he died in gaol. Pavel Mif (1901–1938) was patron of Wang Ming and the so-called Twenty Eight Bolsheviks at Sun Yat-sen University. Arrested in 1937, he disappeared during the purges.

Wang Jiaxiang, and Chen Changhao.⁵ In 1928 the CCP held its Sixth Congress in the Soviet Union. Wang Ming was one of its translators, and played no small role in the meeting. Stalin used him to control the CCP, by interfering in its top appointments. Mif and Wang took steps to rope in people with a working-class background, replacing the relatively independent-minded Qu Qiubai with the malleable Xiang Zhongfa.⁶ This was a first step from controlling the school to controlling the party. Members of the Wang Ming faction began returning to China in 1929. Initially, they took control of the 'practical work faction,' but their hopes were dashed (Wang was only made secretary of the Propaganda Department). In the summer of 1930, Stalin's Third Period philosophy (predicting imminent worldwide revolution) peaked under Li Lisan, but within months it had collapsed. The defeat left many apprehensive and dissatisfied. Wang seized the chance to use Qu Qiubai to attack Li Lisan, and then combined with Mif (head of the Comintern's Far Eastern Bureau) to attack Qu. Soon, the Wang Ming faction, with Stalin's support, was on its way to controlling the entire party.

All these struggles were conducted in secret, in Shanghai. Mao was fighting on the Hunan-Jiangxi border,⁷ far away from the centre of intrigue. He paid scant attention to theoretical and political questions, and basically went along with Stalin's Third Period idea. In principle, he supported the Li Lisan line. His criticisms of it were limited to its technical execution, in terms of military tactics. He knew from personal experience that the Red Army could not directly attack big cities. He is primarily a doer, not a theoretician, so from the start, and throughout his entire life, he has viewed theory from a practical angle. Stalin was the same. In those years, Mao either dismissed the theoretical disputes in Shanghai (the real one between Stalin and Trotsky, or Wang Ming's fake one, actually a cover for his power bid) or had no time to attend to them. In writings by Mao currently available, there's nothing about them, which would seem to confirm my point. His attitude was probably something like: 'Without power, there's no right to speak. The most reliable power is the masses holding guns. You carry on with your back-room power struggles, I will go on accumulating armed force.'

---

5   Qin Bangxian, Wang Jiaxiang, and Chen Changhao were Russia-returned members of the Twenty Eight Bolsheviks.
6   Xiang Zhongfa (1880–1931), a workers' leader, was General Secretary of the CCP from 1928 to 1931, promoted because of his record in the labour movement at a time when the 1927 defeat was being blamed on the shortage of workers in the leadership. He was executed by Chiang Kai-shek despite capitulating after his arrest.
7   Mao and other Communists fought along the Hunan-Jiangxi border between 1927 and 1934.

At first, the Wangites looked down on Mao. The Comintern saw no future for the armed struggle in South China. At the Sixth Congress, Bukharin mocked China's Red Army and said it would 'eat the peasants' last chicken.' The Sixth Congress made the call for soviets a propaganda slogan, meaning peasant risings should be halted. The focus was on workers and the cities. Under Guomindang terror, the party's task was to restore its link to the workers and rebuild party organisations and the trade unions. In this spirit, the Wangites concentrated on seizing control of the Central Committee in Shanghai, and for the time being ignored the army under Mao in Jiangxi. But once the Central Committee was in their hands, and once it became clear that Mao's army was not bound for destruction, as the Comintern had predicted, but was growing by the day, they started using the same methods against Mao that they had used against Li Lisan and Qu Qiubai.

After January 1931, the inner-party struggle was between Mao and Wang. It went on for a long time, with victories and defeats on both sides, until Mao won final victory at the CCP's Seventh Congress in April 1945. The longevity of the struggle had numerous subtle causes that in some cases remain hidden, even from party members. The main reason for it was that behind Wang stood Stalin, representing the Moscow bureaucracy, while Wang represented the *yang* communists as against Mao's *tu*.[8] So the struggle directly and indirectly involved Stalin, the Comintern, and the Soviet Union. Naturally Mao knew this, but for tactical reasons he dared not attack Wang's patron directly, and he didn't even dare attack Wang too obviously.

The fourteen years' struggle between the two factions happened as follows:

In January 1931, at the Fourth Plenum of the Sixth Congress, the Wangites seized the leadership. Backed by Moscow and with the support of Xiang Zhongfa and Zhou Enlai,[9] they ousted Li Lisan, Qu Qiubai, and other old revolutionaries. Wang's slogans were oppose the Lisan line, oppose accommodationism, and oppose rightism. His own position was ultra-left, like Stalin's Third Period. The Wangites set up a temporary Central Committee under Qin Bangxian and started attacking Mao more openly.

In November 1931, a party meeting in the southern Jiangxi base attacked Mao; in August 1932, the same happened at a Ningdu conference. Mao was accused of carrying out a rich-peasant line and of right-opportunist errors, and the leadership was changed. Mao was elected President of the first Soviet Congress in December 1931, but in reality he was a figurehead.

---

8   *Yang*, 'ocean,' a traditional term for foreign; *tu*, 'earth,' for local.
9   Zhou Enlai (1898–1976) was an early CCP leader and later became its best diplomat.

In early 1933, the Wangite Central Committee was forced by pressure from Chiang Kai-shek's secret service to give up its urban strategy and take refuge in one of the party's rural bases.[10] After that, the Wangites grabbed even more power from Mao. In January 1934, at the Fifth Plenum, they announced that the Chinese Revolution had reached an acute stage. A directly revolutionary situation existed in China, and the main danger was right opportunism. Under these and other slogans, they attacked Mao and his supporters.

Between 1930 and the Zunyi Conference of December 1935, Mao wrote no theoretical articles (to judge by his *Selected Works*). Wang Ming called him a right opportunist and denounced his 'rich peasant line.' Logically, Mao should have defended himself, or, like Li Lisan, Qu Qiubai, and Zhou Enlai, confessed his errors, but he does not seem to have done so. His four writings from this period in the *Selected Works* are on economic policy. There is no criticism of the Wang Ming line, nor any attempt at self-defence. The Resolution on Certain Questions in the History of Our Party (April 1945) said that '[t]he comrades who advocated the correct line, with Comrade Mao Zedong as their representative, were diametrically opposed to the third "Left" line during the period of its domination [...] and demanded that it be corrected,' but it did not say how and why they opposed it. Probably Mao opposed Wang's leadership but didn't dare do so openly, since Wang represented Stalin. So the Mao faction wore two faces, playing the old Chinese game of feigning compliance, pretending interest and sympathy, biding one's time, and awaiting change. The change was not long in coming – in the autumn of 1934, the Red Army broke through Chiang Kai-shek's encirclement and went on the Long March.

In January 1935, Mao held a meeting of the Politburo in Zunyi. According to the Resolution on Certain Questions in the History of Our Party, the meeting rectified military and organisational errors. Mao was able to succeed because

> the repeated failures of the 'Left' line in practical work, and especially the repeated defeats in the campaign against the fifth 'encirclement and suppression' in the area where the central leading body was located, had begun to reveal the wrongness of this line to more and more leading cadres and rank-and-file party members and to arouse their doubt and dissatisfaction. After the Red Army [...] set out on the Long March, this doubt and dissatisfaction grew to such an extent that some comrades who had committed 'Left' errors began to awaken and take a stand against

---

10 Wang Ming himself did not follow the Central Committee to Jiangxi. He returned from Shanghai to his 'home country' Moscow, as Chinese representative to the Comintern. He didn't return to China until the winter of 1937 (note by Wang Fanxi).

them. Accordingly, large numbers of cadres and party members who were opposed to the 'Left' line rallied under the leadership of Comrade Mao Zedong.

We still don't know what happened before and after the Zunyi Conference and what it decided.[11] However, the questions raised were military and organisational. Mao did not put forward a different political programme from Wang Ming's. Hu Qiaomu confirmed this in his book *Thirty Years of the Chinese Communist Party*, where he said that the left sectarian line was corrected not at Zunyi but at the Seventh Congress of the Comintern, later in 1935. In other words, the CCP's line could change only when the Comintern's line changed, and both Wang's denouncing of Mao as a right opportunist and Mao's of Wang as a left opportunist were leaps around the palm of Buddha.

In short, the Zunyi Conference put Mao and his people in charge rather than Wang Ming and his people, but it did not solve the other problems. Mao's *tu* communists had come out on top, but Wang's *yang* communists had not yet been defeated. Wang still represented the CCP at the Comintern. He still commanded the CCP politically and continued to lord it over the Chinese communists in the Soviet Union and to oppress Chinese political dissidents there. Li Lisan said at the CCP's Eighth Congress: 'I worked under the direct leadership of Comrade Wang Ming for seven years. I was like a young married woman, constantly on tenterhooks, always worried about making a mistake and getting blamed [by the mother-in-law], but I still got blamed.'[12] Li Lisan confirmed that Mao's works could not circulate in Moscow, and that only after Li's own return to China in 1946 was he able to read them.

So Wang Ming, with Stalin's support, did not lose power and authority immediately after the Zunyi Meeting, not in Moscow nor even in the CCP. Although Mao rose to the top in January 1935, it took years more to exclude Wang from the leadership.

In the decade starting in 1935, the struggle between Mao and Wang can be divided into three periods: (1) Mao engages in advanced study; (2) Mao and Wang clash repeatedly; (3) Mao wins, and Mao Zedong Thought is born.

The Long March ended in October 1935. Before this, the Red Army fought in many places, and often teetered on the brink of defeat. It was internally

---

11   The meeting made decisions about the future of the Long March and its military strategy as well as criticising earlier mistakes, endorsing Mao's position, and electing Mao to the Standing Committee of the Politburo.
12   Wang gives no source.

divided (with Zhang Guotao[13] providing the main opposition) and under hot pursuit by Guomindang armies. Mao held on by the skin of his teeth, against overwhelming odds, and naturally did all he could to concentrate his forces. By 1936, the Red Army had a relatively stable base in northern Shaanxi, and Japan's stepping up of its aggression against China, the rise in anti-Japan sentiment, and the consequences of the CCP's detention and then release of Chiang Kai-shek in Xi'an led to a big drop in Guomindang military pressure. During this period, Mao's circumstances changed. He was able to sum up past debates and to read Marxist-Leninist classics, especially writings by Stalin. It is easy to see why he did so. In his fight with Wang (and the many Chinese and Russian theoreticians behind Wang), he was always on the back foot, for to rebut Wang's dogmas he had first to understand them. Second, the more complex the situation, the more keenly he felt his lack of Marxist education. Third, Mao studied Marxism-Leninism half for tactical reasons, 'to use [Wang Ming's] spear against his shield,' or out of snobbery, to compete with Wang for Stalin's favour by fawning on him, and eventually to remove Wang as the Kremlin's agent; and half because of his real affinity with Stalin on grounds of temperament and ideology (action caps theory, tactics cap strategy). He therefore focused on the Marxism-Leninism represented by Stalin.

In discussing the maturation of Mao thought, I mentioned Chen Boda's comment that Mao began reading Stalin only after the start of the Resistance War. Again I quote Chen:

> Both in 1927 when Chen [Duxiu] was in power and afterwards, the opportunists either intentionally or unintentionally obstructed the dissemination inside the Chinese party of Stalin's many works on the Chinese question. There were also language difficulties and the counter-revolutionary blockade. For these reasons, many comrades in our party who were actually leading the Chinese Revolution did not have an opportunity to make a systematic study of Stalin's many works on China, and Comrade Mao Zedong was among them. It was only after the rectification movement in 1942 that Stalin's numerous works on China were systematically edited by our party. [...] Opportunists intentionally or unintentionally hid Stalin's writings on China issues, in order to spread their own erroneous views and proposals, which for our party was very unfortunate. But despite this, Comrade Mao Zedong on many fundamental issues was able to accord

---

13   Zhang Guotao (1897–1979) was a founding member and leader of the CCP and Mao's rival. He left the party in 1938.

with Marx, Engels, Lenin, and Stalin's fundamental science of revolution, and with his own independent thinking reached the same conclusions as Stalin, thus keeping himself and his comrades on the right path. It was during the War of Resistance to Japanese Aggression that Comrade Mao Zedong had an opportunity to read Stalin's works extensively. He read and pondered over all the available works of Stalin with the greatest enthusiasm. As everyone knows, Comrade Mao Zedong in his 'On New Democracy' made clear what an important enlightenment Stalin's works had been to him.[14]

Chen Boda frankly admits that Mao knew little about Marxism,[15] and that before the Anti-Japanese War he knew only its rudiments. To them he added his 'own independent ideas,' drawn from traditional Chinese thinking. This was Mao's weakness, but it was also, in certain circumstances, his strength. This strength, however, was defined by its alternative, as the lesser of two evils: in other circumstances, it was a weakness, especially when Mao lacked quotes and arguments beyond 'Confucius said' to fire back at the dogmatists.

Mao spent much of the three to four years after 1936 catching up on Marxism, especially Stalinism. The results were impressive. Mao's most important theoretical work is from that period. Judging by it, Mao's research had three parts: a review of strategy and tactics in the armed revolution; the basic philosophy of Marxism; and Stalin's views on China and his position in the disputes inside the CPSU. In all cases, Mao's target was Wang Ming. The research increased his self-confidence regarding theory; equipped him to denounce Wang as a dogmatist; and made him Stalin's even warmer admirer.

Mao's self-study and his conflict with Wang were intimately connected. The *Selected Works* show that his first post-Zunyi theoretical attack on Wang was in December 1936, in 'Problems of Strategy in China's Revolutionary War,' an attempt to sum up a decade of civil war. He said:

> They urged a return to ways suited to the general run of things, refused to go into the specific circumstances of each case, rejected the experience gained in the Red Army's history of sanguinary battles, belittled the strength of imperialism and the Guomindang as well as that of the Guomindang army, and turned a blind eye to the new reactionary prin-

---

14   Chen Boda 1953, pp. 24–5.
15   The early leaders of the CCP branch in Moscow and Wang Ming were said to have deliberately prevented theoretical works from being translated, so they could monopolise them, as Red compradors.

ciples adopted by the enemy. As a result, all the revolutionary bases except the Shaanxi-Gansu border area were lost, the Red Army was reduced from 300,000 to a few tens of thousands, the membership of the Chinese Communist Party fell from 300,000 to a few tens of thousands, and the party organizations in the Guomindang areas were almost all destroyed. [...] This group of people called themselves Marxist-Leninists, but actually they had not learned an iota of Marxism-Leninism. Lenin said that the most essential thing in Marxism, the living soul of Marxism, is the concrete analysis of concrete conditions. That was precisely the point these comrades of ours forgot.[16]

The charge was serious, but Mao named no names. In July of the same year, Mao told Edgar Snow that one reason for the Red Army's invincibility was the competence, loyalty, and bravery of Zhu De, Wang Ming, Luo Fu, Zhou Enlai, Bo Gu, Wang Jiaxiang, and others. So Wang Ming was second only to Zhu De, and several of his supporters were named as 'excellent comrades.' Nearly two years after Zunyi, the Wangites were still a powerful force, able to vie with Mao for supremacy – not to mention that the Kremlin stood behind them. Mao's tactic – anonymous sniping and raising up so as to cast down – was, in one sense, a display of Confucian forbearance, but it was also an accurate measure of Stalin's hold on the CCP.

Wang Ming returned to China in the winter of 1937 and went to Wuhan. He was as arrogant as ever, and both Guomindang and CCP ranked him above Zhou Enlai, because he was seen as representing Moscow as well as Yan'an. It's hard to say whether Wang was again in conflict with Mao's Central Committee in Yan'an.[17] On December 12, 1935, at Wayaobao, Mao gave a report 'On Tactics Against Japanese Imperialism.' This was Mao's first report after his return to power, and the CCP's first elaboration of the Popular Front theory.

The Popular Front was introduced at the Seventh Congress of the Comintern in the summer of 1935. It signalled Stalin's abandonment of the leftist Third Period philosophy that had ruined the German Revolution and helped bring Hitler to power and of Wang Ming's third leftist line in China, and marked the start of a new rightist strategy of cooperation with the bourgeoisie.

The Wayaobao meeting was a response to the Comintern's Seventh Congress. The purpose was to implement the Popular Front (actually an anti-Japanese

---

16 Mao, 'Problems of Strategy in China's Revolutionary War,' SW, vol. 1, pp. 179–254, at pp. 195–6.
17 We now know that he was.

united front in China, called the Second United Front [1937–45] to distinguish it from the disastrous First United Front [1923–7]). The new line met with some scepticism, countered by Mao in his report, which noted 'some comrades'' past errors. Mao and Wang seemed to agree about the new line. Wang dutifully followed the Comintern, while the Popular Front was, from whatever angle, more to Mao's liking than the Third Period.

In May 1937, the CCP held a national conference in Yan'an. At it, Mao clashed not with Wang Ming but with Zhang Guotao, and the leftism he criticised was not Wang's but the Trotskyists'. In August 1937, at a meeting in Luochuan, there were no disputes. However, Mao wrote two texts essential to his fight with the Wangites, *On Practice* and *On Contradiction*. In them, he used the Marxist theory of knowledge and dialectics to counter Wang's dogmatism and others' empiricism.

Mao and Wang's first frontal clash during the Anti-Japanese War came in November 1937, when Mao made his report on 'The Situation and Tasks in the Anti-Japanese War After the Fall of Shanghai and Taiyuan.' The Wangites are said to have attacked this report from the right, particularly its stance on independence within the united front. According to the editors of the *Selected Works*, they advocated 'everything through the united front.'[18] The dispute went on for nearly a year, until the Sixth Plenum in October 1938, which 'substantially overcame' the rightist line. 'Substantially overcame' means Mao won, but not completely. When he talked about 'everything through the united front,' again he didn't name names but simply mentioned 'some comrades.' His diplomacy was aimed mainly at pleasing Moscow, but he was also keen not to offend the Wangites. He stuck to anonymous sniping even after 1949, and even then he used others (chiefly his editors) to do the dirty work.

Wang Ming's rightist thinking is said to have infected the leadership of the New Fourth Army, especially Xiang Ying. In January 1941, the New Fourth Army headquarters was destroyed in the Wannan (New Fourth Army) Incident. Whether or not Wang was really to blame for Xiang Ying's defeat, with it his counter-attack on Mao was over, once and for all.[19] Mao continued his theoretical work, in which, for the first time, he reviewed theoretical problems of the Chinese Revolution, mainly from Stalin's point of view. Before that, apart from his two philosophical essays in 1937, his writings were political, tactical, and

---

18   Wang Ming's policy of 'everything through the united front' contrasted with Mao's more aggressive call for 'independence and initiative' within the united front.
19   The New Fourth was the CCP's second army in the Anti-Japanese War, after its more northerly Eighth Route Army. Wang Ming was not in fact responsible for Xiang Ying's defeat in January 1941.

military. The emergence of Mao thought as a complete system can be dated to 1940, with the appearance of 'On New Democracy.' After that, Mao was unprecedentedly self-confident, in ideology, politics, and organisation. His struggle with Wang had ended in Wang's rout.

In May 1941, Mao gave a report titled 'Reform Our Study' of which his editors said:

> The report and the two articles, 'Rectify the Party's Style of Work' and 'Oppose Stereotyped Party Writing,' are Comrade Mao Zedong's basic works on the rectification movement. In these he summed up, on the ideological plane, past differences in the party over the party line and analysed the petty-bourgeois ideology and style which, masquerading as Marxism-Leninism, were prevalent in the party, and which chiefly manifested themselves in subjectivist and sectarian tendencies, their form of expression being stereotyped party writing. Comrade Mao Zedong called for a party-wide movement of Marxist-Leninist education to rectify style of work in accordance with the ideological principles of Marxism-Leninism. His call very quickly led to a great debate between proletarian and petty-bourgeois ideology inside and outside the party. This consolidated the position of proletarian ideology inside and outside the party, enabled the broad ranks of cadres to take a great step forward ideologically and the party to achieve unprecedented unity.[20]

Wang Ming was yet again not named, but it is clear who was 'masquerading' as a Marxist-Leninist. Wang was not the only target of the Rectification Movement. By the 1940s, Mao was already much stronger than Wang. Wang had backing in the Comintern and even some support in China, but there was little chance of him seriously competing with Mao, even with foreign help. So the main task was not so much to destroy Wang Ming thought as to establish Mao Zedong Thought. The frequent references to a Wang Ming line did not mean that Wang was seen as a threat. The main point, as Mao's editors said, was to sum up, 'on the ideological plane, past differences in the party over the party line.' In the summing up, the Wang Ming line, which had ruled the party longer than any other line, to the party's great detriment, was criticised; but its point was less to settle old accounts than to found a new one, in which everything Mao ever did stood as assets and everything Chen Duxiu, Li Lisan, Zhang Guotao, Wang Ming, and others did as liabilities. All correct thought was attributed to Mao,

---

20   Editors' note to Mao, 'Reform Our Study,' May 1941 SW, vol. 3, pp. 17–26, at 17–18.

all sins and errors to the counterparty. To fix this truth was the main end of rectification, a movement geared to forging Mao Zedong Thought as a spiritual weapon with which to create Stalin-style ideological unity and a Stalin-style personality cult.

We don't know whether this movement encountered any opposition. All we do know is that it lasted until 1944. The Seventh Congress of the CCP convened, after repeated delays, between April 23 and June 11, 1945. Perhaps the delays were caused by resistance to the personality cult by Wangites, we don't know.[21] By the end of 1944 and the start of 1945, Mao had routed all his opponents. A comprehensive victory notice, titled 'Resolution on Certain Questions in the History of Our Party,' appeared as a resolution of the Seventh Plenum of the Sixth Congress, held just before the Seventh Congress.

Thus, Mao Zedong Thought was born. At the Seventh Congress, it was written into the party platform and proclaimed as the party's guideline for all work, while party members were ordered to strive to grasp its foundations. The fourteen-year battle between Mao and Wang, between *tu* and *yang*, ended in a big victory for *tu*, and for Mao thought. However, it was not an outright victory, and the story of Mao thought had not yet run its course.

Wang's story, however, had. At the Seventh Congress, when Mao Zedong Thought was enthroned, Wang joined in singing the praises of the great leader, and publicly owned his errors. Mao, either to show that he really did believe in 'curing the patient' or to give Moscow face, let Wang stay on the Central Committee (second to last, ahead of Qin Bangxian). Wang did not speak at the Eighth Congress,[22] but had to listen to a lot of accusations (especially from Li Lisan), and was named last on the list of those attending. Cao Cao said, 'Under Heaven, only Liu Bei and I deserve the title of hero.' Has Wang a future? He is only a little over fifty. Will he live to fight again against Cao Cao's worshippers or their successors? As things are, it seems unlikely, but it is not impossible.[23]

The Eighth Congress in September 1956 took place eleven years after Mao's victory and seven years after the CCP set up a government in Beijing. Mao's power and prestige were at their peak. However, the Congress adopted a new party constitution that dropped the reference to Mao Zedong Thought as the

---

21 Delegates have said that Mao delayed the Congress until the Rectification Movement had achieved its goal of creating clarity and unanimity within the party (Guoguang Wu 2015, p. 89).
22 The Eighth Congress in 1956 set the scene for the conflicts that later broke out in the Cultural Revolution.
23 Wang Ming did not make a come-back. He died in Moscow in 1974.

guideline for all work. Deng Xiaoping did not mention it in his speech. No one said anything about it. The reason for this change is worth exploring.

Had Wang Ming regained his influence? Had the victory of the revolution made Mao Zedong Thought unnecessary? Had newly enlightened party members risen up against the injunction? The answer to these questions is, of course, no. Quite simply, the Eighth Congress came just a few months after the Twentieth Congress of the Soviet Communist Party, at which Khrushchev, to defeat his rivals, took advantage of Soviet people's craving for democracy to denounce Stalin's autocratic style and personality cult.

Whatever the reasons for the Soviet opposition to the personality cult, it had a huge impact on the world communist movement, especially the CCP. The Chinese leaders were in a dilemma, for they themselves were pushing a Mao cult on the same lines as the Stalin cult of the late 1930s. Among ordinary Chinese, the party was substituting Mao for the idols worshipped in the past. When they ate, they had to thank the Chairman. His image dominated weddings and funerals. In the midst of all this came news of the attack on Stalin, to general dismay. The cult had offended many Chinese and even some party members, or had at least left them uneasy and confused. The reason people tolerated it, and even supported it, was (a) because the revolution was advancing and (b) because of the Stalin cult. But now Stalin's cult had been denounced, what of his disciple's cult? The CCP leaders started to have misgivings, and Mao Zedong Thought was quietly dropped from the party constitution.

The democratic surge in the communist bloc also played a role, especially the Poznan workers' and the Hungarian workers' uprisings. In 1956, Mao launched the Hundred Flowers campaign and, in June 1957, published a speech on 'The Correct Handling of Contradictions Among the People.' For a while, Mao Zedong Thought largely disappeared from view, until 1960, when it was restored to prominence, to great fanfare. Now, in the summer of 1961, the movement continues, and is spreading to all fields. How will it develop? Will it be restored to the Constitution at the Ninth Congress?[24] We have no way of knowing. However, before I end this chapter on Mao Zedong Thought, I would like to try to explain why, after being dropped in 1956, it was briefly revived in 1958 and restored to full glory in 1960. Among many possible reasons, I suggest two: externally, the Chinese leaders' clash with the Kremlin; and, internally, the economic and political difficulties caused by the Great Leap Forward.[25] Strength-

---

24 The Mao cult peaked at the Ninth Congress in 1969.
25 The Great Leap Forward (1958–1962) was an economic and social campaign spearheaded by Mao that aimed at a leap into communism but ended in disaster.

ening the personality cult is not the best way of overcoming difficulties, but the focus of the cult, and those around that focus, are often mistakenly seen as the sole alternative.

The first person to use the term Mao Zedong Thought was Liu Shaoqi,[26] in his report 'On the Party.' The relationship between Mao and Liu is presaged in a passage in Francis Bacon's 'Of Friendship':

> A man hath a body, and that body is confined to a place; but where friendship is, all offices of life are as it were granted to him, and his deputy. For he may exercise them by his friend. How many things are there which a man cannot, with any face or comeliness, say or do himself? A man can scarce allege his own merits with modesty, much less extol them; a man cannot sometimes brook to supplicate or beg; and a number of the like. But all these things are graceful, in a friend's mouth, which are blushing in a man's own.

Writers on CCP history have expressed surprise that Liu is second only to Mao and has been named as his successor, for although Liu is not bad as a thinker and a practical politician, in manner, attitude, and speaking style he lags far behind Mao and even behind Zhou Enlai. Bacon helps throw light on Mao and Liu's relationship. Liu's report to the Seventh Congress was given over entirely to praising Mao and Mao Zedong Thought. He said that in Mao the party had 'a great leader of its own,' who had developed on its behalf 'a unique, integrated and correct theory of the people's revolution and national reconstruction' that had been maturing since the party's founding, in the shape of Mao Zedong Thought. Mao Zedong Thought integrated Marxist-Leninism with the practice of the Chinese Revolution, and was 'communism and Marxism applied to China.' Liu defined its content as Marxism 'improved through its application in China,' 'at once thoroughly Marxist and thoroughly Chinese, […] the highest expression of the wisdom of the Chinese people and the most succinct of theoretical generalizations.'[27] Mao could not have said this of himself. Who better to say it than his best friend?

Liu Shaoqi's analysis of Mao Zedong Thought falls into three parts: (1) revolutionary and military tactics; (2) revolutionary principles and strategies; and (3)

---

26 Liu Shaoqi (1898–1969) was a veteran revolutionary and Mao's named successor, but he fell out with Mao, was purged, and died in 1969. Deng Xiaoping posthumously rehabilitated him in 1980.
27 Liu Shaoqi, 'On the Party.'

thought and culture. I will follow these three categories to explore Mao thought in greater detail, affirming his positive contributions while noting his mistakes and weaknesses. I will recognise his achievements but expose attempts to justify his deification. In that way, I hope to reveal the true face of Mao the person and of his thought, and to determine his true standing in Chinese and world history as a great revolutionary and a thinker.

CHAPTER 4

A Brilliant Tactician

Mao Zedong said 'despise the enemy strategically, take him seriously tactically.'[1] This can be taken in two ways, one right, one wrong. It means you should be bold yet cautious, not that there's no harm in despising the enemy except in small things. Mao's main point was that imperialism and all forms of reactionary rule have, from the point of view of history as a whole, had their day and are bound to die, and are paper tigers. However, they won't die of their own accord. They will fight to the end, so we must stay on our guard. This is true, but it is misleading to use the terms strategy and tactics in this context. We know from Marx that capitalism is doomed and unable to resolve its contradictions. But Marx's and especially Lenin's theory of revolution stresses strategic thinking in the revolution, rather than the tactical means of implementing it. To say that one should 'despise the enemy strategically' does not, of course, mean that one should despise the strategy for defeating the enemy. It simply means that, in one's strategic dispositions, the enemy should not be taken seriously. But even that approach is wrong, for any underestimation of the enemy can lead to failure; and imperialism, which is no dead tiger, needs not capturing but killing. Mao made his point about strategy and tactics because he is, essentially, a brilliant military and political tactician, although he is not an equally outstanding and visionary strategist; and because his tactics have often rescued his far from brilliant strategy, so that it seems to him that tactics can ensure victory in revolution.

Mao's famous saying shows, first and foremost, not only that he is a tactician but how, in the course of the revolution, the relationship between strategy and tactics was distorted. Mao explains the difference between strategy and tactics as follows: 'The task of the science of strategy is to study those laws for directing a war that govern a war situation as a whole. The task of the science of campaigns and the science of tactics is to study those laws for directing a war that govern a partial situation.'[2] But a broader distinction, not just between 'partial' and 'as a whole,' is required. Whoever threads together, comprehensively integrates, and, from a principled position, notes and resolves specific problems

---

1 'More on the Differences Between Comrade Togliatti and Us', by the editorial department of *Hongqi*, nos 3–4, 1963.
2 Mao, 'Problems of Strategy in China's Revolutionary War,' December 1936, SW, vol. 1, pp. 179–90, at 183.

is a strategist; whoever looks at single issues, cannot generalise or synthesise, and answers only specific questions, constantly switching principles, is a tactician. In the narrow military sense, Mao is not just a clever tactician but an outstanding strategist. However, in the broader military and political sense, and especially in the political sense, Mao is less a strategist than a tactician.

Mao's greatest contribution to the Chinese Revolution was to switch the focus of power to the countryside, arm the peasants, establish base areas, and wage revolutionary war. But why was this tactical rather than strategic? Why was Mao a tactician rather than a strategist? Lenin plotted a new strategic course for the Russian Revolution, by which the proletariat allied with the peasants against the bourgeoisie to establish a democratic dictatorship of the workers and peasants in order to complete the bourgeois-democratic revolution and carry out social revolution. So why was Mao's arming of the peasants, establishing base areas, and waging revolutionary war not like Lenin's strategy?

First, Mao's peasant line was, essentially, a method, not a principle. The success or failure of the revolution can turn on whether a method of struggle is right or wrong, but methods cannot, of themselves, decide the nature of the revolution or the way in which its driving forces combine. Mao's armed road to revolution was adopted and implemented under the provisions of a strategic line set by Stalin. When Mao took that road, he said repeatedly that he fully agreed with the Comintern's line on China and the line set by the CCP's Sixth Congress. So Mao's thinking about rural revolution was a tactical means of realising Comintern and CCP strategy and in no way a strategy. Second, Mao did not develop his idea of meeting armed force with armed force on the basis of an analysis of the present era and of the Guomindang's semi-fascist militarisation. It arose because China is politically unstable and factious, leading Mao to conclude that the Red Army and Red power were possible, and to invent, or to induce from armed struggle, appropriate military tactics. So it was not a military strategy based on principle and developed with an eye to the whole situation and how to achieve the revolution but a tactic more or less forced on him by the defeat of the revolution, arrived at by a process of trial and error. It is true that he said, in November 1928, that a 'special characteristic of the revolution in China, a country with a predominantly agricultural economy, is the use of military action to develop insurrection' and recommended that the Central Committee 'should devote great effort to military work,'[3] and that he later, in January 1930, criticized the theory 'that we must first win over the masses

---

3   Mao, 'Struggle in the Jinggang Mountains,' SW, vol. 1, pp. 73–104, at 99.

on a country-wide scale and in all regions and then establish political power' because it did not 'accord with the actual state of the Chinese Revolution.'[4] But he did not make his criticism on strategic grounds and he was not fundamentally opposed to the Central Committee's proposals. He did not say that the party should abandon the mass movement in the cities and concentrate on building bases in the villages from which to liberate the cities and the country by armed force. On the contrary, he wrote as follows: 'Building a proletarian foundation for the party and setting up party branches in industrial enterprises in key districts are important organizational tasks for the party at present; but at the same time the major prerequisites for helping the struggle in the cities and hastening the rise of the revolutionary tide are specifically the development of the struggle in the countryside, the establishment of Red political power in small areas, and the creation and expansion of the Red Army. Therefore, it would be wrong to abandon the struggle in the cities.'[5] He could not have been clearer: like all Marxists, Chinese and non-Chinese, he thought that peasant armies and local governments can only 'help' and 'hasten' the revolutionary struggle as a whole. So the actual way in which the Chinese Revolution happened, its leaving of the cities (after 1933[6]), its reliance on peasant local governments and armies, its victory over the Guomindang in the civil war, and its liberation of the whole of China, was not the result of a pre-planned strategy but went against the CCP's and even Mao's own strategic line. So Mao's theory of 'peasant liberation, armed struggle, and revolutionary bases' is not on a par with Lenin's strategic formulae. Even so, Mao's theory, although tactical in nature, is still of value, and worthy of study around the world, especially in poor countries.

Chinese and non-Chinese Marxists alike have a set of traditional and orthodox ways, or tactics, for organising, promoting, and making revolution. They bring out newspapers, gather cadres in a party, organise the workers, extend organisation to working people outside the proletariat, agitate, make propaganda, and lead economic and political struggles, both legal and illegal, in order to spread their political influence and gain organisational strength, until the ripening of a nationwide revolutionary crisis (with popular support and at a time when the ruling class is collapsing politically and economically) and the launching by workers of one or several revolutions (violent or non-violent, parliamentary or extraparliamentary), the capture of political power in one or

---

4 Mao, 'A Single Spark Can Start a Prairie Fire,' January 5, 1930, SW, vol. 1, pp. 117–28, at 117.
5 Op. cit, pp. 122–3.
6 In January 1933, the Central Committee finally moved from Shanghai to the party's rural base centred on Ruijin.

more major cities, the formation of organs of state power (including an army), and the spreading of the revolution (with or without a civil war) to the rest of the country.

This approach has its source in basic Marxism, in the opposition in capitalist society between capital and labour, and in the idea of urban hegemony over the countryside and working-class leadership of non-proletarian forces. In the first thirty years after the Paris Commune, Western capitalism made great progress. The development of a parliament-based labour politics led at the turn of the century to opportunism and reformism, but parliamentarism had no future in backward Russia, where Lenin's Bolshevik strategy and tactics came into being. Bolshevism took over some practices from the Narodniks and at the same time borrowed methods from the Western European labour movement, absorbing the best bits of both and discarding the worst. From the Narodniks, it inherited vanguard characteristics: tightly organised, centralised, focused, combative, and conspiratorial; but it rejected their peasant standpoint, their elitism and individualism, and their bureaucratic authoritarianism. From the Western European labour movement, it adopted the idea of organising, educating, and leading the masses, but it rejected reformism and one-sided parliamentarism.

From its inception, the CCP adopted this approach, under Comintern guidance. With the party press as its organiser and Shanghai as its base, it fought to educate and organise workers and to embed itself everywhere, starting with the big cities, in order spread its political influence, increase its numbers, and, when the time was right, make revolution. It did this not just before the Northern Expedition but after the defeat of the revolution, under the Guomindang's reign of terror. The Chinese Trotskyists did too, and so did Wang Ming and Mao, though less consistently. Mao embraced the traditional approach to revolution, but he did not always follow it. He was a man of action rather than a theorist. His ideas were mostly rooted in traditional thinking. He knew little about Marxism-Leninism (especially in the 1920s), and was relatively unfettered by foreign dogmas. Pressed by circumstance and the logic of the struggle, he abandoned Marxist tactics. He substituted backward villages for the modern littoral, peasants for workers, a small number of communists in command of peasant armies for the industrial proletariat's influence over the peasantry, and armed secession and protracted war for propaganda, agitation, long-term organisation, and revolution by means of a general strike. In making these substitutions, Mao did not (publicly) abandon the official line, of working-class leadership and the primacy of work in the cities. Whenever he spotted a conflict between knowing and doing, he adapted the former to the latter, but without ever flagrantly violating Marxist-Leninist principles. For example, he never said that peasants do not need working-class leadership, but merely that a firm, tightly organised communist leadership will suffice to lead the peasants' struggle against the Guomindang. Similarly, regarding the establishment of independent regimes, Mao was not always absolutely confident and dared not attach unique importance to it. He always said that the struggle to establish separate regimes depends on the revolutionary situation in China as a whole. In a word, Mao initially adopted novel tactics because he was forced to do so, because things had turned out contrary to his wishes, and he formed his own opinions only gradually. Not until November 1938 did he make a comprehensive theoretical exposition of his views, at the Sixth Plenum of the Sixth Congress. He said:

> The seizure of power by armed force, the settlement of the problem by war, is the central task and the highest form of revolution. This Marxist-Leninist principle of revolution holds good universally, for China and for all other countries. But while the principle remains the same, its application by the party of the proletariat finds expression in varying ways according to the varying conditions. Internally, capitalist countries practice bourgeois democracy (not feudalism) when they are not fascist or not at war; in their external relations, they are not oppressed by, but themselves oppress, other nations. Because of these characteristics, it is the task of the party of the proletariat in the capitalist countries to educate the workers and build up strength through a long period of legal struggle, and thus prepare for the final overthrow of capitalism. In these countries, the question is one of a long legal struggle, of utilizing parliament as a platform, of economic and political strikes, of organizing trade unions and educating the workers. There the form of organization is legal and the form of struggle bloodless (non-military). On the issue of war, the Communist Parties in the capitalist countries oppose the imperialist wars waged by their own countries; if such wars occur, the policy of these Parties is to bring about the defeat of the reactionary governments of their own countries. The one war they want to fight is the civil war for which they are preparing. But this insurrection and war should not be launched until the bourgeoisie becomes really helpless, until the majority of the proletariat are determined to rise in arms and fight, and until the rural masses are giving willing help to the proletariat. And when the time comes to launch such an insurrection and war, the first step will be to seize the cities, and then advance into the countryside and not the other way about. All this has been done by Communist Parties in capitalist countries, and it has been proved correct by the October Revolution in Russia. China is different however. The characteristics of China are that she

is not independent and democratic but semi-colonial and semi-feudal, that internally she has no democracy but is under feudal oppression and that in her external relations she has no national independence but is oppressed by imperialism. It follows that we have no parliament to make use of and no legal right to organize the workers to strike. Basically, the task of the communist party here is not to go through a long period of legal struggle before launching insurrection and war, and not to seize the big cities first and then occupy the countryside, but the reverse. [...] All this shows the difference between China and the capitalist countries. In China war is the main form of struggle and the army is the main form of organization. Other forms such as mass organization and mass struggle are also extremely important and indeed indispensable and in no circumstances to be overlooked, but their purpose is to serve the war. Before the outbreak of a war all organization and struggle are in preparation for the war, as in the period from the May 4th Movement of 1919 to the May 30th Movement of 1925. After war breaks out, all organization and struggle are coordinated with the war either directly or indirectly, as, for instance, in the period of the Northern Expedition when all organization and struggle in the rear areas of the revolutionary army were co-ordinated with the war directly, and those in the Northern warlord areas were co-ordinated with the war indirectly. Again in the period of the War of Agrarian Revolution all organization and struggle inside the Red areas were co-ordinated with the war directly, and outside the Red areas indirectly. Yet again in the present period, the War of Resistance, all organization and struggle in the rear areas of the anti-Japanese forces and in the areas occupied by the enemy are directly or indirectly co-ordinated with the war. 'In China the armed revolution is fighting the armed counterrevolution. That is one of the specific features and one of the advantages of the Chinese Revolution.' This thesis of Comrade Stalin's is perfectly correct and is equally valid for the Northern Expedition, the War of Agrarian Revolution, and the present War of Resistance Against Japan. They are all revolutionary wars; all directed against counter-revolutionaries and all waged mainly by the revolutionary people, differing only in the sense that a civil war differs from a national war, and that a war conducted by the communist party differs from a war it conducts jointly with the Guomindang. Of course, these differences are important. They indicate the breadth of the main forces in the war (an alliance of the workers and peasants, or of the workers, peasants and bourgeoisie) and whether our antagonist in the war is internal or external (whether the war is against domestic or foreign foes, and, if domestic, whether against the Northern warlords or against the Guomindang); they also indicate that the content of China's revolutionary war differs at different stages of its history. But all these wars are instances of armed revolution fighting armed counterrevolution, they are all revolutionary wars, and all exhibit the specific features and advantages of the Chinese Revolution. The thesis that revolutionary war 'is one of the specific features and one of the advantages of the Chinese Revolution' fits China's conditions perfectly. The main task of the party of the Chinese proletariat, a task confronting it almost from its very inception, has been to unite with as many allies as possible and, according to the circumstances, to organize armed struggles for national and social liberation against armed counterrevolution, whether internal or external. Without armed struggle the proletariat and the communist party would have no standing at all in China, and it would be impossible to accomplish any revolutionary task. Our party did not grasp this point fully during the first five or six years after it was founded, that is, from 1921 to its participation in the Northern Expedition in 1926. It did not then understand the supreme importance of armed struggle in China, or seriously prepare for war and organize armed forces, or apply itself to the study of military strategy and tactics. During the Northern Expedition it neglected to win over the army but laid one-sided stress on the mass movement, with the result that the whole mass movement collapsed the moment the Guomindang turned reactionary. For a long time after 1927 many comrades continued to make it the party's central task to prepare for insurrections in the cities and to work in the White areas. It was only after our victory in repelling the enemy's third 'encirclement and suppression' campaign in 1931 that some comrades fundamentally changed their attitude on this question. But this was not true of the whole party, and there were other comrades who did not think along the lines presented here. Experience tells us that China's problems cannot be settled without armed force.[7]

After explaining the importance of armed struggle in the revolution, Mao went on to illustrate his ideas by looking at the role of war in the Guomindang and the CCP. He said:

From the start, when he organized a small revolutionary group, Sun Yat-sen staged armed insurrections against the Qing dynasty. The period of *Tongmeng hui* (the Chinese Revolutionary Alliance) was replete with

---

7 Mao, 'Problems of War and Strategy,' November 6, 1938, SW, vol. 1, pp. 219–36, at 219–22.

armed insurrections, right up to the armed overthrow of the Qing dynasty by the Revolution of 1911. Then, during the period of the Chinese Revolutionary Alliance, he carried out a military campaign against Yuan Shikai. Subsequent events such as the southern movement of the naval units, the northern expedition from Guilin and the founding of the Huangpu Military Academy were also among Sun Yat-sen's military undertakings.

After Sun Yat-sen came Chiang Kai-shek, who brought the Guomindang's military power to its zenith. He values the army as his very life and has had the experience of three wars, namely, the Northern Expedition, the Civil War and the War of Resistance Against Japan. For the last ten years Chiang Kai-shek has been a counter-revolutionary. He has created a huge 'Central Army' for counter-revolutionary purposes. He has held firmly to the vital point that whoever has an army has power and that war decides everything. In this respect we ought to learn from him. In this respect both Sun Yat-sen and Chiang Kai-shek are our teachers. There have also been parties in China, notably the Progressive Party, which did not want to have an army; yet even this party recognized that it could not get government positions without some warlord backing. Among its successive patrons have been Yuan Shikai, Duan Qirui and Chiang Kai-shek (to whom the Political Science Group, formed out of a section of the Progressive Party, has attached itself).

[…]

A few small political parties with a short history, e.g., the Youth Party, have no army, and so have not been able to get anywhere.

In other countries there is no need for each of the bourgeois parties to have an armed force under its direct command. But things are different in China, where, because of the feudal division of the country, those landlord or bourgeois groupings or parties which have guns have power, and those which have more guns have more power. Placed in such an environment, the party of the proletariat should see clearly to the heart of the matter.

Communists do not fight for personal military power (they must in no circumstances do that, and let no one ever again follow the example of Zhang Guotao), but they must fight for military power for the party, for military power for the people. As a national war of resistance is going on, we must also fight for military power for the nation. Where there is naivety on the question of military power, nothing whatsoever can be achieved. It is very difficult for the labouring people, who have been deceived and intimidated by the reactionary ruling classes for thousands of years, to awaken to the importance of having guns in their own hands. Now that

Japanese imperialist oppression and the nation-wide resistance to it have pushed our labouring people into the arena of war, Communists should prove themselves the most politically conscious leaders in this war. Every Communist must grasp the truth, 'Political power grows out of the barrel of a gun.' Our principle is that the party commands the gun, and the gun must never be allowed to command the party. Yet, having guns, we can create party organizations, as witness the powerful party organizations which the Eighth Route Army has created in northern China. We can also create cadres, create schools, create culture, create mass movements. Everything in Yan'an has been created by having guns. All things grow out of the barrel of a gun. According to the Marxist theory of the state, the army is the chief component of state power. Whoever wants to seize and retain state power must have a strong army. Some people ridicule us as advocates of the 'omnipotence of war.' Yes, we are advocates of the omnipotence of revolutionary war; that is good, not bad, it is Marxist. The guns of the Russian Communist Party created socialism. We shall create a democratic republic. Experience in the class struggle in the era of imperialism teaches us that it is only by the power of the gun that the working class and the labouring masses can defeat the armed bourgeoisie and landlords; in this sense we may say that only with guns can the whole world be transformed. We are advocates of the abolition of war, we do not want war; but war can only be abolished through war, and in order to get rid of the gun it is necessary to take up the gun.[8]

I quote Mao at such length because of the importance of his analysis. He wants not only to raise armed struggle from the tactical to the strategic level but to make it a fundamental principle of revolution, in China and the world. He talks not only about the relationship between modern China's parties and armies but also about the development of the CCP's attitude to military struggle. For the first time, he describes his own revolutionary tactics (or strategy) and the relationship, as he sees it, between town and village, class and party, army and party, and so on. Thus he explains, or at least raises, some issues of principle regarding revolutionary strategy. If you are seeking Mao thought or Maoism, here it is at its most representative and general.

Mao took up the gun at the end of 1927, but as a tactic. He engaged in armed struggle from within the strategic loop set by Moscow and in line with Marxist tradition. Even when fighting along the Hunan-Jiangxi border, he did not deny

---

8   Mao, 'Problems of War and Strategy,' November 6, 1938, SW, vol. 2, pp. 219–36, at 223–5.

workers' hegemony, the cities' decisive economic and political role, and workers' leadership of the peasants. He did not deny that only a proletarian party rooted in a proletarian setting can establish and consolidate its position, that without a nationwide upsurge the Red Army and the Red regime will falter, or that armed peasants can only play a supporting role. Before 1938 he never said that what communist parties in the capitalist countries and in Russia had done was not suitable for China, and that China should take an opposite path. Previously, Mao's guns had been compatible with the communists' approach in the capitalist countries, for when revolution fails in the cities it can sometimes, temporarily, adopt this tactic. Now, he says openly that he will make revolution with a peasant army, no longer as a temporary expedient and supplement in the wake of setbacks but because that is what semi-feudal, semi-colonial China needs. He therefore favours an opposite strategy for China to that of communists in the capitalist countries and Russia.

So Mao the tactician turned, gradually and cumulatively, over ten years, into Mao the strategist. There's nothing wrong with that. Practice usually precedes theory, and many strategies grow out of the accumulation of tactical experience. Even an innate strategist must pass the test of battle and constantly review the implementation of tactics to perfect them. So to assess the value of a strategist, attention should be directed to the strategic thinking itself rather than to how it came about. What, then, of Mao's status as a strategist? In a word, it was far lower than his status as a tactician.

To call '[t]he seizure of power by armed force, the settlement of the problem by war, the central task and the highest form of revolution' is to turn a correct principle (or, more accurately, correct principles) into something one-sided, simplistic, mechanical, and wrong. Lenin said that the main problem of any revolution is the problem of state power, and Engels called revolution 'the act whereby one part of the population imposes its will upon the other part by means of rifles, bayonets and cannon – authoritarian means, if such there be at all.'[9] Yes, the seizure of power depends in the final analysis on force, and even on violence, and revolutions that win power by armed uprisings usually turn into civil wars, or revolutionary wars against foreign interference – all revolutionaries would agree on that. But that does not make Mao right. For Mao, the sole task of a revolutionary is to study and organise revolutionary war in order to seize power. Mao declared this idea a 'Marxist-Leninist principle of revolution [that] holds good universally, for China and for all other countries. [However], while the principle remains the same, its application by the party of the pro-

---

9 Engels, 'On Authority,' 1872, MECW, cited in vol. 23, p. xvii.

letariat finds expression in varying ways according to the varying conditions.' But although it is nothing new for wars to resolve revolutions, it doesn't follow that they always do. That revolution, especially deep revolution, usually turns into civil war or revolutionary war is, if you like, a 'law of history.' Even so, it is wrong, despite the close relationship between revolution and war, to confuse the two, and to say that only war can lead to revolution and only by winning the war can you win the revolution.

Mao's assertion is wrong on several scores. First, it counterposes China and the world; second, it confuses revolution and war, especially revolution and revolutionary war; third, it sees all mass-based non-military revolutionary movements (propaganda and organisation) as preparatory to and subordinate to revolutionary war; and, fourth, it suggests that war, violence, guns are all-powerful.

After establishing his general principle, Mao went on to say: 'But while the principle remains the same, its application by the party of the proletariat finds expression in varying ways according to the varying conditions.' He explained that in capitalist countries 'the form of organization is legal and the form of struggle bloodless (non-military),' whereas in 'semi-feudal and semi-colonial' China, 'the task of the communist party [...] is not to go through a long period of legal struggle before launching insurrection and war, and not to seize the big cities first and then occupy the countryside, but the reverse.'[10]

These two passages contain a string of errors. First, the legal and bloodless struggle in the capitalist countries cannot simply be interpreted as a different 'manifestation' of the principle of settling issues by war. When Mao tries to point out the special circumstances of the capitalist countries, it is quite apparent that he, too, 'knew only China, not Greece.' He does not seem to know about (or at least does not mention) the changes in the historical conditions of Europe over the last hundred years, and the adaptations to these changes by the party of the proletariat, the manifestation of the principle. The European capitalist countries before and after 1848 did not unanimously overthrow feudalism internally and national oppression externally. Bourgeois democracy did not spread everywhere. Therefore revolutionary parties in the countries of Europe during that period did not adopt as their basic mission 'legal struggle, utilizing parliament as a platform, economic and political strikes, organizing trade unions, educating the workers,' etc. Those revolutions that did break out took the

---

10 Mao, 'Problems of War and Strategy,' November 6, 1938, SW, vol. 2, 219–36, at 219.

form of riots and street fighting. This went on until the early 1870s, culminating in the Paris Commune. This period saw the rise of Blanquist insurrection and the Marxist art of revolution. The revolution in Western Europe was drenched in blood, and sought to 'settle problems by means of war.' After the 1870s, capitalist industry shot ahead. The working class became increasingly powerful, democracy spread and took root, and what Mao sees as the legal, parliamentary, economic, and political struggle came into its own. People called this the democratic or liberal period of capitalism, which preceded the stage of monopoly finance capital and imperialism – the last stage of capitalism, which started at the turn of the century. This coincided with the birth of a new revolutionary strategy and tactics in Russia, where the economy was backward but the organisation of capital was highly concentrated. It was 'manifested' principally in Lenin's Bolshevism. This ism was, in many respects, a throwback to the years before 1871, to 'conspiracies,' violence, and 'settling problems of revolution by means of war.' For many Social-Democrats, Leninism was a return to Blanquism. In the half century after 1905, revolutionary parties in Europe and America were increasingly forced by militarisation and fascistisation to abandon legal and peaceful methods. So communists in capitalist countries did not follow the legal and parliamentary road to power. Sometimes there were periods of peace, but much blood was shed as well.

Violence has a role in revolution, but to reduce all revolution to violence is wrong. At its fullest point, class struggle, particularly the struggle for state power, must resort to violence and depend on force (armed and unarmed, material and immaterial), but that does not mean that all problems of revolution must be settled by war.

Neither Marx nor Lenin, in theory or in practice, absolutely ruled out the idea of peaceful revolution. In the months leading up to the October Revolution, Lenin said it might turn out to be peaceful and strove to make it so. This was not because he thought the reactionaries would voluntarily give up power, nor simply because he wanted to avoid bloodshed, but because of the balance of class forces and the arming of the people. Lenin was a realist, and did not believe that the ruling class would simply abdicate or that the ballot could replace the bullet, but he did believe that if the struggle developed favourably, and especially if the ruling class began to disintegrate, power (and even arms) might fall into the people's hands, and a wise party could follow a peaceful road to victory. Lenin's peaceful revolution was like Sunzi's 'winning without fighting': 'To win one hundred victories in one hundred battles is not the height of skill. To subdue the enemy without fighting is the height of skill.'

But isn't 'to subdue the enemy without fighting' a kind of war, and the best kind, and the opposite of not fighting? Only the best fighter does not go to war.

Lenin's peaceful revolution is also a kind of war, and also the best kind. This war can be won even without war, and power can be taken peacefully, because arms are in the people's hands. Does Lenin's theory not therefore back Mao's 'settling problems by war'? Does not peace depend on a commitment to settling problems by force and arming the people?

There's nothing wrong with these ideas. However, there is much wrong with simply asserting the principle of settling the question of power by war and excluding the possibility of a peaceful road. The idea that guns decide all or create all is not only wrong but harmful, and has more in common with Blanquism and even Machiavellianism than with Marxism. Mao was not always so simplistic, and did not always say that only guns mattered (if he had, he would not have achieved what he has); even so, this simple idea is a cornerstone of Mao thought.

Revolution is not the same as war, and it is not even the same as revolutionary war. Clausewitz said that 'war is the continuation of politics by other means,' so revolutionary war is the continuation of revolutionary politics by other means. But it is by 'other means' and a 'continuation,' so it differs in form and substance. Revolutionary war grows out of revolution. It has its own methods. Revolution that develops into revolutionary war does not stop being revolutionary, but it will conform more to the laws of war than to those of revolution. These two sorts of laws are not the same. Revolution happens from below. It tends to be excessively democratic, the popular will gains the upper hand, it destroys authority, and its sole fetter is spiritual; war, even revolutionary war, is top-down, centralised, and the product of the will of a few leaders who must establish their authority and coercive power. Because of these differences, even if revolution and revolutionary war are conducted by the same group and to the same end, the outcomes can be very different. Living determines consciousness, while means and ends are closely linked. Whether a revolution can be won without war or only by war depends not on what revolutionaries desire. Revolutionary war is always forced and never sought – to win the revolution, revolutionaries must fight armed counter-revolution. But it is important to tell revolution and revolutionary war apart, and to know their different outcomes. It is particularly wrong to think that a rising without mass support, relying on a handful of revolutionaries, can spark a war and create a revolution, or take the place of a revolution.

Mao does not distinguish revolution from revolutionary war and believes that in China there can be no revolution other than as revolutionary war, so he thinks all non-military mass revolutionary movements are simply in preparation for and ancillary to war. The next logical step is to conclude that guns decide and create everything. 'The guns of the Russian Communist Party created socialism. We shall create a democratic republic. [...] [O]nly with guns can the whole world be transformed.'[11]

In his efforts to raise revolutionary practice and armed struggle to the level of strategy, Mao fails to answer fundamental questions about the relationship between town and village, worker and peasant, and party and class, as well as about the role, limits, and consequences of violence. His comparative analysis of the special features of the struggle of the Western working class does little to clarify their history and present circumstances. When summarising the special features of armed revolution in China, he focuses crudely and one-sidedly on violence and reduces world revolution to the gun. In a word, as a revolutionary strategist, he is weak.

How, then, to explain the CCP's glittering victory on the political and military front? Is not its mere fact the most eloquent illustration of the brilliance of Mao's leadership? Could it be that clever tactics, even when joined to poor strategy, can bring about victory in the revolution?

This is not the place to discuss why the CCP won. Later, when I look at Mao's contribution to the revolution, I will discuss it in greater detail. Here, I want merely to say that the victory of the revolution should never be attributed wholly to the CCP or Mao personally. Mao's personal contribution was great, but that does not change his status as a strategist. A middling strategist can apply clever tactics to win, just as a brilliant strategist might apply poor tactics and lose. Whether in victory or in defeat, people can still distinguish the role played by strategy and by tactics. In victory as in defeat, it enables people to judge whether a leader's genius lies in strategy or in tactics. To evaluate heroes according to success or failure is vulgar and philistine. To evaluate strategy according to victory or defeat is unfair. The process of winning or losing, the cost of it, and the attitude towards it all demonstrate the strategic ability of top leaders. Starting out from these three things, one must sometimes concede that the losers' commander-in-chief is cleverer than the winners'. So victory does not in itself prove that Mao is a superb strategist. One must at least ask how the victory came about, what it cost, and how it is sustained and extended. However, I discuss these points in the next chapter, while here I persevere with Mao the tactician.

Mao's brilliance as a tactician (from a purely military standpoint, many of his tactics should be called strategic) is contrary to many people's intuition, for the impression has always been that Mao was good at politics while Zhu De was good at fighting. However, Mao's writings show that he was a better general

---

11   Mao, 'Problems of War and Strategy,' November 6, 1938, SW, vol. 2, pp. 219–36, at 225.

than a politician. He didn't learn military science from European, American, or Japanese textbooks or even from the Russian communists. He said, with a characteristic mix of arrogance and good sense:

> Some people hold a wrong view. [...] They say that it is enough merely to study the laws of war in general, or, to put it more concretely, that it is enough merely to follow the military manuals published by the reactionary Chinese government or the reactionary military academies in China. They do not see that these manuals give merely the laws of war in general and moreover are wholly copied from abroad, and that if we copy and apply them exactly without the slightest change in form or content, we shall be 'cutting the feet to fit the shoes' and be defeated. [...] Others hold a second wrong view. [...] They say that it is enough merely to study the experience of revolutionary war in Russia, or, to put it more concretely, that it is enough merely to follow the laws by which the civil war in the Soviet Union was directed and the military manuals published by Soviet military organizations. They do not see that these laws and manuals embody the specific characteristics of the civil war and the Red Army in the Soviet Union, and that if we copy and apply them without allowing any change, we shall also be 'cutting the feet to fit the shoes' and be defeated.

The shoes Mao wanted to fashion for Chinese feet were made from native materials, and his military textbooks were the *Zuozhuan*,[12] the *Zizhi tongjian*, and even the *Romance of the Three Kingdoms* and the *Water Margin*. The battles he studied were not Austerlitz, Waterloo, or Sedan, and they weren't even Tsaritsyno or Petrograd. Instead, they were battles of Chinese antiquity – the Battle of Changshao between the Qi and the Lu, the Battle of Chenggao between the Chu and the Han, the Battle of Kunyang between the Xin and the Lülin rebels, the Battle of Guandu between Cao Cao and Yuan Shao, the Battles of Chibi and Yiling between Cao Cao and Sun Quan, the Battle of Fei River between the Qin and the Jin, and even Lin Chong's defeat of Instructor Hong in a bout with staves in the Water Margin. He learned his strategy and tactics not from Clausewitz, Napoleon, or Moltke, nor from Voroshilov, etc., but from Sunzi.[13] Mao himself has never described his relationship with Sunzi, although he called him a 'great

---

12 The *Zuozhuan* ('Zuo's commentary'), China's first great historical work, was a commentary on the *Spring and Autumn Annals*.
13 Moltke (1848–1916) was a German military commander. Voroshilov (1881–1969) was a Soviet military officer and politician in the Stalin era.

military thinker of antiquity,' and nor has anyone else (as far as I know) asked how Mao studied Sun's Thirteen Chapters. However, Mao's strategic and tactical thinking (in the purely military sense) is closely and obviously linked with Sunzi's. Mao summarised the basic principle of the CCP's guerrilla tactics in a sixteen-character formula: 'He advances, we retreat. He camps, we harass. He tires, we attack. He retreats, we pursue.'[14] This formula, adopted in May 1928, 'simple in nature and suited to the conditions of the time,' was 'greatly enriched' after the defeat of the Guomindang's third encirclement in 1931, by which time 'a complete set of operational principles for the Red Army had taken shape.' However, they 'remained the same as in the sixteen-character formula,' for the earlier formula had 'covered the basic principles for combating 'encirclement and suppression'; it covered the two stages of the strategic defensive and the strategic offensive, and, within the defensive, it covered the two stages of the strategic retreat and the strategic counter-offensive. What came later was only a development of this formula.'[15] So the sixteen-character formula is the clearest, most concise summary of Mao's strategic and tactical thinking. Where, then, did it come from? From Sunzi's *Art of War*.

Sunzi said:

1. 'The art of using troops is this: when ten to the enemy's one, surround him; when five to his one, attack him; when twice his strength, divide him; when equally matched, engage him; when fewer in number, be able to withdraw; and, if in all respects unequal, be able to elude him.'
2. 'All warfare is based on deception. [...] Entice the enemy with baits. Pretend disorder, and crush him. If he is secure, be prepared for him, if greater in strength, evade him. If he is angry, irritate him. Pretend to be weak, so he grows arrogant. If he is at ease, give him no rest. If he is united, divide him. Attack him where he is unprepared. Appear where you are unexpected.'
3. 'Avoid the enemy when he is fresh and strike him when he is tired and withdraws. [...] Be disciplined and calm, in expectation of his clamour and disorder. [...] Be near the goal when he is far from it.'

Mao's 'he advances, we retreat' echoes Sun's prescription. So does 'he camps, we harass' and 'he retreats, we pursue.'

Mao's strategy and tactics became fuller and richer in time, but the sixteen-character formula, and thus Sunzi's *Art of War*, stayed at its heart. The history

---

14   Mao, 'Problems of Strategy in China's Revolutionary War,' December 1936, SW, vol. 1, pp. 179–254, at 124.
15   Mao, 'Problems of Strategy in China's Revolutionary War,' December 1936, SW, vol. 1, pp. 179–254, at 213.

of the Chinese Red Army's ten-year civil war was one of resisting encirclement and extermination. This definition is very succinct. All war is a cycle of being encircled and breaking out of encirclement. Strategically, the Red Army was fighting on the interior line: tactically, on the external line. Its strategy was to do all it could to avoid destruction or weakening. Tactically, it sought to wipe out the enemy. Its strategy was to avoid encirclement, its tactic to encircle. To avoid encirclement, it had to be on the initiative at all times, and to be flexible; to retain the initiative when advancing and retreating, while dodging the enemy and raiding him. To encircle the enemy, you must concentrate in one place a force several or dozens of times greater than his, to take him by surprise, to hit him sharply and swiftly, and to wipe him out. These tactics enabled the Red Army to beat back four of Chiang Kai-shek's encirclements but not the fifth, allegedly because Wang Ming and others abandoned them in favour of regular warfare, leading to defeat, evacuation of the Jiangxi base, and the start of the Long March.[16] On the Long March, the Red Army reverted to the old tactics, and reached northern Shaanxi; in the Sino-Japanese War and the Third Civil War after victory over Japan, the CCP continued to apply the same basic tactics, but more explicitly and richly developed, as explained by Mao in December 1947 in 'The Present Situation and Our Tasks,' in the Ten Principles.[17]

Since the Ten Principles are an elaboration on the Sixteen-Character Formula, which was an emanation of Sunzi's military thinking, there is a link between them and the Thirteen Chapters. That does mean that Mao took all his ideas from Sun. It would be silly to say that Mao simply recited what 'the Master said.' As Mao himself pointed out, 'All the laws for directing war develop as history develops and as war develops; nothing is changeless.' What Sunzi said two thousand four hundred years ago cannot be applied word for word today. Mao's military thinking is a product of the age of imperialism and world revolution and of revolutionary war in semi-colonial China under communist leadership. It cannot be equated with warcraft in the Spring and Autumn period. However, although the laws of war, like those of any social phenomenon, change and grow, not everything changes. Total negation is not development, as the Hegelian and Marxist idea of *Aufhebung* (sublation) affirms. That Mao's Ten Prin-

---

16   In reality, the failure of the Chinese Red Army's campaign against Chiang Kai-shek's Fifth Encirclement and the fall of the Chinese Soviet cannot be one-sidedly attributed to the tactics of Mao's opponents in the leadership.

17   Mao, 'The Present Situation and Our Tasks,' December 1947, SW, vol. 4, pp. 157–76, at 161–2.

ciples preserve or embody elements of the Thirteen Chapters should come as no surprise, and is compatible with the whole character of Mao thought and the idea of 'Chinese learning for the foundation, Western learning for application.'

Compare Mao's Ten Principles and Sun's Thirteen Chapters:

Mao's First Principle: 'Attack dispersed, isolated enemy forces first; attack concentrated, strong enemy forces later.'

Thirteen Chapters: 'Avoid the solid, strike the weak.' 'Some armies must not be attacked.' 'When a general unable to estimate the enemy sends a small force against a big one or a weak force against a strong one and does not put picked soldiers at the front, rout will ensue.'

Mao's Second Principle: 'Take small and medium cities and extensive rural areas first; take big cities later.'

Thirteen Chapters: 'There are cities that must not be attacked. There are grounds that must not be contested.' 'Avoid the solid, strike the weak.'

Mao's Third Principle: 'Make wiping out the enemy's effective strength our main objective; do not make holding or seizing a city or place our main objective. Holding or seizing a place is the outcome of wiping out the enemy's effective strength, and often a place can be held or seized for good only after it has changed hands a number of times.'

Thirteen Chapters: No equivalent.

Mao's Fourth Principle: 'In every battle, concentrate an absolutely superior force (two, three, four and sometimes even five or six times the enemy's strength), encircle the enemy forces completely, and strive to wipe them out thoroughly and not to let any escape the net.'

Thirteen Chapters: 'We will be a united body, while the enemy will split into parts. So we will oppose his separate parts, being many to his few. If we can attack a weak force with a strong one, those we fight will be in trouble.'

Mao's Fifth Principle: 'Fight no battle unprepared, fight no battle you are not sure of winning; make every effort to be well prepared for each battle, make every effort to ensure victory in the given set of conditions as between the enemy and ourselves.'

Thirteen Chapters: 'The general who wins a battle makes many calculations in his temple [headquarters] before the battle.' 'So in war let your object be victory, not lengthy campaigns.' 'Fighters in the past first put themselves beyond the possibility of defeat, and then awaited the chance to defeat the enemy.' 'Skilful fighters put themselves in positions where defeat is impossible.'

Mao's Sixth Principle: 'Give full play to our style of fighting – courage in battle, no fear of sacrifice, no fear of fatigue, and continuous fighting (that is, fighting successive battles in a short time without rest).'

Thirteen Chapters: 'Speed is precious in war.' 'The good fighter will be terrible in his onset, prompt in his decision.'

Mao's Seventh Principle: 'Strive to wipe out the enemy through mobile warfare. At the same time, pay attention to the tactics of positional attack and capture enemy fortified points and cities.'

Thirteen Chapters: 'In fighting, the direct method may be used for joining battle, but indirect methods are needed to win.'

Mao's Eighth Principle: 'With regard to attacking cities, resolutely seize all enemy fortified points and cities which are weakly defended. Seize at opportune moments all enemy fortified points and cities defended with moderate strength.'

Thirteen Chapters: 'There are some cities that must not be attacked.' 'The rule is, do not besiege walled cities unless you have to.' 'He captures their cities without laying siege to them.'

Mao's Ninth Principle: 'Replenish our strength with all the arms and most of the personnel captured from the enemy. Our army's main sources of manpower and matériel are at the front.'

Thirteen Chapters: 'The captured soldiers should be kindly treated and kept. This is called using the conquered enemy to increase one's own strength.' 'Then the army will have enough food.'

Mao's Tenth Principle: 'Make good use of the intervals between campaigns to rest, train and consolidate our troops. Periods of rest, training and consolidation should in general not be very long, and the enemy should so far as possible be permitted no breathing space.'

Thirteen Chapters: 'Carefully study your men's well-being, and do not exhaust them. Concentrate your energy and hoard your strength.' 'Without losing a man, the general's triumph is complete.' 'Speed in war is of the essence.'

Mao's principles (especially the third, seventh, and eighth) and Sun's ideas are obviously not identical, for ancient and modern wars are waged under very different conditions. In antiquity, the concept of battles of movement and annihilation and the storming of heavily fortified positions had not yet been fully worked out, so the relationship between the Thirteen Chapters and the Ten Principles is a bud not a fruit. It would be stupid to claim that Mao based his military thinking on Sunzi. However, it is obvious, given the similarities, that he had studied him.

It is interesting to think how Mao learned from the Master, and how, in conditions of modern warfare, he came to deploy ideas formulated two thousand four hundred years earlier, but this is not a question to answer here. I simply note a source of his military thinking, and point out that he achieved in practice a set of military theories suitable for Chinese conditions, and, applying them, won the war. His military writings have not only historical and theoretical value but real practical value for revolutionaries in poor, semi-colonial capitalist countries.

All China's famous generals have revered Sunzi, especially the so-called *ru* generals, the literati who switched careers, but few have applied his thinking successfully. Most were like Ma Su,[18] doltish and useless, muddle-headed and careless, the 'dogmatists' of China's Seven Military Classics.[19] After the West used modern weapons to smash open the door to China, things became even more ridiculous. *Ru* generals who had 'mastered [Sunzi's] *Art of War*' thought that China's old military tactics were as useless against modern military science as the magic incantations of the red-tasselled Great Swords sect,[20] even if not every general made such an exhibition of himself as Ye Mingchen and Ronglu.[21] Arrogant literati at first used armed might to try to subdue the 'barbarians.' They sincerely believed that lack of armed might was their sole failing. So for a long time, while closing their eyes to Western ideas and continuing to vaunt China's spiritual civilisation as the best in the world, they scrambled to achieve 'wholesale westernisation' of their weaponry. The military academies rang with talk about foreign military affairs. The troops did foreign drill, wore foreign uniforms, and used foreign guns. The Thirteen Chapters and the Eighteen Kinds of Weapon were sent to the museum.[22] China's new military command was made up of men trained in Japan and Germany and at America's West Point. After 1911, China's warlords hired foreign advisers to teach them strategies and tactics developed since the Franco-Prussian War, which the warlords practised on the Chinese people. During the Northern Expedition, the Guomindang army was influenced by Soviet strategists, in the civil war by German followers of Ludendorff, and in the Sino-Japanese War by West Point. In short, for decades people fought and died on the Chinese battlefield under foreign military orchestration and command. Most of the CCP's military cadres received their training from Soviet army men, either dir-

---

18   Ma Su (190–228) was a general and strategist in the Three Kingdoms period who committed a famous tactical blunder.
19   The Seven Military Classics were military texts of ancient China, including Sunzi's *Art of War*.
20   The Great Swords sect was a fictional alliance of martial-arts sects and also the name of actual sects.
21   Ye Mingchen (1807–1859) was a Qing dynasty official ridiculed for his inability to resist the British in battle. Ronglu (1836–1903) was a conservative Manchu political and military leader.
22   The Thirteen Chapters are the chapters of the *Art of War*. The Eighteen Arms were the eighteen weapons of Chinese martial arts.

ectly (in Soviet military school) or indirectly (at the Huangpu Academy in China).[23] For a while (mainly while Wang Ming was in charge), Soviet military experts personally commanded the Red Army in Jiangxi. However, 'all are past and gone,' leaving behind no great achievement. In today's China, against the background of these developments, Mao, a self-taught strategist, learned from Sunzi, China's native military thinker, and applied Sunzi's stratagems and tricks to peasant armed struggle, creating his own military theory and using it to win power.

Was Mao a military genius? Was China's ancient warcraft better than today's? Of course not. Mao had a superior military mind, and his case shows that ancient Chinese military science can still be regarded as a precious heritage. However, the reason the *Art of War* as digested and applied by Mao could defeat the enemy was not just military. Chiang was also familiar with Sunzi and drew up a full set of counter-measures, but to no avail. Why? Mao has the answer: 'The reason is that our strategy and tactics are based on a people's war; no army opposed to the people can use our strategy and tactics. On the basis of a people's war and of the principles of unity between army and people, of unity between commanders and fighters and of disintegrating the enemy troops, the People's Liberation Army has developed its vigorous revolutionary political work, which is an important factor in winning victory over the enemy.'[24] This is right. In the end, only mass-based revolutionary war can apply these methods effectively to win power.

Political tactics are usually understood as stratagems, manoeuvres, chicanes, or machinations. That Mao is well qualified in this respect goes without saying. Mao made revolution for forty years, led it, and gave full play to his policies for more than ten years, from 1935 to 1947. This period can be divided into (1) before and after 'reunification' with the Guomindang; (2) before and after the Wannan Incident of January 1941; and (3) between victory over Japan and the outbreak of the civil war.[25] Mao's political operations in these periods, going by his published work, show him to be an outstanding tactician.

In the years between the winters of 1935 and 1938, the Guomindang and the CCP made peace, after a decade of civil war. The decision was Stalin's, an

---

23 The Huangpu Military Academy was set up by Sun Yat-sen in the 1920s. Many of its original instructors were Soviet military officers.
24 Mao, 'The Present Situation and Our Tasks,' December 1947, SW, vol. 4, 157–76, at 162.
25 'Reunification' with the Guomindang, after the First United Front of the 1920s, happened in 1937; the Wannan Incident of January 1941 marked the *de facto* end of the Second United Front; (3) victory over Japan was achieved in 1945 and civil war broke out in earnest in 1946 and lasted until 1949.

adaptation for Chinese enactment of the Comintern's Popular Front. In 1929, Stalin had swung to the left and communists everywhere were told to prepare for the final battle. As a consequence, Hitler took power in Germany and Chiang Kai-shek defeated the Red Army in Jiangxi, causing the Japanese to run even more rampant. Threatened to the east and west, Stalin made communists everywhere support their 'own' bourgeois governments and oppose fascism. In China, where the Long March had taken the Red Amy remnants to the northwest, Mao happily embraced the new line. The old line, implemented by the Wang Ming faction, had brought disaster, and Mao himself had nearly fallen victim to it. The Red Army was saved by a timely switch in strategy and tactics on the Long March. Although worn out, it was now able to take cover, pause for breath, consolidate, and manoeuvre in the Chinese northwest. Had it stayed on the old line of waging separate wars from fragmented bases and not executed a dramatic change of course by issuing a nationwide political appeal, resisting Chiang's siege would have been harder. This is what Mao meant when he said in December 1935: 'The kind of impatience that was formerly displayed will never do. Moreover, sound revolutionary tactics must be worked out; we will never achieve great things if we keep on milling around within narrow confines.'[26] Mao was arguing in support of Stalin's new line, but he unwittingly provided a defence for Trotskyist strategy in that period. Since early 1928, Trotsky had been calling for a Chinese National Assembly[27] with full powers and elected on the basis of universal suffrage, but Stalin rejected this. Having put aside the Soviet slogan, he ended up with no slogan at all, 'milling around within narrow confines.' I will return to this.

I am not, for the time being, concerned with why Stalin turned and why Mao followed him in late 1935, or whether they were right to turn. I am interested only in Mao's attitude to the turn and his tactics in it. The leap from left to right, from fratricide to brotherly love and 'sincere cooperation,' bewildered people and provoked suspicion and opposition even among cadres, who were used to doing what they were told. To still the doubts and neutralise the opposition, Mao's report 'On Tactics Against Japanese Imperialism' tried to justify the new policy in class terms. It was largely wrong and superficial, but two passages carried weight:

---

26   Mao, 'On Tactics Against Japanese Imperialism,' December 27, 1935, SW, vol. 1, pp. 153–78, at 163.
27   Both the Chinese Trotskyists and the CCP used the term *guomin* (national) rather than *lixian* (constituent) because the latter term had been discredited in the late Qing dynasty and the early Republican period.

A BRILLIANT TACTICIAN

1. The special feature on the revolutionary side at present is the existence of a well-steeled communist party and Red Army. This is of crucial importance. Great difficulties would arise if they did not exist.
2. The Communists are no longer political infants and are able to take care of themselves and to handle relations with their allies. If the Japanese imperialists and Chiang Kai-shek can manoeuvre in relation to the revolutionary forces, the communist party can do the same in relation to the counter-revolutionary forces.[28]

Mao was saying the pact with Chiang would not repeat the errors of 1927, for the communists now had guns, and stratagems to support them. Mao did as he said, and did it well. Popular fronts have always failed in revolutions, but this was a trap into which the CCP did not fall, thanks largely to Mao.

The Second United Front between the Guomindang and the CCP began as a cold war, with infighting, but soon hotted up, starting in 1938, and culminated in the Wannan Incident in January 1941. Mao wrote a series of articles on tactics in this period. In March 1940, he said the party should fight the Guomindang only 'on just grounds', 'to our advantage,' and 'with restraint.'[29] In December 1940, he defined its tactical principles as 'neither all alliance and no struggle nor all struggle and no alliance' but a combination of 'alliance and struggle [...] to make use of contradictions, win over the many, oppose the few and crush our enemies one by one, and to wage struggles on just grounds, to our advantage, and with restraint.'[30] He said that in Guomindang areas 'it must have well-selected cadres working underground [and] must accumulate strength and bide its time there.'[31] In the third article, he advocated a tit-for-tat policy and pointed out that 'Chinese politics, which are extremely complex, demand our comrades' deepest attention. [...] A whole range of tactics is needed to combat the Guomindang's anti-Communist policy, and there must be absolutely no carelessness or negligence.'[32] Mao's strategy of manoeuvring among political groupings bore rich fruit, whether or not one agrees with his united front.

---

28 Mao, 'On Tactics Against Japanese Imperialism,' December 27, 1935, SW, vol. 1, pp. 153–78, at 167.
29 Mao, 'Our Study and The Current Situation,' April 12, 1944, SW, vol. 3, pp. 163–76, at 169.
30 Appendix: Resolution on Certain Questions in the History of Our Party, adopted on April 20, 1945, by the Enlarged Seventh Plenary Session of the Sixth Central Committee of the Communist Party of China, in Mao, vol. 3, pp. 177–226, at 202.
31 Mao, 'The Chinese Revolution and the Chinese Communist Party,' December 1939, SW, vol. 2, pp. 305–33, at 318.
32 Mao, 'Conclusions on the Repulse of the Second Anti-Communist Onslaught,' May 8, 1941, SW, vol. 2, pp. 463–8, at 464.

The last of the three periods began in August 1945 and ended in July 1946, with the resumption of civil war. In it, Mao summed up his strategy or tactics in the formula 'give [the enemy] tit for tat and fight for every inch of land.'[33] Helped by the Americans, the Guomindang combined negotiations with attacks; the communists joined peace talks while preparing a counter-offensive. Both sides were realists; each did its utmost to manoeuvre among the political groupings. But leaving aside social class and looking just at tactics, Mao outshone Chiang in skill and courage, thus gaining an unprecedented degree of political influence and a big propaganda advantage.

Mao excels at cold war and power politics, as even his enemies admit. Some say that means he is not a great revolutionary or statesman, just a petty schemer and manipulator. Others, that there's no essential difference between politics and warcraft, for both are based on deception. Those who are good at deceiving win while those who are bad at it lose, and the former are great generals and statesmen – morality doesn't come into it. The same goes for revolutions – what matters is winning, by whatever means, fair or foul. Mao won, so he is a great revolutionary.

Who is right? To say that a great revolutionary values only principles is like saying that a great politician values only righteousness and disdains intrigue – the view of a bookish pedant, or of a young and inexperienced revolutionary. For this disorder, Lenin prescribed these remedies:

> To carry on a war for the overthrow of the international bourgeoisie, a war which is a hundred times more difficult, prolonged and complicated than the most stubborn of ordinary wars between states, and to refuse beforehand to manoeuvre, to utilise the conflict of interests (even though temporary) among one's enemies, to refuse to temporise and compromise with possible (even though transitory, unstable, vacillating and conditional) allies – is not this ridiculous in the extreme? Is it not as though, when making a difficult ascent of an unexplored and hitherto inaccessible mountain, we were to refuse beforehand ever to move in zigzags, ever to retrace our steps, ever to abandon the course once selected to try others?[34]

Lenin valued principles more highly than any other revolutionary, ancient or modern, and set out from principle in all he did, but he also valued political

---

33   Mao, 'The Situation and Our Policy After the Victory in the War of Resistance Against Japan,' August 13, 1945, pp. 11–26, at 14.
34   Lenin 1970, p. 67.

manoeuvres of the sort Mao excels at, and said that revolutionaries should exploit conflicts among enemies, even temporary ones. He favoured compromising with or accommodating potential allies of all sorts (temporary, unstable, vacillating, and conditional), a fact borne out by the whole history of Bolshevism, before and after October. He manoeuvred boldly, to the alarm of party purists. In February 1917, for example, he returned to Russia in a sealed train provided by the Germans so that he could rejoin the revolution, and in 1918 he signed the Treaty of Brest-Litovsk with the Central Powers against party and non-party opposition, to gain a breathing space.

Can any road that heads in the right direction be taken? Can an approach to revolution that depends on manoeuvring between different factions and lacks a grand scheme and base in principle win anyway? Can revolutionaries do as they please? All roads lead to Rome, but not all means lead to revolution. The Jesuit maxim that the end justifies the means has no place in revolutionary politics. In revolutions, especially socialist revolutions, end and means are interdependent. The means determine the end. Some means reach an end or bring it closer, others wreck or defer it. Identical means applied in different circumstances have different outcomes, either serving the revolution or betraying it. In this regard, Lenin distinguished compromises enforced by circumstance from compromises by traitors acting from self-interest.

What about Mao's tactics and alliances? Were they necessary for the revolution? Lenin said that determining whether a compromise is legitimate can be a matter of 'exceptional difficulty and complexity.' To look at Mao's tactics case by case, in fine detail, and in light of the subjective and objective conditions of the time in order to define the true nature of each would be difficult (partly because of lack of information). In any case, it is beyond the scope of this study, which asks instead: What was Mao's attitude when adopting expedients? Was it like that of other revolutionary leaders? When Lenin and others engaged in compromises or changed tack, they did so, at all times and in all circumstances, principally to '*raise* – not lower – the *general* level of proletarian class-consciousness, revolutionary spirit, and ability to fight and win.'[35] For Lenin, this was the nub of it, no matter whether the goal was to harm the enemy, protect themselves, respond to impossible pressures, avoid fighting under adverse circumstances, play off one enemy against another, or ally with wavering forces to beat the enemy. In all cases, he asked when considering an expedient what its effect would be on the toiling classes. Could it be used to teach them and make them more aware? If not, he had no use for it. Lenin was prepared to use

---

35 Lenin 1970, p. 72.

any tactic, but not without conditions. A tactic (for example, individual terror) that might knock the enemy down but at the cost of paralysing revolutionary consciousness was impermissible. So was one that hoodwinked the enemy but also duped the workers. Lenin's tack was bold and meticulous, a fine example of the integration of principle and means. When he had to hurry back to Russia in 1917, he boldly requested safe passage across enemy territory and was offered a sealed train, which he accepted, but not without laying down conditions. To pre-empt slander by his political opponents and (more importantly) to dispel the misgivings of workers at home and abroad, before setting out he invited Paul Levy and other foreign revolutionaries to sign a declaration saying 'the Russian internationalists are [...] going to Russia to contribute to the revolutionary cause and to help us rouse the proletariat of other countries, especially Germany, to oppose their governments.'[36] In return for passage, Lenin's sole concession was to undertake to do what he could to improve the conditions of German POWs and hasten the repatriation of the German sick and wounded. At Brest-Litovsk, the Bolsheviks, unable to fight on at the front or ignore German blackmail, won breathing space in which to await hoped-for rescue by the world proletariat, especially the German proletariat. They explained the situation to workers in Russia and the world and made no attempt, in the talks, to hide the painful truth behind diplomatic words. In that way, they buoyed up workers' consciousness and fighting spirit at home and abroad. Trotsky backed this approach, saying 'the secret of propaganda is to tell the truth.'[37] Only after Stalin took power did machinations replace principle. Stalin schemed against the workers and even more so against comrades. When compromising, he compromised in principle, powdering the enemy's face and pretending he had become a friend. Stalin gave no thought to the impact of his deals.

Mao's attitude to power play was far closer to Stalin's than to Lenin's and Trotsky's. He mocked those who failed to understand compromise as believing that 'If we shake hands with Cai Tingkai, we must call him a counter-revolutionary.'[38] Mao thought it wrong to be rude to temporary allies or to

---

36   Lenin, 'Farewell Letter to the Swiss Workers,' CW, vol. 23, pp. 367–73.
37   This sentence is perhaps a very rough paraphrase of the following passage: 'The superiority of our propaganda lies in its content. Our propaganda invariably united the Red Army, while disrupting the enemy's forces, not by any special technical methods or procedures but by the Communist idea which constituted the content of this propaganda. This military secret of ours we openly divulge, without fearing any plagiarism on the part of our adversaries' (Trotsky, writing in *Yezhegodnik Kominterna* ['Comintern Annual'], May 21, 1922).
38   Mao, 'On Tactics Against Japanese Imperialism,' December 27, 1935, SW, vol. 1, pp. 153–78, 164.

expose their scars, and important to promote goodwill. When shaking hands with Cai Tingkai, at least call him dear friend. This attitude was the opposite of Lenin's, who explained that compromises were temporary, to increase class consciousness and keep spirits high and to avoid confusion. Instead, it was the same as Stalin's. After his deal with Hitler, Stalin tried to beautify him, and although Hitler kept up his hue-and-cry against the Reds, Stalin said he knew that 'the German people love their Führer' and that German-Soviet friendship, 'sealed in blood, has every reason to be long and strong.'[39] After his pact with Japan in 1941, he told Matsuoka, the ferocious Japanese Foreign Minister, 'we are both Asiatics,' and Matsuoka returned: 'I am a moral communist!'[40] For Stalin, a handshake had to be polite and at least superficially sincere, thus fooling both the enemy and the people, or it wouldn't work. He couldn't care less about its impact on workers' consciousness and fighting spirit, for the source of all power was with the few (or even the one) who commanded the army and the state machine, and not with the masses.

Mao, similarly, not only stopped calling Chiang Kai-shek a counter-revolutionary and a national traitor in 1938 but started calling him a great leader and said the CCP accepted the Three People's Principles and subordination to the Guomindang. Obviously, his aim was to firm up the United Front against Japan. He had not turned traitor or surrendered, but was adopting a ploy. Revolutionaries have every right to use ploys, but not to embrace a bandit as one's father and to get everyone to do so, 'in all sincerity.' Mao's aim was to support Chiang's leadership and avoid harming the government's authority, but although he might see ten thousand reasons to do so, it reduced people's awareness and fighting spirit, and thus weakened or destroyed their revolutionary spirit. Sunzi said: 'Humble words and increased preparations are signs that the enemy is about to advance. [...] When envoys are sent with compliments in their mouths, it means the enemy wants a truce.' To deceive the enemy and step up preparations, there is perhaps no harm in a bit of bowing and scraping and tactful verbiage, but more in antiquity than now. Today, politics has become massified and democratised, partly because publishing and broadcasting have become influential, so hypocrisy can backfire. Mao knows this, which is why he has removed all the obvious eyesores from his recently published works.

But is victory not the main thing? Is not any tactic that helps win victory legitimate? Yes, victory is important, more so than anything, but what kind of victory? That depends on how it is achieved. The reason awareness and fighting spirit mattered so much to Lenin and Trotsky was not just that a conscious and spirited proletariat is the only way of winning but, and even more import-

---

39   *Pravda*, December 25, 1939.
40   Bromage 1956, p. 194.

antly, because it was the only way of winning consonant with the interests of world revolution. Today Mao has won, and so has the Chinese Revolution (in part because of Mao's clever tactics). But since it scarcely drew on the capacity and mettle of the working class, the new state born of it has met with many problems and crises and become deeply mired in bureaucratism and narrow nationalism.

CHAPTER 5

A Middling Strategist (Part 1)
New Democracy and Permanent Revolution[1]

When I say Mao is a middling strategist, I am talking about politics, not war. Strategy in revolutionary politics refers, above all, to the revolutionary's or the revolutionary party's understanding of the revolution's motive power, tasks, nature, and future, and especially the attitude to and understanding of revolutionary state power (establishing which is the main and immediate goal of all revolutions). Mao's grasp of it was, to judge by his writings, shaky.

What is revolutionary strategy and what was its role in the October Revolution? Trotsky wrote:

> By tactics in politics we understand, using the analogy of military science, the art of conducting isolated operations. By strategy, we understand the art of conquest, i.e., the seizure of power. Prior to the war we did not, as a rule, make this distinction. In the epoch of the Second International we confined ourselves solely to the conception of social democratic tactics. Nor was this accidental. The social democracy applied parliamentary tactics, trade union tactics, municipal tactics, cooperative tactics, and so on. But the question of combining all forces and resources – all sorts of troops – to obtain victory over the enemy was really never raised in the epoch of the Second International, insofar as the practical task of the struggle for power was not raised. It was only the 1905 revolution that first posed, after a long interval, the fundamental or strategical questions of proletarian struggle. By reason of this it secured immense advantages to the revolutionary Russian social democrats, i.e., the Bolsheviks. The great

---

1 The term 'permanent (*buduande*) revolution' re-emerged in China in the late 1950s. The most accurate translation of *buduande* is 'uninterrupted' or 'continuous,' but it has always been used in China to translate Marx's and Trotsky's idea of permanent revolution. The Chinese usually translate it into English as 'uninterrupted,' almost certainly to avoid the Trotskyist connotation. (Mao said in 1958: 'I advocate the theory of the permanent revolution. You mustn't think that this is Trotsky's theory of the permanent revolution.') Here, following Stuart Schram, I translate *buduande* as 'permanent,' because of the Marxist pedigree of the word, in European languages and in Marx's and Trotsky's own writings. (See Schram 1971, pp. 221–44. The Mao quote is at 222.)

epoch of revolutionary strategy began in 1917, first for Russia and afterwards for the rest of Europe.[2]

The revolution of 1905 became not only 'the dress rehearsal of 1917' but also the laboratory from which emerged all the basic groupings of Russian political thought and where all tendencies and shadings within Russian Marxism took shape or were outlined. The centre of the disputes and differences was naturally occupied by the question of the historical character of the Russian revolution and its future paths of development.[3]

These 'basic groupings' can be roughly summarised as follows:

Narodnikism, in the wake of the Slavophiles, proceeded from illusions concerning the absolutely original paths of Russia's development, and waved aside capitalism and the bourgeois republic. Plekhanov's Marxism was concentrated on proving the principled identity of the historical paths of Russia and of the West. The program derived from this ignored the wholly real and not at all mystical peculiarities of Russia's social structure and of her revolutionary development. The Menshevik attitude toward the revolution, stripped of episodic encrustations and individual deviations, is reducible to the following: The victory of the Russian bourgeois revolution is conceivable only under the leadership of the liberal bourgeoisie and must hand over power to the latter. The democratic regime will then permit the Russian proletariat to catch up with its older Western brothers on the road of the struggle for socialism with incomparably greater success than hitherto.

Lenin's perspective may be briefly expressed as follows: The belated Russian bourgeoisie is incapable of leading its own revolution to the end. The complete victory of the revolution through the medium of the 'democratic dictatorship of the proletariat and the peasantry' will purge the country of medievalism, invest the development of Russian capitalism with American tempos, strengthen the proletariat in the city and country, and open up broad possibilities for the struggle for socialism. On the other hand, the victory of the Russian revolution will provide a mighty impulse for the socialist revolution in the West, and the latter will not only shield

---

2 Trotsky, The Lessons of October, Section I.
3 Trotsky, The Character of the Russian Revolution.

Russia from the dangers of restoration but also permit the Russian proletariat to reach the conquest of power in a comparatively short historical interval.

The perspective of the permanent revolution may be summed up in these words: The complete victory of the democratic revolution in Russia is inconceivable otherwise than in the form of the dictatorship of the proletariat basing itself on the peasantry. The dictatorship of the proletariat, which will inescapably place on the order of the day not only democratic but also socialist tasks, will at the same time provide a mighty impulse to the international socialist revolution. Only, the victory of the proletariat in the West will shield Russia from bourgeois restoration and secure for her the possibility of bringing the socialist construction to its conclusion.[4]

The perspective of Menshevism was false to the core: it pointed out an entirely different road for the proletariat. The perspective of Bolshevism was not complete; it indicated correctly the general direction of the struggle but characterized its stages incorrectly. The inadequacy of the perspective of Bolshevism was not revealed in 1905 only because the revolution itself did not receive further development. But at the beginning of 1917 Lenin was compelled, in a direct struggle against the oldest cadres of the party, to change the perspective.

A political prognosis cannot pretend to the same exactness as an astronomical one. It suffices if it gives a correct indication of the general line of development and helps to orient oneself in the actual course of events in which the basic line is inevitably shifted either to the right or to the left. In this sense it is impossible not to recognize that the conception of the permanent revolution has fully passed the test of history.[5]

Russia's bourgeois-democratic tasks were completed in the October Revolution, which set up a proletarian dictatorship supported by the peasantry. It carried out both a democratic and a socialist agenda. The Russian Revolution proved that the Russian bourgeoisie was unable to complete 'its' revolution, which could be led only by the proletariat (through its party); and that the victorious proletariat could only establish a proletarian dictatorship (with peasant support) and not a democratic dictatorship of workers and peasants, let alone a multi-class democratic government. The Russian Revolution proved Trotsky's theses, later upheld by Lenin.

---

4   Ibid.
5   Ibid.

That the theory of permanent revolution was confirmed in Russia does not mean it applies only there. Trotsky said backwardness is not 'a simple reproduction of the development of advanced countries, with merely a delay of one or two centuries. It engenders an entirely new "combined" social formation in which the latest conquests of capitalist technique and structure root themselves into relations of feudal and pre-feudal barbarism, transforming and subjecting them and creating a peculiar interrelationship of classes.'[6] This 'peculiar interrelationship of classes' also obtains in other poor countries, and gives the same grounds for permanent revolution. A 'bourgeois revolution' that follows its path can win, one that does not will lose. Anyone who cannot grasp this truth, or stumbles on it by trial and error, is not a brilliant strategist.

Most Chinese communists slight revolutionary theory and despise 'academic' ideas about the nature and future of the revolution. For them, a distant goal of communism and a few programmatic points opposing imperialism and feudalism are enough – the rest is down to hard work. Empty chatter and idle talk are pointless and even harmful. So theory is denounced and 'Marxist scholarship' derided. This mindless activism led to wrong Comintern decisions being uncritically implemented in the Revolution of 1925–7, and thus to its defeat. But the revolution was wounded rather than killed off, and the experience led some to draw lessons. As in Russia after 1905, strategic questions occurred to Chinese Revolutionaries only after 1927. However, there was one big difference: the Russians thought things through for themselves and formed their own factions, whereas the Chinese split after 1927 along lines drawn by Stalin and Trotsky. Stalin thought the communists should support the bourgeoisie against imperialism and feudalism and form a democratic union of bourgeois, petty bourgeois, peasants, and workers that would set out on a non-capitalist road under 'proletarian leadership.' In reality, however, that meant that, before 1927, they were made to join the Guomindang, submit to its discipline, and act independently of it, so as not to endanger the 'anti-imperialist, anti-feudal alliance.' Trotsky, on the other hand, said the Chinese bourgeois would not complete their revolution because of their links to imperialists and feudal remnants, and would compromise rather than risk a workers and peasants' rising. The communists should take an independent class line, leave the Guomindang, criticise its Three People's Principles, defy Guomindang discipline, and wage class struggle, especially land war. In places occupied by the anti-warlord Northern Expedition, they should seek armed peasant support and form soviets to set up a peasant-backed dictatorship of the proletariat, solve the democratic tasks,

---

6 Trotsky, 'Revolution and War in China.'

and carry on down the road to socialism. Stalin had already seized power in the AUCP(b) and the Comintern, so he prevailed over Trotsky. When events in China proved him wrong and Trotsky right, he used bureaucratic means and even terror to suppress opposition and maintain authority.

What was Mao's attitude to the Soviet dispute on strategy in China, and which side did he take? Before the 1927 defeat, the Soviet debate hardly figured in the CCP, given that the Stalin faction had twisted it beyond recognition or blacked it out and the Chinese anyway had little interest in or knowledge of theory. Not even General Secretary Chen Duxiu knew that there were other views besides the Comintern's, i.e., besides Stalin's. A handful of leaders like Tan Pingshan sent to Moscow to attend meetings knew, but Stalin's 'China experts' ordered them to oppose Trotsky. They were kept away from Oppositionists and couldn't even read their documents (except for 'quotes' torn out of context). So they were unable to take news of the dispute back to China (assuming they would have dared or wanted to, which is unlikely). After the Chinese defeat, Stalin took advantage of the CCP's ignorance and of the AUCP(b) prestige to heap blame for the defeat on Chen Duxiu (thus 'putting Zhang's hat on Li's head'[7]), and the CCP agreed. So the Chinese communists paid the price of the defeat, but still knew nothing about its strategic causes.

This changed between 1927 and 1930, when hundreds of young communists went to study in Moscow. There they came into contact with the Soviet Opposition. Many joined it, and secretly sent back documents to old revolutionaries in China. Two or three years after the defeat of 1927, a debate started in China on the strategic direction of the revolution. In 1930, an anti-Stalinist faction under Chen Duxiu split from the CCP and formed the Chinese Trotskyist Opposition, which included many leading figures from China's Great Revolution.

What was Mao's attitude to the split and the dispute? Before his Wayaobao report of December 1935, whenever he talked about the reasons for the defeat of the revolution and its nature and future, he did so in generalities, devoid of substance and wide of the mark, reciting snatches of Comintern resolutions with which he seemed minimally acquainted. For example, on October 25, 1928, he said:

> China is in urgent need of a bourgeois-democratic revolution, and this revolution can be completed only under the leadership of the proletariat. Because the proletariat failed to exercise firm leadership in the revolution of 1926–27 which started from Guangdong and spread towards

---

7 Attributing something to the wrong person.

the Yangtze River, leadership was seized by the comprador and landlord classes and the revolution was replaced by counterrevolution. The bourgeois-democratic revolution thus met with a temporary defeat. [...] According to the directives of the Communist International and the Central Committee of our Party, the content of China's democratic revolution consists in overthrowing the rule of imperialism and its warlord tools in China so as to complete the national revolution, and in carrying out the agrarian revolution so as to eliminate the feudal exploitation of the peasants by the landlord class. Such a revolutionary movement has been growing day by day since the Jinan Massacre in May 1928.[8]

This is a schoolboyish recitation. Mao's own view is out of sight. No one – Stalinist or Trotskyist – denied that the Chinese Revolution was democratic in nature and content. Proletarian leadership was a Trotskyist policy – the Stalinists had advocated a revolution jointly led by 'four revolutionary classes' and denounced the Trotskyists for going against the idea of bourgeois-democratic revolution; although they did sometimes talk about proletarian leadership, in practice they instructed Chinese workers and revolutionaries to accept bourgeois leadership, thereby ruining the Chinese Revolution. Did this mean Mao was on Trotsky's side? Obviously not, since he was almost certainly ignorant of the two factions' stance on China. As for taking up arms and insisting on proletarian – read communist – leadership of the revolution, most people would have agreed with this after the defeat of the revolution.

Not long afterwards, Mao wrote:

We fully agree with the Communist International's resolution on China. There is no doubt that China is still at the stage of the bourgeois-democratic revolution. The programme for a thorough democratic revolution in China comprises, externally, the overthrow of imperialism so as to achieve complete national liberation, and, internally, the elimination of the power and influence of the comprador class in the cities, the completion of the agrarian revolution in order to abolish feudal relations in the villages, and the overthrow of the government of the warlords. We must go through such a democratic revolution before we can lay a real foundation for the transition to socialism.[9]

---

8 Mao, 'Why Is It that Red Political Power Can Exist in China?,' October 5, 1928, SW, vol. 1, pp. 63–72, at 64.
9 Mao, 'The Struggle in the Jinggang Mountains,' November 25, 1928, SW, vol. 1, pp. 73–104, at 97.

On April 5, 1929, he returned to this issue:

> The political line and the organizational line laid down by the Sixth Congress are entirely correct: the current stage of the revolution is democratic and not socialist, and the present task of the party is to win over the masses and not to stage immediate armed insurrections.[10]

These passages, while not explicitly prescribing which view on China to follow, clearly backed Stalin. At the time, Stalin claimed, falsely, that Trotsky thought China's bourgeois revolution had already been completed, by Chiang Kai-shek, so a socialist revolution was now due, directed principally against the bourgeois system of private property. Mao, who agreed that the Chinese Revolution was still bourgeois-democratic, therefore opposed Trotsky's supposed position.

After the defeat of the revolution in 1927, Stalin initially denied it, dressing it up as a progression to a 'higher stage.' After the failure of the Guangzhou Uprising, he acknowledged the defeat but denied that it was grave and said it would be short-lived, so he refused to let the CCP rally forces to fight the democratic revolution by calling for a National Assembly. He also denied that the victory of the counter-revolution would affect the revolution's future development. Although the big bourgeoisie under Chiang had turned traitor, the coming democratic revolution would still be led by an alliance of revolutionary classes, including the national bourgeoisie. Although Chiang's counter-revolution would put national state power into the hands of the bourgeoisie, the coming revolution would still be democratic in nature, politically and economically.

Trotsky, on the other hand, promptly recognised the defeat and warned against rash action, arguing instead that Chinese should campaign for an all-powerful National Assembly elected on the basis of universal suffrage, to accumulate forces and prepare the next revolution. The victory of counter-revolution did not mean the revolution was over. Democracy was still to be won, so the revolution was still bourgeois-democratic in nature. However, the bourgeoisie held state power, so the democratic revolution should point its spears first at the regime. To carry out the democratic tasks, a worker-led revolution must seize state power and set up its own dictatorship. The future revolution would be socialist from the start.

---

10 Mao, 'A Letter from the Front Committee to the Central Committee,' April 5, 1929, in Mao Zedong 1995, vol. 3, pp. 153–61, at 153.

Neither Stalin nor Trotsky disputed the democratic nature of the Chinese Revolution. The real disputes concerned the following questions. (1) How to understand the counter-revolutionary period and what slogans to use in it, in order to shorten it and prepare a new revolution. (2) In the future democratic revolution, could the counter-revolutionary bourgeoisie still play a leading role, even if only a partial one? Must the future revolution establish a proletarian dictatorship, or a multi-class dictatorship? Could China's democratic tasks be resolved only by proletarian dictatorship? Must the proletarian dictatorship that resolves the democratic tasks inevitably, immediately, and even simultaneously set up a socialist agenda? (3) Is not a revolution that fights bourgeois dictatorship in favour of proletarian dictatorship already socialist?

At first Mao knew little about the debate, except for some one-sided views on it he got from the Stalinists. He consistently slighted theory in favour of practice and was, like Stalin, a realist at heart, with little interest in distant events in Russia, which he considered a storm in a teacup. In his report of December 1935, he endorsed Stalin against the 'counter-revolutionary' Trotsky (to ensure Stalin's backing) and said the Chinese Revolution was still bourgeois-democratic rather than proletarian. But the Trotskyists never said, before or after 1935, that the Chinese Revolution in its then stage was socialist rather than bourgeois-democratic, for in their view the revolution was, for the time being, anyway over, having fizzled out in late 1927, while the new one had not yet begun. However, though latent, the revolution was most certainly democratic in nature. The Trotskyists never once said 'China has already completed its bourgeois-democratic revolution.' They said instead that counter-revolution had triumphed, but had not completed – could not complete – democratic revolution. As for the next revolution being socialist, they meant that it would, from the outset, oppose bourgeois dictatorship and fight for a workers' dictatorship – thus, politically and principally, for socialist revolution. The further unfolding of its fight for democracy would, from the outset, almost certainly lead to a fight with the rural and the urban bourgeoisie – thus, economically and secondarily, also for socialist revolution.

Mao's attack on the Trotskyists showed his contempt for theory and his calculating approach to principled questions of strategy. More fundamentally, it showed that he was unable, independently, to raise partial, tactical experiences to the strategic plane. Take the first of the three questions in the Stalin-Trotsky dispute, about what slogan to use in a period of counter-revolution. Trotsky told the communists to call for a National Assembly, but Stalin called this 'liquidationism.' But what did Mao's personal experience tell him? In November 1928, he said:

> In the past year we have fought in many places and are keenly aware that the revolutionary tide is on the ebb in the country as a whole. While Red political power has been established in a few small areas, in the country as a whole the people lack the ordinary democratic rights, the workers, the peasants and even the bourgeois democrats do not have freedom of speech or assembly, and the worst crime is to join the communist party. Wherever the Red Army goes, the masses are cold and aloof, and only after our propaganda do they slowly move into action. Whatever enemy units we face, there are hardly any cases of mutiny or desertion to our side and we have to fight it out. This holds even for the enemy's Sixth Army which recruited the greatest number of 'rebels' after the May 21st Incident. We have an acute sense of our isolation which we keep hoping will end. Only by launching a political and economic struggle for democracy, which will also involve the urban petty bourgeoisie, can we turn the revolution into a seething tide that will surge through the country.[11]

This is the best possible argument for the National Assembly slogan. Had Mao been a better strategist, his own experience would have led him to the same conclusion as Trotsky, that revolution had long since given way to counter-revolution and the CCP should call for a National Assembly, that it should put an end to its isolation by launching a struggle (including urban petty bourgeois) for political and economic democracy, thus drowning the counter-revolution in a seething nationwide high tide of revolution. But Mao could not, or dared not, do this – although he strongly affirmed the democratic nature, 'at this stage,' of the revolution, knew the strength of the counter-revolution, felt isolated and lonely, recognised the need, in the towns and villages, for a struggle for political and economic democracy, and was well aware that 'a few small areas' of Red power could be preserved and extended only with the help of a nationwide movement of workers, peasants, and bourgeois democrats fighting for 'ordinary democratic rights.'

There are further grounds on which to fault Mao. When Stalin jumped from left to right in 1935, he replaced the call for soviets in China with the previously 'liquidationist' call for a National Assembly. Cadres must have been surprised, for they had got used to denouncing the latter as counter-revolutionary. However, Mao defended it with the same vigour as he had previously rejected it. On May 3, 1937, at a conference in Yan'an, he said: 'The people of the

---

11   Mao, 'The Struggle in the Jinggang Mountains,' November 25, 1928, SW, vol. 1, pp. 73–104, 97–8.

whole country and the patriots of all parties should throw off their former indifference towards the question of a national assembly and a constitution, and should concentrate on the movement for a national assembly and a constitution.'[12] Mao must have known this 'indifference' was due to Stalin and to Mao himself, and that those who had urged him to throw it off were the Trotskyists. By then, Mao must have been informed about the Stalin-Trotsky dispute, for he called on everyone to fight the 'Trotskyite plotters.' He explained why the National Assembly slogan was so important: 'Why do we place so much emphasis on a national assembly? Because it is something that can affect every aspect of life, because it is the bridge from reactionary dictatorship to democracy, because it is connected with national defence, and because it is a legal institution. [...] [T]he essential thing is still the national assembly and freedom for the people.'[13] This is well said, apart from the reference to national defence, which lacks coherence. But why now, and why not between 1928 and 1935?[14]

This shows Mao blindly followed Stalin. It is also a measure of Mao's strategic incompetence. Mao did not study Marxism seriously and extensively until 1937. From his research he learned about the Stalin-Trotsky controversy. Previously, he had had not known its ins and outs, and had followed Stalin mainly because of discipline. Now, he did so out of conviction, born of a similarity of thinking and temperament (alongside minor things). Mao had little in common with Wang Ming. He wasn't a comprador, he didn't worship foreign things, and he had the mettle to resist authority. So after 1937 he became a Stalin supporter only in part for tactical reasons (to take advantage of Stalin's and the Comintern's material and other resources) and mainly because of his ideological convergence with Stalin and their likeness in temper and nature. Both were great schemers but poor strategists. Both valued practice and slighted theory. Both were empiricists who favoured inductive reasoning and despised deep contemplation conducted on a basis of principle. Both disdained deduction from ideas. Both loved 'common sense' and disliked class-struggle 'pedantry.' Neither knew a foreign language, and both were unfamiliar with Western thinking, which they belittled and despised. They were internationalists in name only, and actually nationalists. Finally, both rated real power (military and civilian) above ideas, both were hugely ambitious, both had leader cults, and both despised

---

12 Mao, 'The Tasks of the Chinese Communist Party in the Period of Resistance to Japan,' May 3, 1937, SW, vol. 1, pp. 263–84, at 268.
13 Mao, 'Struggle to Win the Masses in Their Millions for the Anti-Japanese National United Front,' May, 7, 1937, SW, vol. 1, pp. 285–94, at 289.
14 Mao first spoke publicly of a National Assembly in 1937, but it cropped up in another form (people's republic as opposed to workers and peasants' republic) in the autumn of 1935.

the people's spontaneous creativity, so both tended, in spirit and by disposition, towards thinking that was bureaucratic, heroic, and even imperial. Apart from these commonalities, they had numerous differences – in the origin of their thinking, their relationship with and standing in the revolution and the party, and their competence (Mao's exceeded Stalin's) and temperament (Stalin was harsher and more insidious). However, these differences were dwarfed by the likenesses. Mao sometimes resented Stalin (e.g., for nurturing Wang Ming as a counterweight to him), disagreed with Stalin, and even despised Stalin (for his China directives, which he often found ridiculous and treated either by feigning compliance or by acting first and reporting later). However, he never exposed Stalin, and he even misattributed some of his own better decisions to the Comintern's 'wise leadership.' Ideologically, he followed Stalin, especially his strategic thinking on democratic revolution in poor countries, for although Trotsky's elegance of manner, attitude, and speech might have won his admiration, Stalin's mediocrity and pragmatism were more to his taste, in an elective affinity.

Mao made his debut as a fully fledged Stalinist in the debate on strategic issues in the Chinese Revolution in December 1939, in 'The Chinese Revolution and the Chinese Communist Party.' He explained: '[T]he character of the Chinese Revolution at the present stage is not proletarian-socialist but bourgeois-democratic. However, in present-day China the bourgeois-democratic revolution is no longer of the old general type, which is now obsolete, but one of a new special type. We call this type the new-democratic revolution. [...] The new-democratic revolution is part of the world proletarian-socialist revolution, for it resolutely opposes imperialism, i.e., international capitalism. Politically, it strives for the joint dictatorship of the revolutionary classes over the imperialists, traitors and reactionaries.' New democracy differed from old democracy and socialist revolution in that, politically, it aimed for a 'joint dictatorship of [several] revolutionary classes.'[15]

In January 1940, in 'On New Democracy,' he explained his strategy more fluently (for he was no longer parroting someone else but giving voice to his own ideas) and in greater depth. He said:

> This new-democratic republic will be different from the old European-American form of capitalist republic under bourgeois dictatorship, which is the old democratic form and already out of date. On the other hand, it

---

15   Mao, 'The Chinese Revolution and the Communist Party of China,' December 1939, SW, vol. 2, pp. 305–34, at 327.

will also be different from the socialist republic of the Soviet type under the dictatorship of the proletariat which is already flourishing in the USSR, and which, moreover, will be established in all the capitalist countries and will undoubtedly become the dominant form of state and governmental structure in all the industrially advanced countries. However, for a certain historical period, this form is not suitable for the revolutions in the colonial and semi-colonial countries. During this period, therefore, a third form of state must be adopted in the revolutions of all colonial and semi-colonial countries, namely, the new-democratic republic. This form suits a certain historical period and is therefore transitional; nevertheless, it is a form which is necessary and cannot be dispensed with. [...] The third kind is the transitional form of state to be adopted in the revolutions of the colonial and semi-colonial countries, [...] i.e., a new-democratic state under the joint dictatorship of several anti-imperialist classes.[16]

This, in essence, is a reprise of old-style Menshevism, though with superficial differences. The Mensheviks did not distinguish old from New Democracy, and they said openly that the revolution should be led by the liberal bourgeoisie, whereas Mao's bourgeois democracy was 'new' and would be a 'joint dictatorship of several anti-imperialist classes.' However, taken at its face value, as a principled statement of communist strategy, and given that it would not be allowed to become a proletarian dictatorship, what could this 'joint dictatorship' be other than a dictatorship of the bourgeoisie, with guns? That is why Mao Zedong was, in essence, taking a Menshevik stance.

The Mensheviks thought that the Russian proletariat, having helped the liberal bourgeoisie set up a democratic republic, would then, to even greater effect, go down the socialist road and catch up with its Western brothers. This strategy was never put to the test, but even if it had been and a bourgeois-democratic republic had stabilised in Russia and survived, the Russian workers would still not, under Menshevik leadership, have caught up with the West. What was going to be the future of Mao's joint dictatorship? He explained:

> Without a doubt, the present revolution is the first step, which will develop into the second step. [...] The Chinese Revolution cannot avoid taking the two steps, first of New Democracy and then of socialism. Moreover, the first step will need quite a long time and cannot be accomplished overnight.

---

16   Mao, 'On New Democracy,' January 1940, SW, vol. 2, pp. 339–84, 350.

As to how the second step would come about, and how long it would take, he gave no answer, simply saying again and again that the revolution is divided into stages, and that 'we can only proceed to the next stage of revolution after accomplishing the first, and that there is no such thing as "accomplishing both at one stroke."' The first stage would have its 'specific [...] period' comprising a 'certain historical period,' during which the democratic tasks can be resolved only by means of a democratic dictatorship of various classes, after which 'the present revolution [...] will develop into the second step, that of socialism.'[17]

Actually, Mao had already, when reviving the alliance with the Guomindang, spoken clearly about the timing and conditions of the transition from one type of revolution to the other. In December 1935, in 'On Tactics Against Japanese Imperialism,' he said:

> The change in the revolution will come later. In the future the democratic revolution will inevitably be transformed into a socialist revolution. As to when the transition will take place, that will depend on the presence of the necessary conditions, and it may take quite a long time. We should not hold forth about transition until all the necessary political and economic conditions are present and until it is advantageous and not detrimental to the overwhelming majority of the people throughout China. It is wrong to have any doubts on this matter and expect the transition to take place soon, as some of our comrades did when they maintained that the transition in the revolution would begin the moment the democratic revolution began to triumph in key provinces. They did so because they failed to understand what kind of country China is politically and economically and to realize that, compared with Russia, China will find it more difficult, and require much more time and effort, to complete her democratic revolution politically and economically.[18]

In May 1937, in 'Win the Masses in Their Millions for the Anti-Japanese United Front,' he said:

> We are exponents of the theory of the transition of the revolution, and not of the Trotskyite theory of 'permanent revolution.' We are for the attainment of socialism by going through all the necessary stages of the democratic republic. We are opposed to tailism, but we are also opposed

---

17   Op. cit., p. 358.
18   Mao, 'On Tactics Against Japanese Imperialism,' December 1935, SW, vol. 1, pp. 153–78, at 170.

to adventurism and impetuosity. To reject the participation of the bourgeoisie in the revolution on the ground that it can only be temporary and to describe the alliance with anti-Japanese sections of the bourgeoisie (in a semi-colonial country) as capitulation is a Trotskyite approach, with which we cannot agree.[19]

Mao sketches three theories of transition. The first, represented by Wang Ming (representing Stalin), said the revolution would begin the day it started to triumph in key provinces. The second, represented by Mao himself, said the transition would start when conditions were right, and this could take time – it should not be undertaken lightly, and only if it were to the advantage of the great majority of Chinese. The third, attributed by Mao to the Trotskyists, said there was no need to pass through the stages of the democratic republic, and socialist revolution could start at once. But the Trotskyists never said any such thing. They believed that the revolution would revive through the national struggle, but it would only be able to advance and deepen if led by the proletariat and its party, so the workers would have to fight for state power and this state power could not be limited to democratic tasks. The Trotskyists thought the question of the transition was falsely posed: from the point of view of the revolution's objective tasks, a period of democracy would follow the establishment of proletarian dictatorship, but from the point of view of the revolution's driving force, especially from that of the historical necessity of the proletariat taking power, the transition would be socialist from the start.

Stalin and Mao denied that the proletariat can and must fight for their own dictatorship in the democratic revolution and that in poor countries that revolution's tasks can only be resolved by proletarian dictatorship. They believed that democratic tasks devolve on a democratic regime or dictatorship. Only after their resolution can the transition to socialist revolution start. This is why they floundered on the question of the timing of and conditions for the turn. In the leftist years, they invented the 'key provinces' formula.[20] If the Chinese Soviet Government and Red Army had really acted on behalf of the workers and against the rich peasants, then, even if limited to just a few provinces, the revolution would have made an early transition to social-

---

19   Mao, 'Win the Masses in Their Millions for the Anti-Japanese United Front,' May 1937, SW, vol. 1, pp. 263–84, at 270.
20   This formulation was contained in a letter from the Comintern to the CCP variously dated June and July 23, 1930, in response to what was known in Moscow of CCP policy in China (Stuart Reynolds Schram and Nancy Jane Hodes, 'Introduction,' in Mao Zedong 1995, p. lvii).

ism. Otherwise, it would have been a Soviet and a Red Army in name only, its regime would have been a multi-class alliance, and its policy would have been confined to anti-feudalism. Even if it had gained power throughout China, there would have been no substantial transition. Mao rightly opposed this latter prescription but could come up with nothing better. His idea that the turn would happen when conditions were right was Menshevik, for in a 'poor, blank' country like China to wait for conditions to ripen before talking about socialist revolution was like saying that until the 'new-democratic' republic had raised China's politics and economy to the level of the advanced capitalist countries, socialist revolution might take 'quite a long time.' Or, more likely, a very long time – as long as it took for the revolution to happen in the rich countries. Mao's idea of transition (had he stuck to it) was even more right-wing than Stalin's.

Mao never openly changed his mind. In 'On Coalition Government,' he went even further to the right:

> It is a law of Marxism that socialism can be attained only via the stage of democracy. And in China the fight for democracy is a protracted one. It would be a sheer illusion to try to build a socialist society on the ruins of the colonial, semi-colonial and semi-feudal order without a united new-democratic state, without the development of the state sector of the new-democratic economy, of the private capitalist and the co-operative sectors, and of a national, scientific and mass culture, i.e., a new-democratic culture, and without the liberation and the development of the individuality of hundreds of millions of people.[21]

So the transition from multi-class alliance to proletarian dictatorship and from democracy to socialism could happen only after a lengthy period of rule under a new-democratic unified state with a highly developed capitalist economy, private ownership, cooperative ownership, an advanced culture, and a high degree of individuality, thus providing a base upon which a socialist society could be built. To remove any possible doubts about his loyalty, Mao also said:

> [A] new-democratic state based on an alliance of the democratic classes is different in principle from a socialist state under the dictatorship of the proletariat. [...] The Chinese system for the present stage is being shaped by the present stage of Chinese history, and for a long time to come there will exist a special form of state and political power, a form that is distin-

---

21   Mao, 'On Coalition Government,' April 24, 1945, SW, vol. 3, pp. 255–320, at 283.

guished from the Russian system but is perfectly necessary and reasonable for us, namely, the new-democratic form of state and political power based on the alliance of the democratic classes.[22]

Mao intended to set up a joint dictatorship (different in principle from proletarian dictatorship) of various classes and, under it and for a long time, develop a democratic economy and culture; and then, but only when the time was right, make the transition from New Democracy to socialism. Mao never wavered on this, although his focus changed: before the civil war, he stressed alliance and mutuality within dictatorship; during it, especially when winning, he focused increasingly on proletarian leadership. In March 1948 he still stressed that 'our revolution at the present stage is a new-democratic, a people's democratic revolution in character and is different from a socialist revolution such as the October Revolution.'[23]

In 1949 June, on the eve of victory, Mao wrote 'On the People's Democratic Dictatorship,' in which, according to an official commentator, he 'creatively advanced a number of guidelines and policies concerning the question of the transition of the Chinese Revolution, [...] and, from a theoretical angle, expounded on them in detail.'[24] But I find only this:

> Who are the people? At the present stage in China, they are the working class, the peasantry, the urban petty bourgeoisie and the national bourgeoisie.[25]

'The People's Democratic Dictatorship' comprises these four classes, so nothing has changed since 1935. Where are the new creations? The following paragraph is constantly cited nowadays by ideologists, to show Mao believed in permanent revolution:

> Our present task is to strengthen the people's state apparatus – mainly the people's army, the people's police and the people's courts – in order to consolidate national defence and protect the people's interests. Given this condition, China can develop steadily, under the leadership of the working class and the Communist Party, from an agricultural into an industrial

---

22 Op. cit., p. 284.
23 Mao, 'On the Question of the National Bourgeoisie and the Enlightened Gentry,' March 1, 1948, SW, vol. 4, pp. 207–10, at 208.
24 *People's Daily*, September 30, 1960.
25 Mao, 'On the People's Democratic Dictatorship,' June 30, 1949, vol. 4, pp. 411–24, at 417.

country and from a new-democratic into a socialist and communist society, can abolish classes and realize the Great Harmony [*datong*].[26]

According to an official commentator, Mao is here formally proclaiming that the transition was already happening.[27] But the original text suggests this interpretation was thought up later. Strengthening the state machine referred to the army, the police, and the courts and was designed to 'consolidate national defence and protect the people's interests.' It did not mean that the multiclass People's Democratic Dictatorship should be 'strengthened' into (make the transition to) a proletarian dictatorship. Mao was talking about a People's Democratic Dictatorship, which – according to him – differed 'in principle' from a socialist dictatorship of the proletariat. The one could not turn into the other simply by strengthening the repressive apparatus. So the article is far from proof of Mao's commitment to a theory of permanent revolution.

The passage 'Given this condition, China can develop steadily, under the leadership of the working class' could, I suppose, be taken to mean that the workers control the state and are completing the democratic tasks on that basis, while striking out on the road to socialism, but that would contradict Mao's view of People's Democratic Dictatorship. According to Mao, the democratic revolution has one state system and form of government and the socialist revolution another, the former being a democratic republic and the latter a workers and peasants' republic. Each represents a different historical period and stage in the revolution, and an absolutely different social entity. That is why the former cannot be skipped and the latter cannot be realised ahead of time. Liu Shaoqi says that 'people's democratic state power has, in fact, already become, in essence, a form of proletarian dictatorship.'[28] But is that not Trotskyism? (Trotsky, applying the theory and experience of the Russian Revolution to China, said that the idea of a multi-class dictatorship was theoretically unpersuasive and practically inoperable, both for Chiang Kai-shek's bourgeoisie and for the workers.) How could Mao, who had always fought for a people's dictatorship, suddenly embrace a seemingly Trotskyist approach?

The subsequent attempt to resolve this contradiction by conceding, after the event, that the Chinese Revolution had taken a 'permanent' road was not Mao's but Liu Shaoqi's and Shi Dongxiang's (assuming that Shi Dongxiang is

---

26   Op. cit., 418.
27   *Red Flag*, no. 1, 1961.
28   Liu Shaoqi, 'Political Report of the Central Committee of the Communist Party of China to the Eighth National Congress of the Communist Party of China,' September 15, 1956.

not Mao's *nom de plume*[29]). As far as I know, Mao's strategic approach to the Chinese Revolution was first altered in September 1956, by Liu Shaoqi saying that 'people's democratic state power has, in fact, already become, in essence, a form of proletarian dictatorship.' Liu added:

> Thus, it has become possible for the bourgeois-democratic revolution in our country to be directly transformed, by peaceful means, into a proletarian-socialist revolution. The establishment of the People's Republic of China signifies the virtual completion of the stage of bourgeois-democratic revolution in our country and the beginning of the stage of proletarian-socialist revolution: the beginning of the period of transition from capitalism to socialism.[30]

Except on one or two points, this statement basically accords with the Trotskyist view. It is the CCP's unintended hat-tip, after the event, to Trotskyism, sweeping away Stalin's and Mao's illusory, reactionary idea of New Democracy and People's Democratic Dictatorship.

Liu's report came exactly seven years after the publication of 'On the People's Democratic Dictatorship.' Before October 1949, Mao had not known that the Chinese Revolution could only be a proletarian dictatorship, and after 1949 it took him seven long years (and numerous tragedies) to admit (through the mouth of Liu Shaoqi) that the people's dictatorship was already one. Mao's mediocrity as a revolutionary strategist is clear for all to see.

Mao has never seemed to realise that the question of the revolutionary transition can be resolved only if joined to the question of state power. He has always seemed to think that the nature of the revolution is manifested chiefly in the state system and the form of government, so the transition in the nature of the revolution is also manifested in transitions in those two things. Democratic tasks, People's Republic, and People's Democratic Dictatorship are a trinity, an independent category, the three key elements in the first of two transformatory stages. The second, possible only after the first has been completed, also comprises a trinity – of socialist tasks, workers and peasants' republic, and proletarian dictatorship – and an independent category. The two sets are separated by a long historical period, during which economy and culture rise greatly:

---

29 According to *Jiangsu daxue xuebao, sheke ban* (Jiangsu University journal) (2008), no. 2, pp. 61–8, Shi Dongxiang was the collective name of a group in the editorial department of *Hongqi* (Red Flag) whose membership varied. (Thanks to David Cowhig, who provided this information.)

30 Liu Shaoqi, 'Political Report of the Central Committee.'

the passage from first to second article can happen only when the grounds for socialist revolution have been laid and readied. As for the specific form the change will take and the basis upon which the transition will happen, as for whether or not, after conditions have matured, the communist-led workers will make another, socialist revolution to transform the state system and form of government, or whether instead the People's Democratic Dictatorship will automatically go through a peaceful transition, so that the other classes exit, leaving behind a workers and peasants' state, not a people's one – these are questions to which Mao lacks answers, since he has never seriously considered them.

Were Mao a truly great strategist, he would, whether familiar or not with Marx', Lenin's, and Trotsky's view of permanent revolution and the history of revolutionary thought in Russia, have reflected independently on his practical experience of the Chinese class struggle and, early on, arrived at the theory of permanent revolution. The theory states, first, that since the Chinese can only win the revolutionary struggle for democratic rights under the leadership of the proletariat, victory in it must propel the proletariat into state power. Second, to prevent a reactionary restoration and consolidate their victory, the workers in power (under their own party) must form a dictatorship supported by the urban and rural poor. Third, the proletariat in power cannot stop at democratic tasks but must at the same time adopt socialist measures and set the country on a socialist road. Fourth, establishing a proletarian dictatorship and taking socialist measures does not mean the country is economically and culturally ripe for socialism. Socialism is imaginable only on a world scale – building socialism in China is indivisible from world revolution. Mao has thought about none of these points except for the first part of the first one, about proletarian leadership in the democratic revolution. Now he has been forced by events to favour permanent revolution, but he still doesn't grasp its meaning. He has never seen, perhaps does not want to see, that state power is the key to the revolutionary transition. In poor countries, the democratic revolution, when it wins, must set up a proletarian dictatorship and simultaneously tackle democratic and socialist tasks. The inevitability and necessity of proletarian dictatorship in the democratic revolution make that revolution permanent, thus resolving all the issues around the transition in the nature of the revolution in such countries. Because Mao always trailed behind Stalin, he rejected the idea of the workers seizing power in the midst of the democratic revolution, so he landed himself in endless asinine contradictions on the question of the transition, for example when attacking the theory of permanent revolution and (through the mouths of others) its supporters. In an essay designed to reconcile the CCP's old and new views on revolutionary strategy, Shi Dongxiang defined

Mao's 'integration of the theory of revolutionary stages and the theory of permanent revolution' using the following bizarre formula: 'Before overthrowing the Guomindang's reactionary rule on a national scale, the character of people's state power was a multi-class dictatorship led by the proletariat and shouldering tasks of the democratic revolution. [...] Having overthrown Guomindang rule on a national scale and set up the People's Republic, the character of the all-China people's government was, in essence, that of a proletarian dictatorship shouldering proletarian socialist revolutionary tasks.' Shi goes on to assert that 'after' victory, the conflict between socialism and capitalism had gradually sharpened and become critical – whereas Mao said that, under the People's Democratic Dictatorship, China would go through a long period of national capitalism and cooperatives. Shi argues that 'the establishment of the PRC marked, fundamentally, the end of China's democratic revolution and the start of socialist revolution' – but both Russia and China showed that setting up a revolutionary dictatorship signalled neither the end of democratic nor the start of socialist revolution. Democratic issues such as the land question were not confronted in China until after the revolution. As for socialist revolution, it had already started during the struggle led by the proletariat for state power, if viewed from the angle of politics. Shi gets one thing right: 'The basic question in all revolutions is the question of state power.' But Mao is most myopic, and most vulnerable to brutal refutal by events, on precisely this issue. Mao always harped on about the democratic nature of the revolution, and how China could only set up a People's Democratic Dictatorship and not a proletarian dictatorship, but as a result he ended up with an embarrassing choice: either admit he was wrong and that the victory of the democratic revolution could lead only to proletarian dictatorship,[31] as the Trotskyists had argued, and that a multi-class dictatorship of the sort he and Stalin had predicted could end up only in a bourgeois dictatorship; or insist that all had gone to plan, that the people's government produced by the Chinese People's Political Consultative Conference in 1949 was indeed 'a joint dictatorship of various democratic classes,' and that the latter differed in principle from proletarian dictatorship – while,

---

31   Is the regime the Chinese communists set up after the revolution a proletarian dictatorship? If so, to what extent and in what sense? This question has exercised non-Stalinist communists and socialists throughout the world. I have my own view on it. Initially, I thought it was not a proletarian but a bureaucratic dictatorship. After further study and reflection, I concluded: 'The CCP can still be regarded as representing the working-class tendency and its state, and, from the point of view of its principal major economic measures, can still be said to represent the demands required by history of the working class. Naturally, this "representation" is grotesquely misshapen, brutal, bureaucratic, and dictatorial' (*Sixiang wenti* [Ideological questions]) (note by Wang).

in reality, everything was wrestled into the hands of party members and not only the 'democratic classes' but even the workers were warned to mind their own business. Mao chose the second course, but the duplicity and hypocrisy got out of hand and the communists ran out of tricks, especially when China's capitalists used Mao's theory of democratic coalition to wage a political and economic offensive against the new regime. Relentless events forced the party to change tack. There followed the Three Anti's and the Five Anti's,[32] and the announcement that private capitalism had no long-term future. The revolution had changed in nature, and the form of government must follow suit – the People's Democratic Dictatorship must turn into proletarian dictatorship. How to so turn it? In reality, no changes were required. All power was anyway in party hands. A couple of flower-vase deputy ministers belonging to the democratic parties could have been thrown out of the democratic dictatorship thus turning it into a proletarian dictatorship, but even the communists seemed to think that would have been going too far. How then to effect the 'transformation'? Mao kept quiet on the matter, and so did Liu Shaoqi. It was left to Shi Dongxiang to deal with it. He said:

> The Chinese proletariat, at the same time as leading the revolution to victory, firmly established its own sovereign power, so that after the victory of the democratic revolution it did not need to conduct another struggle for state power in order to achieve socialist revolution. This is because our party, in leading the revolution, never once forgot its goal of socialist revolution and in the democratic-revolutionary struggle took a firm hold on state power, while resolutely establishing and consolidating proletarian leadership.

This is not bad. As a review, it passes muster. However, from the CCP's point of view, it has one major imperfection: it is, in essence, Trotskyist. It smashes to smithereens Mao's theories of the previous ten to twenty years and thoroughly invalidates him as a great revolutionary strategist.

---

32   The Three Anti's (1951) and Five Anti's (1952) were reform movements aimed at ridding Chinese cities of corruption and enemies of the state. They consolidated the new state by attacking its opponents, especially capitalists who had stayed on after 1949.

CHAPTER 6

A Middling Strategist (Part 2)

Armed Revolution and Revolutionary Strategy

In the chapter on Mao as a tactician, I made an assessment of Mao's armed road to revolution. I said that before 1938, it was tactical, but it then became strategic. I argued that his attempt to present it as a unique, comprehensive revolutionary strategy was superficial and full of holes. Here, I want to deal with a question posed but not answered in the previous chapter: if Mao had consciously and comprehensively raised armed struggle to the strategic plane and, even more importantly, if, from the beginning, he had raised and implemented it in the context of a strategy of permanent revolution, how would advancing towards victory, gaining victory, and extending victory have been different?

The question might seem academic. To wave one's arms around and parade one's knowledge after the event, to say what should and shouldn't have happened and what should have been done differently or sooner, is tedious and futile. However, serious historical research is not the same as being a post factum Zhuge Liang.[1] Not just historians have the right to determine the truth about the Chinese Revolution. Trotskyists are particularly qualified and entitled to seek it, since Stalinists and Trotskyists have disputed the issues in the revolution – tactical and strategic – for more than thirty years, practically from the word go. So to look back on events from the angle of Stalinist and Trotskyist texts is neither futile nor academic. The revolution was not completed in China as a result of the victory of the CCP. Transversely, from a world perspective, and vertically, from the point of view of its deepening, victory was just one stage, although an extremely important one, to which basic questions of historical and practical significance attach and will continue to attach.

Facts speak louder than words, especially the fact of victory. Since the CCP won mainly while following Stalin's line, the Stalin-Trotsky dispute would seem to have been resolved in Stalin's favour. However, that is shallow thinking. It is recognised in Chinese culture that heroism does not depend on success or failure. The schemes of Western sages cannot be judged by their outcomes, while the Carthaginians punished their generals for poor planning even though they

---

1 Zhuge Liang (181–234) was an accomplished strategist, likened to Sunzi.

narrowly won victory. Today, the CCP has triumphed, but that does not prove that Stalin and Mao's strategy was superior to that of Trotsky and the Trotskyists.

Mao often quoted Stalin as saying that '[i]n China the armed revolution is fighting the armed counter-revolution. That is one of the specific features and one of the advantages of the Chinese Revolution.'[2] For Mao, these words (1) confirmed Stalin as the founder of the Chinese strategy of armed revolution and (2) showed that Mao's own advocacy and implementation of that strategy was born of careful deliberation, a theory transmitted from Stalin as master to Mao as disciple, a practice based on Mao's own investigation of China's national condition.

Mao always cited Stalin's dictum abstractly and devoid of context, as a Kantian-style categorical imperative, so that one had no way of knowing for sure when and under what circumstances it was said and what were its exact properties. Here it is in full:

> [T]he advance of the [Guangdong Army] means a blow at imperialism, a blow at its agents in China; it means freedom of assembly, freedom to strike, freedom of the press, and freedom to organise for all the revolutionary elements in China in general, and for the workers in particular. That is what constitutes the specific feature and supreme importance of the revolutionary army in China. Formerly, in the eighteenth and nineteenth centuries, revolutions usually began with an uprising of the people for the most part unarmed or poorly armed, who came into collision with the army of the old regime, which they tried to demoralise or at least to win in part to their own side. That was the typical form of the revolutionary outbreaks in the past. That is what happened here in Russia in 1905. In China things have taken a different course. In China, the troops of the old government are confronted not by an unarmed people, but by an armed people, in the shape of its revolutionary army. In China the armed revolution is fighting the armed counter-revolution. That is one of the specific features and one of the advantages of the Chinese Revolution. And therein lies the special significance of the revolutionary army in China.[3]

Stalin said this on November 30, 1926, in a speech on 'The Prospects of the Revolution in China.' The 'revolutionary army' was Chiang Kai-shek's. He said

---

2 Mao, 'Problems of War and Strategy,' November 6, 1938, SW, vol. 2, pp. 219–36, at 221.
3 Stalin, 'The Prospects of the Revolution in China,' November 30, 1926, W, vol. 8, pp. 373–92, at 379.

it to criticise his supporters, Petrov and Mif, who had 'ignore[d] or underestimate[d]' the question of the Chinese revolutionary army. His approach was linked to his dispute with Trotsky. According to Stalin, Chiang's 'people's revolutionary army' was the main factor in the workers and peasants' struggle for liberation. The Guangdong Army's offensive was aimed at the imperialists and their 'Chinese running dogs.' Stalin set the CCP two tasks: strengthen political work in Chiang's army and make it a 'real and exemplary vehicle of the ideas of the Chinese Revolution'; and instruct communists to 'undertake a thorough study of the art of war [...] in order gradually to come to the fore and occupy various leading posts in the revolutionary army.' The Oppositionists, under Trotsky, held an opposite opinion. They did not accept that Chiang's army was a people's revolutionary army, for it was officered mainly by the sons of bourgeois and landlords, who had the upper hand in it. To turn it into a vehicle for emancipation, Trotsky called for soldiers, workers, and peasants' soviets (representative assemblies) and the arming of the workers and peasants. Political work in the army, the system of party representatives, was, in the absence of a revolutionary party and soviets, a cover for bourgeoisie militarism. Communists in leadership positions in it would be powerless to prevent its use by counter-revolutionaries and would probably end up being corrupted by them.

So the Comintern under Stalin opposed organising representative assemblies during the Northern Expedition and arming the workers and peasants, and resolved that the arming of the workers should be kept to a minimum, 'in the interests of the revolution.' Comintern representatives in China opposed arming workers altogether, so as not to offend Chiang or frighten off Wang Jingwei.[4]

Stalin's speech was published four months and twelve days before the 'people's revolutionary army' started massacring workers in China, on April 12, 1927. At the time, he was trying to ward off the Trotskyists' proposal to set up a truly revolutionary army on the basis of workers, peasants, and soldiers' councils, and Petrov and Mif, keen to please him, had omitted all mention of revolutionary armed forces from their outline. But avoiding a problem does not make it go away, and might make people even more willing to give ear to the Opposition, so Stalin set out to correct his supporters' error. He affirmed the importance of armed struggle in China and of a revolutionary army, but he opposed the Opposition's idea of arming the workers and peasants and set-

---

4 Wang Jingwei (1883–1944) was initially a leader of the left wing of the Guomindang and briefly an ally of the CCP.

ting up workers, peasants, and soldiers' councils. He said a revolutionary army already existed, in the form of Chiang's Northern Expeditionary Army, and so did armed struggle, waged between the Guangdong Army and [the warlords] Sun Chuanfang and Zhang Zuolin. To arm the workers and peasants and organise workers, peasants, and soldiers' councils would sabotage that struggle. So by putting the army and the struggle, to great fanfare, at the centre of attention he was rooting for Chiang, not setting a strategic path for revolution. To identify the special feature of the Chinese Revolution as armed revolution versus armed counter-revolution meant identifying the army Chiang commanded against the Northern warlords as the main factor in the workers and peasants' liberation, and woe betide anyone out to sabotage it.

This is the true meaning of Stalin's judgment. It is not the meaning Mao subsequently gave it or the one he wants us to accept. Trotsky said of it:

> On February 25, 1927, a month and a half before the crushing of Shanghai, the central organ of the Comintern wrote:
> 'The Chinese Communist Party and the conscious Chinese workers must not *under any circumstances* pursue a tactic which would disorganize the revolutionary armies just because the influence of the bourgeoisie is to a certain degree strong there.'
> And here is what Stalin said – and repeated on every occasion – at the Plenum of the ECCI on May 24, 1927:
> 'Not unarmed people stand against the armies of the old régime in China, but an armed people in the form of the revolutionary army. In China, an armed revolution is fighting against armed counter-revolution.'
> In the summer and autumn of 1927, the armies of the Guomindang were depicted as an armed people. But when these armies crushed the Guangzhou insurrection, *Pravda* declared the 'oldest [!] shortcoming' of the Chinese Communists to be their inability to decompose the 'reactionary armies,' the very ones that were proclaimed 'the revolutionary people' on the very eve of Guangzhou.[5]

It could not be clearer. Stalin's formula was a revolutionary shop sign on Chiang's mercenary army and a shield to stop workers and peasants dividing Chiang's troops. Eleven years after Stalin came up with it, Mao used it as the basis for his theory of 'revolution at gunpoint.' But if it really emboldened Mao to raise armed revolution from tactic to strategy, the credit is due not to the for-

---

5 Trotsky, 'Stalin and the Chinese Revolution,' August 26, 1930.

mula but to Mao's failure to grasp its meaning. This was not the first time, in China or the world, that a progressive movement, intentionally or otherwise, derived a 'formula' from the holy writ of the ruling class and used it as a defence and rationale. Mao's misquoting Stalin ranks high on the list of such 'inspired errors.'

So Stalin never proposed a way for the Chinese Revolution other than the traditional Marxist one and never said Chinese should act differently from their brothers and sisters in Europe or take the road of armed revolution. When they seemed likely to, he forbade it, and told them to let Chiang make best use of the 'special features' of the Chinese Revolution by meeting 'armed counter-revolution with armed struggle.'

After the defeat, when the CCP skipped on Comintern orders from opportunism to putschism and rose up in Nanchang and Guangzhou,[6] did Stalin prescribe a strategy of armed struggle? I don't know. The available documents suggest that the armed-struggle line adopted after the emergency conference on August 7, 1927, was the result not of a new strategy but of Stalin and co.'s bizarre appraisal of the revolution. They thought that despite repeated defeats, the general trend was still upward, and each setback would lead to a higher stage. When Wuhan under Wang Jingwei suffered the same blood-letting as Shanghai under Chiang, the Comintern said China was in a directly revolutionary situation and called for the 'immediate formation of Soviets of workers' and peasants' deputies.'[7] In the summer and autumn of 1928, Stalin acknowledged, with a mixture of embarrassment and insincerity, that the 'first phase' of the revolution was over, and relegated calls for armed uprisings to a 'propaganda' slogan, thus closing the road of 'armed revolution fighting against armed counter-revolution.' That communists in some places stayed on it had nothing to do with Stalin's formula but was a logical outcome of the Southern peasants' struggle provoked by the Great Revolution. Once peasant struggles well up, they either come to nothing or turn at once into armed conflicts. Such conflicts can be abandoned only at the cost of repression and retaliation – there is no question of backing down. Peasant struggles are inherently difficult to keep going. The reason the peasant uprising on the Hunan-Jiangxi border did so in late 1927 was because of the arrival of communists fleeing Wuhan. These two forces, having converged, had no choice other than to hold out or await slaughter. Their road was not thought through but forced on them by the logic of the struggle. Climbing the Jinggang Mountains, like climbing Mount Liang,

---

6 August and December 1927.
7 Stalin, 'Concerning Questions of the Chinese Revolution: Reply to Comrade Marchulin,' May 15, 1927, W, vol. 9, pp. 236–42, at 236.

was not a choice. Stalin's subsequent 'approval' of Mao's road was part of a general estimate formed during the Third Period ('world capitalism is in terminal decline') rather than an endorsement of a new strategy for China. Communists throughout the world were told to prepare for the 'final battle,' while China, despite the earlier admission of defeat, was now said to be in a 'directly revolution' situation. So although Stalin did not actively encourage peasant armed struggle under the CCP, his approach amounted to passive tolerance. He told the Sixteenth Congress of the AUCP(b) in 1930:

> It would be ridiculous to think that these outrages will be without consequences for the imperialists. The Chinese workers and peasants have already retaliated by forming Soviets and a Red Army. It is said that a Soviet government has already been set up there. I think that if this is true, there is nothing surprising about it. There can be no doubt that only Soviets can save China from utter collapse and pauperisation.[8]

Such a vague, unfocused, slippery, and hypothetical comment on the tongue of the top authority and top decision maker on China's revolutionary strategy, in a formal report, beggars belief. Why did Stalin say it? Mainly because of his fight with Trotsky, but I won't go into that now. Here I want merely to show, using this 'five-sentence review,' that even in the CCP's putschist days Stalin did not, starting out from some 'special feature' of the Chinese Revolution, direct it along a unique road, different from the traditional Marxist strategic road, one of 'armed struggle against armed counter-revolution.' To be sure, he mentions soviets and the Red Army. But that, as Trotsky pointed out, was a stratagem. What kind of stratagem? Shortly before this, the CCP and the Comintern had stopped calling for armed uprisings. Faced with the facts, Stalin had to admit that there was no future, in a counter-revolutionary situation, in the traditional strategy of fighting to organise workers' and peasants' soviets and a Red Army. However, uprisings were still going on in the villages in the South, and the rebels were calling them soviets and claiming to be a Red Army. This was useful for supporting Stalin's view that 'the whole world is already in a directly revolutionary situation.' Stalin felt he might as well let his Chinese comrades continue down the road of armed risings, but he had to watch what he said, in case things went awry. He was in a quandary. The traditional route looked realistic and rational, but the goal was remote; the non-traditional route was risky and unreliable,

---

8   Stalin, 'Political Report of the Central Committee to the Sixteenth Congress of the CPSU(B),' June 29, 1930, W, vol. 12, pp. 242–385, at 258.

but the goal was near. Each had its attractions (at least in terms of the inner-party struggle), so he deemed them equally matched and approved both: the resolution dropped the call for uprisings, the speech praised them. However, the praise was qualified: 'It is said,' 'if this is true', then ... 'there is nothing surprising about it.' In other words, if what's said turns out to be wrong, if the risings end badly, that would be no surprise, and anyway, Stalin had cancelled the call for uprisings in the resolution. No wonder Trotsky called it a 'shameless trick.'

So it is not true that Stalin set China on the strategic road to armed struggle. What about after the AUCP(b)'s Sixth Congress? As far as I know, Stalin never again advised the CCP on matters of principle or strategy. When the Comintern buried the Third Period in 1934–5, China's revolutionary armed forces were told to submit to the command of the armed counter-revolutionary leader Chiang Kai-shek, thus cancelling the strategy of armed struggle altogether.

If not Stalin, then Mao? Should the strategy of armed struggle be attributed to Mao? Mao's contribution is indisputable, but that does not make him a great strategist. Was his decision to switch to the villages, take up arms there, accumulate forces in the long term, and train them to meet force with force a deliberate strategy based on mature reflection or a continuation of the Chinese tradition of revolt? Not until the winter of 1938, after ten years' fighting, did he seriously reflect, on grounds of principle, history, Marxist revolutionary strategy, and the many special features of the revolutionary struggle of the Chinese people, on his own heroic undertaking to 'draw the sword, swish the whip,' and 'bow in homage to this land.'[9] His accomplishments, though still far from final victory, were already exceptional. It is easy, and a matter of course, to make a theoretical review of them. But before doing so, what, in the endless days before he concluded that armed struggle was the only feasible strategic road, especially when the struggle was in its seemingly unavailing early years, drove Mao onto it? China's pitiless and bloody class struggle was the main driving force. As for Mao himself, he was not yet versed in Marxism, and although familiar with Chinese history, he knew little about revolutionary history in the West. That, together with his village background and his personality and thinking, part Confucian, part *youxia*, played a part. In the autumn and winter of 1927, with the Great Revolution in ruins, people's spirits were low, a mixture of grief, pain, and indignation. That, of the CCP's top leaders, it was Mao who strode down the path of armed struggle had much to do with his character and temperament.

---

9   From Mao's poem 'This land so rich in beauty.'

'A person's shortcomings are often a person's strengths.' Because Mao knew little about Marxism-Leninism, he was scarcely bound by it, so he could set the route by resorting to instinct, common sense, personal experience, tradition, and his own best judgment. If he had 'known about Greece' or, worse still, had had a smattering of knowledge about Greece, if he had been well grounded in the ways of workers' revolution in the West, if he had known about the relationship in Marxist doctrine between workers and peasants, town and village, the former leading the latter, if he had known that the Red Army must be a product of a workers and peasants' government at national level, and fettered by it, and if he had adhered strictly to the idea that a workers' party must cleave to the cities, then, like most communist leaders after the 1927 rout in Wuhan, he would have slipped back into Shanghai or gone into hibernation in Wuhan rather than strike deep into the villages of Hunan and Jiangxi and climb the Jinggang Mountains. When Mao left Changsha to renounce the pen for the sword, copies of the *Water Margin* and *Cixuan* (a selection of classical poetry) in his knapsack (according to his comrade He Zishen[10]) and with Song Jiang, Huang Chao, Li Zicheng,[11] Hong Xiuquan, Sun Yat-sen, and even Chiang Kai-shek rather than Marx and Lenin as his teachers, he was settled in his intention. The revolution had been defeated. Many revolutionaries were dead, with counter-revolutionary generals and politicians dancing on their corpses. What should the survivors do? The weak in spirit yielded and turned traitor, the strong crawled from the bloodbath and concluded that they could best avoid further defeats by getting guns. Not just Mao thought this, many others did as well. Where Mao differed from most communists was in his ability to make the change from *xiucai* to bandit rebel, for he was free of the strategic strictures of classical Marxism and could put the idea to work regardless of other considerations. Mao's determination was laudable. He was able to put his strong points, and weak points made strong, at the service of the revolution, to which he contributed mightily. Even so, he was still not a great revolutionary strategist. The path he took was an extension of the Chinese tradition of peasant revolt, a pragmatic and largely unintended choice forced on him by circumstance. It is true that action precedes knowledge. In war and revolution, things change constantly and rules are unreliable, which is why Napoleon said

---

10   He Zishen (1898–1961) succeeded Mao as Secretary of the CCP's Hunan Provincial Committee. He later became a Trotskyist.
11   Song Jiang was an outlaw leader in the Song dynasty and a character in *The Water Margin*. Li Zicheng (ca. 1605–1645) was a rebel leader who dethroned the last Ming emperor. Huang Chao (835–884) led a major agrarian rebellion that severely weakened the Tang dynasty.

on s'engage et puis on voit (you commit yourself, and then you see). But this does not negate the value of knowing before doing, and even less so of systematic induction from the facts as a guide to doing. The genius of generals or revolutionary leaders, and whether they succeed or fail, depends on their mastery of the fruits of the knowledge of people in the past and present and the extent to which it informs their planning and strategic thinking. 'Commit yourself and then see' does not contradict the idea of 'plan first and then move.' They are not different things but sides of the same thing, in mutual complement, each indispensable to the other. To throw out the former is like drawing a circle on the ground to serve as one's own gaol, clinging stubbornly to outworn rules and routines; to throw out the latter is to drift aimlessly and rush blindly into battle. It is hard to say which plays the greater role in success or failure, but in determining the quality of a general or a revolutionary, the former does. Only the master calculating in the temple,[12] the presiding genius, can be commander-in-chief and adapt to changing circumstances, thus deploying the necessary executant talent. But again, the two qualities cannot be separated or counterposed. Decision makers must be good at meeting contingencies and executors must take a lofty view, or they will fail to lay overall plans that are good in all respects and never overtaken by events, plans that, while changing ten thousand times, never depart from the original aim or stand. To rank 'planning first and then moving' above 'committing yourself and then seeing' is simply to say that great strategists, military or political, need to 'think first, then do' more than they need to 'do first, then think.' The distinction is not just between before and after the event. The knowing of those who first know and then do is higher and fuller and can therefore expedite the next doing. The knowing of those who first do and then know might not be true knowing. It is, for the most part, a superficial summary, possibly teeming with errors, of past doing, unable to guide the next step and even a hindrance to it. The thinking of a person mature in all respects is fixed. A person who knows before doing may eventually shrivel into one who does first and then knows, or even one who neither knows nor does. Usually, however, only a tiny number of those who do before knowing can, through study or tempering, become people who first know and then do. Mao's road to a strategy of armed revolution was one of doing before knowing. That being so, was his knowing false or true? Did it guide or hamper his next step? After summing up his thinking about armed revolution in 1938, had he made the progression to first knowing and then doing?

---

12   The general's temple headquarters (Sunzi).

I have tackled some of these problems in the chapter on tactics, I will tackle others later. Here, I return to the question of guns in the ten years up to 1938: can guns make a party, can guns make a revolution, and can guns build socialism? Why did China's communists go in an opposite direction to Europe's communists? Why, before the bourgeoisie was on its last legs, before many workers favoured armed uprisings and war, before the peasant masses had volunteered to help the proletariat, did the CCP stage uprisings and wage wars, and why, in staging and waging them, did it not seize the cities before the villages? Mao has never answered these questions, except perfunctorily. A bare reference to capitalism there, feudal oppression here, no national oppression there, national oppression here, is not enough. This touches on fundamental principles of Marxism: the leading role of the proletariat in revolution, the relationship between party and workers, the workers' and the cities' leadership of the peasants and the villages, and the preparation of the workers and peasants' revolt, i.e., whether it must be by their own determination. The focal point of Marxism is an analysis of the class structure of and class struggle in modern society (mainly Western), from which Marxists conclude that revolution (wherever it happens) is inconceivable without proletarian leadership, realised through the communist party. To become the workers' vanguard, the party must (a) have a revolutionary socialist platform and (b) strike roots among the workers, with the industrial cities as their main stronghold; as for the peasants, they are, through their attachment to private property, their dispersion, and their feebleness, often insufficiently revolutionary and even conservative. They are, at the very least, incapable of independent action, let alone of leadership; historically, especially in China, peasants are the coolies of dynastic change, unable to take society forward. Peasant wars play a propelling role in the social system only under the leadership of an urban revolutionary class, only when the peasants are roused to struggle by urban classes. It doesn't mean that when urban revolution fails, revolutionaries go down to the villages to stoke up the struggle.

These fundamental tenets were first set out in the *Communist Manifesto*. After decades of positive and negative validation in revolutions throughout the world, they finally bore fruit in October 1917, and were then more fully and clearly expounded in the early programme of the Comintern. When applied to China, they suffered severe distortion at the hands of Stalin and Bukharin, but in many respects they retained their original form, in words if not always in deeds. Even after the autumn of 1927, when the Chinese Revolution went from opportunism to putschism and back again, stumbling and reeling along the way, neither Stalin nor Mao expressed doubts or opposition to them (what they did in practice is another thing).

Nineteen-thirty-eight was a year of special significance in this regard, for it was the year in which the line of armed revolution won out. It was also when Mao graduated in basic Marxism, whereupon he raised armed revolution to the strategic plane. But during this exercise, as I have said repeatedly, he did not answer the fundamental questions I have asked, although he did say that the revolution was not following the traditional path. He did not even mention the following problems. (1) Can communists posing as a revolutionary party and fighting far away from their base in the industrial proletariat still be good communists, develop along sound lines, avoid degeneration, and continue to play a revolutionary role? (2) If the answer is no (as it should be from the traditional Marxist point of view) then: if the CCP is compelled by circumstance to do as it does, has it already been corrupted? Or, if it is still in good health, how can that good health be reconciled with Marxist-Leninist thinking on the party? (3) Can a group of intellectuals, committed to socialism, organise the peasants, carry out armed struggle, and replace the proletariat as the peasants' leaders? Can peasant units thus organised and led survive? Can they escape the fragmentation and parochialism of peasant existence? Can they be used to seize the cities, wage civil war on a national scale, and bring proletarian revolution to victory? (4) Can a communist party and communist state power based on an armed peasantry preserve the purity of the workers' political programme and implement it? What ailments might such a revolution bring with it?

Mao has never tried to answer these questions, even since winning the revolution, and even as the special character of his victory results in difficulties and defeats. But it is important to ask and answer them, not just in order to explain the past but to prepare for future crises. Can Mao, not having done so, be described as a great strategist?

'[T]he emancipation of the working classes must be conquered by the working classes themselves,'[13] and the party representing it must share its fate. These two ideas are the nub of Marxist thinking on the matter. Marx and co. said revolutionaries should share the workers' joys and sorrows, understand their thoughts and feelings, make them the party's backbone, and put them in its leadership. The party must join every struggle, grand or humdrum, and unite the whole working class. Only then can it truly become the party of the working class. To be rooted among the workers and subject to their weal and woe guarantees against corruption and betrayal. Without skin, where is the hair? This metaphor can serve to express the relationship between workers and the

---

13   Rules and Administrative Regulations of the International Workingmen's Association 1964, pp. 265–270, at 265.

party. But the CCP comprised mainly peasants and was led, overwhelmingly, by intellectuals. It had long been divorced from the workers and even from the cities. Militarily, it had always insisted on roundabout advance and retreat to take cities and seize ground. Could such a party represent the workers? Even if it carried out a socialist programme and avoided degenerating, could it complete the revolution? For Marxists, the answer would seem to be obvious. However, the CCP not only survived but led the revolution to victory, not just militarily but in the full sense of the word, as deep social revolution, conforming (with all its faults) to workers' interests and securing their liberation.

What happened does not require a revision of Marxism but it does require an explanation other than the traditional one and the correction of a misunderstanding, especially regarding hair and skin. A country must first have a working class if it is to have a working-class party, and that party can only represent that class's interests if it is tightly bound to it in feelings, thought, life, and struggle. But there's more to this than meets the eye. Bondedness and representation, and how to combine them, have been the subject of numerous debates in the labour movement and the socialist movement ever since the start.

The birth of a workers' or socialist party is often understood nationally, but actually it is international. The maturity of a revolution and its dictatorship is determined mainly by the ripeness of the capitalist world system and its contradictions. The world has entered the age of socialist revolution, at least since October 1917. Few countries are sufficiently mature, economically or politically, for socialist revolution, but that doesn't invalidate the assertion, for in poor and colonial countries revolutions for people's livelihood, democracy, and national rights can, if they last long enough, carry on without stopping, propelled forward both by their own internal logic and by external pressure towards becoming, in the long or short term, part of world, i.e., social, revolution. Each poor country, even in the absence of industry and a big working class, can give rise to a party representing working-class interests. In a word, the hair need not grow on national skin, for the world working class and what has become, over the past century or so, international socialist thinking has created the premises and guidance, in thought and action, for workers' parties in each separate country.

So it is wrong to look at the relationship between hair and skin formally and narrowly. Doing so has led to a range of errors, including the following. (1) A workers' party must be in a workers' district. It must consist only of workers, and most of its leaders must have a working-class background. Its main or sole point should be to serve workers' interests. It should focus overwhelmingly on the workers' economic struggle rather than on national questions not directly related to it. This error has led to syndicalism, economism, and tailism. (2)

Countries with few workers do not need an independent workers' party. They need a workers and peasants' party, or workers should join national-bourgeois parties like the Guomindang. Workers and peasants' parties should not act or think independently but should assist, drive forward, and supervise bourgeois revolution. This kind of thinking was represented by Stalin and Bukharin's policy towards the Guomindang.

The reasons for these errors are various, but the narrow view of the working class and its party, a view national rather than international in scope, is the main one. Lenin, in *What Is To Be Done?*, looked at the question from another angle, that of the sources of the socialist and labour movement, and said, against syndicalism and economism, that there could be no social-democratic consciousness among the workers and it would have to be 'brought to them from without.' Workers, alone, see only the need to set up trade unions, fight the bosses, force the government to pass pro-labour laws, etc. Socialist theory, on the other hand, 'grew out of the philosophic, historical, and economic theories elaborated by educated representatives of the propertied classes, by intellectuals.' Lenin also said:

> Working-class consciousness cannot be genuine political consciousness unless the workers are trained to respond to *all* cases of tyranny, oppression, violence, and abuse, no matter *what class* is affected – unless they are trained, moreover, to respond from a Social-Democratic point of view and no other. The consciousness of the working masses cannot be genuine class-consciousness, unless the workers learn, from concrete, and above all from topical, political facts and events to observe *every* other social class in *all* the manifestations of its intellectual, ethical, and political life; unless they learn to apply in practice the materialist analysis and the materialist estimate of *all* aspects of the life and activity of *all* classes, strata, and groups of the population.[14]

With extreme honesty and courage, Lenin argued that workers, in their fight for self-liberation and social liberation, are not self-sufficient, especially in knowledge and ideas, and need external input. The idea of socialism cannot arise spontaneously from workers' lives or be 'objectively' generated. He emphasised the leading role of the party in the workers' movement and explained the relationship between vanguard and class. Here, the skin-hair metaphor holds only in its original and fundamental sense. As the relationship develops, the

---

14 Lenin 1973, p. 86.

life of the party (its thoughts and action) is not a direct, simple reflection of the class it represents, nor are the two indissolubly welded. A strong, mature working class can have a weak, ineffectual party: a puny, tiny one can have a militant vanguard. Some parties are led by workers, grow up among workers, and are closely and long bound up with workers, but, at critical junctures, help the capitalists. Others, especially their leaders, are, for various reasons, forced to leave the workers they represent, sometimes for a long time, but stay true and, in the end, lead them to victory.

So a party that represents the workers does not have to live with them cheek by jowl, inseparably conjoined. Lucky the party that has working-class members, leaders, and cadres and strongholds in working-class areas – but that alone cannot guarantee its integrity. On the other hand, a workers' party whose leaders are gaoled or driven by white terror from the cities, into exile or the remote villages, where they rely mainly on peasants and intellectuals in order to keep up the struggle on behalf of the workers and the people – its lot is tragic, but it cannot merely on those grounds be written off.

Lenin's argument with the Russian economists can help put right the perception in orthodox Marxism that a workers' party must, under all circumstances, give priority to urban work, and if, for whatever reason, it leaves the cities and leads a main force of peasants or intellectuals, it is bound to degenerate or die. This view is, of course, unrelated to the economist idea. It is not only Marxist but Bolshevik. To avoid degeneration or death and to consolidate and even win, a revolutionary party needs a strong urban base, a proletarian membership and cadre, and leaders from working-class backgrounds or steeled in the workers' struggle. There are many proofs, positive and negative, of this. But new facts prompt new questions. If leaders of a party meet the fate sketched out above and their attempt to fight on underground comes to nothing, or they manage to fight on but get nowhere, should they temporarily vacate their main force and, while sticking to their Marxist-Leninist principles, make revolution on a non-proletarian base, to escape degeneration and death? To put it more simply, can, under certain conditions, a staunchly united group of professional revolutionaries that has detached itself from the workers in the short or long term still represent their interests? More simply still: can a group of intellectuals, gripped by socialist ideas that they pass on to non-proletarian toilers, shoulder, over a period of years, the responsibilities of the party of the working class? These are, at bottom, three different ways of saying the same thing. The traditional Marxist answer would tend to be no, for to say yes would seem to stab at the heart of Marxist class theory and the idea that being determines consciousness and life determines thought. The Russian economists, 'adherents of the 'labour movement pure and simple,' worshippers of the closest 'organic' contacts with the proletarian struggle, opponents of any non-worker intelligentsia (even a socialist intelligentsia),'[15] would say no. However, even those who side with Lenin and who believe that socialism and class struggle 'arise side by side and not one out of the other; each arises under different conditions,' that the workers must have socialism 'brought to them from without,' and that revolution needs party leadership would not readily say yes. For they have too often seen intellectuals or communist sects lose touch with the workers and either sell out before the revolution, at the workers' cost, or turn into a new ruling caste of bureaucrats after the revolution, also at the workers' cost.

It is easy to see why they say no, and in some ways they are right. Think of the leaders of the Second International (some of them originally workers) and of Stalin. The corruption is mainly caused by the gap between the leaders and those they say they represent. Keeping close ties between leaders and led is essential, and will perhaps become ever more so. However, this is not, in itself, an argument against the party ever or under whatever circumstance leaving the cities and the workers.

Class struggle in capitalist society has given birth to socialist thought and the labour movement. Together, they create a socialist movement, which for the last hundred years has, with the workers as its main force, tried to change the social system. Socialist thought grows strong only when embodied in the working class, which can only triumph if it embraces socialist thought and the party representing it. That party must rest on a working-class foundation and keep faith with it. But this relationship is not that of substance and shadow,[16] body and soul. Its components are not different functions, or even less so different sides, of the same thing. Socialist thought does not emanate from the workers' movement – each arises alongside the other. Socialism (its ideology and organisation) and the working-class movement can be separated and yet cannot. *Can* because a socialist party forced to leave its working-class base and environment does not have to degenerate or die. It can live and fight on, and even grow – even, for the time being, among non-proletarians – as long as it cleaves to socialist thinking and policies. *Cannot* because a socialist party that leaves the workers for a long time, whether of its own accord or under compulsion, will absorb elements of the style, behaviour, policies, and even fundamental thinking of other classes, so that the party, especially the leadership, spoils or changes in nature.

---

15   Lenin 1973, p. 46.
16   Zhuangzi, 'Letting Be, and Exercising Forbearance,' Paragraph 5.

Separability and inseparability serve different ends in different circumstances, as Lenin showed. At the turn of the century, when the Bolshevik Party was founded, he put the stress on separability; after 1917, especially after NEP, on inseparability. The former, so as to build a professional organisation, resist the lure of working-class spontaneity, and see beyond the workers' narrow economic interests to the grander plan for revolution in Russia and the world. The latter, to prevent the party and the state's contamination by bureaucracy and to ensure that the revolution can proceed soundly. Only Lenin could grasp this fundamental theoretical distinction, thereby, on the one hand, paving the way to a professional revolutionary organisation and, on the other, perceiving the need for it to stay in close touch, in life and thought, with the workers in order to prevent its hardening and corruption.

In separating socialist organisation and the working class, Mao went further than any Marxist. For twenty-four years, from the autumn of 1927 to the spring of 1949, he stayed away from the cities and the workers. He led the party for most of that time, and, with peasants as his main force, strove to make headway in the villages. He saw no harm in it from the point of view of the party or of its continuing to serve the workers and the revolution. But how could a party separated from the workers represent them? Mao never apparently asked this question, either before or after the event. When Lenin wanted to create a party outside and above the working class, he discussed the issue in fine detail, but Mao ignored it. Given that he aimed for an even greater degree of separation, he should have studied the issue even more urgently than Lenin did. But he didn't and hasn't, so he cannot be called a great strategist.

Since Mao failed to explore the separability of class and party from a theoretical point of view, he also failed to understand the deeper meaning of their inseparability. After an absence of 24 years, his party of intellectuals and his peasant army were finally reunited with the class they programmatically represented, a reunion of liberators and the freed. The Husk Wife and her husband were apart for only eighteen years, but in that time he became a high official and was crowned a king. How could he be the equal of his old wife, who had stayed to guard the humble hearth? Of his early love, only pity survived. How could he serve her?[17] This was a complex and tragic problem. For Mao, however, the problem did not exist. He refused to acknowledge that the party had changed in style, thought, and behaviour in its time in the villages and become corrupt, bureaucratic, aloof, and haughty. He had given no thought to

---

17   The Husk Wife or *zaokang zhi qi*, who lives on husks and rice dregs in the long years of her husband's absence, until his return in triumph, is a character in early southern puppet plays and operas.

the theoretical meaning of the inseparability of party and class, let alone to the complementarity of separability and inseparability. Having, in the past, separated without forethought or awareness, he was ill-equipped to deal with the consequences of inseparability. To turn into orderlies charged with the conveyance and execution of directives on behalf of the workers a party that no longer directly relied on the workers but ruled by force of arms, to stop the party being master of the house, was not easy. Had enlightened leaders foreseen the problem and known that the future of the party and the revolution depended on its resolution, how vigilant they would have been when driven from the towns, and, on their return, how scrupulously they would have guarded against violating the people's interests, what strict and detailed steps they would have taken to prevent and uproot bureaucracy.

But Mao did not do this. He made no serious effort to curb bureaucracy after the return. Party, government, and army did not relax their top-down ways and their system of political tutelage and military control. Confucian-style 'notifying superiors of the circumstances of inferiors' took the place of what might have been workers' democracy. Bureaucracy spread unchecked. Today, the economy is in crisis, mainly because democracy has been choked, and bureaucrats make rash decisions without the slightest supervision. If one were to reduce the problem to Mao's personal responsibility and look no further than Mao thought for its causes, one would have to say: this happened because Mao did not know that if a party must, in certain circumstances, separate from its class, it should bear in mind and hammer home the underlying inseparability. Because Mao failed to do this, he cannot be regarded as a great strategist.

Here I set out some thoughts on the Marxist strategy of armed struggle.

1. In modern times (since 1917), the main backdrop to the birth in a country of a socialist or communist party is the existence of the international proletariat and its revolutionary struggle, and only then the existence of the working class and the state of its struggle in that country. The workers' party in each country does not owe its existence completely to its own working class. Socialist and labour movements have separate origins. They 'combine into one' rather than 'divide into two.'[18] The link between them is not, as some people imagine, 'organic,' 'pure,' as body and shadow, but permits separation in both form and thought.

---

18 The view that 'two combine into one' was put forward in the early 1960s by Yang Xianzhen (1896–1992). In July 1964 his formulation was attacked for minimizing the importance of struggle and contradiction and was interpreted as supporting capitalist restoration. It was contrasted with Mao's view that 'one divides into two,' i.e., that struggle constantly re-emerges, even when particular contradictions have been resolved.

2. Since some capitalist countries went fascist or militarised, the sort of socialist workers' movement set up, mainly in Europe, before the First World War has long proved unworkable in many poor countries, and the phenomenon has gradually begun to spread. Socialists and communists follow the traditional method of organising the working class and then uniting the great majority of the people around it to win elections. In some places these are no more than a formality, in others, not even that. Any independent workers' organisation, any active workers' party, is brutally crushed. If the party decides to stick with the workers and stand firm, it must either hibernate or shrink to a flicker.

3. Then, it is right for the party to withdraw some or most of its supporters from the workers' districts to a place where they can escape attention or easily hide. If conditions permit, especially if the ruling class is fighting a civil or foreign war, the party can start to fight back.

4. The strategy of 'armed revolution to oppose armed counter revolution' might, in future, be more widely applied. To carry it out, the party must, as Liu Shaoqi said, let 'hundreds of thousands of its members leave their jobs behind and plunge into the revolutionary life of a military community and a life-and-death struggle, where they will undergo rigorous ideological and organizational education and tempering.'[19] But Liu Shaoqi is wrong to say that this will ensure the party's proletarian character – the opposite is true. Separating the 'vanguard' from its class makes it less proletarian. Leaving their jobs behind, living the collective life of a soldier, living in the countryside, getting used to obeying orders – in many cases, for years on end – will instil the 'hundreds of thousands' with a 'collective will,' but it will not 'raise their class consciousness.' It will 'strengthen their sense of organisation and discipline,' but only at the cost of their sense of democracy and initiative. They will learn to be obsequious towards their superiors and contemptuous of their subordinates and to think no end of themselves, and bureaucracy will run riot. So if a workers' party is forced to take refuge in the villages, its leaders must ensure that it does not lose its bearings. They must be ever vigilant and defend Marxism-Leninism. They must take specific measures to oppose bureaucracy, introduce mechanisms whereby toilers can exercise democratic supervision, and uphold workers' interests in thought, style, and action. If things change and a victorious party returns to the cities and reunites with the workers, it must ensure its proletarian character by

---

19 Liu Shaoqi, *On the Party*, adapted translation.

using democracy to heal its chronic bureaucratic ailments. Above all, it must absorb large numbers of workers. (Liu Shaoqi told the Eighth Congress in September 1956 that only 14 per cent of the party's 101,730,000 members were workers, as against 69 per cent peasants and 12 per cent intellectuals.) It must quickly reverse the militarisation of political life and put the workers in charge. In short, a workers' party long separated from its base must do everything it can to reverse the effects of separation.

5. A worker's party that comes to power by the gun can, if it takes timely steps to mend its ties to the workers, go on to build socialism. However, building socialism, unlike setting up a party or even seizing power, has a massively international dimension, and cannot be done in a single country, whether big (like China) or small, and whether poor or rich. The idea that 'wise leadership,' a 'correct plan,' and spurring on the masses to work hard and leap forward can create an oasis of socialism is criminal folly. The overturned cart of Stalin's 'socialism in one country' is a warning to all, but Mao ignored it and instead defiled socialism with his Three Red Banners.[20]

These five points are designed to assess the strengths and weaknesses of Mao's theory of armed revolution and his standing as a strategist. I now return to the question raised at the start of the chapter: 'If Mao had consciously and comprehensively raised armed struggle to the strategic plane and, even more importantly, if, from the beginning, he had raised and implemented it in the context of a strategy of permanent revolution, how would advancing towards victory, gaining victory, and extending victory have been different?' Put another way, if Mao had pursued his tactics in the framework of Trotsky's theory rather than of Stalin's Third Period and Popular Front, would he still have won? And if so, would the route and the price have been the same?

I don't intend to go into detail or to follow events step by step, pitting a Stalinist Mao against a hypothetical Trotskyist Mao. That would take too much time, and would anyway repeat much of what I've said already. I only want to look at three antitheses: soviets vs national assembly, coalition government vs joint action, and nation-based socialism vs international socialism.

China's soviet slogan was first put forward by Trotsky, in the spring of 1927, when the Northern Expedition reached the Yangtze River and the workers' and peasants' movement in Hunan, Jiangxi, and Hubei was still buoyant. To give strength and coherence to the loose mass movement and to equip it to face down the Guomindang, with its army, and the bourgeoisie, Trotsky's Oppos-

---

20   Including the People's Communes and the Great Leap Forward.

ition proposed organising workers', peasants', and soldiers' soviets. The Stalin faction said no, on the grounds that soviets were incompatible with China's 'bourgeois' revolution, and, as organs of insurrection, with the Guomindang–CCP alliance. Everyone knows what happened. The Guomindang caught the workers off guard and repeatedly betrayed the revolution and massacred the revolutionaries. If, in 1926–7, the CCP, rather than allow itself to be tied hand and foot to the Guomindang, had followed Trotsky, things might have turned out differently. If a government of workers and peasants had been established in 1927 rather than in 1949, there would have been no military dictatorship under Chiang and probably no Japanese invasion (because Japan would have changed under Chinese influence), and even if the Sino-Japanese War had happened, it would have been shorter and less devastating.

After the defeat of the revolution in the winter of 1927, the debate about the soviet slogan underwent an interesting change, for the two sides swapped positions. Stalin declared the defeat a progression to a higher stage of revolution, and called for soviets as the basis for an uprising against the Guomindang. Trotsky said the revolution was spent, and calling for soviets would only deepen the counter-revolution and delay the new revolution. He argued for a democratic slogan, a National Assembly with plenary powers elected on the basis of universal suffrage, as a means of reuniting the revolutionary forces and opposing the Guomindang's military dictatorship.

After a string of defeats in China, Stalin relegated the soviet slogan to the realm of propaganda, but he remained opposed to any sort of democratic slogan. For a long time, from the summer of 1928 to the autumn of 1935, the CCP had no central slogan. The Red Army was defeated and had to go on the Long March. The CCP lost nearly all its urban members and 90 per cent of its troops, not least because of its failure to fight for a democratic programme, which would have relieved the military pressure on it.

Should armed revolution have been combined with the demand for a National Assembly? If it had been, and if the party had started fighting, guns in hand, for thorough-going democracy before and after 1930, how would things have turned out? In the winter of 1928, Mao had been fighting for a year, and the soviet slogan had been withdrawn. In his report on 'The Struggle in the Jinggang Mountains,' he said:

> We have an acute sense of our isolation which we keep hoping will end. Only by launching a political and economic struggle for democracy, which will also involve the urban petty bourgeoisie, can we turn the revolution into a seething tide that will surge through the country. [...] The Central Committee wants us to issue a political programme which takes into

account the interests of the petty bourgeoisie, and we for our part propose that the Central Committee work out, for general guidance, a programme for the whole democratic revolution which takes into account the workers' interests, the agrarian revolution and national liberation.[21]

These passages explain, clearly and succinctly, the need for a 'programme for the whole democratic revolution' of the sort represented by a National Assembly, and vividly describe the revolutionaries' isolation as a result of its absence. Given Mao's testimony, the relevance of the National Assembly slogan is obvious. If Mao had adopted it, what might have happened? Arbitrarily hypothetical or conjectural history has little point, but being a hypothesis does not necessarily make it wrong in all respects. Mao's express wish for an early end to the 'acute sense of isolation' and a 'seething tide that will surge through the country' as a result of 'a political and economic struggle for democracy [involving] the urban petty bourgeoisie' justifies the surmise that the isolation might have ended and the tide might have risen sooner.

So Mao's victory does not prove Stalin right and Trotsky wrong. In fact, the opposite is true. Yes, Trotsky never approved of the communists leaving the cities to fight with guns. In the autumn of 1930, when the CCP already had quite an army and was starting to attract international attention, Trotsky said:

> The Chinese communists now need a suitable relatively long-term policy, their task is not to disperse their forces in a blaze of undisciplined peasant uprisings – a numerically small and weak party can never cover these areas. The communists' task is to concentrate on the factories, workshops, and workers' districts, and to explain to the workers the significance of the incidents in the countryside and raise their flagging spirits, and to unite them on economic demands and democratic slogans and the fight for land revolution. That is the only way of awakening and uniting the workers. Only the communist party can lead the peasant revolts, the peasant revolution.[22]

This is the orthodox Marxist-Leninist position. I've already talked about it, and won't go into it again here. All I will say is that although Trotsky took this position, he did not absolutely exclude such a struggle, if the conditions were right. He said:

---

21   Mao, 'The Struggle in the Jinggang Mountains,' November 25, 1928, SW, vol. 1, at pp. 73–104, at 97–8.
22   Trotsky, 'The Question of the Chinese Revolution,' retranslated from the Chinese.

> The rising tide of peasant uprisings will undoubtedly promote the advance of the political struggle in the industrial centres, of that there can be no doubt. [...] No one can say in advance whether the flame of peasant uprisings will continue in the long term, up until the time when the proletariat becomes strong and solid, so that leading the working-class struggle and causing the workers to take power can happen in concert with the peasants' struggle against their closest enemy.

Trotsky explained how that armed struggle could be brought to victory:

> The peasant movement, even under a soviet signboard, is still dispersed, locally oriented, and province-based. To raise it to the national plane, the fight for land and against warlord taxes and oppression must be joined to the idea of China's independence and national sovereignty. The democratic reflection of that tie is the plenary National Assembly, under which slogan the communist vanguard can unite around itself the workers, the oppressed urban populace, and the hundreds of millions of poor peasants and broad popular masses, to rise up against oppressors at home and abroad.[23]

Trotsky wrote this in September 1930. It concurs with what Mao had said two years earlier. But because Mao was not a strategist or theoretician, he was unable to propose the democratic programme he thought was urgently needed and he could not help chiming in with Stalin's description of the National Assembly slogan as 'liquidationist.' As a result, he spent the next five or six years in even greater suffering and isolation, until Stalin switched from adventurism to opportunism. This gave him the chance he needed. Under the cover of Stalin's turn, he tactfully conceded past mistakes: 'The people of the whole country and the patriots of all parties should throw off their former indifference towards the question of a national assembly and a constitution.'[24] Naturally, he could not say that the 'indifference' was due to Stalin. But if he had done from the start as Trotsky said, things might have turned out differently.

---

23   Trotsky, retranslated from the Chinese.
24   Mao, 'The Tasks of the Communist Party of China in the Period of Resistance to Japan,' May 3, 1937, SW, vol. 1, pp. 263–84, at 268.

CHAPTER 7

Theory and Practice

Mao has written two short books on philosophy, *On Practice* and *On Contradiction*, the first in July and the second in August 1937. According to their editors, they were written to oppose dogmatism in the party. In other words, their main aim was to attack the Wang Ming faction. At the time, Mao was studying Marxist theory. At the start of the Anti-Japanese War, Wang and co. had not yet fallen into complete disgrace, despite their ouster at Zunyi,[1] and they still posed a threat to the Maoists. To consolidate his victory, Mao had to continue fighting on all fronts, not just those of military and political leadership (where he had already scored big victories) but also of theory and ideology, to overcome Wang's 'dogmatism.' In the theory war, the main front Mao now opened was philosophical. Wang had long called Mao an 'empiricist.'[2] To remove that inglorious hat, Mao had to get to grips with basic Marxist theory, to raise his own stature and slap hats back onto his rivals.

This shaped the nature of the two books. They were not so much treatises on Marxist philosophy as a systematic narrative based on the notes Mao made while doing his research, and they are far more about politics than about philosophy. To call them reading notes is not to belittle them. Writing should be judged by its genre. Lenin's *Philosophical Notebooks* are in no way inferior to his *Materialism and Empirio-criticism*, just as Marx's *Theses on Feuerbach* are no less valuable than Engels' *Ludwig Feuerbach and the End of Classical German Philosophy*. The focus must be on the content of the thinking rather than on the formal genre. Some notes are slavish copying, others extract and purify at a high level, sparkling with wisdom and intelligence. Some are feeble-minded and error-strewn, turning essence into dross, others magically transform dross and error into truth (as Marx and Lenin did with Hegel), or unearth and polish hidden treasures and apply universal truths to specific instances (as Lenin did with Marx and Engels). Many of Lenin's most famous writings can be described as reading notes, especially *State and Revolution*, much of which is copied from Marx's and Engels' theories of the state, 'with lots of annotation and com-

---

1 The CCP held conference at Zunyi in January 1935 during the Long March. At it, Mao defeated Bo Gu and Otto Braun in a power struggle and thus laid the grounds for his later rise to unchallenged power.
2 Wang Ming saw Mao as a 'narrow empiricist,' in contrast to his own supposed mastery of theory.

mentary' (as Lenin told Kamenev). So my description of Mao's two booklets as reading notes is not meant to belittle them.

Nor is the conclusion that the books are far more political than philosophical detrimental. Lenin put it well: 'Marx and Engels were partisans in philosophy from start to finish.'[3] The idea of philosophy as detachment is a hoax, intentional or not. Philosophy is, to a greater or lesser extent, overtly or covertly, in the interests of this or that class and in the service of this or that political ideology. The question is not whether politics are integral to philosophy, but in what way they are.

What about Mao's notebooks? Are they slavish copying, feeble, and error-strewn, or do they extract and purify at a high level? The CCP's Propaganda Department says they are a 'brilliant, creative further development' of Marxism-Leninism. That is nonsense. However, one must admit that Mao's achievements are a cut above Stalin's, whose writings on dialectical materialism had more in common with a court verdict, a catechism, or the Ten Commandments than with philosophy, and whose method of presenting his thoughts, to quote Plekhanov (speaking of the philosopher Berdyaev, in Plekhanov's Preface to Engels' *Feuerbach*), is best 'described by the word *decree*. [...] – and when a muddle-head like Mr Berdyaev takes to issuing decrees, absolutely nothing instructive will come of them.'[4] That is Stalin in a nutshell.

Mao studied Marxist philosophy not as a philosopher but as a practitioner of revolution. Unlike Engels and Lenin, who engaged with Marxist philosophy from all angles, he focused on one aspect of Marx's epistemology, the meaning of practice, and one law of dialectics, the theory of contradictions. Starting out from these two questions, he aimed to master if not the whole of Marxist philosophy then a big part of it. In doing so, he showed his lack of training, but he also – and more importantly – displayed his self-knowledge, which was greater than Stalin's, his reluctance to pretend to knowledge he did not have, and his ability to make the best of his strengths, so that in study and research he was not without achievements.

Stalin's writing is worthless, and increasingly seen as such. However, *On Practice* and *On Contradiction*, despite not adding to Marxist knowledge, have value, as a philosophical foundation for Mao thought and practice. *On Contradiction* is more important than *On Practice*, for the latter is merely a systematic narration of general Marxist knowledge, with nothing new to say. If it has meaning, it is as an indicator of Mao's fight to educate and defend himself. Before

---

3 Lenin 1972, p. 411.
4 Plekhanov 1976, vol. 3, pp. 64–83, at 83.

1935, everyone in the CCP, Mao included, was still in the 'perceptual stage of cognition' where basic questions of the Chinese and world revolutions were concerned. They called themselves Marxists and representatives of the Chinese proletariat. They opposed imperialism, 'feudal forces,' and comprador capitalism and took up arms against the Guomindang. However, as Mao said in *On Practice*, they were 'vulgar "practical men" [who] respect experience but despise theory' (at the time, "practical work" was a common term). They lacked a comprehensive view of the objective process, lacked clear direction and a long-range perspective, and were 'complacent over occasional successes and glimpses of the truth.' Mao concluded: 'If such persons direct a revolution, they will lead it up a blind alley.'[5] He was right. There was no end of blind alleys, but less because of 'practical work' than because of the lack of a clear compass and theoretical discernment, so that fake theoreticians in Moscow could use their faulty compasses to misguide the Wangites from afar. Mao was in a double bind, beset by the facts of the revolution and theory handed down by fake foreign devils.[6] His suffering drove him to consider studying, and to 'make the leap from perceptual to rational cognition.' *On Practice* and *On Contradiction* were signposts along that road.

Mao was, first and foremost, a man of action, as I have already shown. Wang Ming called him an empiricist, and not without reason. Mao thinks highly of real power and believes most of all in the gun. Whatever the state of his Marxism, he has scored many passing achievements in practical work. That is why, in his bones, he was never likely to set great store by theory. However, he knew that in Marxist vocabulary empiricism was a term of abuse, and when the 'dogmatists' started showing off their theory, he found it hard to answer back. In the endless struggle, as someone 'unable to take a comprehensive view of the objective process as a whole and lacking a clear guiding principle and a long-term outlook,' he, as a serious revolutionary, could not but resolve to study theory. So his motivation was various: first, to get a defence for himself, having always in the past stressed practicalities; second, to clarify the relationship in classical Marxism of knowing to doing; and, third, to charge the Wangites with the crime of dogmatism. With that in mind, he not surprisingly started his philosophical studies by looking at practice and focusing on knowledge and action.

Dialectical materialists value practice as the criterion of truth in cognition and perceptual experience as its source and basis. However, these fundamental

---

5 Mao, 'On Practice,' July 1937, SW, vol. 1, pp. 295–310, at 301.
6 A disparaging term for Chinese who ape foreigners' attitudes and behaviour.

notions are not the same thing as the CCP's, and even less so Mao's, idea of 'practical work,' and are not even in the same category. The former are important for establishing the objectivity of truth and the temporality of thought, the latter for the debate about which comes first in revolutionary work, theory or practice. When this debate arises in Marxist parties, there is at least consensus on the basic philosophical postulates, that practice is the criterion of truth and perceptual knowledge (experience) the basis of rational knowledge. However, people often argue about whether a revolutionary should be better at theoretical discernment and the ability to generalise than at practical investigation or the other way round. Is standing high and seeing far, like a strategist, better than suiting one's actions to changing conditions, as a tactician does? Should one stick to principles or engage in tactical adjustments and manoeuvres? Obviously the two cannot be mechanically separated. Both are valuable and necessary for the revolution, and form a complementary set. But as I have said more than once, revolutionaries can, broadly speaking, be assigned to one camp or the other, and that camp defines the extent of their contribution. Mao tried to abolish the distinction and resented apportioning precedence. He stressed the unity of knowing and doing, and opposed both chattering theoreticians and empiricists who get bogged down in daily routine. So a good revolutionary should prize theory and value practice and wield pen and sword with equal ease, as a consummate all-rounder. But that does not end the problem. At the very most, apart from expressing the view that Mao was not the empiricist Wang said he was, that he was not single-mindedly and one-sidedly committed to practical work but was instead both an inspired theorist and man of action, it says little. For in reality, no one is equally good at everything. Nature and nurture conspire to make us able in different ways. Revolutionaries are human, and cannot escape this truth. To deny the distinction between theory and practice is to deny reality. To treat them equally without discrimination, to refuse to rank them, is to slight theory and put undue emphasis on practice.

I do not uphold the view that 'to know is easier than to do.' However, one must admit that the ability, 'through the exercise of thought, to reconstruct the rich data of sense perception, discarding the dross and selecting the essential, eliminating the false and retaining the true, proceeding from the one to the other and from the outside to the inside, in order to form a system of concepts and theories'[7] is rarer than the mastery of mere perceptual knowledge, and even those who manage the reconstruction do so with varying degrees

---

7 Mao, 'On Practice,' July 1937, SW, vol. 1, pp. 295–310, at 303.

of competence. That being so, how can we not value even more highly those theoretical 'prophets' who make the leap from perceptual to rational knowledge!

Mao has never openly said that it is right to look down on theory. He says that theory and practice should be equally stressed. In *On Practice*, as elsewhere, he strongly commended this sentence of Stalin's: 'Theory becomes purposeless if it is not connected with revolutionary practice, just as practice gropes in the dark if its path is not illumined by revolutionary theory.'[8] But this dualist approach does not answer my question, which was: which comes first and which matters most, theory bound up with revolutionary practice or practice that takes revolutionary theory as its guide? One answer might be that they cannot be distinguished and each is equally important. That is not necessarily wrong. Another, even more tenable, is that in some situations, theory is more important, and in others, practice is more important. But neither answer can avoid the problem of dualism. Marx once wrote, in a letter: 'Every step of real movement is more important than a dozen programmes.'[9] This sentence has been used as a talisman by 'practical workers' and routinists of all kinds to argue that Marx put practice above theory. But, as Lenin later pointed out, the letter '*sharply condemns* eclecticism in the formulation of principles. If you must unite, Marx wrote to the party leaders, then enter into agreements to satisfy the practical aims of the movement, but do not allow any bargaining over principles, do not make theoretical "concessions."' In fact, Marx was speaking ironically. In *What Is To Be Done?*, Lenin made his famous remark that 'without revolutionary theory there can be no revolutionary movement.' He suggested three reasons why theory mattered in Russia. (1) The party was still in the process of formation, and it had not yet settled accounts with other trends of revolutionary thought that might divert it from the correct path. (2) As an incipient movement in a young country, it could succeed only if it made use of the experiences of other countries, but it must treat those experiences critically and test them independently. (3) The national tasks facing it were such as had never before been confronted by any socialist party in the world. Why do I raise these points? Because the conditions 'special to Russia' were shared by parties of the East that later started springing up one after the other, so Lenin's assertions apply to them too. Settling accounts with trends of thought that might deflect revolutionaries from the right path was not just a problem for incipient parties. With the growth of the world socialist movement, the deepening

---

8   Mao, 'On Practice,' July 1937, SW, vol. 1, pp. 295–310, at 305.
9   Marx, 'Letter to Wilhelm Bracke,' May 5, 1875, MECW, vol. 24, 7.

crisis of capitalism, and the sharpening of the class struggle throughout the world, trends of thought that might knock new parties off course, or already had knocked them off course, abounded, so revolutionaries must be good at identifying them – Lenin's dictum was, and is, widely applicable. Members of a modern socialist party must put studying and mastering Marxist-Leninist theory above all else. Theory is the compass, without which one will stray ever further from the destination.

Mao quoted Lenin's famous remark, but then said that 'Marxism emphasizes the importance of theory precisely and only because it can guide action,' as if Lenin, by stressing theory, had been advocating idle chatter. Mao went on to praise Stalin's comment that 'theory becomes purposeless if it is not connected with revolutionary practice,' thus silencing Lenin's chatter, and, by playing on the safe side and putting equal weight on each, cancelling out Lenin's supposed bias (in fact an insight of great profundity) in theory's favour.

Such even-handedness in philosophy is usually an indication of eclecticism and, in the social sciences, a disguised way of rendering the trivial important. Stalin's 'six of one and half a dozen of the other' was a cover for his habit of doing without particularly knowing, and the reason Mao appreciated this 'dualism' was that it let him shake off the 'empiricist' hat while continuing to belittle theory.

'Discover the truth through practice, and again through practice verify and develop the truth' is materialist epistemology and a basic tenet of Marxist philosophy. Here, Mao's description of Marx's philosophy is right. But he goes on to say: 'Start from perceptual knowledge and actively develop it into rational knowledge; then start from rational knowledge and actively guide revolutionary practice to change both the subjective and the objective world.'[10] This is mechanical induction, and wrong. According to Mao, human understanding is a matter of '[p]ractice, knowledge, again practice, and again knowledge [...] in endless cycles.'[11] But that does not mean that each particular group of people, and even each individual, must, at all times and under all circumstances, do so in the prescribed order, until the process is over. Human experience and knowledge accumulated over aeons is ceaselessly handed down. People's understanding (as individuals or in groups) does not start from their own perception but by studying and digesting the rationality of their predecessors and contemporaries. Do today's revolutionaries first become Luddites and then Fourierites and Owenites before finding their own way to Marxism? Of course not. Instead,

---

10   Mao, 'On Practice,' July 1937, SW, vol. 1, pp. 295–310, at 308.
11   Ibid.

they start with Marxism-Leninism, the highest form of knowledge. So socialists should found their practice in revolutionary theory, gained from past achievements, and thus get twice the result with half the effort, rather than waste time and energy on 'perceptual' revolutionary activity. For in today's conditions, defeat is practically inevitable without a grounding in 'rational' revolutionary theory.

That being so, why does Mao insist on the formula 'practice, knowledge, again practice, and again knowledge'? Because this is how he himself, unwittingly, came by knowledge, and how he, wittingly, aims to defend himself. In fact, the formula belongs to the infancy of both humankind and the individual. When humans (and groups) grow into adulthood, the cycle of practice and knowledge is no longer the main starting point, but knowledge is. If Mao were talking about general and low-level knowledge, then the advanced formula would be 'knowledge, practice, again knowledge, again practice.' The second formula does not negate the first but supplements and develops it. Without the second, the first can serve as a general formula. However, it is quite wrong to see it as a special law, for example, for describing the maturation of a revolutionary or a revolutionary party. Therein lies the 'philosophical basis' of the empiricist and the person of action, the denial of the truth that 'without revolutionary theory there can be no revolutionary movement.' Such, however, is the message of *On Practice*.

On Contradiction is much richer in content than *On Practice* and the part played in it by Mao's own thinking much clearer, even though it is still mainly reading notes. It is, in essence, his reflections on and insights gained from Lenin's *Philosophical Notebooks*. I do not intend to look at Lenin's ideas as retold by Mao, for I am interested mainly in how Mao used them to develop his own thinking. In *On Practice*, Mao also developed his own ideas, but less rigorously and fully. I have already said why – because he wanted to borrow Marxism-Leninism's criterion of practice to defend his own modest 'doctrine of practical work' and disparagement of theory. Hence the hemming and hawing, hiding the head but showing the tail,[12] and putting Mr Zhang's hat on Mr Li's head,[13] for there is no way Mao cannot have known that honouring the criterion of practice is not the same as promoting practical work at the cost of theory. But once he had leapt into the field of 'contradictions,' his reflections were of quite a different order. A shrewd and agile tactician, he had apparently lit on a formula that generalised his tactics and on laws of thought that lent system and

---

12   Half truths.
13   False attribution.

theoretical form to his Machiavellian propensity. This caused him to rejoice, so that he dived straight in and soared straight up, his thoughts boldly flowing and brimming over.

Mao focused on 'the particularity of contradiction, the principal contradiction and the principal aspect of a contradiction, the identity and struggle of the aspects of a contradiction, and the place of antagonism in contradiction,'[14] and devoted a section to each. He described Lenin's views on them and voiced his own opinions, using many arguments and historical examples. His ideas are well worth scrutinising, not because of their contribution to the science of dialectics but because, in their basic method, they elucidate Mao's political position and strategy, both then and later. Everyone, no matter who, is, in a certain sense, a philosopher. Everyone has thoughts, and each person's thought has its own individual methods and characteristics. To the extent that the thinker is conscious of them, to that extent he or she is a philosopher. To grasp a person's thought, starting from that person's philosophy, one can always deduce many things from single instances, thus achieving relative fullness and depth. Mao is a brilliant tactician, both politically and militarily, as I have already said. In his nurturing and training, he gained this ability (so I argued) from his steeping in Confucianism. Confucius was an outstanding dialectician. His Middle Way[15] was, in effect, a philosophy proper to middle classes. What was his social class? Chinese Marxist historians hold different views, but all agree he belonged to a middle class. A social thinker rooted in a middle class tends, by nature, to be a 'born dialectician.' Marx said this early on. Such thinkers are sometimes swayed by the ruler, sometimes by the ruled. They swing from side to side, without necessarily persisting in an opinion. They usually attend to each and every aspect of a matter, striking water right and left. In a certain sense, that leads to dialectics. But as Marx said, it is the dialectics of opportunism, not of revolution. Confucianism in China undoubtedly has a dialectical component, Taoism even more so. However, both belong to the category of subjective idealism, both are opportunist. Marx established his dialectics on a material basis, and linked it to revolution. Such was Marx's genius. Even more important, it was due to the rapid progress of natural and social science and the rise of an awakening proletariat.

In his early years, Mao absorbed some dialectical thinking from Confucianism. Add that to his innate artfulness and his knowledge, gained from his-

---

14 Mao, 'On Contradiction,' August 1937, SW, vol. 1, pp. 311–47, at 311.
15 The Middle Way or *zhong yong*, also translated as the Doctrine of the Mean, is a doctrine of Confucianism and the title of one of the Four Books of Confucian philosophy. It represents moderation, rectitude, objectivity, sincerity, honesty and propriety.

tory books, of ways of conducting oneself in society and of ruling people, and you will see why he was an outstanding tactician and man of action. By the same token, however, he was ill-equipped to become a similarly brilliant strategist and theorist. His intrinsic *tu* dialecticity, rooted in Confucianism, prevents him from grasping in an all-sided way its materialist *yang* equivalent.[16] The essence of his dialectics is opportunism. His intellectual and his political opportunism are each other's outside and inside. His opportunistic practice shaped his opportunistic thought, and vice versa. The third section of *On Contradiction* expresses this with utmost clarity:

> Qualitatively different contradictions can only be resolved by qualitatively different methods. For instance, the contradiction between the proletariat and the bourgeoisie is resolved by the method of socialist revolution; the contradiction between the great masses of the people and the feudal system is resolved by the method of democratic revolution; the contradiction between the colonies and imperialism is resolved by the method of national revolutionary war; the contradiction between the working class and the peasant class in socialist society is resolved by the method of collectivization and mechanization in agriculture; contradiction within the communist party is resolved by the method of criticism and self-criticism; the contradiction between society and nature is resolved by the method of developing the productive forces. Processes change, old processes and old contradictions disappear, new processes and new contradictions emerge, and the methods of resolving contradictions differ accordingly. In Russia, there was a fundamental difference between the contradiction resolved by the February Revolution and the contradiction resolved by the October Revolution, as well as between the methods used to resolve them. The principle of using different methods to resolve different contradictions is one which Marxist-Leninists must strictly observe. The dogmatists do not observe this principle; they do not understand that conditions differ in different kinds of revolution and so do not understand that different methods should be used to resolve different contradictions; on the contrary, they invariably adopt what they imagine to be an unalterable formula and arbitrarily apply it everywhere, which only causes setbacks to the revolution or makes a sorry mess of what was originally well done.[17]

---

16 See footnote 8 on p. 89.
17 Mao, 'On Contradiction,' August 1937, SW, vol. 1, pp. 311–47, at 321.

This passage demonstrates Mao's understanding of the particularity of contradiction and the stages in its general process, as well as the way in which he uses the dialectic to explain historical events and applies it to them in practice. But it also reveals his deep underlying opportunism. 'Qualitatively different contradictions can only be resolved by qualitatively different methods.' This assertion is, at first sight, very dialectical, but not on closer inspection. The formula A becomes not A and B becomes not B is, in essence, merely a mutation of the formula A is equal to A and B to B. It perfectly matches the formal logic of common sense. It stands to reason that when a contradiction changes in nature, so must the way of resolving it. That is one aspect of the truth. On the other hand, the nature of the resolution does not necessarily change with the nature of the contradiction, and the nature of the resolution may change even when the contradiction stays the same. That is also true, and accords even more with the dialectic. The proposition that contradiction A can be resolved only by method A may hold, but to deny outright that contradiction A can and sometimes must be resolved by method B is to get stuck in a quagmire of mechanical formal logic. So Mao's understanding of the particularity of contradiction and how to resolve it is mechanical. This mechanicalism is the root in thought of his chronic political opportunism.

The examples Mao uses to validate 'the dialectic' smack little of it. In the textbook of dialectics, 'resolving the contradiction between the proletariat and the bourgeoisie by the method of socialist revolution, resolving the contradiction between the great masses of the people and the feudal system by the method of democratic revolution, etc.,'[18] can only be cited as counter-examples. A real example would be: even if a resolution of the contradiction between proletariat and bourgeoisie is ceaselessly sought in democratic revolution, the contradiction between the popular masses and the feudal system must, in the present age, be resolved by socialist revolution. This statement might, on the surface, look absurd, but in fact it is dialectical. It accords with contemporary class relations and has been repeatedly validated over the past half century by victory and defeat in revolution. Comparing Russia's February and October revolutions, Mao says that the contradictions and the methods used to resolve them differed in each case. He either doesn't know what he's talking about or he was hoodwinked by Stalin, for although the contradictions differed,[19] the Bolsheviks resolved them using the same basic methods: the workers, with peasant support, attacked the bourgeoisie, took power, and set

---

18 Ibid.
19 Even the contradictions were in some ways the same. There were similarities (in February,

up a revolutionary dictatorship. The dispute between Lenin and the Mensheviks boiled down to this: the Mensheviks said the revolution would be bourgeois, because it was against feudalism, and democratic – an alliance of the workers and the bourgeoisie; while Lenin said the workers should stay independent in the democratic revolution, unite with the peasants, carry out revolution to the end, and set up a democratic dictatorship of workers and peasants, thus resolving the contradiction between the people and the Tsar by socialist revolution. The Mensheviks attacked Lenin for using methods alien to the target. In formal logic, Russia couldn't skip capitalism, the main contradiction was between capitalist development and the feudal obstacles to it, the revolution was bourgeois in nature, and the bourgeoisie also wanted revolution, so why not cooperate with it against autocracy and for bourgeois democracy? But although Lenin agreed that the revolution was bourgeois, he differed on how to resolve the contradiction, and advocated a workers and peasants' democratic dictatorship – in other words, use anti-bourgeois methods to resolve an essentially bourgeois revolution, and replace tsarism not with bourgeois democracy but with a democratic dictatorship of workers and peasants. For the Mensheviks, this was crazy. As for Lenin, he initially said the dictatorship was still part of the democratic revolution and would carry out purely democratic tasks, but he later recognized that if it was to differ from bourgeois dictatorship, it must see itself as socialist. So while the Mensheviks said the contradiction should be resolved by democratic revolutionary means, Lenin said the same goal should be achieved by socialist revolutionary means. In other words, the Menshevik approach bore out Mao's dialectic while Lenin's contradicted it.

At first, nearly everyone opposed Lenin for calling on the workers and peasants to seize power in a bourgeois revolution – not just the Mensheviks, who had always opposed him, but even his old Bolshevik followers. They said he was mad, 'divorced from reality,' an 'adventurist,' and even a 'Blanquist.' Some Mensheviks and others called him a 'Russian traitor' and a 'German spy.' The reason his political opponents, especially his comrades (including Stalin, Kamenev, and Zinoviev), were so upset was that he was violating a rule Mao later said must be 'strictly observed,' 'that different methods should be used to resolve different contradictions,' i.e., the democratic revolution should be resolved by democratic revolutionary methods. Lenin's previous followers thought the democratic, i.e., bourgeois, revolution had not yet been completed, and that to

---

the democratic tasks were not resolved, which was one reason why the October Revolution happened) and differences (in October, the proletariat took power, and resolved the socialist contradictions) (note by Wang).

call on the workers and peasants to seize power was like matching horses' jaws to cows' heads – or, as Mao might say, Lenin did not know he was supposed to use different methods for different contradictions. But the truth was that the masses spontaneously rose up in February and started a revolution that led to soviets and to the workers and peasants' government Lenin had foreseen. It was only because various kinds of socialist leader 'strictly observed' the principle of 'using the methods of democratic revolution to resolve the contradiction between the popular masses and the feudal system' that a Provisional Government 'conforming to the democratic republican system' arose, and only because the soviets, which held real power, 'dogmatically' yielded, handing power to the 'historically legitimate' bourgeois government, that a strange phenomenon arose after the February Revolution: the soviets and the Provisional Government existed side by side, in a situation of dual power.

So using the democratic (i.e., bourgeois) Provisional Government to 'resolve' the democratic contradictions in the February Revolution in line with a supposed dialectical law of historical development was definitely not necessary and inevitable but an artificial approach that violated the course of history and thus the interests of the revolution. The theory behind this approach was metaphysical and mechanistic. It would have derailed the Russian Revolution in 1917 but for Lenin, Trotsky, and others, who stood firm and eventually convinced most of the Bolsheviks to seize power and carry out socialist revolution. Even though the contradictions in February and October differed in some ways, Lenin resolved them in basically the same way, by uniting the workers and peasants under working-class leadership and establishing a dictatorship. At all times, in February, in October, and even in 1905, the method was socialist, for there has never been, and never will be, a workers and peasants' dictatorship that does not oppose the capitalist system.

The greatest misfortune in history was the failure of Lenin's successors to understand that the February Revolution could be saved from ruin and the October Revolution could triumph only because of Lenin's resolving of democratic revolution by socialist revolution and Marx's and Trotsky's advocacy of permanent revolution. Although the Russian Revolution of 1917 had shown, both positively and negatively, that the old way of resolving the contradictions of democratic revolution by democratic-revolutionary means was bankrupt, Stalin and other Bolsheviks refused to see this. They continued to insist that two quite distinct revolutions resolved two quite distinct contradictions and forced this theory on a number of poor countries, including China, bringing many revolutions to ruin. The Chinese Revolution of 1925–7 failed for several reasons, but the first and most fundamental one was Stalin and Bukharin's adherence to the method of democratic revolution. They said that because the Chinese Revolution was bourgeois, the workers should do as the bourgeois political parties told them, and the CCP should join the Guomindang and not act independently. In a word, it should not transcend the scope of bourgeois-democratic revolution. The result was that when the revolutionary forces upon which the bourgeoisie had been relying started to demand concessions, the bourgeois forces carried out a massacre of the workers and the communists, delivered to them in chains by Stalin. To put it 'philosophically,' the top leaders at the time had abided by the instruction to 'resolve contradiction A with method A and not with method non-A.'

Mao never drew the lessons from the defeat, never dropped the formula, and always insisted on 'strictly observing' its principles. How was the new revolution that opened up after the Second World War (and that Mao dominated) won? As with the previous defeat, the reasons were many and various. But looked at from the subjective point if view, Mao and the party centre said one thing and did another. They verbally adhered to the method of people's democratic revolution to resolve the tasks of democratic revolution but in reality, under the sway of events, they took a path other than that of democratic revolution and, within the areas they controlled, reignited the land war. They hit the bourgeoisie and the Guomindang with full force, 'dared to win,' and 'dared to seize power at national level.' They 'resolved by means of socialist revolution the contradictions of democratic revolution' and thus, in a sense, implemented a strategy of permanent revolution. This was the main reason for their victory. In the next seven years,[20] when trying to explain their victory from the point of view of theory, their constant inveighing against permanent revolution was the best measure of its pertinence. That the CCP later took everyone by surprise by subscribing to it doesn't mean they understood it. Their astonishing about-turn had ulterior motives (which I mentioned earlier and will return to later). However, if permanent revolution as the only plausible theory of the course of revolution in poor countries had not, like a force of nature, taken the CCP by storm, Mao would never have made the slightest concession to it, even in words.

Sadly, Mao failed to see that resolving the democratic contradiction by permanent revolution was the opposite of the 'strictly observing' principle. Had he stuck with it in fact rather than on paper, in obedience to the 'dialectical law' that different methods must be applied to different contradictions, then the revolution, however favourable its circumstances, would have faltered at the

---

20 In September 1956, Liu Shaoqi told the Eighth Congress that the People's Democratic Dictatorship had 'already, in essence, become a form of proletarian dictatorship.' Since the Second Plenum (in May 1958), the term 'permanent revolution' has been openly used (naturally it is explained in a special way) (note by Wang).

point of completion or soon afterwards. But Mao cannot see that, so if he were to rewrite *On Contradiction* now, he would not change the mechanical theorem that 'contradiction A must be resolved by method A.'

Does all that have anything to do with philosophy, or do I make too much of it? In fact, *On Contradiction* provides the philosophical basis for Mao's tactical genius. 'Pure' philosophers may pooh-pooh the relationship between revolutionary tasks and revolutionary methods, but for theorists of practical revolution it is a supremely philosophical issue. Since in that respect I am at one with Mao, I have every right to dwell on the issue.

To illustrate the principle of 'using the same means to resolve different contradictions,' I pointed out that Lenin applied the strategic line of socialist revolution to resolve the contradictions in both February and October, and that Mao, in leading China's democratic revolution between 1947 and 1949, went against his own subjective wishes and led an essentially socialist rather than a democratic revolution to victory. So it is not true that '[q]ualitatively different contradictions can only be resolved by qualitatively different methods.' Why could Mao not accept the theory of permanent revolution in an all-sided, consistent, principled way? At least in part, because he failed to grasp the general law of contemporary world revolution, especially in poor countries.

An A-type contradiction can be resolved only by an A-type method. That's true as far as it goes, as I have already said. But like the formula 'A is equal to A, A is not equal to B,' it is true only within limits. It is preliminary, and it belongs to formal logic. In more advanced logic, i.e., in dialectics, the formula 'A is not equal to A, A might be equal to B' is not only not absurd but even truer, and even more in line with the innate objective laws of things and of reason. So an A-type contradiction cannot, perversely, always be resolved by an A-type method and must sometimes be resolved by a B-type one – this is not formal logic, but it is fully in line with dialectical thinking. Mao's argument that an 'A-type contradiction must be resolved by an A-type method' is high dialectics and a principle that must be strictly observed shows how little he knows about it.

Does dialectics therefore mean that the same stereotyped, repetitive, and immutable formula can be mechanically and arbitrarily applied anywhere, at will? Of course not. In fact, the question applies far more so to those who apply democratic methods to democratic revolutions and socialist methods to socialist revolutions against all the evidence. Sometimes contradictions in democratic revolutions must be resolved by democratic means and sometimes by socialist means. By mechanically and arbitrarily applying his rigid formula to a fundamental strategic issue in democratic revolution, that of permanent revolution, Mao forfeits elevation to the status of a great strategist and will be remembered only as a great tactician and man of action.

According to Lenin, 'In specific conditions one must raise specific political tasks. All is relative, all is fluid, all is mutable.'[21] Mao ignored half of this and complied with the other half. In one sense, he failed to understand it: in another, he fully mastered it. He failed to understand it in its most fundamental, significant, and principled strategic sense. Human history has already entered the era of world proletarian revolution, but Mao still clings to the old idea that democratic revolution in poor countries must by resolved by democratic-revolutionary methods, a fatal weakness. He fully masters it in its secondary, tactical sense. In that sense, he is highly intelligent and elastic. He is even better at nominating tasks to suit conditions than Stalin was. Tactical skills like the ability to change according to the situation, stoop or stand, give tit for tat, and act 'rationally and with restraint' indubitably reflected a dialectical approach, as I argued in the chapter on tactics. In *On Contradiction*, particularly in the fourth section on 'the principal contradiction and the principal aspect of a contradiction,' Mao summed up his own tactical genius. He gave examples of the application of dialectics to tactics, which, though not philosophical, are well worth studying, and he revealed in abstract philosophical language, and with great clarity, the roots in thought of his political opportunism. He said:

> There are many contradictions in the process of development of a complex thing, and one of them is necessarily the principal contradiction whose existence and development determine or influence the existence and development of the other contradictions. For instance, in capitalist society the two forces in contradiction, the proletariat and the bourgeoisie, form the principal contradiction. The other contradictions [...] are all determined or influenced by this principal contradiction.

This is true, but he then went on to say:

> In a semi-colonial country such as China, the relationship between the principal contradiction and the non-principal contradictions presents a complicated picture.
> When imperialism launches a war of aggression against such a country, all its various classes, except for some traitors, can temporarily unite

---

21 The source of this quotation is unknown. Matthew Zhang, in a personal communication, thinks it might be a mangling of Lenin's quoting in 'The Economic Content of Narodism and the Criticism of it in Mr Struve's Book (The Reflection of Marxism in Bourgeois Literature)' of a sentence by Mikhailovsky ('But life,' he [Mikhailovsky] adds, 'is never made up of absolute contradictions: in life everything is mobile and relative, and at the same time all the separate sides are in a state of constant interaction'), but notes that Lenin is rather critical of the statement.

in a national war against imperialism. At such a time, the contradiction between imperialism and the country concerned becomes the principal contradiction, while all the contradictions among the various classes within the country (including what was the principal contradiction, between the feudal system and the great masses of the people) are temporarily relegated to a secondary and subordinate position. [...]

But in another situation, the contradictions change position. When imperialism carries on its oppression not by war, but by milder means – political, economic and cultural – [...] the masses often resort to civil war.[22]

These sentences are riddled with errors. But because they are the philosophical rationale for thirty years of Mao and Stalin's joint management of the Chinese Revolution, they merit detailed study.

Social contradictions are always complex, especially in colonial or semi-colonial countries. To know these societies, as Mao said, one must first know the contradictions and grasp the main one. In circumstances in which social and national relations change constantly, the contradictions keep swapping places, with the primary becoming secondary and vice versa. As a merely abstract, algebraic formula, this makes perfect sense. Problems arise when one substitutes real values for the variables. According to Mao, the relationship between the national and the class contradiction over the past thirty to forty years has, because of various forms of imperialist oppression, kept changing. When the national contradiction becomes primary, class contradictions are relegated to a secondary position and must become subordinate. In other words, when the ruling class of colonial or semi-colonial countries is forced to fight foreign invaders, the ruled class at home must stop class struggle and solidarise with the ruling class against the external foe. Once the war is won and the national crisis is over, the national contradiction becomes secondary and the class contradiction automatically becomes primary. At that point, class interests reign supreme, and the workers and peasants' revolutionary party can go all out in leading the class struggle.

This idea of Mao's is not new. In Europe's Great War, the social-traitors of the Second International also advocated 'civil peace,' using a Mao-style theory of transposed contradictions. Lenin, however, proposed using the war to topple the ruling class, and was denounced as a 'German agent' or, less stridently, for 'ignoring the distinction between primary and secondary contradictions.' Obviously Mao stood with Lenin on this point of history, but why, following Stalin,

---

22   Mao, 'On Contradiction,' August 1937, SW, vol. 1, pp. 311–47, at 331.

did he call in the Second World War for 'civil peace'? Why did the CCP stop the civil war during the Resistance to Japan? Because the main contradiction was with German fascism and Japanese imperialism. To catch the bandits, first catch the king – first resolve the main contradiction, by relegating class struggle in the democratic camp (whether in imperialist or colonial countries) to a secondary position and subordinating domestic revolutionary interests to those of the foreign war. But would that not also have held in the Great War? According to the social-patriots, it did. Socialists in the Entente countries said German militarism was the main threat to world peace, so the principal contradiction was between militarism and anti-militarism; members of the Triple Alliance denounced the Tsar's brutal rule, and declared that the principal contradiction was between the barbaric East and Western civilisation represented by Germany. Lenin disdained this search for the 'principal contradiction' and said (a) that both two sides were imperialist and (b) the revolutionary contradiction was ripening everywhere, so it was the job of socialists in every country to overthrow the ruling class and end capitalism by means of revolution. Before the main contradiction between socialist revolution and capitalist rule, all other contradictions paled into insignificance. That's how Lenin decided his basic strategy. Should we blame him for not ranking the contradictions into major and minor? In the Second World War, had the transformation of militarism into Nazism made Lenin's approach outdated and redundant? Obviously, Stalin and Mao seemed to have abandoned Lenin's teachings on this point and to have gone over to the position of the Second International.

In China, however, Mao could speak with greater boldness and assurance, for China was a semi-colonial country, Japan was imperialist, and the Chinese war, under whatever leadership, was just, progressive, and even revolutionary. Had not Lenin said that we should oppose both sides with revolution in an imperialist war but support colonial countries in an anti-imperialist war? Clearly, the Sino-Japanese War was not a war between imperialists. Chinese revolutionaries should firmly support China. But how to support China? By keeping up class struggle, or ending class struggle? That was the main question. To answer it, one must review the second focus of attention in Lenin's strategy of civil war: had the Chinese workers been faced with revolutionary tasks, in particular the seizure of power? If not, as a result of international and domestic conditions, and if they were unlikely to be in the near future, then they could participate in a progressive war under bourgeois leadership against imperialist invaders only in an ancillary role, hell-bent on victory and going all out to win patriotic sympathy, in order to improve their political and social standing. For in this war, the class contradictions would come second to the national one. Otherwise, even in a semi-colonial country fighting a foreign war, if capitalism is rampant and class struggle highly developed, if the democratic revolution is already underway, if it has already split into two, if the big bourgeoisie already has state power, so that the workers' party has already proposed seizing power in alliance with the peasants, the workers' party should put class first in any war with imperialism. For in war as in peace, the revolutionary party's central task is to gain power in order to complete first the democratic and then the socialist revolution. In wars, the rapacity and corruption of the ruling class is exposed far more clearly than usual, and the conditions are more favourable for revolution than in ordinary times, so to give up class struggle would be a crime. The policies adopted by a workers' party in such a war would be unlike those adopted in a reactionary imperialist war. In the former, it would aim to win victory in the revolution or to defend the revolution, in the latter, to bring about the defeat of its own ruling class. In the first sort of war, the party continues to fight for revolution because only revolution can rouse the toilers to join the war and only a workers and peasants' government, instead of a rotten government of the bourgeoisie, can win the war and overthrow imperialism. In the second, the party continues to fight for revolution for a simpler reason: the war is imperialist and for the ruling class, and only by overthrowing the government of the ruling class can the war be ended, in revolution. The specific application of these two approaches will vary; in essence, however, national contradiction (even in the form of war) should never exclude class contradiction, whether in colonial and semi-colonial or in imperialist countries. The workers' party's general strategy is to prepare for revolution, launch revolution, and achieve revolution. The two sorts of war differ only in the conditions in which the tactics form to realise it.

So from the point of view of the relationship of revolution and war, including in anti-imperialist wars led by the bourgeoisie, Mao's assertion that the principal contradiction constantly changes place is wrong. Instead, in any given historical era, the social contradiction continues to occupy the main position, or, even better, the most fundamental position, to which other contradictions are subordinate, it is the axis by which they are set and shaped and around which they spin. In the imperialist age, the age of world proletarian revolution, the main contradiction is between the bourgeoisie and the workers. This is true not only of capitalist countries but also of backward countries, as long as capitalist relations predominate (politically and economically) and there is a prospect of the working class, with peasant support, taking power. So Mao's argument that in semi-colonial countries like China 'the relationship between the principal contradiction and the non-principal contradiction is complex' and that China has no principal contradiction fixed for a specific historical period but just a whole number of complex contradictions (of which that between the bourgeoisie and the proletariat is merely one), that the primary and secondary ones change places in line with changes in the international and domestic political situation, is mistaken, and the theoretical source of his opportunism. There are many reasons why workers' parties become opportunist, but the most profound reason in thought is that their leaders forget that the contradiction between labour and capital is the contradiction of our times, the principal and central contradiction. On the other hand, a revolutionary party that knows and remembers only the main contradiction and ignores the contradiction between domestic and foreign interests and among and between social classes and strata other than the capitalists and the workers, that is not alive to changes in the situation, that eats without digesting, sees only red and white, and treats potential friends as enemies, with the aim of carrying out the purest, most ideal working-class revolution are also mistaken, and are dogmatists, 'infantile leftists,' and revolutionary Quixotes. Of the two, however, opportunism is the most pernicious.

The philosophical source of Mao's opportunism lies in his opportunistic or nihilistic understanding of the dialectical method. Different people have interpreted the dialectic in different ways, in antiquity and today and in China and the world. The dialectic has featured in philosophy for thousands of years, starting with Heraclitus and Plato in Europe and the *Book of Changes* and Laozi in China. The exposition of its laws was generally similar (though it differed in quality and depth), and its multifarious forms can be explained by the different times in which thinkers were seeking to grasp and apply it. Some were idealists, others materialists, some passive, others active, some opportunists, others revolutionaries. The dialectic in Hegel's and Marx's hands was more or less the same, except that Marx turned it on its head. Throughout the ages many idealist philosophers have striven to understand the dialectic. Their writings burst with the bright light of knowledge and intelligence, and they lay bare magical secrets of human life and the universe. But almost all of them are negative, sceptical, and sophistic. They tend to interpret natural history abstrusely and nihilistically; human history, in terms of cycles. That was because of the times they inhabited: the struggle with nature had, as yet, won few victories, and social relations had not yet become simplified, as they now are. As for class struggle, there was little cause for optimism. So the cyclical and repetitious properties of natural and social phenomena drove them (a) to think in dialectical terms and (b) to develop an abstruse, nihilistic world view, and a negative, sceptical, cynical, unconventional, and even brazen view of human life. The dialectic came into its own with Hegel, in whose hands it became for the first time positive and active. Although Hegel was an extreme idealist, his understanding of the dialectic was positive and revolutionary. The leap forward in natural science as a result of the industrial revolution and the liberation of the mind promoted by the French Revolution could not but have a positive and revolutionary effect on Hegel's great mind. After reviewing the history of dialectics, he pointed out that '[t]he fundamental prejudice here is that the dialectic has *only a negative result*.' He also said:

> But the Other is essentially not the empty negative or Nothing *which is commonly taken as the result of dialectics*, it is the Other of the first, the negative of the immediate; it is thus determined as mediated – and altogether contains the determination of the first. The first is thus essentially *contained* and *preserved* in the Other. – To hold fast the positive in *its* negative, and the content of the presupposition in the result, is the most important part of rational cognition.[23]

Lenin believed that Hegel's theory of 'sublation'[24] is crucial for understanding the dialectical method. He said: 'Not empty negation, not futile negation, *not sceptical* negation, vacillation and doubt is characteristic and essential in dialectics, – which undoubtedly contains the element of negation and indeed as its most important element – no, but negation as a moment of connection, as a moment of development, retaining the positive, i.e., without any vacillations, without any eclecticism.'[25] Marx richly applied Hegel's positive dialectical method, especially his 'negation as a moment of connection, as a moment of development,' to the study of the history of human society, and Lenin to the practice of world socialist revolution.

But that did not put and end to the negative, sceptical, opportunistic, and even non-revolutionary dialectic. Just as scientific advances have never eradicated superstition, so materialism has not ruled out idealism and the revolutionary dialectic has not put an end to the non-revolutionary, opportunistic, eclectic, negative, and nihilistic dialectic. In what follows, I look only at opportunism and the dialectic, given its importance for understanding Mao thought.

Earlier, I mentioned Marx's comment about dialectics and the petty bourgeoisie. Here's what he said:

> Proudhon had a natural inclination for dialectics. But as he never grasped really scientific dialectics he never got further than sophistry. This is in

---

23 Hegel's Science of Logic: The Absolute Idea, § 1795, quoted from Lenin's *Philosophical Notebooks*.
24 Wang uses the word *yangqi*.
25 Lenin, CW, vol. 38, p. 236.

fact connected with his petty-bourgeois point of view. Like the historian *Raumer*, the petty bourgeois is made up of on-the-one-hand and on-the-other-hand. This is so in his economic interests and *therefore* in his politics, religious, scientific and artistic views. And likewise in his morals, IN EVERYTHING. He is a living contradiction. If, like Proudhon, he is in addition an ingenious man, he will soon learn to play with his own contradictions and develop them according to circumstances into striking, ostentatious, now scandalous now brilliant paradoxes. Charlatanism in science and accommodation in politics are inseparable from such a point of view.[26]

There is much overlap between Mao and Proudhon, Raumer, and the petty bourgeois. Unlike Proudhon, Mao did his best to come to terms with the dialectic as a scientific method, but although he got quite a long way, 'he never got further than sophistry.'[27] He knows all about 'on the one hand' and 'on the other,' and he can always distinguish seventeen or eighteen different sides to a thing. Being quick-witted and resourceful, he quickly learned how to juggle contradictions, either to play scandalous tricks or to mount dazzling arguments. Although he never applied his charlatanry to natural (as opposed to social) science, he is a master of accommodation in politics. That is because, like Proudhon, he is a petty bourgeois. How is it that a communist leader who has worked for years to liberate the workers and peasants by revolution cannot rid himself of petty-bourgeois thinking? To a large extent because of his pre-Marxist social and intellectual background and the CCP's peasant base, but also because of the bureaucratic degeneration of the Soviet Union under Stalin and the spread of Stalinist bureaucracy and ideology throughout the world communist movement, which greatly contributed to Mao's Proudhon-style sophistry. Stalinist bureaucracy was initially based in the petty bourgeoisie. The main feature of its bureaucratic style is that it 'attends to each and every aspect of a matter' and 'transcends individual classes,' as a supposedly impartial arbiter. Mao's 'acting according to circumstances' is a consummate example of it.

If so, how could Mao lead the Chinese Revolution to victory? I tried to answer this question earlier. Let me now suggest another reason. Many factors, subjective and objective, contributed to the victory of the Chinese Revolution in 1949, and not all can be completely attributed to Mao's political line. Second,

---

26   Marx, 'On Proudhon [Letter to J.B. Schweizer],' January 24, 1865, MECW, vol. 20, p. 33.
27   Marx, Appendix to *The Poverty Of Philosophy*, MECW, vol. 20, p. 33.

although Mao's ideas and actions played a decisive role in the victory, opportunistic (or bureaucratic) political leaders can only play a negative role, unless they are forced to give up their opportunism. But in what way are they forced to give it up? This is the third point that needs explaining. Mao, as I have argued, acts first and thinks later. He is a man of action rather than a theorist. For him, theory justifies action rather than informs it. He is a tactician rather than a strategist. As a result, he is prone to empiricism and lacks foresight born of a lofty vision, so he is not a great revolutionary like Lenin. However, the same qualities ensure that, when acting, he is not constantly bound by wrong theories: he can improvise, accommodate his theories to his actions, or even divorce action and theory or set them at odds with each other. This disparity between words and deeds has greatly damaged Mao's reputation and status as a radical thinker, but in many respects, especially on occasions of rapid revolutionary advance, it helped him succeed, by counteracting the noxious effects of opportunism.

So the root cause, in terms of way of thinking, of Mao's political opportunism lies in his opportunistic understanding of the dialectic, which derives in turn from his inherent petty-bourgeois stance and his acquired 'supra-class' bureaucratic view. From such an angle, all contradictions are equivalent and can gain or lose in importance according to circumstance. To 'attend simultaneously to two or more things,' 'to benefit all sides,' to attend to all quarters and in all directions, far and near, left and right, and to be clear, logical, and persuasive: this ingeniously and exquisitely wrought approach, whereby anything is possible, has the outer shine of the dialectic but belongs in reality to the most contemptible sophistry. A fundamental reason for this approach is that such people completely deny absoluteness and immobility. For them everything is relative and in flux, and hence 'dialectical.' But to go one step further and conclude, even under given circumstances and within given temporal limits, that no absolute standard can apply, and, even within absolute change, simply to deny relative immobility, is to lapse into incurable sophistry. One must recognise that, in the age of capitalist imperialism and world proletarian revolution, the contradiction between capital and labour is principal and basic, the contradiction of contradictions. That is a conditional absolute. As long as historical circumstances remain unchanged, that will continue to be the case, the constant axis. That is the meaning of the dictum 'to change ten thousand times without leaving the original aim or stand,' 'to meet all changes by remaining unchanged.' If the conflict between capital and labour is presented as just one among many, class struggle can be dropped at will, to suit party policy – but then the party risks losing the people's trust and forfeiting its own reason for being.

CHAPTER 8

Literature and Art

In November 1905, Lenin wrote an article on 'Party Organization and Party Literature' that is constantly cited by Stalinists writing about literature and art. However, a close reading of it reveals big differences between his view and theirs.

In European languages, the word literature is the equivalent, in many contexts, of Chinese *wenxue*, meaning creative literature. However, it also has other meanings, such as 'documents,' 'publications,' and publishing in general. In ordinary political discourse, it is more likely to mean the latter than the former, but both meanings occur. In the first part of his article, Lenin uses it in the broad rather than the narrow sense, to mean documents or publications, while in the second, longer part he uses it more narrowly, to refer to creative writing. Those who quote him wrongly understand the term exclusively in the narrow rather than the broad sense. They also quote him out of context, in a one-sided and distorted way, as the opening paragraphs show:

> The new conditions for Social-Democratic work in Russia which have arisen since the October Revolution have brought the question of party literature to the fore. The distinction between the illegal and the legal press, that melancholy heritage of the epoch of feudal, autocratic Russia, is beginning to disappear. It is not yet dead, by a long way. [...]
>
> So long as there was a distinction between the illegal and the legal press, the question of the party and non-party press was decided extremely simply and in an extremely false and abnormal way. The entire illegal press was a party press, being published by organisations and run by groups which in one way or another were linked with groups of practical party workers. The entire legal press was non-party – since parties were banned – but it 'gravitated' towards one party or another. Unnatural alliances, strange 'bed-fellows' and false cover-devices were inevitable. The forced reserve of those who wished to express party views merged with the immature thinking or mental cowardice of those who had not risen to these views and who were not, in effect, party people.
>
> An accursed period of Aesopian language, literary bondage, slavish speech, and ideological serfdom! [...]
>
> The revolution is not yet completed. While tsarism is *no longer* strong enough to defeat the revolution, the revolution is *not yet* strong enough

to defeat tsarism. And we are living in times when everywhere and in everything there operates this unnatural combination of open, forthright, direct and consistent party spirit with an underground, covert, 'diplomatic' and dodgy 'legality.' This unnatural combination makes itself felt even in our newspaper. [...]

Be that as it may, the half-way revolution compels all of us to set to work at once organising the whole thing on new lines. Today literature, even that published 'legally,' can be nine-tenths party literature. It must become party literature. In contradistinction to bourgeois customs, to the profit-making, commercialised bourgeois press, to bourgeois literary careerism and individualism, "aristocratic anarchism" and drive for profit, the socialist proletariat must put forward the principle of *party literature*, must develop this principle and put it into practice as fully and completely as possible.

What is this principle of party literature? It is not simply that, for the socialist proletariat, literature cannot be a means of enriching individuals or groups: it cannot, in fact, be an individual undertaking, independent of the common cause of the proletariat. Down with non-partisan writers! Down with literary supermen! Literature must become *part* of the common cause of the proletariat, 'a cog and a screw' of one single great Social-Democratic mechanism set in motion by the entire politically-conscious vanguard of the entire working class. Literature must become a component of organised, planned and integrated Social-Democratic Party work.

[L]iterature must by all means and necessarily become an element of Social-Democratic Party work, inseparably bound up with the other elements. Newspapers must become the organs of the various party organisations, and their writers must by all means become members of these organisations. Publishing and distributing centres, bookshops and reading-rooms, libraries and similar establishments – must all be under party control. The organised socialist proletariat must keep an eye on all this work, supervise it in its entirety, and, from beginning to end, without any exception, infuse into it the life-stream of the living proletarian cause, thereby cutting the ground from under the old, semi-Oblomov, semi-shopkeeper Russian principle: the writer does the writing, the reader does the reading.[1]

---

1 Lenin, 'Party Organisation and Party Literature,' CW, vol. 10, pp. 44–49, at 46.

Lenin does not mean *belles lettres* but publications in general. That is why 'literature [...] can be nine-tenths party literature.' Those who claim that Lenin wanted to make creative writing 'part of the common cause of the proletariat' must explain the reference to '[p]ublishing and distributing centres, bookshops and reading-rooms, libraries and similar establishments' coming under party control. Why did he want to put political publications under party leadership? So they would fight for revolution, eschew slavish speech, and embrace party goals.

When Lenin published this article, in November 1905, the revolution was in full spate. Of all the new things the revolution caused to happen, the best was when the voice of big dumb Russia, mute for centuries, suddenly boomed out, on the streets and in the meeting places, and especially in the newspapers. Newspapers of all kinds, including *Izvestia* (the organ of the St Petersburg Soviet), the *Russian Gazette* (run by Trotsky and Alexander Parvus), and *New Life* (run by Lenin, Gorky, and Lunacharsky)[2] sprang up on all sides, founded by individual revolutionaries or literati or with a factional or party affiliation. However, few were 'open, forthright, direct and consistent' and most were meek, mealy-mouthed, and inhibited. This was mainly because the revolution had, at the time, gained only a partial victory, but it was also because of the immaturity of the parties and their members, whose bowing and scraping reflected their failure to keep pace with the revolution; or, in the case of steeled revolutionaries, because they feared the consequences of speaking out, so they beat about the bush, hid their views from sight, or spoke in a cryptic or ambiguous way, in order (as they themselves explained) to retain their legal status.

The latter attitude (commonplace in the early days of any revolution) was Lenin's main target. Lenin also attacked the non-party newspapers, which he said should become 'organs of the various party organisations, and their writers [should] become members of these organisations,' just as publishing and distributing centres, bookshops, reading-rooms, and libraries should come under party control. Lenin's contribution to the revolution was both as a political thinker and as an organiser. He said the party should be rigorously organised and disciplined and that it should lead and supervise all aspects of the revolution. His idea of organisation played an exceptionally important role in the

---

2 *Novaya Zhizn* (New Life) was a Bolshevik legal newspaper. Maxim Gorky (1868–1936) was a Russian and Soviet writer and activist and a founder of socialist realism. Anatoly Vasilyevich Lunacharsky (1875–1933) was the Soviet People's Commissar responsible for culture and education, and a poet, art critic, and journalist.

victory of the revolution. He fought at all times to realise his concept of the party. In November 1905, his excursion into the 'literary' field was part of that struggle. That is why he derided 'non-partisan writers' and 'literary supermen' and said that literature should become '"a cog and a screw" of one single great Social-Democratic mechanism set in motion by the entire politically conscious vanguard of the entire working class.'

Lenin was not calling for the overthrow of poets and novelists who failed to join the communist party. He was arguing that writers in or close to it should act under its leadership, in coordination with the revolutionary machine, as its 'cog and screw.' Otherwise, they would not be able to serve the revolution but would cause it losses.

After October 1905 in Russia, the relationship between literature and revolution (and the revolutionary party) became acute, which is why Lenin wrote his article. His target in the party was probably Gorky or Lunacharsky. At the time of *New Life*'s founding in St Petersburg, Lenin was still in Stockholm. The St Petersburg Soviet had just been set up and was becoming more and more influential, but the Bolsheviks took a sectarian attitude towards it, arguing that it should be organised on the basis of a strong party rather than as a workers' council. Lenin opposed the Bolsheviks on this, and wrote a long letter from Sweden for publication in *New Life*. The letter never actually appeared at the time, either because Lenin reached St Petersburg first or because it was suppressed by other Bolsheviks whose approach it contradicted. Whatever the case, within days Lenin had written 'Party Organization and Party Literature.' The temporal sequence perhaps explains Lenin's comment about 'legal' publications ignoring party supervision and leadership, and why he wanted to put the question of party literature on the agenda and settle the relationship between illegal and legal publications, party leadership and the party's publishing enterprise, and party leadership and special party literary activities. This is more or less what happened. However, Stalinist literary theorists have taken Lenin's article out of context, ignored its actual intention, and used snippets of it to tell the world that Marxist-Leninists want to put literary creation under party leadership.

In revolutionary periods, all literary (publishing) work by revolutionary writers bearing on the revolution must be closely monitored, put under party leadership, and coordinated with other revolutionary work; and the press must comply with party spirit and speak plainly of its intentions, without hemming and hawing, so as not to paralyse the masses' revolutionary awareness – this is what Lenin's article meant. However, at no point does it say that creative writing must be under the party's control and command and conform to its policies and slogans. That was Stalin's view, not Lenin's.

That is not to say that, in his article, Lenin ignored the question of the relationship between the party and creative writing, literature in the narrow sense. Lenin's reply to those who accused him of denying the absolute freedom of individual creation was as follows. (1) '[W]e are discussing party literature and its subordination to party control.' Naturally, '[e]veryone is free to write and say whatever he likes, without any restrictions,' but a revolutionary party is also free to 'expel members who use the name of the party to advocate anti-party views.' The party would inevitably break up, 'first ideologically and then physically,' if it did not stick to its platform and require its members, in all spheres (including literary work), to follow its leadership. Anyone who refuses to do so will be asked to leave. (2) 'Absolute freedom' is sheer hypocrisy. 'The freedom of the bourgeois writer, artist or actress is simply masked (or hypocritically masked) dependence on the money-bag, on corruption, on prostitution.' Socialists must 'expose this hypocrisy and rip off the false labels, not in order to arrive at a non-class literature and art (that will be possible only in a socialist extra-class society), but to contrast this hypocritically free literature, which is in reality linked to the bourgeoisie, with a really free one that will be *openly* linked to the proletariat.'[3]

So according to Lenin, writers keen to make revolution and help bring about human progress must join a revolutionary party and, in their literary work, comply with its platform, constitution, and resolutions. They cannot do as they please or write against the party, or they will be expelled from it, and lose the chance of serving the revolution. Second, socialists believe that literature exists in a class society and cannot but reflect or represent a class position. Supraclass non-class literature is an illusion. In revolutions, revolutionary writers must reflect and represent the interests of the proletariat, support the revolution, and create writing that is worthwhile and truly free. These two points of view, although linked to specific problems in the 1905 Revolution, are true everywhere, in essence, of a socialist party's attitude to writers and their writing. Sadly, though, Lenin's views have been distorted and abused. Stalin used them to justify imposing crude and extreme controls on literature and art, while ignoring these two passages:

1. There is no question that literature is least of all subject to mechanical adjustment or levelling, to the rule of the majority over the minority. There is no question, either, that in this field greater scope must undoubtedly be allowed for personal initiative, individual inclination, thought and fantasy, form and content.

---

3 Lenin, 'Party Organisation and Party Literature,' p. 46.

2. Far be it from us to advocate any kind of standardised system, or a solution by means of a few decrees. Cut-and-dried schemes are least of all applicable here.[4]

It is not difficult to see that Stalin's and Mao's policy on literature and art is poles apart from Lenin's. Stalin said of himself, 'I am not an expert in literature and, of course, not a critic.'[5] This sentence, while bathing the writer's sense of absolute superiority in self-deprecatory light, is in fact a painful confession of the truth, even though Stalin's writings, especially after the Second World War, were paraded as a model of Russian rhetoric and his views on literature and art as highest criticism. He did not even like literature and art, empty, helpless things, of no use in extending one's power and influence. So although touted as supreme authority in the art of language, he made no systematic, formal contribution to party policy (apart from a handful of letters). In fact, the spokesman for 'Stalin's view on literature and art' was Zhdanov,[6] his right-hand man.

Stalin first took notice of the problem of literature and art after his rival Trotsky made a speech on it, in the early 1920s. The civil war was over, NEP[7] had just started, and the Soviet literary and artistic scene was beginning to revive. Some young writers, and some old revolutionaries in charge of cultural and educational work, came up with the idea of 'proletarian culture' and 'proletarian art.' They argued that proletarian dictatorship, just like feudalism and capitalism, should have a culture that accorded with its own class views. They dismissed the cultural heritage of past class societies, severed all ties to tradition, and set out, solely on the basis of writers with a proletarian background, to create out of thin air a specifically proletarian culture. Lenin strongly opposed this revolutionary infantilism and artistic nihilism and denounced it as 'harmful.'[8] Rebuked by Lenin, the 'proletarians' turned to Trotsky, who said they were free to pursue their ideas, but he agreed with Lenin that proletarian literature and art was harmful and meaningless. In the summer of 1922 and the following summer, he wrote *Literature and Revolution*,[9] where he explained the party's view and set out some policy suggestions.

---

4 Ibid.
5 Stalin, 'Letter to Bezymensky,' March 19, 1930, translated in Kemp-Welch 1991, p. 84.
6 Zhdanov (1896–1948) was Stalin's close associate and helped develop his cultural policy.
7 In 1921 Lenin replaced war communism with NEP, which he called 'state capitalism.'
8 '[T]he All-Russia Proletcult Congress rejects in the most resolute manner, as theoretically unsound and practically harmful, all attempts to invent one's own particular brand of culture, to remain isolated in self-contained organisations' (Lenin, 'On Proletarian Culture,' October 8, 1920, CW, Vol. 31, pp. 316–17).
9 Trotsky 2005 [1925].

At first, Trotsky thought that 'proletarian literature' and 'proletarian culture' were impossible. Unlike feudal and bourgeois rule, which lasts for an entire historical period, the dictatorship of the proletariat would be over in decades, and would not have time to form a special culture. For culture, in Trotsky's view, was not the outstanding product of a specific writer in a specific work but 'the organic sum of knowledge and capacity which characterizes the entire society, or at least its ruling class.' Moreover, 'the dictatorship of the proletariat is not an organization for the production of the culture of a new society, but a revolutionary and military system struggling for it.' Under it, dynamic change focuses on politics and on revolution and war, both highly destructive of technology and culture. Finally, proletarian dictatorship differs from past forms of class rule in that its historical mission is not to consolidate class but to eradicate it; to create not a class culture but a classless culture, a socialist culture. However, a socialist culture is possible only on the basis of a socialist society, so it can only begin where proletarian dictatorship ends.

Does that mean that there is no cultural and artistic work during the transitional period in which proletarian dictatorship is the dominant form? Trotsky does not deny that a new culture must be constructed. However, he believes that '[t]he main task of the proletarian intelligentsia in the immediate future is not the abstract formation of a new culture regardless of the absence of a basis for it, but definite culture-bearing, that is, a systematic, planned and, of course, critical imparting to the backward masses of the essential elements of the culture which already exists.' He says: 'The working-class strives to transform the state apparatus into a powerful pump for quenching the cultural thirst of the masses. This is a task of immeasurable historic importance.' In short: 'Our epoch is not yet an epoch of new culture, but only the entrance to it, [...] to such an extent, at least, as to be able to pave the way for a new culture.'[10]

In the transitional period of the dictatorship of the proletariat, Trotsky argued that what can and must be produced is revolutionary literature and art – not proletarian literature and art, but literature and art for the proletariat. Such a literature and art would start 'from the point of view of what the proletariat reads, what it needs, what absorbs it, what impels it to action, what elevates its cultural level and so prepares the ground for a new art.'[11]

As for what attitude a workers' government should take towards writers and literature, Trotsky's advice was 'to allow them complete freedom of self-determination in the field of art, after putting before them the categorical

---

10   Trotsky 2005 [1925], pp. 158–9.
11   Trotsky 2005, p. 175.

standard of being for or against the Revolution.' The party should beware of taking sides between rival literary groups and should repel none, 'even from the intelligentsia, insofar as [such a group] tries to approach the revolution and to strengthen one of its links – a link is always a weak point – between the city and the village, or between the party member and the non-partisan, or between the intelligentsia and the workers.'[12]

That does not mean that the party should adopt a laissez-faire approach. It should play the leading role in culture too, but while taking into account its special nature:

> Marxism affords an opportunity to estimate the development of the new art, to trace its sources, to help the most progressive tendencies by critically illuminating the road, but it does no more than that. Art must make its own way and by its own means. Marxist methods are not the same as artistic methods. The party leads the proletariat but not the historic processes of history. There are domains in which the party leads, directly and imperatively. There are domains in which it only cooperates. There are, finally, domains in which it only orients itself. Art is not a domain in which the party is called upon to command. It can and must protect and help it, but it can only lead it indirectly. It can and must confer additional trust on art groups striving sincerely to approach the revolution and so help establish a revolutionary artistic form.[13]

Finally, Trotsky talked about the attitude revolutionary art should take. He deemed realism appropriate, but understood in his own way, as 'a realistic monism, in the sense of a philosophy of life, and not a "realism" in the sense of the traditional arsenal of literary schools.' Realism 'in the sense of a philosophy of life' meant 'a feeling for life as it is, [...] an artistic acceptance of reality, and not a shrinking from it, [...] an active interest in the specific stability and mobility of life.'[14] So Trotsky's realism meant that artists should take as their target life as it is lived, and should actively care about it. To realise this approach, revolutionary artists need not wrest realism from the literature of the past, but 'the new artist will need all the methods and processes evolved in the past, as well as a few supplementary ones, in order to grasp the new life [and] a preoccupation with our life of three dimensions as a sufficient and invaluable theme for art.'

---

12   Trotsky 2005, p. 180.
13   Trotsky, 'Communist Policy Toward Art,' 1923 (translation here adapted).
14   Trotsky 2005, ch. 7.

How to treat the theme? You can strive 'either to picture life as it is or to idealize it, either to justify or to condemn it, either to photograph it or generalize and symbolize it.'[15]

Trotsky was the first Marxist to discuss cultural policy in detail, in a book published more than forty years ago. Has *Literature and Revolution* stood the test of time? Trotsky was wrong about how long proletarian dictatorship would last, but he was right about proletarian art and culture, both in the Soviet Union and in the communist countries that have come into being since his assassination. If it has existed at all, it has simply been in the shape of an accelerated embrace of bourgeois culture, or in the inglorious shape of praise for the regime and its leaders.

When *Literature and Revolution* first appeared, Trotsky was under attack from Stalin and his then allies, who used every means to discredit him, including unscrupulous alliances with Trotsky's opponents. Trotsky had made enemies in the cultural world, whom Stalin befriended and protected. However, he did so not personally but through agents, principally Bukharin and Lunacharsky, together with some young and inexperienced 'proletarian writers.' With their help, he had Trotsky denounced as an anarchist and Menshevik at the First Conference of Proletarian Writers in January 1925, and for saying that 'the Marxian methods are not the same as the artistic.'[16] This criticism was trivial in itself, but it subsequently influenced Soviet policy on literature and art. Trotsky believed that Marxist method was not the same as artistic method. Mastery of the former was not necessary for mastery of the latter. A work of art might be good Marxism but bad art, and vice versa. Trotsky's opponents, on the other hand, believed that Marxist method and artistic method were one and the same, and that, in politics as in art, the 'law of class struggle' trumps all. The sole criterion for artistic excellence was the artist's grasp of Marxism. Poems and novels that read like *Pravda* editorials were declared works of genius. Tens of thousands of writers and artists were sent to labour camps – not least because of this 'political criterion.'

It took nearly ten years for this criterion to become firmly established. In June 1925, the Soviet leaders passed a resolution rejecting proletcult and largely adopting Trotsky's position. It proclaimed the freedom of literary factions, opposed the use of bureaucratic and 'commandist' methods to resolve literary problems, and denounced party arrogance, illiteracy, pomposity, and 'arbitrary and incompetent administrative interference' in literary affairs.[17] The resolu-

---

15   Trotsky 2005, p. 192.
16   Trotsky 2005, ch. 7.
17   Quoted in Serge 1932, pp. 50–1.

tion showed that the democratic plebeian spirit of October was not yet dead and that Lenin's view that literature and art is 'least of all subject to mechanical adjustment or levelling, to the rule of the majority over the minority,'[18] continued to hold sway.

The transition from Lenin to Stalin did not happen overnight. The political climate was changing, but not everywhere at the same speed. Thermidor came first in the party, government, and army, and only later in literature and art, though the direction was the same. Under the party's relatively liberal and laissez-faire cultural regime, literature and art flourished in the 1920s, so that since Stalin's death many Soviet literary historians look back on the period as a paradise lost, whether in poetry, fiction, drama, film, music, or painting. The achievements could never match those of Russian classical literature, but in style, breadth of spirit, boldness of vision, and aspiration, they surpassed those of earlier generations. The new cultural army, given time, would have dazzled not just Russia but the world. Sadly, however, reaction had triumphed by 1930. Stalin's bureaucratic dictatorship had taken over. In all areas of Soviet life, the spontaneous creativity of the people had been extinguished. The early literary and artistic harvests had come to an end. In 1930, the poet Mayakovsky committed suicide, a richly symbolic comment on the death of Soviet literature in the 1920s.

In those years, Stalin used the methods he had earlier used against Trotsky to eradicate the extreme left wing in literature and art, i.e., members of proletcult, who were accused of being saboteurs, enemies of the people, and Trotskyists and were either gaoled or killed. Most of the better-known writers and artists were criticised at meetings and forced to make a self-criticism, as a warning to others. They then had a choice – dance to the official tune or face destruction. The early 1930s were terrible years for men and women of talent in the Soviet Union.

On April 23, 1932, the AUCP(b) resolved to 'restructure' its literary and artistic organisation, and it set about purging Soviet cultural circles.[19] In August and September 1934, the first Congress of Soviet Writers passed its statutes and published a speech by Zhdanov,[20] which thereafter formed the supreme instruction on literature and art, in the Soviet Union and abroad, including in the CCP. The spirit of the 1925 resolution on literature vanished from sight. The new statutes decreed for the first time that literature must serve the party and

---

18 Lenin, 'Party Organisation and Party Literature,' p. 46.
19 Resolution of the Central Committee of the All-Union Communist Party, 'On the Restructuring of Literary Artistic Organisations,' April 23, 1932.
20 See Zhdanov 1977.

the regime. A new principle of Soviet literary creation was announced – socialist realism. To borrow Hu Feng's[21] metaphor, knives dangled over the heads of Soviet writers, cutting off creativity in the bud and many a creative head.

Mao's ideas about literature and art are entirely inherited from Stalin. Next to none of them can be called his own, except for their narration and explanation, which has a Sinified veneer. Stalin's policy on literature and art claims to be based on Lenin's 1905 article and in opposition to Trotsky's theory. The same goes for Mao's. Mao cites Lenin to show that proletarian literature and art is one part of the entire revolutionary cause, a cog and a screw in the machine; and attacks Trotsky, for advocating 'politics–proletarian; literature–bourgeois.'[22] But in reality, Mao never really understood Lenin and had never read Trotsky. He had merely allowed himself to be deceived by Stalin and Zhdanov, who misinterpreted Lenin to him, and accepted Stalin's slanderous attack on Trotsky. Although he is always telling people to 'investigate and research,' he failed to follow his own advice, at least in this case.

Immediately after his comments about cogs and screws, Lenin wrote: '"All comparisons are lame," says a German proverb. So is my comparison of literature with a cog, of a living movement with a mechanism.' To point out the defects in his comparison, he went on to say:

> There is no question that literature is least of all subject to mechanical adjustment or levelling, to the rule of the majority over the minority. There is no question, either, that in this field greater scope must undoubtedly be allowed for personal initiative, individual inclination, thought and fantasy, form and content. All this is undeniable; but all this simply shows that the literary side of the proletarian party cause cannot be mechanically identified with its other sides. [...] There is no question that literature must by all means and necessarily become an element of Social-Democratic Party work, inseparably bound up with the other elements.

However, he denied that he was advocating 'any kind of standardised system, or a solution by means of a few decrees. Cut-and-dried schemes are least of all applicable here.'[23]

---

21 Hu Feng (1902–1985) was a Chinese writer and literary theorist gaoled in 1955 as the alleged ringleader of an anti-party clique and was not cleared until 1980.
22 Mao, 'Talks at the Yenan Forum on Literature and Art,' May 1942, SW, vol. 3, pp. 69–98, at 86.
23 Lenin, 'Party Organisation and Party Literature,' p. 46.

So Lenin did not want to subject literature and art to party control. There were limits to his cog-screw metaphor. The relationship between writers and artists and the party should be one of mutual benefit – the party must respect the specificity of each sector of its work and guarantee individual creativity; while writers and artists, for their part, should, of their own accord, on the basis of a clear understanding of what is needed, and while retaining their full independence, put literature and art at the service of the revolution. For Lenin, the two things were inseparable: literature must be 'a cog and a screw' in the revolutionary machine, and under party control; and the party, while exercising control, must see that literature remains free and independent. Why inseparable? Because, without the first, literature ran the risk of degenerating into 'bourgeois literary careerism and individualism, 'aristocratic anarchism' and drive for profit,' and the revolution would lose one of its most powerful weapons; and without the second, writing would stay mechanical, flat, and uniform. Any bias either way would harm (1) literature and art and (2) the revolution. Lenin never subsequently returned to the issue, but his late articles on Tolstoy and his attitude to proletcult show that he stuck by his position.

Although not himself a writer (in the creative sense), Lenin appreciated literature and had a good grasp of Marxist aesthetics, though 'Party Organization and Party Literature' was not a meticulous exposition of the latter but purely political in scope. However, his unfocused comments specify two essential preconditions for good writing and painting: (1) greater scope for 'personal initiative [and] individual inclination' and (2) greater scope for 'thought and fantasy, form and content.' His main purpose was to turn individualistic literature and art into collective literature and art – metaphorically, into cogs and screws of a machine. However, because he was neither ignorant of nor indifferent to literature and art, he switched, after first talking of the need for revolutionary collectivism, to a discussion of the need for literary and artistic 'individualism,' in a display of dialectical genius. The revolution required collectivism and discipline, to which writers and artists should submit. Otherwise, they not only cannot help the revolution but might even hinder or prevent it. That is why writers and artists must openly support the revolution, as its cogs and screws. On the other hand, even as cogs and screws they must not forget that they are writers and artists, and must strive to excel as such. How should this be done? Obviously not by submitting to party orders, for literary and artistic creation is inseparable from individual talent and natural endowment and the process of creation is individual not to say individualistic. Nowadays, quite a lot of creative writing in China is collective, as is most architecture and film. However, if collective literature and art is to have a unified style, it needs a guiding spirit of the sort that comes in ones, to which extent it remains individual.

Writing and painting is the product of 'individual initiative, individual inclination.' Without the former, collective creation is impossible: without the latter, there can be no creative enthusiasm. That is why Lenin, while advocating party literature, asked that the writer's and the artist's 'individual initiative, individual inclination' be given 'greater scope,' greater leeway, greater freedom of movement. He also said that 'greater scope' should be given to 'thought and fantasy, form and content.' In other words, literature and art should not come under party constraints. It was as if Lenin had taken a look into the future, in which leaders of the revolution forbid fantasies and stipulate the one possible form of 'socialist literature and art.'

Stalin's and Mao's idea of literature and art was, at its simplest, an appropriation of Lenin's cogs-and-screws metaphors but without the corrections and qualifications, and taken to absurd lengths. In September 1934, the Soviet Writers' Association issued a set of guidelines on literature and literary criticism, which boiled down to two criteria: it must be directly and closely linked to the current policy of the party and the Soviet government; and socialist realism is the main principle of literary creation in the Soviet Union. In his famous speech on literature and art at the Yan'an Forum, Mao repeated the criterion as follows: 'Party work in literature and art occupies a definite and assigned position in party revolutionary work as a whole and is subordinated to the revolutionary tasks set by the party in a given revolutionary period.'[24]

The idea that literature and art must serve the party and the government can be explained as an application and extension of Lenin's cogs-and-screws idea, but only by distorting and toxifying it. The first harmful effect of this attitude is that literary activity becomes mere propaganda. Art is not for art's sake. A good book or painting must have deep ties to human life and mirror its times. In a revolutionary age, writers and artists who do not join the revolution cannot be good and even less so great. On the other hand, deep and successful revolutions are prefigured in literature and art and give rise to a new literature and art that conforms to their spirit. In contemporary revolutions,[25] revolutionary parties

---

24   Mao did not mention socialist realism, but that was because China was still in the New Democratic stage. However, he went along with it in spirit though not in name (note by Wang).

25   The revolutionary focus on literature and art is a modern phenomenon. The CCP's massive and systematic organisation of song-and-dance troupes and its intimate linking of mass cultural activities with military and political work in the revolution is practically unprecedented. After the October Revolution in Russia, during the civil war, cultural troupes worked in some war zones and even at the front, but never on the same scale as in China. This 'cog-and-screw' cultural work started in the Stalin era in the Soviet Union, at more or less the same time as the party took absolute control of literature and art. In

use all forms of literature and art to engage in propaganda and create a cultural army to match the other army. The relationship between culture and revolution is always close, and necessarily so. But that does not mean that revolutionary literature and art, and even general literature and art, can and should be no more than singing and dancing for the revolution, that it should perform to order, as camp-followers of the revolution, and produce a song or playlet for each new movement and each new slogan.

It is right that revolutionary literature and art should contribute richly to the revolution. In an age in which theatre, film, radio, television, and the press, including books and newspapers, have become part of people's daily lives, writers need not put down the pen to join the revolution. The revolution offers them a broad field on which to battle with their weapons of choice. They know it not from the outside but from the inside. They experience life at war not indirectly but directly.

But are 'cultural assignments' and song-and-dance troupes the only possible form of revolutionary literature and art? Is all other literature and art by definition not revolutionary and destined to be overthrown? These are questions I will try to answer later.

The second harmful effect of bending literature and art to the service of the party is that their specificity is ignored. In his Yan'an Talks, Mao talked about two criteria for literary artistic criticism, political and cultural. There's nothing wrong with that in principle, but the problem is how to apply and treat them. Trotsky's view was as follows:

> Our standard is, clearly, political, imperative and intolerant. But for this very reason, it must define the limits of its activity clearly. For a more precise expression of my meaning, I will say: we ought to have a watchful revolutionary censorship, and a broad and flexible policy in the field of art, free from petty partisan maliciousness.[26]

---

the past, revolutionaries' attitude towards literature and art was one of either indifference or contempt. After England's Puritan Revolution in the seventeenth century, theatres were closed and actors and playwrights were threatened with prosecution. However, the lack of a 'cultural army' did not prevent the emergence of a new culture. Although the Puritans were hostile to literature and art, they had a great poet in John Milton. Revolutionary parties in different times have taken different attitudes to literature and art, a fact for which there are many explanations. I intend to look no further into it, except to remind readers of the adage 'plant a garden and no flowers grow, poke a stick in the mud and it becomes a tree' – such, too, is the case in the relationship between the revolutionary party and literature and art (note by Wang).

26 Trotsky, 'Communist Policy Toward Art.'

Mao's view was:

> [A]ll classes in all class societies invariably put the political criterion first and the artistic criterion second. The bourgeoisie always shuts out proletarian literature and art, however great their artistic merit. The proletariat must similarly distinguish among the literary and art works of past ages and determine its attitude towards them only after examining their attitude to the people and whether or not they had any progressive significance historically.[27]

At first sight, they look the same. Both identify two criteria, both put politics first. However, each has a fundamentally different spirit. Trotsky limits the party and the government's intervention to politics. He wants a watchful censorship and explicit political constraints, so that writers and artists can see at a glance what is allowed and what not. Beyond that, they can write and paint what they like, each after his or her own fashion, without being ordered about by the authorities, for the party's role is that of passively guarding against mistakes in the political sphere rather than actively applying political criteria to literature and art. With Mao, it is the other way round. Politics takes precedence over literature and art, so political criteria are at the same time literary and artistic criteria. Politics takes command, not only of art and literature's political content but of its artistic content. As a result, there are only political criteria and no literary or artistic criteria. For all the talk about 'the unity of politics and art, of content and form, of revolutionary political content and the perfection of artistic form,' as long as politics has the right to interfere closely and extensively with writing and painting, then no matter how the 'struggle on two fronts' is waged, the sole outcome will be that politics reigns and literature and art is reduced to sloganising.

Trotsky's prescription sticks strictly to political questions and only allows the political criterion to intervene in a clearly defined and circumscribed way, thus guaranteeing the artistic criterion, i.e., ensuring the vigour and integrity of the development of literature and art. Mao's, in contrast, is both political and artistic, and sets no clear limits in either regard. It concerns itself with everything under the sun. It requires writers and artists to obey the party in all things. The subject matter of writing and painting must conform with the party's needs at any given moment. Its 'thoughts and fantasies, form and con-

---

27   Mao, 'Talks at the Yenan Forum on Literature and Art,' May 1942, SW, vol. 3, pp. 69–98, at 89.

tent' must always obey orders and submit to the leadership. As for Lenin's 'individual initiative, individual inclination,' and the like, it is 'bourgeois' or 'petty-bourgeois' and must be cast aside.

The relationship between political and artistic criteria as conceived by Mao can only mean the destruction of the latter by the former. Artistic criteria are irrelevant. Perfection is beyond reach, greatness even more so. To advocate political leadership of literature and art down to the smallest detail and subordinating artistic criteria to political criteria is to deny that literary and artistic creativity has its own unique path. Some high-up politicians believe that works of literature and art are products like any other. First lay your plans and make known your commands and specifications, then sit back and wait. But although literature and art are the product of labour, they are a special kind of product, delicate and subtle. They have special characteristics, and (as Lenin pointed out) resist convention, mechanical levelling, uniformity, and majoritarianism. They cannot be reduced to simple labour.

Mao tackles the question from a different angle. He told the Yan'an Forum: 'In discussing a problem, we should start from reality and not from definitions. We would be following a wrong method if we first looked up definitions of literature and art in textbooks and then used them to determine the guiding principles for the present-day literary and artistic movement and to judge the different opinions and controversies that arise today.' He ignored the specificity of literature and art, and started out 'from objective facts, not from abstract definitions, [to] derive guiding principles, policies and measures.'[28]

But is it enough, in formulating party policy on literature and art, simply to lay out the current political situation and class relations? Unless one starts by recognising that literary and artistic creation have special properties, how can one formulate a plan 'in accordance with the objective needs of the situation' for this special 'production department'? How can one issue commands and set targets? Of course one must study the political situation before drafting propaganda outlines and political resolutions, but not as a premise for directing literary and artistic work. For the latter purpose, the main (though not sole) thing is to start out not from 'objective facts' but from the definitions – definitions derived not from textbooks but from a study of the unique properties of literary and artistic work. Without that, how can the party form an attitude and policy, exercise leadership, and use literature and art to promote revolution? In the absence of such an understanding, the cogs and screws of literature and art

---

28   Mao, 'Talks at the Yenan Forum on Literature and Art,' May 1942, SW, vol. 3, pp. 69–98, at 74.

will be treated in the same way as all other cogs and screws in the revolutionary machine, using the same methods of command, leading not to a bumper harvest but to a cultural famine.

What is literature and art? There is no need to trot out the classic definitions. However, one question does require an answer: what are the special features of literary and artistic production? Because only when those special features have been identified can the party avoid violating them, cause literature and art to flourish, and, in so doing, benefit the revolution.

According to Marxism, literature and art are 'superstructure.' Their form and development are, to a certain degree, determined by society's material foundation. They conform to this foundation, and reflect the society and times built on it. However, this relationship cannot be understood mechanically. In his *Contribution to the Critique of Political Economy*, Marx said: 'As regards art, it is well known that some of its peaks by no means correspond to the general development of society; nor do they therefore to the material substructure, the skeleton as it were of its organisation.'[29] So mechanical determinism and reflection have no place in Marxism. These relations of production will not necessarily produce that kind of book or painting; the level of development (high or low) of production does not determine whether a book or painting is good or bad; class relations in a society or an epoch are not faithfully produced, as in a photograph, in books and paintings. In a fundamental and long-term sense, literature and art may be shaped by 'objective facts' and adapt to or reflect them, but in another, not insignificant sense, they are apparently unfettered by them, and act independently and of their own accord. This is always true of superstructures: they drift free of the base on which they rest, to a greater or lesser extent. And literature and art are freest and drift furthest.

Why? Because of their special properties. Among past Marxists, Russia's Plekhanov had the greatest affinity with literature and art. He applied Marxism to the history of literature and art in Europe to outstanding effect. He argued that only historical materialism can explain the history of the development of literature and art. However, he also said that some 'reservations' applied. Literature and art's 'reflecting' of the objective world was not just a matter of understanding or becoming acquainted with it. He said in his *The Development of the Monist View of History*:

> [W]e shall tell Mr Mikhailovsky that it is possible that in questions affecting the development of ideology, even those best acquainted with the

---

29   Marx, MECW, vol. 28, p. 46.

'string'[30] will sometimes prove powerless if they don't possess a certain particular gift, namely artistic feeling. Psychology adapts itself to economy. But this adaptation is a complex process, and in order to understand its whole course and vividly to represent it to oneself and to others, as it actually takes place, more than once the talent of the artist will be needed.[31]

So artistic feeling and artistic talent are not the same as grasping objective or historical facts. Marxism, political education, or 'political criteria' can provide such an understanding, but they cannot bestow feeling or generate talent. Starting out from 'objective facts' can, at most, lead to a right understanding of the needs of the times.

Marxism does not use the same methods as literature and art. Is art therefore unfathomably subtle, inexplicably mysterious? I think not. Literary and artistic activity is emotional rather than rational, imaginative rather than documentary, subconscious rather than conscious, simple and natural rather than analytical, image-borne rather than theory-borne, and expressive and performative rather than expository and discursive. It tends to be individual rather than collective,[32] inwardly rather than outwardly driven, sincere and voluntary, and free of hypocrisy, affectation, and unnaturalness. These qualities are inherent in literary and artistic creation. In their absence, or if they are violated, writers and painters become mere lapdogs.

Lenin, like Marx and Engels, always treated political and artistic criteria separately, rather than confuse the two or rank them. As a revolutionary politician, he was very strict about ideological questions. Regarding literature and art, especially works with a strong intellectual content, he focused first on the writer or artist's ideological stance and the work's ideological content, dissecting it with his Marxist scalpel. However, he applied artistic as well as political and ideological criteria to establish its status and value. He scrupulously distinguished between the two, and strove to keep them apart. For example, he said of Tolstoy:

> The contradictions in Tolstoy's works, views, doctrines, in his school, are indeed glaring. On the one hand, we have the great artist, the genius who

---

30   Used here to denote development of the productive forces (note by Wang).
31   G.V. Plekhanov, *The Development of the Monist View of History*, ch. 5, pt. 4.
32   Great writers speak for their times. Literary and artistic geniuses are not divorced from their communities and do not come from nowhere. Their thinking and creative passion are not just their own. That is not to say that art must be collective (note by Wang).

has not only drawn incomparable pictures of Russian life but has made first-class contributions to world literature. On the other hand we have the landlord obsessed with Christ. [...] On the one hand, the most sober realism, the tearing away of all and sundry masks; on the other, the preaching of one of the most odious things on earth, namely, religion, the striving to replace officially appointed priests by priests who will serve from moral conviction, i.e., to cultivate the most refined and, therefore, particularly disgusting clericalism.

Lenin focused on two aspects of the Tolstoy contradiction, his genius as a writer and his reactionary and confused politics. Tolstoy bitterly opposed social injustice and reflected both the strengths and the weaknesses of the 'great ocean' of the Russian peasantry, redeemable only by social revolution. But Lenin described Tolstoy's doctrine as 'certainly utopian and [...] reactionary in the most precise and most profound sense of the word.'[33] Lenin did not ignore Tolstoy's reactionary ideas because of his artistic genius, but nor did he deny his artistic achievements because of his reactionary ideas.

Engels was an outstanding artist in his own right, a writer of great talent whose letters and articles on literary themes are models of Marxist literary criticism. His writings on Balzac and Goethe were in the same vein as Lenin's on Tolstoy and Gorky, and confirm that political and artistic criteria are not the same thing. Engels knew Balzac was a royalist, but he called him 'a far greater master of realism than all the Zolas *passés, présents et a venir* [past, present and future].' How could such a reactionary create great works of art? Because, according to Engels, he adopted the right methods. Engels (writing in English) said: 'The realism I allude to may crop out even in spite of the author's opinions.'[34] A writer's creative style is not a matter of conscious choice. It is shaped by nurturing and innate artistic talent rather than by a writer's ideas. Good ideas do not necessarily make for good art, or bad ideas for bad art. The quality of a book or painting depends on the writer's or artist's creative method, which the writer or artist chooses on the grounds of his or her artistic talent and nurturing.

Engels said of Goethe:

> In his works Goethe's attitude to contemporary German society is a dual one. Sometimes he is hostile towards it; he attempts to escape from

---

33　Lenin, 'Leo Tolstoy as the Mirror of the Russian Revolution,' CW, vol. 15, pp. 202–9.
34　Engels, 'Letter to Margaret Harkness in London,' April 1888, in Marx and Engels 1953.

what he finds repulsive in it. [...] But then sometimes he is on friendly terms with it, 'accommodates' himself to it. [...] [T]here is a continuing battle within him between the poet of genius who feels revulsion at the wretchedness of his environment, and the cautious offspring of the Frankfurt patrician or the Weimar privy-councillor who finds himself compelled to come to terms with and accustom himself to it. Goethe is thus at one moment a towering figure, at the next petty; at one moment an obstinate, mocking genius full of contempt for the world, at the next a circumspect, unexacting, narrow philistine.

Engels makes the following points: (1) Goethe's rare genius is not composed exclusively of great prime materials, his greatness has a petty side; (2) his genius does not mean one should tolerate and even praise his faults (Engels' main purpose in writing this passage is to prevent that happening), but nor should one deny his towering genius on account of his narrow philistinism; (3) perfect, correct thought is not a precondition for perfect, great art; great writers and artists cannot be vulgar and small-minded by temperament, but they can sometimes be so by circumstance, for art and thought, art and morality, are not all of a piece.

'We criticise [Goethe] not from a moral or from a party point of view, but at the very most from the aesthetic and historical point of view.'[35] Engels was right. It was as if he knew in advance that a century later, people claiming to be his disciples would be insisting that there is no aesthetic perspective independent of morality and political partisanship.

Mao recognised that contradiction is absolute and harmony relative. All Stalinists acknowledge that contradiction drives progress. However, they require their writers and artists to be absolutely free of contradictions in thought and temperament and are not prepared to tolerate the slightest error in it, however exquisite the writing or painting. According to Mao, '[t]he more reactionary their content and the higher their artistic quality, the more poisonous they are to the people, and the more necessary it is to reject them.'[36] So it is even more necessary to overthrow Tolstoy, Balzac, and Goethe than to overthrow literary minnows.

Contradiction is the engine of progress, absolute compliance is the cause of stagnation and decline. If this is true in nature and society, it is truer still of art

---

35 Engels, 'Karl Beck, *Lieder vom Armen Mann*, Or The Poetry of True Socialism,' 1846 and early 1847, *Deutsche-Brüsseler-Zeitung*, no. 95, November 28, 1847, MECW, vol. 6, pp. 235 and 259.

36 Mao, 'Talks at the Yenan Forum on Literature and Art,' May 1942, SW, vol. 3, pp. 69–98, at 89.

and literature. A writer or artist's inspiration is due, first of all, to the contradiction between him or her and the world, or between him or her and the past or present. To call literature and art 'a symbol of depression'[37] is to go too far, but it is true that literature and art are inspired by contradiction. To ban contradictions is to block the source of the literature and art, and Stalin and Mao's requirement that writers and artists display absolute political obedience and swallow every slogan is to stifle their creativity.

What if Goethe, Balzac, and Tolstoy were writing in China now, with their wrong politics? How would they be treated? According to Mao's criteria, which put politics first, the answer is obvious. First of all, they would have to revise their work in line with the prevailing political criteria, i.e., with specific political tasks and slogans. If their thinking deviated from CCP thinking, they would have to reform first their thoughts and then their writing. In doing so, they would have to chop away everything, however outstanding from an artistic point of view, that does not conform one hundred per cent to the party's political criteria. That is the first gate. They must then pass through the artistic gate. Although it is called artistic, the weapons brandished by the gate-keepers are still political, but even more vague and general and without clear limits, because each gate-keeper has a different interpretation of what 'socialist realism' means. Mao did not say what it is, only what it is not, by listing a number of 'moods' and calling on writers to destroy them in order to build something new. He mentioned 'feudal, bourgeois, petty-bourgeois, liberalistic, individualist, nihilist, art-for-art's sake, aristocratic, decadent or pessimistic, and every other creative mood that is alien to the masses of the people and to the proletariat.'[38] These ten counter-commandments are so broad and elastic that they are almost impossible to follow. Worse still, their interpretation is in the hands of literary officials, each with his or her own tastes, so you 'satisfy your brother but not his wife' and end up offending everyone. Can you see a Chinese Goethe, Balzac, or Tolstoy doing that?

Starting with the Wang Shiwei incident,[39] the CCP has shown on numerous occasions that no one with a truly artistic temperament (let alone a genius) could pass through either of the gates. Most would fail at the first gate, on

---

37 Lu Xun translated Kuriyagawa Hakuson's *A Symbol of Depression* into Chinese.
38 Mao, 'Talks at the Yenan Forum on Literature and Art,' May 1942, SW, vol. 3, pp. 69–98, at 94.
39 In 1942 Wang Shiwei wrote essays, including 'Wild Lily,' criticising the communist party in its wartime bases for its perks and privileges. At the Yan'an Forum in May, Mao said art should serve politics. Wang was subsequently expelled from the CCP as a Trotskyist. He was subjected to a 'trial' and sent to prison. Five years later, he was executed on a river bank outside Yan'an.

account of supposed 'political crimes,' not only losing their lives as artists but risking their physical lives as well. The time has come to talk about the third harmful effect of Stalin's literary and artistic policy.

That is, the avenging of personal grudges in the name of public interest and people prostrating themselves before the leader, in fawning adulation. These are one and the same thing. Obsequiousness towards superiors goes hand in hand with arrogance towards inferiors. Talentless scribblers who like to turn their noses up at their peers and to bully and humiliate their fellow writers and who want to make a name for themselves without having to work hard for it use extra-literary means to gain literary recognition and boost their standing by attending to the all-important 'political criteria.' Stalin's literary policy was as if made for 'literary activists' of this sort, as an easy path to fame.

But although literary commanding officers do not need to write well, they do need to know how to be an official. To climb onto the stage and avoid falling off it comes at a price, and that price is flattery. Otherwise, how could a cultural officer with neither revolutionary credentials nor literary achievements establish a reputation?

So a strange relationship ensues. In order to safeguard its criteria and enforce strict control over literature and art, the party has to set up a whole range of institutions and maintain a large number of cultural bureaucrats. These cultural bureaucrats will stop at nothing to consolidate their position by celebrating the leaders in print, paint, and song. Stalin and Mao's leader cult has many causes, but their praise-singing literary and artistic policy and the atmosphere of flattery and toadying that it has generated are far from the least.

In the Soviet Union, the Stalin cult, the unification of writers' organisations, and the subjection of literature to bureaucratic control all happened at the same time. In China, the Mao cult is inseparable from the struggle on the literary and artistic front and its Chinese factions. Mao's Yan'an Talks, published in May 1942, were partly in response to Wang Shiwei's essay 'Wild Lily,' published in March. The 'Wild Lily' incident was a major battle on the CCP's literary and artistic front, and far more important in its consequences than the handful of essays written by Wang and his comrades. Wang Shiwei, like Hu Feng thirteen years later, was important above all for the trend and faction that, knowingly or unknowingly, he represented. 'Wild Lily' was not, in itself, of profound significance. The reason it caused an uproar, brought about the CCP's first literary inquisition, and led Mao to intervene personally was mainly because it represented Lu Xun's literary tendency.[40]

---

40 Lu Xun (1881–1936) was China's most influential twentieth-century Chinese writer. He cri-

The CCP's attitude to Lu Xun bristles with contradictions. The CCP was naturally happy that Lu Xun opposed the Guomindang and supported the communists, so it treated him with respect. However, Lu Xun was a dauntless and unyielding man with his own firm ideas. He liked to criticise and hated being told what to do. He caused the CCP many a headache, and they itched to tell him off and rein him in. Lu Xun was lucky to die when he did, at the peak of his positive influence and on the brink of being invited to play a role he loathed. So the CCP could raise him up and had no need to dash him down. His image is stamped on communist history in China as that of a person of consummate moral quality. Relations between him and the party are invariably described as harmonious and congenial, without the slightest hint of estrangement.

But Lu Xun's death did not expunge the conflict between his style and its. As the CCP consolidated, expanded, and perfected its literary and artistic policies and control system, Lu Xun's style rubbed more and more against it. Until 1942, Lu Xun (who died in 1936) enjoyed supreme authority among left-wing Chinese writers. Young intellectuals who joined the revolution in those days were, without exception, his disciples. They embraced his anti-imperialist and anti-feudal spirit and his satirical tone and style. During the Anti-Japanese War, large number of young people went to Yan'an, and Lu Xun's style blew in with them. As a result, the latent conflict between him and the CCP finally broke out into the open.

Lu Xun was not the main leader of the May Fourth Movement, although the CCP liked to say he was, but he represented the spirit of May Fourth more fully than anyone. Later in life he espoused some elements of Marxism, but his spirit, to its very depths, remained that of a radical democrat, a liberal humanist, an individualist, a rebel against Confucianism, an admirer of Western civilisation. An artist of his stature can, like Gorky, be seen as 'a bad Marxist' and even 'irresponsible,' but whatever his faults, his contribution was immense.[41] Lenin did not expect Gorky to do general revolutionary work but to make his own special

---

ticised social problems and shortcomings in the 'Chinese national character.' His vision was dark, intense, and often bleak. Mao greatly admired him, but would not allow Lu Xun's many followers to apply his methods to China under communism.

41 Gorky was by his own admission 'a bad Marxist.' Lenin wrote, 'The author of these lines has had many occasions, in meetings with Gorky in Capri, to warn and reproach him for his political mistakes. Gorky parried these reproaches with his inimitable charming smile and with the ingenuous remark: "I know I am a bad Marxist. And besides, we artists are all somewhat irresponsible." It is not easy to argue against that. There can be no doubt that Gorky's is an enormous artistic talent which has been, and will be, of great benefit to the world proletarian movement. But why should Gorky meddle in politics?' (Lenin, 'Letters From Afar,' CW, vol. 23, pp. 333–4).

mark, by using his literary talent. In letters to Gorky, Lenin criticised his confused ideas, but his respect for him as a writer never dimmed. Lenin constantly asked him to write for the party press and even got him to draft pamphlets, while at the same time urging him to keep working on his 'big' books. In a letter to Lunacharsky, he put it even more clearly:

> I 'do not know' the nature of Gorky's work (and his intentions). If a person is busy with some important work, and if he's then dragged off to engage in trifles, to write for the newspaper, to write political commentary, to the detriment of that work – then it's criminal and idiotic to bother him, to drag him away from his work![42]

So Lenin hoped Gorky would play a cog-and-screw role and link his literary work to the party cause, but if Gorky had better things (i.e., creative literary work) to do, he should be allowed to get on with it, as his contribution to the workers' movement. Lenin respected the unique nature of artistic activity, and distinguished between it and political activity. He did not shrink from criticising a writer's thinking, but he was determined to guarantee the writer's creative freedom.

Had Lenin met Lu Xun, there is no doubt that he would have taken the same attitude towards him. He would have criticised his shortcomings, in a strict but friendly way, but he would have shown absolute respect for his artistic talent and refrained from interfering with his literary work. But is that not how the CCP and Mao treated Lu Xun? It's how they treated the dead Lu Xun. However, they took a different attitude to Lu Xun's spirit, which had not died with him.

Some commentators restrict his disciples to Hu Feng, Feng Xuefeng,[43] and co., but that is too narrow. In the 1920s and the 1930s, a whole generation of young left-wing Chinese saw themselves as his disciples. They copied his style, his way of life, and his indifference to fame and wealth. Lu Xun's spirit can be summed up as resistance to darkness, resistance to authority, a critical attitude to tradition, and sympathy for the weak. As I said earlier, this spirit was formed mainly during the May Fourth era. Its ideological foundation was, first and foremost, bourgeois democracy. However, as Chinese society changed, Lu Xun's spirit changed with it. Elements of Marxism and proletarian ideology were joined to its core of Enlightenment-style thinking. The late Lu Xun's spirit was built on a rather solid intellectual foundation, fused seamlessly with revolu-

---

42 Retranslated from the Chinese.
43 Feng Xuefeng (1903–1976) is best known for having been Lu Xun's close friend.

tionary socialist thinking. However, the party in Yan'an in 1942 was already fully Stalinised and bureaucratised. Its regime was incompatible with Lu Xun spirit. To set up a Stalin-style cult, Mao first had to get rid of the spirit of Lu Xun.

The 'Wild Lily' incident and the Forum on Literature and Art in the spring of 1942 should be seen mainly in this light. Wang Shiwei studied at Peking University, where he was Hu Feng's classmate and Lu Xun's admirer.[44] That Wang could be the occasion for a struggle between the party and Lu Xun was highly symbolic. 'Wild Lily' was written as a *zawen*,[45] and was not in itself sufficient to trigger an 'incident.' The reason it was selected as the object of a full-scale frontal assault was because it was deemed to represent the Lu Xun tendency.

So when Mao made his speech in 1942, he had nothing at all to say about Wang Shiwei or 'Wild Lily' and concentrated his fire instead on Lu Xun and the Lu Xun spirit. He cited various 'muddled ideas': '[t]he theory of human nature'; and the view that '[t]he fundamental point of departure for literature and art is love, love of humanity'; that '[l]iterary and artistic works have always laid equal stress on the bright and the dark, half and half'; that '[t]he task of literature and art has always been to expose'; that '[t]his is still the period of the satirical essay [*zawen*], and [that] Lu Xun's style of writing is still needed'; that '[t]he works of people who eulogize what is bright are not necessarily great and the works of those who depict the dark are not necessarily paltry'; that '[i]t is not a question of stand; my class stand is correct, my intentions are good and I understand all right, but I am not good at expressing myself and so the effect turns out bad'; and that '[t]o call on us to study Marxism is to repeat the mistake of the dialectical materialist creative method, which will harm the creative mood.'[46]

These eight 'muddled ideas' boil down to one: a writer should not criticise the darkness but should eulogise virtues and achievements, while writing should be not 'burning satire and freezing irony' but fervent praise. Mao thought the age of the *zawen* was over, and that Lu Xun-style writing should no longer be tolerated. Naturally, he didn't say so outright. And not everything he said was wrong. For example, he was right to criticise the theory of human nature and love of humanity, while his comments on Lu Xun were measured and his call for the abolition of the 'abuse' of *zawen* was qualified. But if one looks beyond the text at the spirit of the text and the context, Mao's speech was plainly aimed at deterring what had become the mainstream of China's new

---

44 He was also Wang Fanxi's classmate.
45 *Zawen* were arrestingly polemical essays written in a style typical of Lu Xun, who pioneered them, and by his followers.
46 Mao, 'Talks at the Yenan Forum on Literature and Art,' May 1942, SW, vol. 3, pp. 69–98, at 90–1.

literary movement, which wanted above all to expose malpractice. Mao's main target was Lu Xun and his disciples. In 1942, Mao had already won a decisive victory in his war against Wang Ming,[47] so he did not need to make a speech to consolidate his power in that direction. His aim, instead, was to destroy the Lu Xun literary tradition and Lu Xun spirit. Lu Xun spirit was against authority and repression and for criticism and democracy. It was the main obstacle to deifying the leaders and to bureaucratic totalitarianism, so it had to be extinguished at whatever cost. Mao's speech was the bugle-call for all-out war against the 'Lu Xun wind.'

Literary factions inside and outside the party were thrown into disarray. Each jockeyed to accommodate to the new line, and new struggles flared. Some writers influenced by Lu Xun were purged as Trotskyists, while members of the 'critical faction' turned into the Goethe Faction.[48] A group under Hu Feng seemed to accept Mao's strictures but in reality stayed loyal to Lu Xun. Communist literary bureaucrats in non-communist parts of China[49] used the banner of revolution as a tiger-skin to intimidate people and accuse them. They included Zhou Yang and Xu Maoyong, with whom Lu Xun had often been at war.

Literary censorship did not stop in 1942. Over the years, many writers have fallen foul of it, including Hu Feng, Ding Ling,[50] and Feng Xuefeng. Here, I want merely to point out its historical origins. None of these struggles was ever anything more than the abuse of public power to settle old scores. Zhou Yang and his associates, who had been rebuffed by Lu Xun in 1936, 'grabbed a new flag and saw themselves as a cut above the others, behaving like the head slave' and sending those who had been more or less protected by Lu Xun and kept faith with Lu Xun spirit (they included Hu Feng, Feng Xuefeng, and Ba Ren[51]) for 'training' or into 'exile [...] or to be executed.'[52]

---

47 Wang Ming's political career suffered a fatal blow in January 1941, at the time of the Wannan Incident and the destruction of the headquarters of the New Fourth Army, whose leader Xiang Ying had been associated with Wang Ming's faction.
48 The Goethe (from *gede*, 'singing about virtue') Faction said whatever the party wanted to hear.
49 I.e., parts of China still under Guomindang rule.
50 Ding Ling (1904–1986) was a writer and revolutionary who joined the CCP after the Nationalists executed her husband, the poet Hu Yepin, in 1932. She was gaoled by the Nationalists in the 1930s and again, by the communists, during the Cultural Revolution. Her *Miss Sophie's Diary* tells the story of a young woman's battle against the old society. She was a follower of Lu Xun.
51 Ba Ren (Wang Renshu) (1901–1972) was a literary theorist and humanist.
52 See Lu Xun, 'Reply to Xu Maoyong and on the Question of the United Front,' in Lu Xun 1956–60, vol. 4.

Zhou Yang and his associates were accurately portrayed by Lu Xun as a bunch of 'noisy writers' and 'vagabond members of bankrupt families,' used to making 'irresponsible remarks, slandering people, and acting unscrupulously.' They were entirely capable of playing the dirty tricks Lu Xun predicted. No one who knows even a little about Chinese literary circles in the last three decades will be surprised. But why did Mao, who admired Lu Xun and had no part in the old scores this literary circle was so keen to settle, hand Zhou Yang the banner and the tiger-skin with which they committed their outrages and humiliated and framed Lu Xun's disciples?

The main reason was the start of the Mao cult and Stalinist literary policy. That was far more important than Mao's personal likes and dislikes. Mao liked Lu Xun as a writer, but he had to stamp out his political spirit. Art had to serve politics and policy. The CCP put Zhou Yang rather than Lu Xun's disciples at the literary helm because he was best suited for the job. Who better to snap artists' spines than someone himself without a spine? Deified dictators might not value sycophants, but they need them to run their cults. This is an irresolvable contradiction of the system of personal dictatorship, often to the dictators' great regret. All dictators want to decorate their reign with outstanding art – even Mussolini did, though to no avail, for art, as Ignazio Silone told him, is 'a wild flower.' Mao is no Mussolini, for he is a progressive dictator. But having trampled Wang Shiwei's wild lily underfoot, his hothouse is unlikely to grow even one fine flower, let alone one hundred.[53]

'Socialist realism' became the main creative model in writing, art, and drama after 1949. To limit the subject matter writers and artists are allowed to treat is bad enough: to prescribe one creative method as standard and order everyone to follow it is the height of madness. Perhaps dictating content is in the interests of the revolution, but to stipulate what form to use is excessive, even from the point of view of 'revolutionary utilitarianism,' and harmful. Is a realistic revolutionary story better and more progressive than a romantic one?

The first duty of a revolutionary government is to safeguard the revolution and protect it from attack. Art matters from that point of view. The government should ask what is the attitude of a given piece of writing, or of this or that literary trend, to the revolution, not what its style is. For a government to issue orders, to require writers and artists to follow one creative method and

---

53 An ironic reference to Mao's 1956 slogan, soon betrayed, 'Let a hundred flowers bloom, let a hundred schools of thought contend.'

no other, is not only futile but fundamentally fatal to creative work. It brings no benefit to the revolution, and great harm to the arts. So why did Stalin do it, and why did Mao copy him? Because the bureaucratic system of control extends to the field of literature and art.

Stalin and Mao's idea of socialist realism is, in reality, just another way of saying 'sing praises, don't criticise.' Stalinists and Maoists claim that realism was first advocated by Engels, and then by Trotsky in *Literature and Revolution*. But Engels and Trotsky were not talking about a particular literary school. Engels said, in a letter to Margaret Harkness, that the struggles of the working class 'belong to history and must therefore lay claim to a place in the domain of realism.' On the other hand, he thought that a novel that 'faithfully describes real relations,' regardless of its standpoint, can show the true face of history and the trend of social development and be a good work of art. Engels is applying materialist methods of cognition to literature and art. He does not exclude other creative methods, or seek a special and exclusive status for realism. In *Literature and Revolution*, Trotsky expressed this idea even more clearly when he wrote that '[i]n this large philosophic sense, and not in the narrow sense of a literary school, one may say with certainty that the new art will be realistic.'

In recommending realism, Engels and Trotsky are not seeking to limit or reduce the scope of artistic creation. They are simply pointing, as socialist revolutionaries and literary critics, to the value of a realistic approach for understanding life and the world. They are not saying that realism is the only road, or the only permissible method, like Stalin and Mao. For the latter, socialist realism was the prescribed vehicle for praising the 'supreme leader' and for drab propaganda about the regime's initiatives – and thus, for the rest of us, one of the most hypocritical and least realistic forms of art imaginable.

The best way to promote rather than hinder literary and artistic creativity, serve the revolutionary cause, and guarantee writers and artists 'greater scope' is to recognise, with Trotsky, that 'the new artist will need all the methods and processes evolved in the past, as well as a few supplementary ones, in order to grasp the new life,'[54] and to urge new artists to study and grasp the general meaning, in philosophy and the philosophy of life, of the realist approach. Setting rules can only suffocate artistic creation, put weapons in the hands of sectarians, and allow one clique to entrap the other. Hu Feng took up such a weapon to attack the 'romantic' Guo Moruo. Guo, in turn, flaunting the banner of 'romanticism and realism joined together,' dropped stones down the

---

54   Trotsky 2005, pp. 192–3.

well into which the Hu Feng group had fallen.⁵⁵ Thus a dispute about literary method turned into an opportunity to slander and frame one's literary opponents.

∴

Has the effect of Mao's policy been merely negative, or have more than twenty years of party rule led to worthwhile developments in literature and art? Mao got most of his ideas about it from Stalin, but he thought up some himself. The former had a negative effect, the latter a positive one. In Mao thought, 'Marxist-Leninist universal truths' combined with national factors, national particularities. In many fields, Mao's national particularities were more wisely applied than his 'universal truths,' which were in reality Stalinist. In areas where Mao was able to display originality, his inventiveness sometimes benefited the revolution and even took it on to victory, whereas the things he copied from Stalin either failed outright or succeeded but with a reactionary sequel. This was true in all areas, but especially in literature and art.

If the 'universal truths' in Mao's thinking about literature and art damaged it, what about his *tu* ideas? The critical affirmation of traditional culture, the advocacy of national forms, and the promotion of folk art were not all due to Mao, but they are inseparable from Mao thought. China's early communists had been leading lights in the New Culture Movement in the 1910s. May Fourth,

---

55 Mao has never talked about socialist realism, but he clearly approves of it. The CCP's literary theorists, from Hu Feng to Zhou Yang, have all supported it and attacked dissenters. Later, when Mao, 'giving voice to his lingering enthusiasm,' intervened in the literature and art field, the flag-wavers found themselves in a tight corner. In his poetry, particularly 'Butterflies like Flowers,' Mao uses non-realist mythical allusions with a strong romantic flavour. This jars with the official advocacy of realism, at least in its official interpretation. Guo Moruo, who in the past received some beatings by the realists, was jubilant. He said he was 'very happy,' because 'the publication of Comrade Mao's poems and song lyrics has propelled the romantic spirit to new heights and restored the reputation of romanticism. For example, I dare at this moment to confess: I am a romantic. In my past thirty years of work in literature and art, I have never had such feelings.' Guo Moruo took the opportunity to take revenge on his critics: 'If we were to rewrite Chinese literary history since May Fourth, I think we should adopt a scientific method to look squarely at reality, and that we should thoroughly smash the likes of Hu Feng, Feng Xuefeng, et al.' (Guo Moruo, 'The Romantic and Realism,' *Hongqi* [Red Flag], July 1, 1958). This tells us a lot: (1) Mao violated his own literary prescriptions (a point to which we will return); (2) the party's authority had a terrible impact on writers and artists: people didn't dare confess that they thought differently from the official line; and (3) once a leader cult has been established, the leader can personally influence the factional struggle, especially in literature and art (note by Wang).

under the banner of anti-Confucianism, had sought to create a new culture by means of 'wholesale Westernisation.'[56] They indiscriminately worshipped and introduced into China Western bourgeois culture, and just as indiscriminately rejected China's own cultural heritage. When May Fourth split into left and right, leading in 1921 to the founding of the CCP, its leaders denounced China's traditional culture, so from 1921 until the defeat of the revolution of 1925–7, communism looked, to the overwhelming majority of Chinese, like a foreign import, without deep roots and ill-suited to bearing fruit. This was true politically, socially, and culturally. After the defeat, some revolutionaries fled to the villages, where they had no choice other than to give up their 'fake foreign devil'[57] attitudes and steep themselves in Chinese culture. The communist movement began to acquire national form, get close to the peasants, and strike roots in local soil. I've already discussed the effect of this process on the CCP, its role in the victory of the Chinese Revolution, and Mao's part in it. Here, I look only at the way in which Mao, with immense intelligence and skill and aided by his character and past nurturing, adapted Stalin's brand of communism to China's indigenous culture. He said:

> Our national history goes back several thousand years and has its own characteristics and innumerable treasures. But in these matters we are mere schoolboys. Contemporary China has grown out of the China of the past; we are Marxist in our historical approach and must not lop off our history. We should sum up our history from Confucius to Sun Yat-sen and take over this valuable legacy.[58]

> To advocate 'wholesale westernization' is wrong. China has suffered a great deal from the mechanical absorption of foreign material. Similarly, in applying Marxism to China, Chinese communists must fully and properly integrate the universal truth of Marxism with the concrete practice of the Chinese Revolution, or in other words, the universal truth of Marxism must be combined with specific national characteristics and acquire a definite national form if it is to be useful, and in no circumstances can it be applied subjectively as a mere formula.[59]

---

56 Advocates of the repudiation of Western ideas criticised what they called 'wholesale Westernisation.'
57 Chinese who ape foreigners.
58 'The Role of the Chinese Communist Party in the National War,' October 1938, SW, vol. 2, pp. 195–212, at p. 209.
59 Mao, 'On New Democracy,' January 1940, vol. 2, pp. 339–384, at 381.

The attitude expressed in these two passages says much about the communist movement in China, especially the imposition of national form on China's literature and art. Ever since May Fourth, writers had taken their cues in grammar, genre, subject matter, and ideas from Western models, which they mimicked. In the late 1930s and the early 1940s, a new spirit arose in Yan'an, first in novels and then in poetry, drama, and music. *Tu* writing read fluently and easily, transcending the world of petty-bourgeois intellectuals and their feelings. New musical compositions sounded familiarly Chinese. They took rural class struggle as their main theme, adopted traditional forms, and used the everyday language of ordinary people in the villages. Folk tunes were reworked and refined. The results were impressive.

After 1949, this nationalising of literature and art gathered pace, and was expressed in the slogan 'push out the old, bring in the new – let a hundred flowers bloom.' Letting 'a hundred schools of thought contend' later turned out to be a trap,[60] but in literature and art it represented progress. It revived Chinese drama, dance, music, and painting, and stimulated mass creativity.

Sadly, the movement had only just got going when it was cancelled by another element in Mao's literary and artistic thought, a toxic import from Stalinist Russia, which stamped the life out of it. Literature and art was required to serve political slogans, 'performed' in print, paint, song, and on the stage. This requirement reversed the achievements of the initial stages of the campaign, especially after the leader cult got underway.

∴

Mao is a talented writer, with a training in classical literature. Extraordinary experiences can produce extraordinary emotions, and extraordinary emotions can result in moving poetry. 'Liu Bang and Xiang Yu were not men of letters,' but nine years after returning home with honour after defeating Xiang at Gaixia, Liu composed the 'Song of the Great Wind,' while Xiang wrote the 'Song of Gaixia' before committing suicide after his defeat. Mao is as good a writer as Changli and as good a poet as Su Shi and Xin Qiji, so, inspired by his own accomplishments, why should he not write passionate and graceful verse?[61] No doubt Mao's poetry will last forever, like that of Emperor Gaozu.[62]

---

60 The Hundred Flowers was a brief period of liberalisation that changed course and led to suppression of the critical views voiced.
61 Han Yu (Han Changli, 768–864), Su Shi (Su Dongpo, 1037–1101), and Xin Qiji (1140–1207) were famous writers and poets.
62 Emperor Gaozu (256–195 BC) founded the Han dynasty.

I am not qualified to talk about Mao's poetry as literature, and in any case there is no need to do so. The extreme praise lavished on it by Guo Moruo, a professional in the field, makes all further comment redundant. I want to say two things about it: it violates Mao's own literary policy; and it tells us more about Mao thought than his articles.

In his Yan'an Talks, Mao asked two main questions: whom to serve, and how to serve? The answer to the first question is: literature and art should 'serve the masses of revolutionary workers, peasants, and soldiers.' To the second, by 'popularisation' and by providing 'fuel in snowy weather' rather than 'more flowers on the brocade.' Mao is basically right, especially from the point of view of the needs of the revolution. But to reject all literature and art that is 'non-proletarian' and to confine literary and artistic creation to song-and-dance ensembles is to kill it off.

Mao has so far published thirty-seven poems in the classical style. According to Guo Moruo, he has 'added immeasurably to China's literary treasure house.'[63] Be that as it may, one must admit that Mao's poems are high art and a happy event in Chinese literary history. The only problem is, how to square them with Mao's line on literature. They are not written 'for the masses' and they are not devoted to 'popularisation.' That means they belong to the category of art that 'pleases only the few but is useless or even harmful to the majority' and is 'force[d] on the market' – in this case amid great excitement, with even more coverage than a major party resolution, thus 'not only insulting the masses but also revealing your own lack of self-knowledge.'[64]

I don't intend to hit Mao's shield with his own spear[65] or to talk yet again about the Mao cult. I simply want to point out that the publication of Mao's poems shows that it is wrong to limit literary activity to propaganda. Yes, the poems are about revolution, so indirectly they are for the 'masses.' But in what way are they 'popularising'? There are many different interpretations of the poem 'Send Away the God of Plague.' Zang Kejia interprets it differently from Guo Moruo, and Shen Yinmo interprets it differently from both of them.[66] Zang, Guo, and Shen are not workers, peasants, and soldiers with a 'low level of literary appreciation' and they are not even ordinary cultural cadres but poets and experts in the field. If they can't agree on the poem, what about the masses?

---

63   Guo Moruo (1892–1978) was an author, poet, historian, and government official under Mao and Mao's sycophant.
64   Mao, 'Talks at the Yenan Forum on Literature and Art,' May 1942, SW, vol. 3, pp. 69–98, at 85.
65   A pun on *maodun*, 'contradiction,' literarily 'spear-shield.'
66   Zang Kejia (1905–2004) was a poet, Shen Yinmou (1893–1971) a calligrapher.

If anyone other than Mao had written it, what would have been their fate? Luckily, Mao wrote it, so it can join the treasure house of Chinese literature.

Mao might argue that he wrote merely to vent his feelings, and gave no thought to form, content, or audience, or to 'forcing it on the market.' He might also argue that although he has always said that new poetry is more important, he learned the classical style at school, and it's the only style he knows. All this may be true, but one is entitled to ask why the same arguments do not apply to others, and to point out that if the prescriptions Mao imposed on others were applied to him, he would not have been allowed to publish his poems.

Poetry expresses will, song resonates with the heart, prose excels at reasoning. So poetry connotes with purity, prose with posturing. In prose and expository writing, the author must still be present, so that the reader can make out his individual style; but its subjectivity is far less evident, far more hidden, far less direct than in poetry. Poetry is not necessarily subjective, especially not epic verse, where the poet is not omnipresent. However, in lyric poetry, in poems of the heart, the writer's thoughts and feelings are to the fore. Most Chinese poetry is of the heart and always has been, especially Mao's. So if Mao is invisible in his articles, in his poems he is unmistakable.

The image conveyed by Mao's poems is not that of a contemporary revolutionary, however much one might want it to be. Even a modern figure like Sun Yat-sen does not spring to mind. The rhythmic, sonorous language summons up instead men like Qin Shi Huangdi, Han Wudi, Tang Zong, and Wei Wu; certainly no one more recent than Hong Xiuquan or Shi Dakai, leaders of the nineteenth-century Taiping Revolution.[67] Why is this? One is drawn to the metaphor of new wine in old wineskins. It is impossible to draw a hard and fast line between form and content. China's classical poetry, especially its vocabulary, sets the content in advance: either effete, effeminate, and sentimental: or daggers drawn and trumpets blaring. Other matters or sentiments defy description by it, or are exceedingly hard to capture. Modern, relatively complex thoughts and emotions are particularly difficult to render. Even construed in a demotic register and shorn of the connotations of valiant heroes, gifted scholars, and beautiful women, matters of sentiment seem incompatible with it. Gifted individuals can break new ground, 'make the past serve the present,'[68] and impose novelty

---

67 Han Wudi (156–87 BC) was the seventh emperor of the Han dynasty and its most important ruler. Tang Zong, Emperor Xuanzong (810–859), was a later emperor of the Tang dynasty. Wei Wu was Emperor Wu of Wei (155–220), a posthumous name of Cao Cao, a hero and central figure of the Three Kingdoms period. Shi Dakai (1831–1863) was a leader of the Taipings and a poet.

68 In a letter sent to students of the Central Conservatory of Music in February 1964, Mao wrote, 'Make the past serve the present, make the foreign things serve China.'

on the established order, but at a cost. To inject new content, one must first shed the mortal body, bones included, until nothing remains intact.

The reason classical poetry has become a problem and new poetry 'the main form' is that one needs new forms to vent new thoughts and feelings. Without them, the new content takes shape from the old form. Mao's poems bring to mind antiquity, not modernity; emperors, kings, generals, and ministers, genius and beauty, not the common people. This focus is promoted, in no small measure, by classical poetry's formal properties. However, it is promoted in even greater measure by Mao's thoughts, aspirations, and feelings.

If Mao had not resorted to classical poetry, he would almost certainly have found it impossible to express his feelings, for modern vernacular poetry is not suitable for the sort of things he likes to say. Mao strikes an imperial and heroic pose for which classical poetry is more appropriate, so that outside and inside can complement each other.

I argued earlier that Mao was strongly influenced by Confucianism and the *youxia* tradition and only to a lesser extent by Marxism. He absorbed the first two components at an early age, so they sank deep into his soul and stole into his subconscious, where they became almost instinctual. He was 27 when he embraced Marxism, and although Marxism became the most powerful element in his thought, it was always conscious, never truly fluent or unprompted, and likely to go wrong unless he paid particular attention to it.

In literary and artistic creation, sentiment and the subconscious play a greater role than reason. Although Mao talked a lot about Marxism, called on petty-bourgeois writers to side with the workers and peasants, and claimed personally to have undergone a 'change in feelings, [...] from one class to another,' a 'remoulding,' all this failed to show in his poetry.[69] Under a hail of fine words, abstract phrases, obscure and abstruse allusions, and ready-made idioms and phrases, Mao deceives not only the reader but himself, venting emotions that are the opposite of the spirit of democracy and the people.

Mao's poems reveal the 'innermost soul' not of a petty-bourgeois intellectual (of the sort Mao excoriated in his Yan'an Talks) but of a feudal general, brandishing his sword and shooting eagles with his stretched bow, while displaying an elegance of manner, attitude, and speech, as overlord of the hegemons. Everyone knows that writers exaggerate, although romantic fantasy has no place in revolutionary literature. However, boasting and romanticising can reveal unintended truths. A revolutionary leading an army out of battle who arrives at the

---

69   Mao, 'Talks at the Yenan Forum on Literature and Art,' May 1942, SW, vol. 3, pp. 69–98, at 73.

Yellow River by the Great Wall and sees (like Mao in his poem 'Snow') a 'north country scene, a hundred leagues locked in ice, a thousand leagues of whirling snow, [...] the mountains dancing like silver snakes, the highlands charging like wax-hued elephants' might, like Mao himself, 'muse over things of the remote past' and spit out lofty ideals; but most would not. Most would mourn the countless thousands of abandoned wives, deserted villages, and commoners and dissident scholars forced to build the Great Wall, or conscripts like Chen Sheng and Wu Guang who staged the first peasant revolt there.[70] That would have been more in keeping with a revolution against oppression and exploitation. For recalling the past and thinking of the present are not two separate things.

Mao, on the other hand, thinks first of heroes and of Qin Shi Huangdi and Han Wudi, and not of their crimes but of their achievements. He compares them, unfavourably, with himself, as 'lacking in literary grace.' In the same poem, he says of three dynasty-founding emperors, Tang Taizong, Song Taizu, and Genghis Khan,[71] that the first two 'had little poetry in their souls' and the latter 'knew only about shooting eagles.' So for 'truly great men,' who wield pen and sword with equal skill and are both intelligent and brave – and who, in one case, found a reign – one must 'look to this age alone.'

Mao's imperial thoughts are not confined to 'Snow' but crop up in almost all his poems. While in Beidaihe escaping the summer heat, he recalled how Cao Cao had 'cracked his whip' there. When a fellow poet wanted to go back to his hometown, Mao reminded him of the story of Yan Ziling, a statesman in the Eastern Han dynasty and Emperor Guangwu's old friend, who had once fished with a hook and line on the bank of the Fuchun River, and warned him not to fish there. Some such references are due to the limitations of classical poetry, in which 'living people are captured by the dead.' But most are dictated by Mao's thoughts and feelings, which slip out unintentionally.

'My goal is not yet reached, the people suffer still. Everywhere in the southeast their weeping can be heard.' This poem, by Shi Dakai, voices the compassion of a revolutionary leader in pre-socialist times. Ever since antiquity, leaders of popular rebellions have cherished lofty aspirations and set high aims, but their motivation has not always been the same, because of differences of character and situation. Some were for the people and the common good and moved by sympathy for the oppressed; others sought personal enrichment.

---

70   The uprising of Chen Sheng and Wu Guang (209 BC) was the first uprising against Qin rule following the death of Qin Shi Huangdi.
71   Founders of the Tang and Song and grandfather of the founder of the Yuan.

When Liu Bang was in Xianyang and saw Qin Shi Huangdi's pomp and extravagance, he sighed and said: 'Ah, what a way to be a man.' When Xiang Yu saw the same in Kuaiji, he reacted similarly, saying: 'I can replace him.'[72] Liu and Xiang were not men of letters. They spoke bluntly and to the point, making no secret of their intentions. Most founders of dynasties and most heroes in the last days of dynasties were motivated by personal ambition. They raised the banner of 'ridding the people of a scourge' and 'righting wrongs in accordance with heaven's decree' to gain support but, once in power, they behaved badly. This historical cycle was due to the long-term stagnation of society and the economy. Personal goals played only a minor role, but they were not entirely absent. The leaders' words and deeds were either virtuous and wise or foolish and unworthy.

The idea of 'benevolent government' and the spirit of 'going to hell'[73] is in itself a lofty ideal, but in class society it is used by tyrants as a mask or by the people to mock a stupid ruler. Heroes who rise up because they cannot bear to see the people suffer often end tragically due to the compassion in their hearts, or they abandon their original intention in adverse circumstances and compromise, or give up their sympathy and reign as emperors.

In the past, it was always thus. Now, in the age of proletarian revolution, the world is ripe for an end to human suffering, and wise leaders can act on their compassion. Some people say humanity and compassion is incompatible with socialist revolution, that they are no more than magic incantations used by the ruling class to cheat the exploited classes. They propose instead promoting hatred and ruthlessness. They are half right, but only half. In class society, morality has a class nature. There is no supra-class love or supra-class compassion. In class struggle, especially at its most intense, slaves cannot love their oppressors or pity their fallen enemies. In such a situation, socialists must stoke up class hatred, fight the class enemy resolutely and mercilessly, and put it out of action.

In that sense, there is no room for humanity and compassion. However, that does not rule out the idea of a 'greater good' or of compassion for the oppressed. It is one thing to ask for mercy from the oppressor and tell the oppressed to be humane, and another to show compassion for the oppressed, to arouse their hatred for the oppressor by expressing sympathy with them, to join with them

---

72 Xiang Yu (232–202 BC), a warlord of the late Qin dynasty, saw Qin Shi Huangdi pass by on an inspection tour and said, 'I can replace him.'
73 Probably a reference to the phrase 'if I don't go to hell, you will go to hell,' usually attributed to the Sutra of Bodhisattva Ksitigarbha's Original Vows, paraphrasing a passage about altruism and sacrificing oneself for others.

in the struggle, and to lead it. The latter is entirely compatible with resolute class struggle and inimical to the leaders' personal ambition. Sympathy for the oppressed does not lessen their resentment of the oppressor but deepens it. In the past, few revolutionary leaders belonged to revolutionary classes. Most were outstanding members of the ruling class. They 'turned traitor' to their class partly because they were ashamed of it and partly because they sympathised with the oppressed. This was true of the leaders of the democratic revolution and of the utopian socialists, and also of Marx and Engels. Only a fool would say that they reached their socialist conclusion on the basis of cold scientific analysis without any emotion. *Das Kapital* is a scientific study in which Marx puts capitalism under the microscope, but one has only to read the chapters on primitive accumulation to see that he was not aloof from or indifferent to his subject but moved by grief, burning indignation, infinite pity for the exploited, and the urge to expose capitalist apologists to ridicule. In that sense, he was driven by love, humanism, and compassion.

In Mao's poems, one finds none of this. They brim with high aspirations and ideals, but are not founded in compassion; they are impassioned and heroic, but lacking in altruism. Unless constrained by compassion, heroic aspirations become personal ambition. 'Tying up the grey dragon of the seven stars,' 'driving away tigers and leopards,' 'turning heaven and earth upside down,' and 'inviting the sun and the moon to change place' is the acme of aspiration and ambition, but without a firm base in the democratic spirit of the common people and a commitment to the common good, it leads at most to an enlightened despot or a sage leader.

CHAPTER 9

Self-Reliance and Communism in One Country

All Mao's theories are a summation of his and the party's actions, in politics as in economics. Mao's economic thinking can only be grasped from the point of view of economic practice.

Mao has spent most of his life on the battlefield. His understanding of military affairs is rich and special. He has spent much less time attending specifically to economic affairs, probably no more than a couple of years in all. But even though his record is limited and his *Selected Works* include fewer than a dozen articles about economics, those articles provide a clear indication of his views on economic work.

Mao's economic work can be divided into (1) the early Chinese Soviet era; (2) the period of economic construction in the Chinese Soviet era; (3) self-reliance during the War of Resistance against Japan; and (4) the years since 1949.

His role in the early years of the first period, from early 1928 to the autumn of 1931, is relatively well documented. In 'Why Is It That Red Political Power Can Exist in China?', written in October 1928, he said:

> The shortage of necessities and cash has become a very big problem for the army and the people inside the White encirclement. Because of the tight enemy blockade, necessities such as salt, cloth and medicines have been very scarce and dear all through the past year in the independent border area, which has upset, sometimes to an acute degree, the lives of the masses of the workers, peasants and petty bourgeoisie, as well as of the soldiers of the Red Army. The Red Army has to fight the enemy and to provision itself at one and the same time. It even lacks funds to pay the daily food allowance of five cents per person, which is provided in addition to grain; the soldiers are undernourished, many are ill, and the wounded in the hospitals are worse off. Such difficulties are of course unavoidable before the nation-wide seizure of political power; yet there is a pressing need to overcome them to some extent, to make life somewhat easier, and especially to secure more adequate supplies for the Red Army. Unless the party in the border area can find proper ways to deal with economic problems, the independent regime will have great difficulties during the comparatively long period in which the enemy's rule will remain stable. An adequate solution of these

economic problems undoubtedly merits the attention of every party member.¹

The article explains the effects of the economic blockade and the general economic plight in soviet areas.

In November 1928, in 'The Struggle in the Jinggang Mountains,' Mao described the 'pressure of daily life' as follows:

> The Red and the White areas are now facing each other like two countries at war. Owing to the tight enemy blockade and to our mishandling of the petty bourgeoisie, trade between the two areas has almost entirely ceased; necessities such as salt, cloth and medicines are scarce and costly, and agricultural products such as timber, tea and oil cannot be sent out, so that the peasants cash income is cut off and the people as a whole are affected. Poor peasants are more able to bear such hardships, but the intermediate class will go over to the big landlord class when it can bear them no longer. Unless the splits and wars within the landlord class and among the warlords in China continue, and unless a nation-wide revolutionary situation develops, the small independent Red regimes will come under great economic pressure and it is doubtful whether they will be able to last. For not only is such economic strain intolerable to the intermediate class, but some day it will prove too much even for the workers, poor peasants and Red Army men. In the counties of Yongxin and Ninggang there was at one time no salt for cooking, and supplies of cloth and medicines, not to mention about other things, were entirely cut off. Now salt can be had again but is very expensive. Cloth and medicines are still unobtainable. Timber, tea and oil, which are all produced abundantly in Ninggang, western Yongxin and northern Suichuan (all within our areas at present), cannot be sent out.²

About economic hardship in the army, he sad:

> The Hunan Provincial Committee has asked us to attend to the material conditions of the soldiers and make them at least a little better than those of the average worker or peasant. Actually they are worse. In addition to

---

1 Mao, 'Why is it That Red Political Power Can Exist in China?' October 5, 1928, SW, vol. 1, pp. 63–72, at 69.
2 Mao, 'Struggle in the Jinggang Mountains,' SW, vol. 1, pp. 73–104, at 89.

grain, each man receives only five cents a day for cooking oil, salt, firewood and vegetables, and even this is hard to keep up. The monthly cost of these items alone amounts to more than ten thousand silver dollars, which is obtained exclusively through expropriation of the local tyrants. We now have cotton padding for winter clothing for the whole army of five thousand men but are still short of cloth. Cold as the weather is, many of our men are still wearing only two layers of thin clothing. Fortunately we are inured to hardships. What is more, all of us share the same hardships; from the commander of the army to the cook everyone lives on the daily food allowance of five cents, apart from grain. As for pocket money, everybody gets the same amount, whether it is twenty cents, or forty cents. Consequently the soldiers have no complaints against anyone. After each engagement there are some wounded. Also many officers and men have fallen ill from malnutrition, exposure to cold or other causes. Our hospitals up in the mountains give both Chinese and Western treatment, but are short of doctors and medicines. At present they have over eight hundred patients. The Hunan Provincial Committee promised to obtain drugs for us, but so far we have received none. We still hope the Central Committee and the two Provincial Committees will send us a few doctors with Western training, and some iodine.[3]

Mao added that without appropriate countermeasures, the Guomindang's economic blockade would result in great suffering. The 'small independent Red regimes' would 'come under great economic pressure and it is doubtful whether they will be able to last.'[4] If anything, Mao was understating the difficulties. His troops were on the brink of starving or freezing to death, and the Soviet might have fallen anyway, even without a Guomindang offensive.

According to his own account, Mao and his comrades overcame the difficulties by collecting a land tax (but this was difficult for a guerrilla regime, frequently on the move in 'hilly areas [...] where the peasants are so poverty-stricken that any taxation is inadvisable'); and by 'expropriating' (i.e., kidnapping) *tuhao* (local tyrants). In the Jinggang Mountains, the guerrillas had

to rely on expropriating the local tyrants in the White areas to cover the expenses of the government and the Red Guards. As for the provisioning of the Red Army, rice is obtained for the time being from the land tax in

---

3 Ibid.
4 Ibid.

Ninggang, while cash is obtained solely from expropriation of the local tyrants. During our guerrilla operations in Suichuan in October, we collected more than ten thousand yuan, which will last us some time, and we shall see what can be done when it is spent.[5]

'Beating *tuhao*' and 'kidnapping the god of wealth' was convenient and practical in the short term, but as a long-term expedient it would have led eventually either to corruption and banditry or to defeat and annihilation. The CCP escaped both fates and grew stronger by following other paths, economic and non-economic. The main one, according to Mao, was democracy in the army. He said:

> Apart from the role played by the party, the reason why the Red Army has been able to carry on in spite of such poor material conditions and such frequent engagements is its practice of democracy. The officers do not beat the men; officers and men receive equal treatment, soldiers are free to hold meetings and to speak out; trivial formalities have been done away with; and the accounts are open for all to inspect. The soldiers handle the mess arrangements and, out of the daily five cents for cooking oil, salt, firewood and vegetables, they can even save a little for pocket money, amounting to roughly six or seven coppers per person per day, which is called 'mess savings.' All this gives great satisfaction to the soldiers.[6]

Such were the party's early economic problems, and its manner of dealing with them. Mao was not the only leader at the time but one of several, so the responsibility for these achievements was not solely Mao's, but he was the main leader and bore most responsibility. The methods were simple and the stock-in-trade of rebels ancient and modern, Chinese and foreign, regardless of whether they ended up as kings or bandits. They were not Mao's invention, and do not in themselves qualify him as an economist.

However, they do tell us something about him. First, he does not easily take fright at economic difficulties. Second, he is not bound by traditional law and morality, as a scholar might be. He does not shrink from 'crime' and is prepared to follow bandit ways. Third, he is a member of the brotherhood of the marshes of Mount Liang, tied to primitive communism's spirit of absolute equality and democracy, which he used to maintain his army's morale. These three points do

---

5 Op. cit., p. 90.
6 Op. cit., p. 83.

not, in themselves, touch on economics, but as solutions to extreme economic hardship suffered by a revolutionary army under siege they are worth studying. If Mao and his comrades had lacked these strengths, or possessed just one or two of them, the independent red regimes would have fallen.

The second period of Mao's economic work, from 1931 to 1934, in the middle of the ten-year civil war of 1927–37, saw him thwarted and disappointed. In August 1932, at Ningdu, he was ejected from the leadership by the Wang Ming faction, and accused of right opportunism and narrow empiricism. We don't know what exactly he did after his ejection, but it seems he was sent to do economic work in the Soviet. For the period from January 5, 1930, to December 27, 1935, we have only four articles by him, three about economics and one an analysis of rural classes. No great weight was attached to economic work at the time. Mao said, 'The economic departments of the local governments are not yet well organized, and some are still without a director; in others some incompetent has been assigned simply to kill the post.'[7] Mao was apparently among those regarded as 'incompetent.'

However, the three articles suggest that, far from being incompetent, he developed special insights into the problems faced in soviet areas. By 1933, the economic situation in the Jiangxi Soviet was better than that described by Mao in 1928. The Soviet had a much bigger population (of around three million) and many more soldiers and cadres. The economy could no longer be run by primitive means but required strategy and system, including conventional taxation to ensure a steady flow of income, an effective plan to restore and develop production, and active steps to deal with the Guomindang blockade, so as to stabilise the region economically or, at the very least, mitigate the suffering caused by Chiang Kai-shek's economic encirclement of the Red areas. However, Mao's speech in August 1933 to an economic conference speech suggested that little had been achieved, at least before his arrival:

> Salt is very dear, and sometimes even unobtainable. Rice is cheap in the autumn and winter, but it becomes terribly dear in spring and summer. [...] About three million piculs of unhusked rice are sent out yearly in exchange for necessary consumer goods, or an average of one picul a head of the three million population; it cannot, surely, be less than this. But who is handling this trade? It is handled entirely by the merchants who exploit us ruthlessly in the process. Last year they bought unhusked rice from the peasants in Wan'an and Taihe Counties at fifty cents a picul and sold it in

---

7 Mao, 'Pay Attention To Economic Work,' August 20, 1933, SW, vol. 1, pp. 129–36, at 130.

Ganzhou for four yuan, making a sevenfold profit. Take another instance. Every year our three million people need about nine million yuan worth of salt and six million yuan worth of cotton cloth. Needless to say, this fifteen million yuan trade in salt and cloth has been entirely in the hands of the merchants; we have done nothing about it. The exploitation by the merchants is really enormous. For instance, they go to Meixian and buy salt at one yuan for seven catties, and then sell it in our areas at one yuan for twelve ounces. Is this not shocking profiteering?[8]

Local Jiangxi products such as wolfram, camphor, paper, tobacco, hemp cloth, peppermint oil, etc. ceased production because of the military blockade, deepening the economic crisis.

The Chinese Soviet government responded with three measures promulgated by Mao: it set up a grain regulation bureau, developed a cooperative movement, and expanded and strengthened the Soviet's external trade (i.e., with non-Soviet areas). The grain transfer bureau worked as follows: 'On the one hand, within our Red areas we should send grain from places with a surplus to those with a deficit, so that it will not pile up in one place and become unobtainable in another and its price will not be too low in one place and too high in another; on the other hand, we should send our grain surplus out of the Red areas in a planned way (i.e., not in unlimited quantities) and bring in necessities from the White areas, thus avoiding exploitation by unscrupulous merchants.'[9] The cooperatives' main objective was to restore handicrafts and mining and assist farming, for example by organising oxen cooperatives and mobilising peasants to purchase oxen jointly and for common use, by voluntarily subscribing to shares. The main job of the external ('foreign') trade bureau was to stop excessive exploitation by independent traders and to break the blockade, by selling excess grain and local products to White (i.e., Guomindang-controlled) areas in exchange for daily necessities such as salt and cloth.

The success or failure of these policies was a life-and-death matter for the Red government. Many people contributed to their formulation – they cannot be attributed to Mao alone. However, conceiving them was one thing and implementing them, to good effect, another. We have no way of knowing Mao's precise role, or whether, between August 1933 and the start of the Long March in the autumn of 1934, the Chinese soviet economy improved or weakened. Mao himself claimed, in January 1934, that the economic blockade had been broken.

---

8 Ibid.
9 Op. cit., p. 131.

He also said that '[i]n the last two years, and especially since the first half of 1933, many handicrafts and a few industries have begun to look up because of the attention we have begun to devote to them and the gradual development of producers' co-operatives by the people.' Regarding external trade, he said: 'Such work was first undertaken in the Fujian-Zhejiang-Jiangxi border area and was started in the Central Area in the spring of 1933. With the establishment of the Bureau of External Trade and other agencies, initial successes have been achieved in this connection.'[10]

Mao probably took charge of economic affairs in the spring of 1933 or slightly earlier, so he takes that date as the point at which the Chinese Soviet economy began improving. It's hard to confirm or to deny his claim. However, one thing seems clear: the Red Army abandoned the Soviet and went on the Long March mainly because of military setbacks and only partly because of economic problems. One should perhaps conclude that Mao played an important part in economic administration in this period, and accumulated much experience in it.

From the point of view of the formation of Mao thought, what matters is less the various measures as such than his basic thinking about economic construction. These ideas continue, even now, to shape his economic policy. His commitment to the idea of socialism in one country, even communism in one country, was due partly to his deep-seated nationalism but also to the experience he accumulated at that time, and later in northern Shaanxi,[11] in this matter, and his theorisation of it.

In the Chinese Soviet era in Jiangxi and Fujian, communist bases were scattered across more than twenty counties with a population of around three million. It was a poor, secluded, and unstable region. At the time, Mao was as yet unable to come up with the concept of economic self-reliance, expressed in the slogan 'regeneration through one's own efforts,' let alone with that of independent socialism in a separate regime set up by force of arms. However, sifting through his three articles, it is clear that Mao was already thinking in terms of 'regional socialism.' In all his writings of the period, Mao is wrestling with an unmentionable notion. Mao said: 'Some comrades have thought it impossible to spare time for economic construction because the revolutionary war keeps people busy enough, and they have condemned anyone arguing for it as a "Right deviationist." In their opinion economic construction is impossible in the midst of a revolutionary war and is possible only in the peaceful, tranquil conditions prevailing after final victory.' Those comrades, Mao concluded, 'are utterly

---

10 Mao, 'Our Economic Policy,' January 23, 1934, SW, vol. 1, pp. 141–6, at 144.
11 Yan'an, the CCP's northern wartime capital, was in northern Shaanxi.

wrong.' Instead, Mao proposed 'an immediate campaign on the economic front' and the undertaking of 'all possible and necessary tasks of economic construction.'[12] He explained why:

> Because all our present efforts should be directed towards gaining victory in the revolutionary war and, first and foremost, towards gaining complete victory in the fight to smash the enemy's fifth 'encirclement and suppression' campaign they should be directed towards securing the material conditions which will guarantee food and other supplies for the Red Army, towards bettering the life of the people and so stimulating their more active participation in the revolutionary war, towards organizing the masses on the economic front and educating them so as to provide fresh mass strength for the war, and towards consolidating the worker-peasant alliance and the democratic dictatorship of workers and peasants and strengthening proletarian leadership by building up the economy.[13]

When a revolutionary army occupies a place that already has an established government, the economic and financial policy its adopts matters greatly. Is enough attention paid to it? Is the right policy followed, and effectively implemented? The survival of the army and the revolutionary regime can depend on these questions. In wars, it is essential to pay attention to the economy and to take long-term economic measures. The army and the government can't rely on emergency tactics and muddling through, and solving economic problems can't be put off until after the revolution. If a faction in the Chinese Soviet had indeed been advocating such an approach, then Mao was right to dissent and propose his own rounded, positive set of economic measures and policies.

What was Mao's view on the economy in those years, and how did it influence his later ideas, particularly his theory of socialism in one country? Some seeds of that theory were already visible in his approach. This matters for understanding the history of his economic thinking.

Mao called economic work and economic policy in the Soviet period economic construction. In fact, 'construction' consisted, in its entirety, of no more than three million yuan of government bonds – one million for the Red Army and two million for the cooperatives, the grain regulation bureau, and the

---

12 Mao, 'Pay Attention To Economic Work,' August 20, 1933, SW, vol. 1, pp. 129–36, at 129.
13 Ibid.

external trade bureau. These four items were, as Mao said, 'urgently demanded by the war. Every one of them should serve the war; none is a peace-time undertaking separate from the war.' Even so, he insisted on calling them 'economic construction.' What did he mean by that?

As long as the content is clear, the name is of secondary and even of no importance. If Mao was simply using an inappropriate term, there is little more to be said. However, the term stood for a wider element in his thinking. It represented the idea, at the time still embryonic but later to become full-blown, that whatever the conditions and regardless of the economic basis and its geographic extent, the construction of an economy can happen only if the ruling power sets out to build a socialist economy.

In 1933, Mao said: 'The principle governing our economic policy is to proceed with all the essential work of economic construction within our power and concentrate our economic resources on the war effort, and at the same time to improve the life of the people as much as possible, consolidate the worker-peasant alliance in the economic field, ensure proletarian leadership of the peasantry, and strive to secure leadership by the state sector of the economy over the private sector, thus creating the prerequisites for our future advance to socialism.'[14] This is a clear statement of intent. When and under what conditions might the 'prerequisites for our future advance to socialism' be realised? The answer is obvious. A true socialist must think about the ideals and goals of socialism whenever and wherever possible, and whatever work he or she does. On the other hand, it is wrong, and harmful, to describe every step forward as socialist revolution and every measure taken as socialist construction. Marxists should call things by their right names, so that the correct strategy is applied. Revolution is an objective process in which subjective factors can play a big and even a decisive role, but subjective schemes must be consistent with objective laws. Otherwise, they might, in the best of cases, have no effect on the revolution, which will follow its own course: or, in the worst of cases, lead to a defeat. It is therefore crucial that subjective schemes do not take over from objective truths.

Subjective schemes took over from objective truths in almost all aspects of the CCP's armed struggle in and around 1930. The communists called their army a Workers and Peasants' Red Army and their government a Soviet, and they talked of 'economic construction' and 'creating the prerequisites' for an advance to socialism. Why the confusion? First, because Stalin wanted to cover up his criminal errors in China, made in line with his Third Period think-

---

14   Mao, 'Our Economic Policy,' January 23, 1934, SW, vol. 1, pp. 141–6, at 141.

ing, so that after the defeat of the Chinese Revolution he ordered the CCP to set up soviets and a Red Army. Second, because the leaders of the CCP, though largely ignorant of the history of the October Revolution, admired the Soviet Union and 'took Russia as their teacher,' with the results that we have seen.

Mao's idea of building the economic foundations for socialism under conditions of extreme poverty was a surreal fantasy, impossible to realise even as an experiment in miniature, but the very fact that it was never tested in reality meant that its seeds could be all the more preserved. Therein took root the notion of economic construction regardless of objective conditions, blind reliance on subjective initiative, and bureaucratic idealism in the form of 'humans conquering nature.'

Mao's economic thought entered its third period at the beginning of 1936, and lasted until 1949. These were the years in in which Mao thought matured and took shape. After a period of relatively systematic Marxist study and immersion in Stalin's works, Mao began to systematise his own political and military thinking, as well as his economic thinking. For the latter, most important was the theory of New Democracy, developed at the start of the period, and the slogan of self-reliance.

The term New Democracy first occurred in the textbook *The Chinese Revolution and the Communist Party of China*, co-authored by Mao and others in the winter of 1939. The original plan was to write three chapters. The first chapter, 'Chinese Society,' was drafted by others and revised by Mao. The second, 'The Chinese Revolution,' was written by Mao himself. A third chapter, scheduled to deal with 'Party Building,' was left unfinished. In the fifth section of the second chapter, 'The Nature of the Chinese Revolution,' Mao used the term New Democracy for the first time. He said:

> [T]he character of the Chinese Revolution at the present stage is not proletarian-socialist but bourgeois-democratic. However, in present-day China the bourgeois-democratic revolution is no longer of the old general type, which is now obsolete, but one of a new special type. We call this type the new-democratic revolution and it is developing in all other colonial and semi-colonial countries as well as in China. The new-democratic revolution is part of the world proletarian-socialist revolution, for it resolutely opposes imperialism, i.e., international capitalism. Politically, it strives for the joint dictatorship of the revolutionary classes over the imperialists, traitors and reactionaries, and opposes the transformation of Chinese society into a society under bourgeois dictatorship. Economically, it aims at the nationalization of all the big enterprises and capital

of the imperialists, traitors and reactionaries, and the distribution among the peasants of the land held by the landlords, while preserving private capitalist enterprise in general and not eliminating the rich-peasant economy.[15]

Not long afterwards, in January 1940, Mao published 'On New Democracy,' in which he expounded more fully on these points. For a long time, New Democracy was promoted as Mao's creation. The term seems not to have appeared in documents of the Comintern. Its meaning is therefore worth exploring, especially its economic meaning, for the Chinese Revolution and Mao thought.

New Democracy was not Mao's idea or a 'creative development' of Marxism-Leninism in Chinese conditions. Instead, it is a Chinese application of Stalin's worldwide Popular Front theory, adapted to Chinese conditions. As theory, it copied Stalin's perversion of Lenin's position on the Russian Revolution, with some cosmetic alteration. Lenin's idea a 'worker-peasant democratic dictatorship' was consigned to the museum and replaced by the Menshevik idea of an 'alliance of all revolutionary classes' and, even more laughably, by Sun Yat-sen's Three People's Principles. Just a little earlier, after his Marxist studies, Mao had systematised his military thinking, and written up the results in 'Problems of Strategy in China's Revolutionary War,' 'Problems of Strategy in Guerrilla War against Japan,' and 'On Protracted War', works that embody many of his unique and creative insights. By comparison, his theory of New Democracy says nothing new or original, and amounts to vulgar popularisation.

Mao made no secret of the fact that New Democracy's economic programme was the same as Sun Yat-sen's Three People's Principles, i.e., capital control and equalisation of land ownership. It was a combination of a petty-bourgeois reformist fantasy and big-bourgeois state capitalism. He put it forward partly for tactical and partly for principled reasons. It was partly insincere, partly meant. The CCP claimed at the time to believe in the Three People's Principles, although in reality it did not. It therefore used various artifices and sophisms to prove that it espoused not the Three People's Principles as such but a new Three People's Principles in the form of New Democracy. Thus, it cleared the way on the plane of theory for its apparent surrender in 1936–7 to the Guomindang while at the same time keeping its members on side. This is an excellent example of Mao's subordination of principle to tactic. So it is important

---

15   Mao, 'The Chinese Revolution and the Communist Party of China,' December 1939, SW, vol. 2, pp. 305–33, at 327.

to study the theory of New Democracy but not to take it too seriously. Even its inventor did not really value it, or even believe in it.

In what ways was the theory 'truly meant'? Mao was speaking from the heart when he said the Chinese Revolution had to go through the historical stage of New Democracy; that, in it, capitalism should be allowed to develop but not to 'dominate the livelihood of the people'; that the stage 'will need quite a long time and cannot be accomplished overnight'; and that the idea of New Democracy was a refutation of the 'theory of a single revolution,' of 'Trotskyism,' etc.[16] He believed that this was Leninism, and in line with China's national conditions. How did these ideas shape his thinking? I have already argued that the theory was inherently wrong, and proved such by the actual course of the Chinese Revolution, so that Mao was ultimately forced to steal the sky and put up a sham sun – to replace New Democracy with permanent revolution. Mao, a pragmatist, did not flinch from dropping the theory he had previously cherished once things changed or the theory collided with the facts, and then replacing it with a theory he had been attacking just the day before; but when he did so, he took the new theory to absurd lengths, and committed the opposite mistake of yesterday's.

Mao's leap from New Democracy to permanent revolution, from allowing capitalism to develop for an entire historical period to, all of a sudden, realising communism in the short term and within a single country reveals his consistent lack of principle and empirical approach, void of all theory. However, no one is completely unconstrained by theory, so what were Mao's constraints? A deep and principled theorist acts under the guidance of consistent and systematic thoughts; a shallow and impressionable person of action is constrained by thoughts accumulated experientially. Mao is bound not by any consistent dogma but merely by insights he has gained in the course of action. He has numerous prejudices, of which the greatest is that 'guns are all-powerful,' followed by the theory of economic self-reliance. Self-reliance is completely different from New Democracy. These prejudices are fixed constituents of Mao thought, unaffected by time and place. They have acquired room in his subconscious, where they dwell as an analytical given. They are the starting point of his conscious ideology, the base upon which he arrives at his decisions.

Self-reliance is an authentically traditional idea. Whether Mao learned it from his teacher Yang Changji, inherited it from Zhu Xi, or formulated it on the basis of a Buddhist-inspired popular saying, it has long served as a motto

---

16   Mao, 'On New Democracy,' January 1940, SW, vol. 2, pp. 339–84, 359.

by which Chinese intellectuals like to conduct themselves. In the 1920s, the Chinese Revolution was seen as part of world revolution, and the promotion of self-reliance receded. Although Mao tended to look for home-grown solutions to political problems and was not too fond of looking to Moscow for guidance, he would not have dared do or say anything that suggested such a thought. When the Red Army was fighting for its life in Jiangxi and was forced back on its own military and economic resources, Mao did not invoke the slogan, mainly because it was all too obvious that the communists had no future without outside support. Although the Red Army was unable to get arms or other forms of material assistance from the Soviet Union, it continued to rely to some extent on outside forces. Some of its commanders were trained in Moscow, and it purchased essential medical items in the cities, mainly with funds supplied by the AUCP(b).[17] So however much Mao only believed in forces he could see, touch, and grasp, still he did not dare to propose a theory of self-reliance.

In 'On New Democracy,' Mao took an opposite theoretical tack. In the seventh section he said:

> All the imperialist powers in the world are our enemies, and China cannot possibly gain her independence without the assistance of the land of socialism and the international proletariat. That is, she cannot do so without the help of the Soviet Union and the help which the proletariat of Japan, Britain, the United States, France, Germany, Italy and other countries provide through their struggles against capitalism. Although no one can say that the victory of the Chinese Revolution must wait upon the victory of the revolution in all of these countries, or in one or two of them, there is no doubt that we cannot win without the added strength of their proletariat. In particular, Soviet assistance is absolutely indispensable.[18]

Mao's remarks were meant to refute the idea of bourgeois dictatorship, but they can just as well be used to counter the theory of proletarian self-reliance. Why did Mao say this? In the early days of the war against Japan, when he was composing his theory of New Democracy, Mao was hoping for foreign aid, and

---

17   I don't know how the Soviet Union helped fund the CCP in the period between the 1927 defeat and the start of the Long March in October 1934. I only know (from personal experience) that in 1929–30 Moscow remitted a monthly sum of $20–30,000 to Shanghai through private channels, and that Zhou Enlai told Chinese students in Moscow that the Leningrad party dues were donated each month to the CCP (note by Wang).

18   Mao, 'On New Democracy,' January 1940, SW, vol. 2, pp. 339–84, 355.

there was 'rice to eat and clothes to wear' in his base in northern Shaanxi. Self-reliance was not yet a pressing issue, and there was, as yet, no need for a theory of it.

Mao first put forward the idea of self-reliance as a guiding principle of economic policy in revolutionary areas in 1942, at a time when the CCP's base in the northwest was under economic blockade by the Guomindang and the Japanese, from different directions. Mao described the situation as follows:

> In the last five years we have passed through several stages. Our worst difficulties occurred in 1940 and 1941, when the Guomindang created friction by its two anti-Communist drives. For a time we had a very acute scarcity of clothing, cooking oil, paper and vegetables, of footwear for our soldiers and of winter bedding for our civilian personnel. The Guomindang tried to strangle us by cutting off the funds due to us and imposing an economic blockade; we were indeed in dire straits. But we pulled through. Not only did the people of the Border Region provide us with grain but, in particular, we resolutely built up the public sector of our economy with our own hands. The government established many industries to meet the needs of the Border Region, the troops engaged in an extensive production campaign and expanded agriculture, industry and commerce to supply their own needs, and the tens of thousands of people in the various organizations and schools also developed similar economic activities for their own support. This self-supporting economy, which has been developed by the troops and the various organizations and schools, is a special product of the special conditions of today. It would be unreasonable and incomprehensible in other historical conditions, but it is perfectly reasonable and necessary at present.[19]

So the CCP's drive for self-sufficiency started in 1940–1, during the Guomindang's 'anti-friction' campaign against the CCP. The experiment tided the communists over the crisis, and the outcome boosted Mao's confidence and caused him to pay greater attention to self-sufficiency, to systematise it and give it theoretical form. Even so, he was not yet fully prepared to give up seeking external support. Immediately afterwards, he pointed out that 'the subsistence economy is a special product of today's special conditions, and would be unreasonable

---

19   Mao, 'Economic and Financial Problems in the Anti-Japanese War,' December 1942, SW, vol. 3, pp. 11–16, at 112.

and inconceivable in other historical circumstances.'[20] So in 1942 Mao had not completely gone over to the theory of self-reliance.

Only in 1945 was self-reliance raised openly, in fundamental contradistinction to the idea of 'hoping for international aid' and as the CCP's sole future way of solving economic problems. Only after encouraging 'workers, peasants, merchants, students, and soldiers' and government organs to practise economic self-sufficiency in the following couple of years did Mao, drawing on the experience, propose the slogan. In January 1945, in a speech titled 'We Must Learn to Do Economic Work,' addressing labour heroes and model workers in the Shaanxi-Gansu-Ningxia border area, he said for the first time: 'We stand for self-reliance.'[21]

Since then, this traditional exhortation, used in the past about 'setting up a family and going into business,' a notion that has always lurked in the depths of Mao's soul, climbed into the open and pushed out of sight the new imported thinking about international aid and cooperation. From then on, the idea of reconstruction through one's own efforts became a fixed part of his economic thinking.

Mao himself explained self-reliance as a reaction to the Guomindang, 'which does not lift a finger itself but depends entirely on foreigners even for such necessities as cotton cloth.' He added: 'We hope for foreign aid but cannot be dependent on it; we depend on our own efforts, on the creative power of the whole army and the entire people.'[22] He was not proposing self-reliance as a point of principle and was not talking about economic construction, let alone about building socialism. Self-reliance was a way of coping with an emergency. It was an expedient. In the twenty years since Mao first proclaimed the idea, he has changed his attitude on several occasions, but his basic approach has been consistently in the direction of self-reliance.

I don't intend to describe these changes in detail, but simply to point out that when Mao thought that foreign aid was available, he stressed its importance in socialist construction; and when he thought it was not, he stressed self-reliance. The question of whether socialism can be built in a single country is a basic one, at the dividing line between internationalism and nationalism. For Mao, however, internationalism is a tactic that can be used or not, depending on circumstance, and that can be bent this way or that, in accordance with the possibilities. This is because he is, at heart, a one-country socialist, a national-

---

20   This passage is omitted from some editions of the text in vol. 3 of the SW.
21   Mao, 'We Must Learn to Do Economic Work,' January 10, 1945, SW, vol. 3, pp. 239–46, at 241.
22   Ibid.

ist, a supporter of the idea of self-reliance. Self-reliance is his abiding principle, while international aid and cooperation and the world division of labour is a tactic, useful for pursuing and realising principles but not absolutely necessary.

On the eve of victory, in June 1949, Mao wrote 'On the People's Democratic Dictatorship,' in which he put forward the slogan 'lean to one side.'[23] He called for unity with 'those nations of the world which treat us as equals' and criticised the idea that '[v]ictory is possible even without international help.' He concluded:

> In the epoch in which imperialism exists, it is impossible for a genuine people's revolution to win victory in any country without various forms of help from the international revolutionary forces, and even if victory were won, it could not be consolidated.[24]

This is the opposite of self-reliance. The idea that victory and consolidation is impossible without help was a reference to initial construction, especially economic construction, after the victory of the revolution. If economic consolidation and construction was impossible without international aid, then long-term socialist economic construction would have to rely on international aid and was imaginable only within an international context. Self-reliance was out of the question.

Why, on the threshold of national power, did Mao, who for years had advocated self-reliance, suddenly say the opposite? Had his ideas about economic construction changed during the passage from the third to the fourth stage? When his army won its surprise victory, Mao was catapulted into power, almost overnight, in 'poor, blank' China, after half a century of wars and disasters. He did not need to be a brilliant economist or theorist of international socialist revolution to think as he did. Anyone with a sense of responsibility would. To create something out of nothing, to set about reconstruction when all is in ruins, requires a measure of external support, at least in the initial stage, so that the self has something to rely on and can play a role in the regeneration. Mao's talk about 'leaning to one side' and international assistance and his trip to Moscow, where he personally requested Stalin's help and advice, did not mean he intended to abandon self-reliance and saw China's socialist revolution and construction, then and in the future, in global terms. Instead, he resorted to

---

23 The side of the Soviet Union.
24 This passage is omitted from some editions of this article.

international aid in order to create the conditions for rehabilitating and reconstructing the economy within a single country. So the international route led in the direction of self-reliance.

A Lenin in charge of the Soviet Union might have offered China selfless assistance in the common interests of both countries. Unfortunately, Stalin's theory of 'socialism in one country,' his Great-Russian chauvinism, his eagerness to recover tsarist privileges in China, and his attachment to naked national self-interest disabused Mao, in the course of their personal encounter, of his momentary adherence to an 'internationalist' approach and convinced him that 'internationalism' was a mere ideal and that socialism, no less than capitalism, needed a solid national foundation and should rely on itself alone in its quest for wealth and power. As long as Soviet aid continued to flow, he would not say so openly and immediately. After Stalin's death, Khrushchev was initially much more generous towards China, and thus gave a new lease of life to Mao's internationalism. However the gradual deterioration of Sino-Soviet relations put a stop to the aid, so the call for self-reliance became ever louder. In June 1963, it was written into the Proposal Concerning the General Line of the International Communist Movement, as a proposition not just for China but for all socialist countries: 'Every socialist country must rely mainly on itself for its construction.'[25] Therewith, Mao made the final passage, as a theorist, from regional to national self-reliance.

∵

Self-reliance has two distinct meanings, one ethical and the other social and economic, and the two must not be confused, in theory or in practice. This is true of individual self-reliance and even more so of national self-reliance. Ethical self-reliance, whether personal or national, regardless even of which people and which countries, conforms with moral norms. Not to affirm it is to advocate idleness, dependency, entrusting one's fate to heaven, exploiting others, and sharing the spoils without joining in the robbery. Rejecting that self-reliance will lead to corruption and decline, of both the individual and the nation, and Mao is right to warn against it. He was right in Jiangxi and in Shaanxi and is still right now, in the period of socialist construction, and anyone

---

25 *A Proposal Concerning the General Line of the International Communist Movement. The Letter of the Central Committee of the Communist Party of China in Reply to the Central Committee of the Communist Party of the Soviet Union of March 30, 1963*, Beijing: Foreign Languages Press, 1963, p. 21.

who opposes him in that sense is an idler and slave of a foreign master. Social and economic self-reliance, however, is synonymous with building socialism in one country, which is wrong.

All true socialists want to overthrow capitalism and build socialism, and to do so on a world scale, for socialism is incompatible with the nation state. However, not everyone agrees about how to overthrow capitalism and build a socialist world.

The achievement of a socialist world of great harmony (*datong*) will depend largely on socialists in individual countries and, in particular, on those that have already won power. So should the focus be on the world situation, international cooperation, and the planning and construction of the temporarily divided separate socialist economies of each individual country from a global perspective, or should each socialist nation state, big or small, first reconstruct its own economy and then come together with the others as in a Chinese tangram? Marx and Lenin believed the former. Stalin believed the latter, and called it socialism in one country.

Marx believed that the concerted efforts of the international working class were necessary to overthrow capitalism, even more so during the period of socialist construction after the revolution. Lenin thought the same, and put the theory into practice. After founding the world's first workers' state, he called on workers everywhere to rise up in revolution, and took practical steps to help them. The Soviet Federative Socialist Republic (1917–22) was seen as a first step towards world socialist unity. Lenin believed the Russian Revolution would soon collapse without international support, and that if workers seized power in a number of countries, they would set up Soviet Socialist Republics and form a close federation. Otherwise, they would come under siege and 'the productive forces which have been ruined by imperialism cannot be restored and the well-being of the working people cannot be ensured.' More fundamentally, they would be unable to participate in 'the creation of a single world economy, regulated by the proletariat of all nations as an integral whole and according to a common plan.'[26] This was a powerful argument, *avant la lettre*, against Stalin's idea of 'socialism in one country.'

In the early 1920s, the civil war was over, the danger of foreign armed intervention had passed, and the Soviet economy had begun to stabilise. In and around 1924, after the death of Lenin and the ebbing of the revolutionary tide in Western Europe, two opposite opinions formed within the AUCP(b) regarding

---

26   Lenin, 'Preliminary Draft Theses on the National and the Colonial Questions,' CW, vol. 31, pp. 144–51.

Soviet economic policy. A faction led by Trotsky argued that since the Russian working class had seized power, the Soviet Union should start building socialism regardless of its isolation, or it would not survive. However, it was essential to uphold the principle of internationalism, for while one could start building socialism in a single country, one could never hope to complete the process. Trotsky and his comrades believed that in an age when capitalism is no longer limited to a single country, socialism can be even less so. They reached two conclusions: a country's economic construction comes second to the interests of world revolution; and nothing achieved within national limits can be called socialist and even less so communist without devaluing the word. The other group, represented by Stalin, argued that Russia's vast territory and abundant resources meant, as long as there was no imperialist interference, that the Russian working class could successfully build socialism in the Soviet Union. They too reached two conclusions: the interests of world revolution must come second to those of the socialist motherland, while the workers' main task was to 'defend the Soviet Union'; and, after the nationalisation of the means of production and the collectivisation of agriculture, society is classless and socialism already exists.

As everyone knows, Stalin defeated Trotsky and built 'socialism in one country.' The Comintern became a tool of the Kremlin and world revolution became Stalin's bargaining chip, leading to a string of defeats. Regarding the Soviet economy, Stalin behaved high-handedly, leading to a great loss of life and wealth, especially as a result of the collectivisation of agriculture. Stalin then declared that the Soviet Union had basically achieved socialism, 'the first phase of communism.' However, democracy vanished, most old Bolsheviks were killed, and society was placed under strict control. Such were the consequences of 'socialism in one country.'

∴

Mao's idea of self-reliance is the same as Stalin's socialism in one country, in its social origins and nationalist intellectual content. If there is a difference, it is that the former focuses on 'subjective initiative' and the 'wisdom and efforts of the people' while the latter emphasises 'objective reality' and the fact that Russia has 'all the necessary material conditions' to build socialism. However, the two theories are essentially the same. The criticism of socialism in one country applies, line for line, to the theory of self-reliance, and Mao is certain, in the name of self-reliance, to commit the same mistakes and crimes as Stalin did in the name of socialism in one country – some he has committed already, others will follow sooner or later, as long as the policy is maintained.

Mao's worst crime up to now has been the Three Red Banners: the General Line (1956), the Great Leap Forward (1957), and the People's Communes (1958). The three banners comprise Mao's strategy of self-reliance. They sent a huge wave through China's political and economic life and lasted for three years, creating a disaster comparable to the famine caused in the early 1930s by Stalin's collectivisation of agriculture.

Here, my focus is not on the Three Red Banners themselves, a topic beyond the scope of this study (and which I have written about elsewhere, in some detail), but on Mao the economist. By exploring how Mao deals with economic problems and outcomes, his attitude and methods, one can begin to assess his abilities as a policymaker. In the mid 1920s, when Stalin launched his theory of socialism in one country, his standing and reputation as a theorist of socialist economics and a strategist of world revolution was already fully established and required no further confirmation in the next twenty to thirty years. The same goes for Mao, whose standing as a Marxist economic thinker was established by brandishing the Three Red Banners.

Launched in 1956, the General Line first took shape in Mao's mind towards the end of 1955. At the time, the period of economic rehabilitation (1950–2) was over, and the First Five-Year Plan was in its third year. For various reasons – aid from the Soviet Union and other fraternal countries, the positive and negative lessons of the early days of the Soviet Union, and China's industrial backwardness and low starting point – the recovery had proceeded rather smoothly. Sound methods were applied, and there were some remarkable achievements.

The focus was on industry, which shot ahead according to government statistics. By 1955, its total output value had risen by 65 per cent, almost a year ahead of quota. This rate of growth was higher than at any time in Chinese history, and rare even in advanced capitalist countries. A similar picture obtained in sectors other than industry, e.g., construction, transportation, handicrafts, and commerce, which had also expanded, though not all at the same rate.

Agriculture was the main exception to the general pattern of rapid growth. In 1953–4, agriculture failed to meet its targets. The total output value of farming was scheduled to rise by 4.3 per cent, but it barely exceeded the level of 1953. To catch up with industrial development and keep the various sectors of the economy in balance and maintain appropriate proportions, in 1955 the CCP launched a movement for the socialist reform of agriculture, handicrafts, and capitalist industry and commerce, aimed at accelerating production in those spheres, especially agriculture, that were lagging behind industry.

The movement was well intentioned, from a Marxist standpoint, but it turned out other than expected. Economic sectors that had originally been on a steady course reacted to their 'transformation' like racehorses spurred on by madcap jockeys along a rough and uneven course. Chaos ensued, with collisions, rash advances, and blind retreats, ending in disaster. The economy and the political reputation of the CCP took a major blow.

In December 1955, Mao wrote a Preface to *The Socialist Upsurge in China's Countryside*, a sourcebook of articles on the rural cooperative movement aimed at promulgating the achievements of the socialist reform movement,[27] personally edited by him. It was a large-scale realisation of his favourite method, 'investigation and research.'[28] It was edited twice, in September and December, and Mao wrote a preface for each. The prefaces show how the CCP progressed from the movement for socialist reform to the general line of 'going all out, aiming high, and gaining greater, faster, better, and more economical results in building socialism.' They also show how Mao did his 'investigation and research' and drew conclusions from it.

In the second Preface, Mao said:

> [T]he situation in China underwent a fundamental change in the second half of 1955. Of China's 110 million peasant households more than 70 million (over 60 per cent) have up to now (late December 1955) joined semi-socialist agricultural producers' co-operatives in response to the call of the Central Committee of the Chinese Communist Party. In my report of July 31, 1955 on the co-operative transformation of agriculture, I put the number of peasant households in co-operatives at 16,900,000, but in the space of a few months that number has been exceeded by well over 50 million. This is a tremendous event. This event makes it clear to us that we need only the calendar year 1956 in order basically to complete the semi-socialist co-operative transformation of agriculture. In another three or four years, that is, by 1959 or 1960, we can in the main complete the transformation of semi-socialist co-operatives into fully socialist ones. This event makes it clear to us that we must try to accomplish the socialist transformation of China's handicrafts and capitalist industry and commerce ahead of schedule in order to meet the needs of an expanding agriculture. And this event makes it clear to us that in scale and tempo China's industrialization and the development of its science, culture, edu-

---

27 Mao's prefaces to this book are collected here: 'Prefaces to *Socialist Upsurge in China's Countryside*,' September and December 1955, SW, vol. 5, pp. 235–41.
28 Mao's writings on 'investigation and research' include 'On Investigation Work,' spring 1930, 'Preface to *Rural Surveys*,' March 17, 1941, and 'Reform Our Study,' May 1941.

cation, health work, etc. can no longer proceed exactly in the way previously envisaged, but must be appropriately expanded and accelerated.[29]

This had an enormous effect on the CCP's subsequent policy, as Liu Shaoqi explained in May 1958 at the Second Session of the Eighth Congress:

> As a matter of fact, in the winter of 1955, when it was apparent that a decisive victory of the socialist revolution in the system of ownership of the means of production was to be won in a short period of time and when a mass upsurge in production and construction was beginning, the norms set in the First Five-Year Plan should have been breached. Comrade Mao Zedong issued a timely call for a speedier tempo to replace that in the First Five-Year Plan In December 1955, he wrote his Preface. [...] Comrade Mao Zedong subsequently summed up the ideas in the slogan of building socialism by achieving 'greater, faster, better, and more economical results.' He pointed out that the urgent task confronting the whole party was to overcome rightist conservative ideas. [...] In January 1956 the party put before the people a Draft National Programme for Agricultural Development, 1956–67. This is a programme for developing socialist agriculture by achieving 'greater, faster, better, and more economical results.' Not only did it set great goals for rural work but it gave a correct line for the development of the entire work of socialist construction.[30]

Mao's Preface is the key to understanding the sudden upward revision of the 'norms' of the Five-Year Plan, 'the entire work of socialist construction,' and CCP economic policy over the last ten years and more. It marks the moment of transition from a relatively steady to a reckless course, from respect for objective circumstances to the breaching of routine norms, from coordinating the sectors of the economy to unhinging them and throwing them completely out of kilter, from measuring growth year by year to staging great leaps forward and backward, from careful scrutiny of material conditions and actual possibilities to rank idealism and blind reliance on subjective initiative – and, finally, from a relative emphasis on international cooperation to an exclusive emphasis on

---

29 Mao, 'Prefaces to *Socialist Upsurge in China's Countryside*,' September and December 1955, SW, Beijing: Foreign Languages Press, 1977, vol. 5, pp. 235–41, at 239.
30 Translated from Wang's citation. For a different version of Liu Shaoqi's speech, see http://www.bannedthought.net/China/Individuals/LiuShaoqi/LiuShaoqi-1958-ReportOnWorkOfCC-580505.pdf

China's human and material resources. A document of such weight requires close study, but here I focus on just three questions.

(1) Within months, more than 50 million peasant households had joined cooperatives, equal to more than 60 per cent of China's peasant population. This was no doubt a 'great event,' but was it a 'fundamental change'? Did it fundamentally transform China's agricultural backwardness and heal its ailments?

An advance in the organisation of production implies higher productivity. Cooperative farming offers better prospects than household farming. But in the last analysis, raising productivity depends on an improvement in technology, and cooperatives work best when people join of their own accord. If agricultural organisation does not accord with the state of technology and if most participants don't accept it, productivity might even fall.

So an 'advanced production organisation' should be a natural result of the development of productive forces. When technology improves, productivity rises, and the old mode of production and organisation of production are no longer in agreement, a larger, more collective, more advanced system of production will result as a matter of course.

This progression is not fixed. The relationship between base and superstructure that obtains between forces of production and relations of production does not change, but their interaction does. In relatively backward countries, mainly due to special factors in the domestic class struggle, a socialist revolution can take place and be followed by the building of a socialist economic base. Similarly, in a relatively backward economic sector, a relatively advanced system of production can be adopted, thus accelerating the sector's productivity. But if one changes the base by first changing the superstructure, whether in a country or in a sector of the economy, one must ensure that the two don't diverge too far from one another, and that the base keeps pace with the leading superstructure. Otherwise, the superstructure will collapse.

Mao seems to understand this point, for in talking about 'fundamental change,' he said that the scale and pace of industrialisation, and of other aspects of development, should be 'appropriately expanded and accelerated, in order to adapt to the needs of agricultural development.'[31] This seemed to imply that although an advanced framework had been put up around agricultural organisation, the technical base still lagged a long way behind. To stop the framework collapsing and to promote agricultural production, industry must

---

31 Mao, 'Prefaces to *Socialist Upsurge in China's Countryside*,' September and December 1955, SW, vol. 5, pp. 235–41, at 239.

develop even more quickly than in the past, to shore up agriculture with new technology and furnish the advanced system of agricultural production with an advanced basic.

But this was not Mao's meaning. What he meant was that collectivisation was in itself a fundamental change, sufficient to ensure that agricultural production could leap ahead. He wanted greater and faster industrialisation not so that agricultural technology could catch up with its advanced organisational form but so that industry and agriculture could advance side by side.

He could hardly have been more wrong. This was one of the causes of the reactionary economic policy implemented by the CCP starting in 1956. Originally, collectivisation was designed to help agriculture catch up with industry, but suddenly a 'fundamental change' happened in agriculture and everything was the other way round: industry was expected to catch up with agriculture. Because the 'fundamental change' was neither fundamental nor real, the 'friendly emulation' led to disaster; agriculture, already backward, became even more backward, while industry, which had originally been speeding ahead, stumbled and collapsed.

(2) How did all this come about? How is it that Mao mistook the appearance of 'fundamental change' for reality? In the Preface, he asked: 'Is agricultural co-operation, now proceeding at such a high tempo, going forward in a healthy way?' This is a good question. Had he answered it calmly and objectively, he might have seen the truth and retracted the announcement, but he didn't. Instead, he concluded: 'It certainly is.' He cited two grounds: 'Party organizations everywhere are giving over-all leadership to the movement'; and 'the masses already see a great future lying before them.'[32] His argument shows poor judgment and a complete failure of Mao-style 'investigation and research.' Everything is in 'good health' as long as it is under party leadership. The party leader is always right, so the party organisation under him is also always right. Because the party organisation is always right, nothing done under its leadership can be wrong. According to this logic, party leadership is synonymous with what is right and sound, and the party organisation itself is right and sound. So to 'investigate and study' whether something is right or wrong, all you need to do is ask whether it is under party leadership. The party, like the Pope, is infallible. Yes, Mao compiled a large amount of primary data, and not only conducted 'investigation and research' of local organisations but purged them repeatedly. But to what avail?

---

32   Ibid.

Because of the leader cult and the all-powerful bureaucracy, Mao is less likely to find a sentence in his subordinates' articles or reports that deviates in any way from his own than to get a live fish in a bowl of soup. Reports from below are either memorials to the throne or attempts to anticipate and attend to the wishes of those in authority. Dissent is fatal, criticism even more so. Memorialisers craft their reports to fit and reflect the current line. If directives from above are feasible, they strive to implement them, and thus win praise; if not, they try to implement them anyway, or pretend to, to show that they are capable and resourceful, and thus to gain recognition. If it finally proves impossible to 'overcome difficulties,' the bad news is swept under the carpet, and the leadership is yet again shown to be infallible. In such a system, and with such an ethos, it matters little whether Mao is sincere or insincere about 'investigation and research,' for the reports received are a mere simulation of his own thoughts, likes, and dislikes, the only difference lying in the skill with which they are presented. What those in power like, those out of power strive to deliver. All Mao gets from these reports is the echo of his own voice.

When Mao did his 'investigation and research' in Hunan in the 1920s, he approached cadres of the middle and lower ranks, a poor *xiucai*, a bankrupt ex-president of the local chamber of commerce, a petty official in charge of county revenue who had lost his job, and a petty gaoler. He got 'a great deal of information,' perhaps because he introduced himself as 'their pupil' and was 'respectful' in his attitude.[33] By 1955, he had become China's most powerful ruler ever, and Mao Zedong Thought reigned supreme. Under such circumstances, 'investigation and research' meant nothing.

Mao's second reason is also false. He said: 'The peasants are taking part in the movement whole-heartedly and in excellent order. Their enthusiasm for production is rising to unprecedented heights. For the first time the broadest masses know clearly what the future has in store for them.' They saw their 'great future' in the Five-Year Plan:

> When three five-year plans are completed, that is, by 1967, the production of grain and many other crops will probably double or treble the highest annual output before the founding of the People's Republic. In a relatively short time, say seven or eight years, illiteracy will be wiped out. Many of the diseases most harmful to the people, such as schistosomiasis, diseases formerly considered incurable, can now be treated.[34]

---

33   Mao, 'Preface and Postscript to *Rural Studies*,' March 17, 1941, SW, vol. 3, 11–16, at 12.
34   This and the following quotations are from Mao, 'Prefaces to *Socialist Upsurge in China's Countryside*,' September and December 1955, SW, vol. 5, 235–41.

Mao implies that Chinese peasants are fundamentally different from peasants elsewhere. Peasants elsewhere only give up their petty-bourgeois prejudices and embrace semi-socialist or socialist methods after years or decades of painful experience, but in China they submit to the party and join the campaign immediately they hear about the Five-Year Plan. However, it is easier to drive peasants into cooperatives than to make them produce more.

(3) In the Preface, Mao made a rash promise. He said: '[W]e need only the calendar year 1956 in order basically to complete the semi-socialist co-operative transformation of agriculture. In another three or four years, that is, by 1959 or 1960, we can in the main complete the transformation of semi-socialist cooperatives into fully socialist ones.' A revolutionary thinker's greatest strength is foresight, but predictive power depends on an accurate analysis of past and current conditions, especially when setting dates and times. Otherwise, the prediction is not only useless but harmful, because it destroys trust and causes material loss.

Mao loves putting dates and numbers to things, but rarely does so on the basis of sober analysis. He relies instead on intuition. Dates and numbers trip casually off his tongue, for propaganda effect. They have the same predictive value as Liu Bowen's Pancake Poem,[35] but they do a lot more harm. Astrologists charge at best a few pence when predicting what will happen to you, but when a head of state makes predictions that fail repeatedly, hundreds of millions suffer.

Old-style Chinese scholars treated numbers either as something mysterious or as a form of literature, but never as a science. They viewed them as mystical symbols rather than as exact concepts. Mao is not superstitious, but he is a poet, and his maths are 'terrible' (according to what he told Edgar Snow), so it is not surprising that he has inherited this tradition. It has played no small role in his sinification of communism. For example, the Three Greats, the Eight Points, the Five Oppositions, the Four Clean Ups, etc., figure not just in slogans but in political programmes.

This is acceptable in propaganda, since numbers are easy to grasp and remember and using them accords with traditional Chinese language and ideas. However, when Mao makes pronouncements on economic policy and economic construction as the supreme authority, his poet's style of mathematics leads to disaster. Whatever the numbers – dates, economic data, or statistics – Mao the poet displays the same slapdash attitude and informality, follow-

---

35   The Pancake Poem is said to have been written in the Ming dynasty. It is full of cryptic phrases later taken as references to future happenings.

ing his own inclinations and casually tossing out estimates along the way. 'Ten thousand years are too long, seize the day, seize the hour'[36] is fine in rhetoric, but not in an economic plan.

In his Preface, he said semi-socialist cooperatives could be established in a year, and fully socialist ones in another three or four years, i.e., by 1959 or 1960. These figures followed the claim that 'in the space of a few months' more than 50 million peasant households had joined up. But what is the logical relationship between 'a few months' and one, three, or four years? The article does not say.

He sets time limits, but is not bound by them; the limits he sets are overtaken by events, but he offers no explanation; he shortens or lengthens them, but never says why. In the Preface, he said: '[W]e need only the calendar year 1956 in order basically to complete the semi-socialist co-operative transformation of agriculture.' But it had already been completed, for after Mao's call, cadres simply abandoned conventional procedures and leapt directly to 'fully socialist advanced cooperatives.' What was supposed to take 'three to four years,' i.e., until 1959 or 1960, was completed in 1956, in less than one year. But Mao offered no explanation. He made no further investigation or even mention of it, but seemed simply to forget about it. In February 1957, just fourteen months after writing the Preface, Mao referred to collectivisation, but he said nothing about its rapid completion, merely that it would 'probably take five years or a little longer' to consolidate.[37] In other words, although the transition to 'fully socialist advanced cooperatives' had been completed years ahead of time, they had not yet been consolidated, and consolidating them would 'probably take five years or a little longer.'

In August 1958, when, according to the original timetable set by the Preface, the transition from lower to higher cooperatives would not yet have been completed and, according to the timetable set out in February 1957, the 'consolidation' of the fully socialist advanced cooperatives would still take another three, four, or five years, Mao shocked the world by announcing the establishment of People's Communes in rural areas. It was no longer a question of cooperatives or consolidation or rectification but of People's Communes, which had not only already emerged but would soon sweep the country. A new timetable was announced: Communism would be realised in China 'in the not too distant future.'

---

36   From Mao's poem 'Reply to Comrade Guo Moruo – to the Tune of *Man jiang hong*,' January 9, 1963.

37   Mao, 'On the Correct Handling of Contradictions Among the People,' February 27, 1957, SW, vol. 5, pp. 384–421.

So in just three years, Mao had come up with three different schemes for China's rural areas. In December 1955, he had vowed to turn the great majority of low-level cooperatives into advanced cooperatives within the year; in February 1957, he said the 'consolidation' of the 'fully socialist advanced cooperatives' would start, also within the year; but when the year was up, in January 1958, he said cooperatives were out of date, People's Communes were now needed, and communism would soon be realised.

In the resolution setting up People's Communes, Mao said that in some places in China socialism 'could be completed in three or four years,' while in other places it might take between three and six years. By then, it would be a case of 'from each according to his or her ability, to each according to the work done.' But it would take a while for that system to reach the point of 'from each according to his or her ability, to each according to his or her need.' How long would it take? Mao didn't put a precise figure on it. He simply said it would take 'a number of years.' But he then went on to say that communism would be realised in China 'in the not too distant future,' so it would clearly not take centuries or even decades. Five years later, in March 1963, by which time socialism in China should have been 'built,' at least in rural areas, and communism should have been on its way, he said:

> In their present level of economic development all socialist countries are still far, far removed from the higher stage of communism in which 'from each according to his ability, to each according to his needs' is put into practice. Therefore, it will take a long, long time to eliminate the class difference between worker and peasant.[38]

According to the first timetable, communism would be realised in poor, blank China, just nine years after the revolution, in the 'not too distant future.' According to the second, the realisation of communism in the Soviet Union, 46 years after the October Revolution and with an economy far more developed than China's, was 'far, far away.' A year later, in July 1964, Mao came up with another timetable. According to this new timetable, 'Here a very long period of time is needed to decide "who will win" in the struggle between socialism and capitalism. Several decades won't do it; success requires anywhere from one to several centuries. On the question of duration, it is better to prepare for a longer rather

---

38   *A Proposal Concerning the General Line of the International Communist Movement. The Letter of the Central Committee of the Communist Party of China in Reply to the Central Committee of the Communist Party of the Soviet Union of March* 30 1963, p. 18.

than a shorter period of time.'[39] So 'socialist society is a very long historical period.' Communism would take longer still, although, just six years earlier, Mao had thought it 'not too distant.' Mao's inconsistency confirms his weakness as a theorist. For the figures Mao announced, though reckless, were not arbitrary. Each deadline was based on Mao's experience at the time. When 'the situation is excellent,' communism will reach China soon; when the situation changes, and the Three Red Banners come crashing down, socialism will take hundreds of years to be realised.

∴

Up to now, I've looked mainly at Mao's methods in the years since 1955 and his attempts to deal with basic problems of building a socialist economy, in line with my goal of assessing Mao as an economic theorist. Because the People's Communes are the biggest and last of the Three Banners, and one of Mao's 'greatest contributions' to Marxism-Leninism, 'in theory and in practice,' his road and approach to them is important for understanding his thinking.

When more than 60 per cent of China's peasants joined cooperatives between the summer and autumn of 1955, Mao spied a 'fundamental change' and began advocating break-throughs in the economy and culture and an all-round acceleration of the pace of development. China should 'go all out, aim high, and gain greater, faster, better results in building socialism.' He identified iron and steel together with irrigation and water conservancy as key targets in his Great Leap Forward. Led by the party and the mass organisations, a massive production and construction movement started up. Victories and miracles were announced on all sides. Marx's saying that 'one day equals twenty years' was widely quoted. Now, the peasant cooperatives were seen as obstacles to agricultural production, and became People's Communes.

I have already discussed, elsewhere, the circumstances in which the Three Red Banners were thought up. Here, I want to talk about only one question, the thesis that the cooperatives stood in the way of a break-through in agricultural production and therefore had to be replaced by People's Communes; and the 'investigation and research' Mao did before acting on it.

The CCP leaders based their assessment of the rate of development of agricultural production on the 'glad tidings' of their subordinates and, even more importantly, on their own fantasising. Collectivisation was completed in early 1956, when agricultural production grew by 4.9 per cent, according to Liu

---

39 Mao, 'Refutation of the So-Called Party of the Entire People,' July 1964.

Shaoqi. 1956 was also the year of the 'rampant right-wing offensive.' Again according to Liu Shaoqi, some people had misgivings in 1957 about the agricultural programme, which 'dampened the initiative of the masses and hampered progress on the production front' in farming. In other words, agricultural production either stagnated or fell in 1957, though no figures were published. In May 1958, the year in which the Great Leap Forward started, Tan Zhenlin said that 'if there are no floods or droughts, [...] grain output might grow by between 10 and 20 per cent.' In August, just three months later, the CCP's report 'On the Establishment of People's Communes in Rural Areas' announced that 'after overcoming rightist conservative thinking,' farm yields were 'doubling or increasing by several, a dozen, or scores of times.'[40]

These figures were given not in a propaganda speech at a mass rally but in a major resolution of the CCP, and were meant to rewrite the whole of human history. How can we explain this? The main explanation is Mao's rash, bold, romantic, and unscientific approach. This approach helped him score some victories but it also led to quite a few disasters, the biggest of which was the Great Leap Forward.

Before Mao announced the decision, the Chinese press carried a number of reports of Mao's visits to the countryside. The reports were designed to show that Mao sought truth from facts, followed the mass line, and carried out on-the-spot investigations, how he was not ashamed to learn from his subordinates, how kind he was, how modest and self-effacing, how he liked to learn while at the same time teaching. They were also meant to prove that the People's Communes came first 'from the masses' and were later 'returned to the masses,' in the form of policy.

On August 29, at Beidaihe, the CCP passed its 'Resolution on the Establishment of People's Communes.' Earlier, Mao had gone on rural visits. Even before his visits, communes had already started up in one or two places in Hebei, Henan, and Shandong. However, although the visits cannot be said to have sparked the movement, they consolidated his view on communes and convinced him to extend them to the whole of China (including, initially, the cities) and to write the Beidaihe resolution. There follow excerpts from contemporary reports on the visits.

At half past four in the afternoon, Chairman Mao, accompanied by Xie Xuegong and Zhang Minghe, [...] first visited an agricultural cooperative in Dasige Village

---

40   'Greet the Upsurge in Forming People's Communes,' editorial in *Red Flag*, September 1, 1958, in n. a. 1958, pp. 9–15, at 9.

SELF-RELIANCE AND COMMUNISM IN ONE COUNTRY

in Nanliyuan township. Chairman Mao was full of enthusiasm. [...] He already knew Zhan Dengke, secretary of the township party committee, Yan Yuru, the cooperative branch secretary, and director Li Jiangsheng. [...] He raised his head and asked:

'Was this year's wheat harvest good?'

'Very good! Much better than any other year,' said Li Jiangsheng.

Chairman Mao asked: 'How many jin per mu on average?'

Secretary Yan Yuru replied: 'Seven hundred and fifty-four!'

Chairman Mao laughed, said 'ah,' and added: 'That's a lot!' He then asked about the forecast for the autumn crops, in the cooperative and the county. The county party secretary Zhang Guozhong said: This year the planned summer and autumn grain output will reach 1200 million jin, an average yield of two thousand jin per mu. [...] Chairman Mao smiled and said:

'You will have to harvest a lot of grain!' Chairman Mao recalled what Zhang Guozhong had told him earlier. [...] He stretched out his big, strong hand and said: 'Your summer harvest is 90 million jin! Your autumn harvest will be 1100 million jin! Your entire county has a population of just 310,000, how can you eat so much grain? What will you do with the surplus?'

Everybody was stumped by Chairman Mao's question. After a while, Zhang Guozhong said: 'We will exchange it for machines.'

Chairman Mao said: 'And what if you are not the only ones with a surplus, what if every county has a surplus? You might exchange it for machines, but no one will want your grain!'

Li Jiangsheng said: 'We can turn our yams into alcohol.'

Chairman Mao said: 'What if every county did that? Where would so much alcohol go!'

Chairman Mao laughed, looking round at everyone. Everyone laughed. Zhang Guozhong laughed and said: 'We're only thinking about how to get a lot of grain!'

Chairman Mao: 'You must also consider how to eat the grain!'

People were whispering together: 'Chairman Mao looks at problems from all sides and so thoughtfully!'

'In fact, more grain is good,' Chairman Mao laughed. 'But the state won't want it, and nor will anyone else! The members of the cooperative will have to eat five times a day!'

Chairman Mao, smiling cordially, got up to go and look round the village.

Reading this, I can't help thinking of Lady Jia's visit to the Grand View Garden in the *Dream of the Red Chamber*.[41] Surrounded by ladies, girls, young wives,

---

41 In this scene from the classic novel, Lady Jia is enchanted by life in the Grand Prospect Garden.

and servant girls, standing like 'a myriad stars clustered around the moon,' they flock to the side of this luminous authority of the Ningguo Mansion, seeking in every way possible to ingratiate themselves with her, cater to her every wish, and make her happy at heart 'like flowers in full bloom.' Her Old Ladyship is elated, and makes some little jokes. The maids and young wives whisper to one another: 'Her Old Ladyship can see so far ahead, she is so thorough and attentive.' In order to please Her Old Ladyship, Wang Xifeng is telling a visitor, Grannie Liu, a peasant and a distant relative of the family, that she manages the house thriftily. Her Old Ladyship laughs at this thriftiness, and says that a wealthy family like Wang Xifeng's can afford five meals a day.

∴

Coming out of the canteen, they went into the fields. Members of the cooperative clapped and cheered, and Chairman Mao constantly waved and nodded, greeting everyone. Chairman Mao perhaps noticed that there were many women in the fields, so he said to the people accompanying him: 'Women's labour power has been liberated very thoroughly here.'

Li Ruinong, the Baoding party secretary, told the Chairman that none of the women any longer did baking, cooking, grinding, or husking. The Chairman said: 'Yes, everyone eats in the canteen, all the cooperatives have kindergartens.'

For several months, peasants all over China abandoned their family stoves and traipsed twice a day, in the hot sun or the cold wind and along bumpy paths, to the local temple or ancestral hall, which had been turned into a canteen, to get a bowl of badly cooked food. Here is the 'investigation and research' that preceded the system's national extension.

∴

Chairman Mao saw the corn and millet, and the pile of yams. [...] When he heard that each mu *yielded two hundred and fifty thousand* jin *of yam, and some as much as one million* jin, *he could not help laughing, and asked:*

'If you can't eat it all, what will you do?' To the township and cooperative cadres he said: 'If you get more grain, then plant less. Do one day's work and then use the next day for culture, science, and entertainment, or do school work, what do you say to that?'

Everyone said yes, they were happy to hear this. Someone told the chairman that this cooperative had already set up a communist Red-Expert University. The Chairman said 'ah,' and kept laughing and nodding. Then he said goodbye.

SELF-RELIANCE AND COMMUNISM IN ONE COUNTRY 263

∴

Chairman Mao went to the county party committee. The first thing he said to the provincial party secretary Xie and his deputy Zhang was: 'People are really enthusiastic here!' He then said to everyone: 'Over the past thousands of years, the yield has been one or two hundred jin *per* mu, *see, suddenly it's become thousands or even tens of thousands!'*

Chairman Mao asked about the crops elsewhere in Hebei, and was told about irrigation and drought control in Xushui last winter and this spring. Finally, he directed Xushui county officials to do early planning for next year's grain, plant more wheat, and plant more oil-bearing crops and vegetables to meet the people's needs. He also said the wheat fields should be ploughed deep, by a foot or more; afterwards, people should eat mainly wheat, while maize and yams should be fed to the animals and the pigs; if the pigs ate more, people could eat their meat. Finally he said, 'It's really good! What a lot of things have been produced!' Smiling at everyone, he said: 'Beijing doesn't produce things. What does Beijing produce?'

'Beijing produces political leadership,' said Zhang Guozhong. 'It produces the party's general line!' Chairman Mao laughed and nodded.

∴

It is half past seven, and Chairman Mao has already gone. Chairman Mao's face radiates his commanding presence, reflecting the rich array of colours on the western horizon. [...]

At night, the county committee held a county telephone conference. All the townships and cooperatives swore to the party and to Chairman Mao that they would ensure that this year's harvest would exceed two thousand jin *of grain per* mu. [...]

It is night time. [...] *Things that could not be done by morning were, a dozen or so hours later, not only done but more than done. All the villages in Dasi had joined communes, formally established that same night. All the trees were collectively distributed by the commune. So were the houses, and members of the commune implemented a wage system.*

These reports reveal the style of Mao's investigation and research on the eve of the resolution to set up People's Communes and show the extent to which the CCP has become a bureaucratic machine. The machine is quite efficient. It is tightly structured and quick to act. It is highly manipulable, and under Mao's absolute control. So far, so good. If Mao has a good idea, he just needs to press the button and the machine springs into action. But the machine is exclusively top-down, which accounts for its speed and efficiency. The bigger and more complex it becomes, the greater the arrogance of those who operate it, and the blinder the obedience. Because of this arrogance and the concomitant lack of criticism, what seems to upper levels like a great achievement might count as a disaster to those below.

If top leaders ask their subordinates about the effects of their policies, they are not told the truth. Mao-style investigation and research amounts to little more than a press interview, all the more so since Mao's recent deification. I don't question his motives. He is still 'seeking truth from facts,' and he still believes that without investigating and researching, no one has the right to speak, so even though he enjoys imperial esteem, he braves the heat to go down into the countryside and spend a few hours in the villages. Perhaps he really does want to learn from the villager elders, as their student. But the bureaucratic machine won't let him. He is surrounded by yea-sayers and sycophants. The emperor's wish has been made known. All spin the same general line, embroidered with local colour, to prove his foresight and to surprise and delight him. To 'confirm' the miracle of the 'agricultural leap' his investigation and research brought to light, news of even bigger miracles flood in on all sides, so that he can feel that everything has turned out just as he expected, or even better than he expected, and just nod and laugh.

Those wielding supreme power also have their troubles. They are cut off by walls from the surrounding world, and even from their intimates. No matter how clever, once isolated behind the walls, the ears and eyes of others are deaf and blind to them. Mao's gullibility at Xushui after hearing the party secretary's report beggars belief, and his failure to ask simple and obvious questions about it of the sort that anyone would ask disqualifies him as an 'investigator' and 'researcher.' When told about harvests dozens of times bigger than any ever seen before seen, he expresses not the slightest surprise, but accepts what he is told as a matter of course. He is less interested in studying the 'miracle' than in propagating it as a model, with People's Communes as 'the best organisational form' for building socialism and achieving the transition to communism. The People's Communes caused indescribable suffering and incalculable material loss. They are the most concentrated and complete illustration of Mao's thinking and of his methods.

In economic matters, as in other things besides, Mao is a nationalist who believes in socialism in one country, and his method is empiricism. These qualities, in economic affairs and economic construction, have been a major factor in his achievements, as a gifted tactician. However, because of the CCP's increasing bureaucratisation and ever tightening grip on the state machine, Mao is less and less able to gain direct experience by means of investigation and research, and is instead fed 'facts' that are in reality grotesquely exaggerated fantasies. As a result, his tactical skills are neutralised and even become a brake. But the CCP no longer rules over its own small independent territory, and its economic problems are no longer confined to how to overcome hardship in order to win the revolution. Now its mission is not only to survive within an imperialist military siege or to restore and build the economy in in poor, blank China but to move towards 'the creation of a single world economy, regulated by the proletariat of all nations as an integral whole and according to a common plan.' In the face of such a task, Mao's policy of self-reliance is ever less appropriate, and his weakness as a strategist ever clearer.

CHAPTER 10

Mao in History

'Who has passed judgment on the good and ill you have brought these thousand autumns?'[1] To weigh a person or a thing requires a scale. Human greatness or smallness is hard to express absolutely, and is usually expressed relatively. To weigh a revolutionary, the scale must be another revolutionary – there is no point in comparing Sun Yat-sen with Yuan Shikai[2] or Marx with Bismarck. That is why the Summary of the Rules of Propriety in the *Book of Rites* says that 'when comparing things, compare things of a like nature.'

Politicians who compare themselves to people in history let slip, without equivocation, the sort of people they are. Confucius dreamed of Duke Zhou, Zhuge Liang likened himself to Guan Zhong and Yue Yi,[3] Stalin admired himself in the mirror of Ivan the Terrible, and Chiang Kai-shek liked to imagine that he had personally penned Zeng Wenzheng's *Letters Home*,[4] revealing a commonality not just of temperament and aspiration but of class stand.

In Lenin's case, 'the Marx scale was the most titanic for measuring human personality.'[5] Although, according to Lunacharsky, Lenin 'never looks at himself, never glances in the mirror of history, never even thinks of what posterity will say of him,'[6] Nadezhda Krupskaya (Lenin's wife) said that shortly before his death he returned again and again to Trotsky's article likening him to Marx, and was perhaps touched by it. But the Marx scale cannot apply to Stalin and Mao, for although they see themselves as Marxist-Leninists, or even as today's Marx or today's Lenin, they also posture as latter-day sovereigns, affecting the literary and martial genius of their 'great ancestors.'

Lenin represented pure, thorough-going revolution, while Stalin and Mao mixed revolution and counter-revolution. So the historical worth of Lenin, and

---

1 Mao poem, 'Kunlun.'
2 Yuan Shikai (1859–1916), a Qing military commander and president of the first Chinese Republic from 1912 to 1916.
3 Duke Zhou (Zhou Gong) (d. 1032 BCE) was a member of the royal family of the Zhou dynasty famed for acting as a loyal regent, for suppressing rebellions, and for his writing. Zhuge Liang (181–234) was a statesman and strategist. Guan Zhong (c. 720–645 BCE) was a chancellor and reformer of the State of Qi. Yue Yi was a military leader of the State of Yan in the Warring States period.
4 Zeng Wenzheng is another name for Zeng Guofan, a nineteenth-century statesman and Confucian scholar.
5 Quoted in Trotsky 2012, p. 510.
6 Anatoly Lunacharsky, quoted in E.H. Carr 1950–78, 3 vols, in vol. 3, p. 164.

of Lenin-style visionaries, can be weighed on a Marx scale, while Stalin, Mao, and their like need a dual standard. They can be weighed against revolutionaries like Marx and Lenin, but also against progressive and reactionary rulers of the past. (In this book on Mao, we talk only about Mao.)

Alongside Marx and Lenin, Mao might reach to their knees but hardly to their waist. Mao himself knew this, and rarely cited the two greats. This was partly because he knew only Chinese, but the barrier was mainly one of approach. Mao felt that China's indigenous theory and experience offered a wealth of knowledge in the fields of politics and warfare. Only a handful of foreign imports – a few Comintern resolutions and some of Stalin's writings – were needed to supplement it. These things, in Mao's eyes, were nothing special. Their chief role was to provide theoretical guidance or defensive cover, for his actions. Mao knew little about Marx, Engels, and Lenin before joining the front in the modern war of ideologies, not to mention about other thinkers in the world socialist movement. He had read Stalin, as I said earlier, but only his *Questions of Leninism* together with some articles about the Chinese Revolution. As a theorist, Mao was too inferior to bear comparison, even with leaders of the Second and Third Internationals like Kautsky, Luxemburg, Mehring, Plekhanov, Trotsky, Zinoviev, and Bukharin. He had only a smattering of Marxist knowledge, a few general principles and organisational or executive methods, made in the Stalin factory of ideas and given a Lenin varnish. So Mao's name occupies a tiny place on the spectrum of revolutionary thinking, or, by comparison with Marx, no place at all.

Put theory to one side, and the discrepancy between Mao and revolutionaries of the stature of Marx and Lenin is smaller, though still there. This is mainly because Marx and Lenin always applied principles to problems, whereas Mao (like Stalin) was ready to barter them for temporary advantage. I have given many examples.

Weighed against Marx and Lenin, Mao's slightness is also manifested in his lack of internationalism. He knew from the *Communist Manifesto* that 'proletarians of all countries should unite,' but the spirit of internationalism never entered his soul. The world outside China existed for him only as a concept. Its proletariat meant nothing, in terms of material contact or spiritual exchange, to this intellectual grown up in a village in central China. During the Chinese Revolution, the first time Mao experienced the true meaning of proletarian internationalism was when the CCP received material and spiritual aid from the Soviet Union. But because of Stalin's errors and reactionary intent, this aid caused defeats in China, leading Mao to conclude that the Chinese Revolution must be self-reliant and reinforcing his national prejudice and his anti-internationalism. The victory of the Chinese Revolution and the ensuing relationship between China and the Soviet Union under Stalin finally dispelled Mao's belief in the ideal of 'proletarian unity.' Today, although Mao poses as the leader of a revolutionary faction in the world communist movement, his internationalism is for show only: in reality he represents Chinese national or state interests.

Another marker of Mao's minor status alongside Marx and Lenin is his cult of personality. Marx and Lenin valued leadership and authority, but as materialists and true workers' leaders, they knew the place of greatness and genius in history. They were neither excessively humble nor arrogant and self-righteous, and never vaunted their role. Marx remained poor throughout his life and never once tasted authority, so his humility was never on display; Lenin came to lead a state, a party and even a world party, but his modesty and plain living survived his elevation and he continued to resist and warn against personal aggrandisement. By the 1930s, however, the habits and style he had so strongly opposed in the party and state while alive had reappeared one by one, dwarfing the arrogance of ordinary bureaucratic states. Whereas Lenin had acquiesced only reluctantly in his fiftieth birthday celebrations in 1920, at which he called for 'a more suitable method of celebrating anniversaries' in future and gently warned against 'swelled heads' and (quoting Kautsky) the 'spirit of flabby philistinism and temperate politics which is beginning to spread in our midst,' Stalin's sixtieth birthday in 1938 was a realisation of Lenin's fears of a party 'stupid, shameful, and ridiculous.'[7]

To all appearances, Mao is a modest and humble person. Up to now, he has never made much of his birthday, and party resolutions have even forbidden celebrating leaders' birthdays and naming factories and streets after them. But that has not stopped the Mao cult.

How can this paradox be explained? The main reason is China's material and cultural poverty and the CCP's base among the peasants, a fertile soil for hypocrisy, bureaucracy, and the personality cult. It has roots, too, in Mao's Confucian thinking. Confucians prize modesty but do not practise it. Confucian modesty, like the whole system of rites, is strictly based on class and stratum. It is practised only among *junzi* (ethical people, 'gentlemen'), and inapplicable to the lives of ordinary Chinese, especially toilers. Confucian modesty is decreed by destiny. The idea that 'life and death are ruled by fate, and wealth and rank are matters of destiny' underpins the Confucian theory of class. It has neutralised some reformist elements in Confucianism, for example, Mencius' prescriptions, and choked off any democratic buds, and it is a talisman

---

7 Lenin, quoted in Tumarkin 1983, p. 103.

for the successful tyrant. But at the same time, the belief in fate and that 'Heaven begat the mind in me' can sometimes make tyrants behave modestly, even beyond their class. The more they believe in their own destiny and in the need for backing from on high, the more likely they are to behave modestly towards ordinary people, to condescend to them, and to share weal and woe with them. This explains the tyrants' superficial humility and actual immodesty. This is why their extreme sense of superiority is often expressed in modest ways.

Naturally, the class constraints on Confucian ethics have a different quality in Mao's case. He represents not the old-style landed aristocracy but a new aristocracy, a bureaucratic aristocracy centred on the CCP. To understand it, one must understand the ways in which Lenin's and Stalin's views on the communist party differed.

For Lenin, the party is the workers' vanguard, different from the class itself and other toilers only in the sense that it is more class conscious and politically aware. The great majority of members of the vanguard give up their jobs and devote all their efforts to socialist revolution. Although Lenin distinguished members of the vanguard (including himself) from non-members, he did not rank them separately or argue that there was an insurmountable difference between them.

Stalin had another approach. He thought that Bolsheviks were made 'in a special mould, [...] of a special stuff.'[8] The relationship between the party and the workers was not that of vanguard and rearguard but of two inherently different sorts of people, one made from superior and the other from inferior stuff. The former commanded, the latter took commands; the former ordered others to do work, the latter did the work; the former were endowed with privilege, the latter not. By extension, the party leader was made of the finest stuff, and Stalin of incomparable stuff.

Stalin's view echoed proposals voiced in the seventeenth and eighteenth century by thinkers of the French Enlightenment and reactionary Christian talk about 'God's chosen people' and 'prophets.' Mao fully accepted Stalin's approach, and combined Stalin's 'truths' with the Confucian idea of 'fate.' The CCP turned into a party that handed down 'liberation' from above and from outside, and Mao became the fated 'saviour.' Stalin and Mao's 'modesty' is a constraint on the new 'class,' on the privileged status of the communists, but it is also a product of the most reactionary theocracy, which mouths modesty while practising extreme dictatorship, and is poles apart from Lenin's idea of

---

8   Quoted in Žižek 2014, no pagination.

workers' democracy and true frugality and modesty. So Mao falls hopelessly short of 'the titanic scale,' especially because of his cult of personality and the leader.

However, on the scale of Yu, Tang, Wen, Wu,[9] Duke Zhou, and Confucius through to Sun Yat-sen, his weight changes. If the measure of Marx and Lenin is revolution, internationalism, and the spirit of the common people, that of Yu and the others is Han nationalism, autocratic monarchical absolutism, and hierarchical bureaucracy. This scale is that of thousands of years of Chinese 'orthodoxy.' The warp of the fabric thus weighed is the rise of the Chinese nation and its consolidation, its struggle to survive, and its expansion; its woof is the Confucian ethical code, with its Three Cardinal Guides and Five Constant Virtues.[10] The two are inextricably interwoven. Throughout Chinese history, this tradition has remained essentially unbroken,[11] embodied in the great figures of dynasty after dynasty, whose sages have embraced it as their orthodoxy and weighed others against it.

In more recent times, Mao named four 'advanced Chinese' who, despite hardship, 'sought truth from the West' but, even so, remained governed by this orthodoxy. They were Hong Xiuquan, Kang Youwei, Yan Fu, and Sun Yat-sen. To complete the list with Sun Yat-sen was not just Dai Jitao[12] and Chiang Kai-shek's anti-communist prejudice, for Sun Yat-sen remained firmly attached to Confucian tradition.[13] Two of his Three People's Principles were democracy and people's livelihood,[14] but they were essentially subordinate to the third, which was nationalism. For Sun Yat-sen, as for all late-Qing men and women of ideals

---

9   Together with Yao, Shun, and Duke Zhou, Yu, Tang Wen, and Wu were celebrated as the founders in ancient times of the Chinese political order.
10 The three cardinal guides governed relations between ruler and minister, father and son, and husband and wife. The five constant virtues were benevolence, righteousness, propriety, knowledge, and integrity.
11 On many occasions, China's Han people have come under non-Han rule, especially in the Yuan and Qing Dynasties. However, Chinese society did not change, and Confucianism retained its functions, even in the hands of non-Han rulers. Han nationalism as concocted by the Confucians was conceived elastically rather than narrowly, and could incorporate 'barbarians' (note by Wang).
12 Dai Jitao (1890–1949) was a Guomindang theoretician who believed China's crisis was rooted in morality.
13 In *Son Bun-shugi no tetsugaku kiso* ('The Basics of Sun Yat-sen's Philosophy', 1925), Dai Jitao said Sun Yat-sen's philosophy 'originated in the orthodox thought of the *Doctrine of the Mean*.' Chiang Kai-shek had a similar view. See Kawata Teiichi, *Confucianism and Sun Yat-sen's Views on Civilization*. This view ran counter to the CCP's image of Sun Yat-sen, as pro-Soviet and pro-communist.
14 Sometimes interpreted as socialism.

and integrity, the principle of national rejuvenation was the watchword and the goal, to which all else was ancillary. To achieve it, he bent every effort to overthrowing the 'alien' Manchu tyranny that had ruled the Han people for more than two hundred years, while striving to replace the Manchus' corrupt and incompetent Qing with western bourgeois democracy (and even social reformism). In a new era and on a new class basis, he adopted and tried to carry forward existing orthodoxy.

In a certain sense, orthodoxy adopted and propagated in this way is, in part, negated. Generally speaking, however, Sun Yat-sen must, because of his role in Chinese history, be weighed in its scale and in no other.

Mao is, of course, further away than Sun Yat-sen from orthodoxy, and the extent of the negation is greater, but even he can be weighed in its scale. In it, Mao can be seen to use methods pioneered by the Russians to raise the Han Chinese to unprecedented heights. Thus weighed, Mao, adopting the form of a people's government, has clearly taken totalitarianism to an extreme, with hierarchies of seniority at all levels and in all fields.

From the point of view either of his weight as an individual or of that of the Chinese people as a whole, Mao belongs on the same scale as Wen, Wu, Duke Zhou, and Confucius. As an individual, he is a proud hero who founded an empire; from the point of view of the nation, he saved the Red Territory and the Divine Land[15] from perdition and returned pride and confidence to the Chinese people. Even if his exploits have not matched those of Genghis Khan, they have certainly overtaken those of the founders of the Han and Tang.

Ever since the start of the global age, the Chinese people led by the Han have been enslaved, despised, and viewed as pitiful and submissive. Ever since Chinese politicians at the end of the Qing dynasty were catapulted by capitalism into the world they have been ridiculed and seen as clowns. They have allowed themselves to be bullied and China to lose face. As a result, they lost confidence in themselves, admitted failure and defeat, and became slaves. But the great majority of Chinese reacted furiously to humiliation, oppression, and loss of national pride, and rose up against the foreign invaders and their Chinese compradors. Over the past century, China has witnesses a succession of upheavals, revolts, and revolutions in which countless Chinese have lost their lives. The main reason is that people are seeking to restore national pride by standing up to free themselves, so that the Han people, even if they do not occupy a dominant position among modern states, can at least occupy an equal position.

---

15 Names for China.

To achieve this end, they have had to go through a long and tortuous struggle, including the Opium War, the Taiping Revolution, the Reform Movement, the 1911 Revolution, and the Revolution 1925–7, right through to Chiang Kai-shek's 'victory' in the War Against Japan. During these years, hopes were constantly dashed by defeats. Events staged to elevate China's national status, like joining the Big Four after the Second World War, were manipulated by the Americans, and ended in ridicule and humiliation. The Guomindang's failure to retain the confidence of the people was due in no small measure to its opposition to the movement to restore national pride.

Conversely, Mao and the CCP owed their victory in no small measure to their honouring of it. When the communists' army marched into the cities, the foreigners, normally arrogant, suddenly become submissive, for the first time in one hundred years. When Chinese leaders attended international conferences for the government, they met with either respect or hatred, but no longer with ridicule or manipulation. They could glare back at the enemy and apply the penalty of tooth for tooth. They no longer bowed and scraped to China's 'friends,' and they refused to give up their own position when 'leaning to one side.' When necessary, they were able to say 'no.' Since all these things happened under a party and state led by Mao, he can clearly be said to bear comparison with Yu, Tang, Wen, Wu, Duke Zhou, and Confucius.

Obviously, China owes its new international standing to the victory of the revolution of its workers and peasants and not to Mao personally, or to his nationalism. However, in ordinary people's eyes the opposite perception holds, and Mao uses it to boost his cult.

But if Mao Zedong is indisputably a good son of his 'great ancestors,' he is even more so a bad student of Marx and Lenin. The two measures are not necessarily in conflict or incompatible. It depends on which great figures one sees as one's forebears and what position nationalism occupies in internationalism, what is its specific gravity; and whether, once nationalism as a progressive force in the revolution has run its course and has begun to play a reactionary and harmful role, it can be promptly and resolutely shut down.

On the first point, Lenin's comments about 'The National Pride of the Great Russians' bear quoting:

> Is a sense of national pride alien to us, Great-Russian class-conscious proletarians? Certainly not! We love our language and our country, and we are doing our very utmost to raise *her* toiling masses (i.e., nine-tenths of *her* population) to the level of a democratic and socialist consciousness. To us it is most painful to see and feel the outrages, the oppression and the humiliation our fair country suffers at the hands of the tsar's butchers,

the nobles and the capitalists. We take pride in the resistance to these outrages put up from our midst, from the Great Russians; in *that* midst having produced Radishchev, the Decembrists and the revolutionary commoners of the seventies; in the Great-Russian working class having created, in 1905, a mighty revolutionary party of the masses; and in the Great-Russian peasantry having begun to turn towards democracy and set about overthrowing the clergy and the landed proprietors.[16]

This paragraph answers the first question. The forbears in whom Lenin took pride were not Ivan the Terrible, Peter the Great, or some wise Romanov – even though some tsars did play a role in the formation and development of the Russian people and Russia's Westernization, to which extent they could be said to be progressive. Nor does Lenin name distinguished generals like Suvorov and Kutuzov as symbols of 'national pride,' despite their illustrious military exploits, or bishops, although some did much for Russia's culture and language, which Lenin mentions. Lenin was a dialectician, and was able to make an objective assessment of the value of these people. However, he was first and foremost a proletarian revolutionary, so instead he names Radishchev,[17] the Decembrists, and revolutionary commoners.

Stalin's approach was the opposite of Lenin's, and Mao reached the same destination as Stalin but by a different route. Like Lenin, Mao took pride in China's uprisings, and he also praised China's Radishchevs, Decembrists, and revolutionary commoners. However, he focused even more so on those heroes who 'made countless bows in homage to this land so rich in beauty.' Lenin, in contrast, found it 'most painful' to see how in 'our fair country' such people committed outrages.

The second question can be answered even more briefly, since we have already touched on it. In a nutshell, in Mao thought internationalism is always subordinate to nationalism. It is method and a tactic, whereas nationalism is the goal. Mao's speeches and writings, especially after the Sino-Soviet split, abound with professions of loyalty to proletarian internationalism. I have written elsewhere about why the CCP came out against revisionism, so here I will limit myself to this: a true internationalist cannot adhere to the doctrine of socialism in one country, the view that socialism can be successfully construc-

---

16   Lenin, 'On the National Pride of the Great Russians,' December 12, 1914, CW, vol. 21, pp. 102–6, at 103.
17   A.N. Radishchev (1749–1802) was one of Russia's earliest democratic thinkers. Born into an aristocratic family, he advocated the abolition of serfdom and opposed autocracy. He was exiled to Siberia, and later committed suicide by drinking poison.

ted country by country, in independent political and economic units. Those who think it can are not internationalists, however high they raise the banner of proletarian internationalism.

Mao is now in his seventies. His thinking will not change. However, one cannot pass judgment on a person's life until the lid is on the coffin. Events can sway anyone, however strong. At present, the CCP is in an argument with the CPSU in which Mao bears the banner of internationalism and world revolution. Mao's new role has been forced on him by circumstance – outside and inside do not tally. Does that rule out future events driving this revolutionary leader of the internationalist faction, who once chose to climb Mount Liang, from turning play-acting into reality and acquiring greatness even in the scales of Marxism? In theory, no. However, one condition must first obtain: a group of true revolutionary internationalists must first arise, especially in China, inside and outside the CCP, and must be in a position to exert an influence before Mao's fake internationalism is made real. That would already imply a political revolution in China and in other places. It would lead to a thorough reform of the party leading to China's democratisation, to which Mao, because of his deep-rooted imperial thinking and his national orthodoxy and absolutism, would be unable to respond and whose target he would probably become.

Here, I am reminded of Shelley, who wrote

> that Virtue owns a more eternal foe
> than Force or Fraud: old Custom.

Shelley was talking about Napoleon, who proclaimed himself emperor. Shelley called him 'a most ambitious slave' who chose 'a frail and bloody pomp,' which has poisoned virtue ever since ancient times. Stalin was deluded by such pomp and became an even more ambitious slave and victim of the 'eternal foe.' Mao had the same ambition. Will he, one hundred years from now, be seen as a slave of old custom and belie my view of him?

This will depend not on Mao as an individual but on the struggle of communists throughout the world, especially that of China's revolutionary internationalists. In it, Mao might swing this way or that, but however far he swings, it will not be far enough to disqualify him as the prime target of future revolutionaries.

Completed in August 1964

APPENDIX 1

Seven Theses on Socialism and Democracy (1957)

In theses written in Macao, Wang Fanxi recalled positions that he had advanced between 1936 and 1940 in exchanges with Chen Duxiu, founder of the CCP and also of its Trotskyist offshoot. In the mid to late 1930s the Moscow show-trials and Stalin's alliance with Hitler caused Chen to conclude that Lenin's denial of the value of democracy was in part responsible for Stalin's crimes and that dictatorship of any sort, revolutionary or counterrevolutionary, is incompatible with democracy. Whereas for Lenin proletarian dictatorship was simultaneously – at least for the workers – the most extensive form of democracy, Chen no longer bothered to distinguish the various democratic rights from democracy as the bourgeois governing form. Wang and other Trotskyists believed that democracy was not abstract but bounded by class and time, but for Chen after 1938 it was a transcendental concept embodied in universal institutions. Even so, Wang did not dismiss from hand Chen's formulations, but strove to develop along Marxist lines what he found in them to be perceptive and valuable. In the course of their exchange, Chen and Wang raised – decades in advance of the mainstream of communist dissent – issues that bear directly on the vexed relationship between socialism and democratic freedoms. I include them here as an illustration of the Chinese Trotskyist critique of the Maoist political system (Source: Gregor Benton, ed., *Prophets Unarmed*, pp. 773–74.).

1. Under present historical conditions if the proletariat through its political party aims to overthrow the political and economic rule of the bourgeoisie, it must carry out a violent revolution and set up a dictatorship to expropriate the expropriators. So in nine cases out of ten it is bound to destroy the bourgeoisie's traditional means of rule – the parliamentary system. To complete such a transformation 'peacefully,' through parliament, is practically if not absolutely impossible.
2. A proletarian dictatorship set up in such a way neither must nor should destroy the various democratic rights – including habeus corpus; freedom of speech, the press, assembly, and association; the right to strike; etc. – already won by the people under the bourgeois democratic system.
3. The organs of the dictatorship elected by the entire toiling people should be under the thorough-going supervision of the electors and recallable by them at all times; and the power of the dictatorship should not be concentrated in one body but should be spread across several structures so

there is a system of checks and balances to prevent the emergence of an autocracy or monocracy.
4. Opposition parties should be allowed to exist under the dictatorship as long as they support the revolution. Whether or not they meet this condition should be decided by the workers and peasants in free ballot.
5. Opposition factions must be tolerated within the party of the proletariat. Under no circumstances must organisational sanctions, secret-service measures, or incriminatory sanctions be used to deal with dissidents; under no circumstances must thought be made a crime.
6. Under no circumstances must proletarian dictatorship become the dictatorship of a single party. Workers' parties organised by part of the working class and the intelligentsia must under no circumstances replace the political power democratically elected by the toilers as a whole. There must be an end to the present system in the communist countries, where government is a facade behind which secretaries of the party branches assume direct command. The ruling party's strategic policies must first be discussed and approved by an empowered parliament (or soviet) that includes opposition parties and factions, and only then should they be implemented by government; and their implementation must continue to be supervised by parliament.
7. Finally, [...] since political democracy is actually a reflection of economic democracy and no political democracy is possible under a system of absolutely centralized economic control, [...] to create the material base for socialist democracy a system of divided power and self-management within the overall planned economy is essential.

All these points are not in themselves enough to save a revolutionary power from bureaucratic degeneration; but since they are not plucked from the void but rooted in bloody experience, they should – if formulated with sufficient clarity – (a) help workers and peasants in countries that have had revolutions to win their anti-bureaucratic struggle when the conditions for the democratisation of the dictatorial state have further ripened; and (b) enable new revolutionary states from the very outset to avoid bureaucratic poisoning.

APPENDIX 2

Thinking in Solitude (1957)

This chapter, omitted from the 1980 Oxford University Press edition of Wang's memoirs, was reinstated in 1991 by Columbia University Press. It looks at the causes of Mao's victory and of the Chinese Trotskyists' defeat (This is the closing chapter of Memoirs of a Chinese Revolutionary, *second revised edition, New York: Columbia University Press, 1991.).*

At the time of writing these lines, in July 1957, I am fifty years old. For the past eight years I have been living on a tiny island off the south China coast, with more than a little time to think. To earn my living I have had to devote much of my energy to writing plays, but this has in no way changed my basic calling. I have remained a revolutionary, keeping a close watch on the changes that have taken place in the world at large and particularly in China. Since December 1952, when my comrades inside China were rounded up by the CCP's secret police, I have no longer been able to play an active part in political life, but this has not prevented me from thinking. In absolute isolation and solitude a person's thinking usually gains in intensity, and so it was with me. The pity is that so much of my time has been taken up with the problem of earning a bare living that up to now I have never had the chance to record all my thoughts over these last few years.

Although I have no intention in what is essentially a book of memoirs of making a detailed examination of the recent development of my thinking, still a short account of some of the problems I have engaged will not be altogether out of place here, particularly since thinking has been more or less my sole political activity in recent times. In an epoch such as ours, however few people may actually share my positions, there must be many addressing similar questions and searching just as anxiously for answers. To such people, I hope my opinions will be of some value.

My thinking over the last few years has focused mainly on two questions. Why, if in terms of overall strategy the Chinese Stalinists were wrong and the Chinese Trotskyists were right, did they end up victorious and we in defeat? And what are the main lessons for the world socialist movement of their victory and our failure?

'Ah-Q-ism'[1] is a harmful affliction, particularly in a revolutionary, but revolu-

---

1 Ah-Q is the antihero of Lu Xun's *The True Story of Ah-Q*. The usual meaning of Ah-Q-ism is to seek consolation by fantasising defeat into victory.

tionaries are particularly prey to it, for the very qualities that mark them out – perseverance, tenacity, and an unbounded confidence in one's cause – often prevent them from recognising their own defeats and admitting their enemies' successes. It is hard, of course, to draw a clear distinction between self-confidence of this sort and revolutionary firmness, for the one is an essential ingredient of the other. But carried to excess, what may originally have been a virtue ends up as 'Ah-Q-ism' of the worst sort. To defend one's beliefs blindly and to dress up others' victories as defeats and our defeats as victories is positively harmful to the revolution. A fact remains a fact whether or not we recognise it as one. People who deliberately close their eyes to reality sooner or later end up bumping their heads against it, whereupon they usually surrender unconditionally to the very facts that only yesterday they so stubbornly denied.

True revolutionary confidence comes only on the basis of a cool assessment of how things really are. To recognise defeat is not at all the same as to surrender to the enemy: there is no reason why it should automatically lead to demoralisation. In all social struggles – particularly the bitter and complex struggles of modern class society – victories and defeats invariably alternate, so the path to socialism is never straight but zigzag and uneven. Those who travel it must be able to draw the lessons of the defeats through which it inevitably passes.

'What is known as calamity is often good fortune in disguise. What is called good fortune is often a cause of calamity.' This is Mao Zedong's favourite quotation from the ancient Chinese philosopher Laozi; he often took heart from it in his darkest hours. Perhaps we too can profit from an examination of the 'good fortune' of the Chinese Stalinists and the 'calamity' of the Chinese Trotskyists in the light of Laozi's teaching. But good fortune is only bestowed on those capable of grasping reality. Here Laozi reminds us of Spinoza's 'not to laugh, not to cry, but to understand,' advice we would do well to bear in mind in attempting any such assessment.

As I said earlier, the Chinese Trotskyist movement entered a period of intellectual ferment in late 1949 and early 1950. Shaken to the core by the unexpectedness of what had happened (for none of us had ever reckoned with the possibility of a CCP victory), we began in the light of the new situation to reconsider our fundamental positions and beliefs. In this atmosphere of intense turmoil and in the heat of events, I made my own attempt to come to grips with the causes of the CCP victory, and noted some of my conclusions in a booklet published in early 1950.[2] In it I said that the Soviet Union had turned into a bureaucratic

---

2 Yi De (Wang Fanxi) 1950.

collectivist state, and the Stalinist party into a party of collectivist bureaucrats. From this I concluded that the victory of the CCP was merely the victory of a collectivist bureaucratic party and in no way the victory of a Chinese proletarian party, that is, of proletarian revolution.

This analysis seemed to me to explain many features of the Stalinist parties and to solve the riddle of the CCP victory. Gradually, however, I discovered that for all its advantages and its theoretical consistency, once applied to revolutionary practice (such as which side to take in the civil war between the CCP and the Guomindang) it proved to be wholly inappropriate and plainly wrong. Armed with this discovery, I returned again from the realm of politics to sociology and from practicalities to theoretical research, and eventually I arrived at the conclusion that among the numerous theoretical analyses of the Soviet Union and Stalinism advanced both inside and outside the Fourth International, Trotsky's was by far the strongest and in the best interests of socialist revolution. I had launched my soul onto unknown seas only to land again at the port where I had embarked. Some may mock me for this. Let them. All that matters to me is the search for truth, and for the key to the completion of the revolution.

To tell the whole story of how I travelled this ideological circuit, with its various periods and stages, would require more lines than I have room for here, and in any case I intend to devote a special study to this question.[3]

So I will confine myself here to a brief discussion of the class nature of the CCP and the historical role of Stalinist parties in general, for it was on these two questions that we Chinese Trotskyists developed a number of positions from which flowed our wrong analysis in and around 1949. Perhaps this discussion will serve as a warning example of how easy it is for revolutionaries to fall captive to their own prescriptions if they do not continually check them against events.

For many years up to and even after 1949 we Chinese Trotskyists had believed that the CCP represented the interests of the petty bourgeoisie (mainly peasants and intellectuals) and was no longer a party of the working class. None of us had ever considered why – we simply took it as self-evident. That the CCP had withdrawn from the big cities, lived in and drawn its forces from the countryside, and abandoned class struggle in favour of class peace was more than enough to confirm us in our opinion.

---

[3] This study, titled *Sixiang wenti* ('Some ideological questions') was mimeographed in 1962 and printed in Hong Kong in 1982. It comprises three articles: 'On Chen Duxiu's Opinions Expressed in His Last Years' (1957); 'On the Twentieth Anniversary of the Transitional Programme' (1958); and 'A Letter to Friends' (1958).

It is impossible to say who first advanced this analysis. In his report to the International Secretariat of the Fourth International in November 1951, Peng Shuzhi tried to attribute it to Trotsky, arguing that 'beginning with 1930, Trotsky repeatedly pointed out that the CCP had gradually degenerated from a workers' party into a peasant party.'[4] But this assertion is quite groundless. In the letter to the Chinese Left Opposition that Peng quotes ('Peasant War in China and the Proletariat'), Trotsky never once argued that the CCP had 'gradually degenerated from a workers' party into a peasant party.' Instead he simply talked about the possible outcome of the struggle between the two factions of the CCP, that is, if a civil war were to break out between a peasant army led by Stalinists and a proletarian vanguard led by Leninists 'the Left Opposition and the Stalinists would have ceased to be communist factions and would have become hostile parties, each with a different class basis.' But he went straight on from this theoretical hypothesis to ask if such a perspective was inevitable. His answer was unequivocal: 'No, I don't think so at all. Within the Stalinist faction (the official Chinese Communist Party) there are not only peasant, that is, petty bourgeois tendencies, but also proletarian tendencies.'[5]

Trotsky's letter was written on September 22, 1932, nearly a whole year before he decided to call for new communist parties and a new International. So at a time when we still considered ourselves a faction of the CCP, Trotsky was allegedly arguing that this same CCP had degenerated from a workers' into a peasants' party!

It was precisely our wrong understanding of the class nature of the CCP that to a large extent determined our positions on it – in particular the significance of its eventual victory over the Guomindang – both before and after 1949. Having once established that it was a petty bourgeois party, we were logically driven to conclude that it could never lead a genuine revolution, still less lead to victory: for it is a fundamental theorem of Marxism (and of Trotsky's theory of permanent revolution in particular) that in the modem age and in a backward country even the bourgeois-democratic tasks of the revolution can only be solved by a thoroughgoing revolution led by the proletariat and its party. Even during the civil war between the CCP and the Guomindang from 1946 to 1949 we invariably argued that a peasant army led by a petty bourgeois party was almost bound to lose, and that even if by some remote chance it won, it would inevitably end up in a blind alley. When facts proved otherwise and the revolution led by the CCP not only triumphed but deepened, we remained

---

4 'The Causes of the Victory of the CCP over Chiang Kai-shek, and the CCP's Perspectives,' in P'eng Shu-tse (Peng Shuzhi) 1980, p. 108.
5 P'eng Shu-tse 1980, p. 530.

tightly bound by our old preconceptions. Instead of promptly recognising the revolution for what it was, we continued to cling to our old assessment and to look for theoretical supports to bridge the growing gap between what had really happened and what we thought had happened. We now argued not only that the CCP was no longer a proletarian party but that it was not even a petty bourgeois party; instead, it represented the interests of an entirely new class – a class Zheng Chaolin called state capitalist and I called bureaucratic collectivist. We believed that such classes were the product of a whole series of defeats of the revolution on a world scale and of the overgrowth of the capitalist system, so they were powerful but reactionary. Unlike the petty bourgeoisie, they were strong enough to overthrow the old bourgeois regimes – in China, the Guomindang – and to turn society on its head. But unlike the proletariat, they were incapable of moving onward in the direction of socialism, and would at best establish a regime of state capitalism or bureaucratic collectivism.

In this way, Zheng Chaolin and I built further on our old assessment of the CCP.

Peng Shuzhi and a number of his followers responded to the situation in a different way, clinging to the same old formula and flatly denying that China had had a revolution. For two years, right up to November 1951, Peng argued that the new regime was 'actually a naked Bonapartist military dictatorship of the petty bourgeoisie and bourgeoisie, based on the armed peasantry,' and that 'such a military dictatorship will never change its bourgeois character.'[6] In May 1952, however, he suddenly discovered that it had lost its bourgeois character and acquired a 'dual character' because 'the worker elements have increased in number in the last two years ... (during the agrarian reform and the campaign against corruption).'[7] However, he continued to insist that the party up to then had been a party of peasants, and that its earlier seizure of power had been not a revolution but an accident resulting from a conjuncture of exceptional historical circumstances.

Like Zheng Chaolin and me, Peng was unable to wrench himself free from the old formula, but unlike us he continues to insist to this day that we Chinese Trotskyists were absolutely right to apply it to the theory and practice of the

---

6 Quoted from 'The Political Resolution,' written by Peng on January 17, 1950, and adopted at a meeting of Peng's group in Hong Kong. In his report to the Third Congress of the Fourth International, Peng formulated the same idea in a slightly different form. See P'eng Shu-tse, 'The Causes of the Victory of the CCP over Chiang Kai-shek, and the CCP's Perspectives,' in P'eng Shu-tse 1980, p. 110.

7 Op. cit., p. 136.

Chinese Revolution at each stage in its development. I am not concerned here with whether Peng's claim to infallibility is valid, and will return to it in a future study.[8]

I said earlier that we had based our assessment of the CCP on the observation that it had (a) withdrawn from the cities into the countryside and recruited its forces almost exclusively from the peasantry rather than the working class and (b) capitulated in 1937 to the Guomindang in the name of unity against Japan, by declaring its conversion to Sun Yat-senism, accepting the reorganisation of its armed forces into the armed forces of the Guomindang, and promising to give up class struggle. On the face of it, this was decisive enough proof of the charges we were making: a party that had torn itself away from the working class, left the main battleground, and given up its revolutionary platform could no longer be called working class.

So when we first declared in the mid-1930s that the CCP had degenerated into a party of the petty bourgeoisie, we were acting on entirely reasonable assumptions. Where we went wrong was in failing to check our assessment against reality, and in closing our eyes to developments that might falsify our analysis. Looking back, I can now see we ignored four key facts. First, the CCP withdrawal from the cities was neither voluntary nor deliberate, but mainly the result of Guomindang persecution and repression, so it could not be taken as proof that the CCP had committed itself to a new strategic orientation to peasant war rather than proletarian revolution. Second, after withdrawing into the countryside the CCP did not forsake, in either words or deeds, the platform of 'a revolutionary united front under the leadership of the proletariat.' Third, while it is true that the CCP abandoned class struggle during the second united front, that is, it called off land revolution and submitted to the leadership of Chiang Kai-shek in a decisive turn that we rightly denounced at the time as a final capitulation, by and large the turn was at the level of tactical manoeuvre rather than of strategy and was never carried to its logical conclusion, the main reason being that there were still revolutionary tendencies in the CCP that opposed Stalin's policy of capitulation. Fourth, during both the 'soviet and Red Army' period and the 'united front and Eighth Route Army' period, the CCP all along remained an organisation of highly disciplined revolutionaries and carried out its recruitment (both political and military) on a class basis. If we Chinese Trotskyists had kept a closer eye on these developments and constantly checked our assessment of the CCP against them, we would have understood the true meaning of the victory of the CCP and would have

---

8   I.e., this present volume.

made fewer mistakes in developing our own work and ideas. Lenin once said something of relevance in this connection. Discussing the problem of British Communists joining the Labour Party, he said: 'Of course, most of the Labour Party's members are working men. However, whether or not a party is really a political party of workers does not depend solely upon a membership of workers but also upon the men that lead it, and the content of its actions and its political tactics. Only this latter determines whether we really have before us a political party of the proletariat. Regarded from this, the only correct, point of view, the Labour Party is a thoroughly bourgeois party.'[9]

Following Lenin's method, we Chinese Trotskyists should have paid more attention to the 'men [and women] that led' the CCP. We should have kept a close eye on the struggle between the various tendencies (particularly the Maoists and the Wang Mingites) in its leadership and tirelessly analysed the 'content of its actions and political tactics.' But instead we put too much emphasis on its social composition, which was overwhelmingly peasant, and so concluded that it was a petty bourgeois party; which later led me to adopt the theory of bureaucratic collectivism. So we were unable to foresee a great many of the developments in the Third Chinese Revolution or to understand them even after they had happened. Had we followed Lenin's method, we would early on have developed a different view of the CCP. We would have admitted that in spite of its massive bureaucratic degeneration and its oppressive internal regime, its overwhelmingly peasant composition, its unprincipled manoeuvres, and its distortions of Marxism, it was still a working class party of sorts, though it was more so in some periods than in others and it acquired a number of grotesque and repellent features.

It is precisely because we failed to follow this procedure that we fell so wide of the mark in our criticism of the CCP in the 1940s and immediately after the establishment of the new regime.

The extreme confusion sown in the ranks of the Trotskyist movement in both China and the world by the victory of the CCP in 1949 was due not only to our wrong analysis of the class nature of that party but also to one crucial mistake in our view of the historical role of Stalinism in general.

Ever since the task of creating a new International was first broached in 1933, we had analysed the Third International as historically spent and no longer capable of playing the role of headquarters of the world revolution. The parties affiliated to it, organisationally and ideologically rotted by the Stalin canker,

---

9   Lenin, 'Speech on Affiliation to the British Labour Party,' August 6, 1920, CW, vol. 31, p. 257.

could no longer be renovated or revitalised into revolutionary parties. They never led a revolution to victory, and they would go out of their way to sabotage, betray, and suppress any revolutionary upsurge not under their direct control. However incredible it might seem, they not only could not but would not take victory for themselves, for any victorious revolution outside the USSR would in the long run weaken and destroy Moscow's bureaucratic control over its 'vassals and dependencies' in the Third International.

This analysis is fundamentally sound and was in the main borne out by a number of events of world importance between 1934 and 1945. However, in our exaggerated and mechanical interpretation of it, the view that Stalinist parties will refuse to make revolution even if to do so puts the helm of state into their hands developed into a sheer prejudice, and explains our utter confusion in the face of the CCP victory in 1949.

This is not the place for a detailed account of the overall evolution of Trotskyism on a world scale – how it grew from a faction of the communist party into an independent organisation, and how it broke from the Third International and launched the Fourth. Suffice it to say that in the summer and autumn of 1933, after Stalin's 'Third Period' policy had paved the way for Hitler's triumph in Germany and the whole of the Third International had supported his positions, Trotsky's decision to call for new communist parties and a new International was just as necessary and had the same historic significance as Lenin's call for a new (Third) International in 1914, when the parties of the Second International came out in support of their respective ruling classes in the imperialist war.

In making the analogy, however, we should note that the history of the past twenty years has shown that the actions of the Third International (which we declared dead in 1933) have differed in significant ways from those of the Second International after 1914. There are a number of fundamental differences between the parties of Stalinism and of social democracy. Even today the former are actually still not reconcilable with capitalism, for they fight to maintain and consolidate state property in the Soviet Union and at the same time work for the creation of a similar system in the capitalist countries. To judge by what they say and write, they are scarcely distinguishable from classical Menshevism, but whereas classical Menshevism is a position of principle and strategy, 'Menshevism' of the Stalinist variety has (at least since 1930) been little more than a series of tactical measures, a smokescreen behind which to carry out political manoeuvres. We Trotskyists have never taken this difference seriously, so we have tended to overlook or underestimate the anti-capitalist aspect of Stalinist parties and have been taken unawares by at least three important developments over the past ten years: first, instead of reverting to capitalism (as we had predicted), the system of state property in the Soviet Union emerged from the Second World War stronger than ever; second, the economic and political system of the Soviet Union was exported (at bayonet point) to Eastern Europe; third, the Chinese Communist Party defeated the Guomindang and began to reconstruct the Chinese economy on the model of the Soviet Union.

So we must admit that we have underestimated the anti-capitalist potential of these parties, which even now is still not entirely exhausted. What then of Trotsky's decision to establish a new International?

Judged from the point of view of the long-term interests of world socialist revolution, we were right to argue that the Third International no longer had any positive role to play, that its thinking, politics, and organisation had degenerated to the point where it would never again complete a revolution like the one in Russia or establish a workers' government like in the early days of the Soviet Union. The path of internal reform had been blocked: a new revolutionary International had become necessary.

This was the only conceivable solution to the problems posed by historical circumstance, and we must continue to defend it now and in the future as stubbornly as we ever did in the past.

But the way in which we understood and interpreted the 1933 decision must be judged separately. Our contention that the Stalinist parties would do no more than serve the Kremlin directly and the world bourgeoisie indirectly, squander the fruits of revolution (especially state-owned property) in the Soviet Union, and betray or crush revolutions that might break out elsewhere in the world even where this would place state power in their hands was demonstrably wrong.

Perhaps one or two of these views can be ascribed to Trotsky, but most of them are mechanistic derivatives from or even caricatures of Trotsky's original positions. Here I am not interested in who authored these mistakes. What does concern me is that, over the last twenty years or more, precisely these views have decided our attitude as Trotskyists toward Stalinism throughout the world; and we Chinese Trotskyists were at the very least among their most stubborn proponents.

This is why, even after the CCP's stunning victories around Xuzhou and Bengbu in late 1948, Trotskyists like Liu Jialiang argued that the Chinese Stalinists would never inflict a nationwide defeat on the Guomindang; why, even after the fall of Guangzhou in the autumn of 1949, they declared that the CCP would decline to reap the fruit of victory; and why, even after the new regime had been established in Beijing and land revolution had been extended throughout China, they asserted that the CCP was not only unable but unwilling to retain state power, and that agrarian reform would (for some unspecified reason) stop at the northern bank of the Yangtze.[10]

But if we renounce such seemingly essential parts of our analysis of Stalinism, how can we continue to argue that the 1933 decision to create a new International was and remains correct and necessary? Should we not admit that since the analysis upon which this decision was based has been undermined, the International should disband and surrender to the Stalinists?

No few Chinese Trotskyists have done so, including veterans like Li Ji and Liu Renjing. A few surrendered under pressure, but most did so from conviction. Before they finally went over to the CCP in the early 1950s I had a chance to discuss this with a number of them, either face to face or through letters. My arguments can be more or less reduced to the following two points.

First, while it is true that Stalinist parties are far less easily reconciled to capitalism than are the social democratic parties, there is still no reason to believe they can adopt a strategy and tactics of the sort necessary for socialist revolution.

Second, even if Stalinist parties can under certain circumstances fight capitalism and carry out a revolution, we should not neglect the equally fundamental question of how they do so, and what sort of regimes they form. As the newly established Stalinist states multiply, this aspect of the problem will increasingly eclipse the other in importance.

Revolutions cannot be made to order and along a predetermined path, but we should still recognise that goal and means are interdependent and that means to no small extent determine goals. The difference between one means and another can amount to hundreds of thousands of human lives, so the choice between them is crucially important and deserves our closest consideration. Moreover, bureaucratic rule will never create a truly socialist society. In the absence (however unlikely) of a successful anti-bureaucratic upsurge by the workers, bureaucratic rule, with its inevitable inter-state wars and conflicts, will spell the collapse into barbarism of human society as a whole.

Needless to say, I did not succeed in convincing my old friends or in preventing them from going over (some from Hong Kong) to the new regime in China. To their great misfortune and disappointment, the authorities doubted the sincerity of their conversion, so few of them got jobs and some were even arrested and cast into jail. In the light of their own experience and of recent develop-

---

10   Liu Jialiang 1949.

ments in the Soviet Union, Poland, and Hungary, most must now realise that their decision to surrender to the Stalinists was wrong.

The Yugoslavian experience, Khrushchev's exposure of Stalin's crimes at the Twentieth Congress of the CPSU, and the tragic events in Poland and Hungary have posed in all its immediacy the problem of how to establish and maintain genuine workers' power.

In his famous speech of December 7, 1956, E. Kardelj, Vice-President of the Federal People's Assembly of Yugoslavia, said: 'It should be noted that since the progressive socialist forces have thus far lacked experience in combating bureaucratism, to induce a form of true democracy from experience is out of the question. Before the Twentieth Congress of the CPSU only the Yugoslavian party had ever seriously searched for and eventually found a series of political measures to resolve the contradictions of the period of transition and established institutions of mass self-management in various areas of social activity, thereby enabling our society to get rid of those political forms and measures used by bureaucratic elements in their attempt to reduce the whole of society to stagnation.'[11]

Kardelj rightly emphasised the importance of combating bureaucratism (though it is another question whether Yugoslavia itself has succeeded in doing so). But he forgot to say that Trotskyism was born from precisely such a struggle and has accumulated valuable experience from the fight for a 'form of true democracy.' For although the Fourth International has so far achieved little of real significance in practical politics, it has contributed richly to theoretical research into the problems of the transition to socialism, in which sense it represents the pinnacle of contemporary Marxism.

Recent experience in the Soviet Union and Eastern Europe shows that there has been no serious or successful attempt to resolve the problems of bureaucratic rule, although the struggles that have broken out there have in general been against bureaucracy. This suggests that without the programme advocated over the years by the Fourth International, the efforts of those currently raising a hue and cry against bureaucratism will surely fail. But although such people have still not broken in practice with Stalinism, what they say is still encouraging. It proves that we Trotskyists have not been fighting in vain over the last thirty years, that our ranks will swell and that Stalinist domination of the world communist movement is coming to an end. In coming years whether we actually achieve anything will depend in part on how far we suc-

---

11   This quotation is retranslated from the Chinese.

ceed in integrating our programme and membership with anti-bureaucratic mass movement in countries under communist rule. But we must never forget to check our positions in the light of events, to hold firm to those that are right, and to right or discard those that are wrong. A Fourth International full of life and energy is more necessary now than it ever was, and must be strengthened and expanded. We have no reason to be pessimistic, still less to desert our organisation.

We first launched the campaign for a new International in 1933, mainly because of our political appraisal of Stalinism but also because of the internal structure of Stalinist parties, which brook no opposition. Now, however, we have begun to notice for the first time (beyond the isolated example of Yugoslavia) that a general process of differentiation is taking place within the Stalinist parties and the countries under their rule, so there is a slight prospect of some degree of internal reform. Should we change our attitude toward them accordingly? Should the world Trotskyist movement return to its old pre-1933 position, which looked to reform existing communist parties rather than set up new ones? I think not. The events in Hungary in 1956 showed how stubbornly those in power in the party and the state will fight to defend themselves and that they will not make the slightest concessions except under the direct revolutionary pressure of the mass movement. So we should continue to propagate unwaveringly the necessity of anti-bureaucratic political revolution in these countries. But at the same time we should avoid interpreting and applying this position mechanistically. The various communist parties and the states they control are no longer Stalinist to an identical degree, and conflicts and struggles are breaking out among them. We should not stand aside from these fights, like passive onlookers. Rather than indiscriminately attack each side with equal force, we should distinguish between them and tirelessly pay attention to the conflicts and struggles, no matter how small, that divide them; and we should give critical support to those that prove the more progressive. In so doing, our revolutionary attitude towards the faction or party concerned should be fairly flexible in its tactical application.

In sum, with our fundamental tenets unrevised, that is, sticking firmly to the position of preparing political revolution in all degenerated or deformed workers' states (whether Stalinist, semi-Stalinist, or 'de-Stalinised') by siding with the toiling people in their fight for democracy and against privilege, we should at the same time pay more attention to the specific application to different circumstances of our basically identical position. A right policy is not enough – it must be supplemented by elastic and flexible tactics.

Is the CCP a Stalinist party, to what extent has it been Stalinised, and what position does it occupy within Stalinism as a world system? Is Mao a Chinese

Tito, or will he become one? What is the nature of the People's Republic of China and what stance should we adopt towards it?

These questions have haunted me in recent years, so I will briefly deal with them. I pointed out in an earlier chapter that it is clear from the history of the factional struggle in the CCP ever since the mid-1950s that Mao has never been a Stalinist in terms of faction. The Stalinists would never have recruited anyone as opinionated as Mao into their inner circle, and he is in any case by nature incapable of acting like a Wang Ming. I have never had the chance to work closely with Mao, but we have no few mutual friends, among them Xu Zhixing (Mao's childhood friend) and He Zishen (who worked closely with Mao for many years and has been in prison under him since 1952). From them I learned many things about Mao's character, his learning, and his way of thinking and working. Combining these indirect impressions with my own knowledge of Mao's life and writings, I conclude that as a man he has many traits in common with Chen Duxiu, the founding father of Chinese communism. Both had their first love of learning in Confucianism; both built their ideological foundations in the Chinese classics; both acquired their knowledge of modern European thought, in particular Marxism-Leninism, in the same way, by building a rough superstructure of foreign style on a solid Chinese foundation at a time when they were physically as well as intellectually fully matured. So both Chen and Mao take 'Chinese learning as substance, western learning for practical application' (to quote the words of the Qing dynasty reformer Zhang Zhidong). They can never become 'thoroughly Europeanised,' nor will they ever cast aside that self-conceited pride peculiar to old-style Chinese scholars. I pointed out in an earlier chapter that Chen Duxiu had a poor opinion of foreign Communists, all the more so after Moscow had shamelessly heaped the whole of the blame for the defeat of 1927 on his shoulders. He always spoke with hatred and contempt of those Chinese Communists who kowtowed to foreign comrades, and dismissed them as 'red compradors.' Mao, being more diplomatic, substituted the word 'dogmatist' for 'comprador,' but he looked down just as deeply on men like Wang Ming who could only quote from the works of Marx, Lenin, and Stalin and from resolutions of the Comintern. He Zishen once told me an interesting anecdote in this connection. While he and Mao were carrying out underground work for the Hunan Provincial Committee of the CCP in Changsha in the autumn of 1927, at a time when the revolution was in chaotic retreat and hundreds of communists were being sent to Moscow to study, Mao once said to him: 'I won't go to Moscow until the revolution triumphs.'

Even at that early date Stalin must have been aware of the recalcitrance of this leader of equal ambition, desperately struggling for survival in the faraway mountains of Jiangxi. That is why he unfalteringly placed his confidence in Wang Ming and finally planted him as leader of the CCP and the Red Army in 1931. But this 'red comprador' proved unequal to the job, so Mao and other 'indigenous' leaders squeezed his followers out of the leadership at the Zunyi conference in 1935. After that, Mao (in the words of Zheng Chaolin) was a 'Titoist before Tito.'

Mao has all along remained outside the clique transplanted into the CCP from Moscow, but that has not prevented him from being a staunch Stalinist, just as it has not prevented the CCP from becoming Stalinised and the People's Republic of China from being organised and constituted after an essentially Stalinist model. Historical and social factors are incomparably stronger than individual likes and dislikes in determining the character of states and institutions. The extreme backwardness of Chinese economy and society, the peasant environment in which the CCP was forced to live and grow, its protracted involvement in a predominantly military struggle, the ebb of the world revolution, the ever-deepening bureaucratic involution of the Soviet state between 1930 and 1945, and (last but not least) Mao's undemocratic disposition and training – all these factors combined to force the Chinese Communist Party and its leading figure onto the Stalinist road. In fundamental ideological terms Stalinism means the substitution of nationalism for internationalism, of tactical inter-class manoeuvres for class struggle, and of bureaucratic dictatorship for the democracy of the toiling people. In practical terms, it means that all initiatives from lower levels of party and government organisations are stifled, that everything is done according to instruction, that political and social life is dominated by a frantic personality cult and a hierarchy of privilege, that all forms of thinking are controlled by the secret police, that all oppositions are purged, that all factions and parties are forbidden, and so on ad nauseam – all these measures have already been copied from Stalin and the CPSU by Mao and the CCP.

I am told that some Marxists in the Fourth International believe that since the victory of the CCP was due mainly to its having broken successfully from Stalinism, or to its freedom from Stalinist influence and domination, the CCP can no longer be regarded as a Stalinist party. Such a view is one-sided and unsound. True, under the direct impact of class struggle the CCP, with Mao Zedong at its head, tactically violated Stalin's directives and at crucial junctures took an opposite path to that of Stalin by going all out to mobilise the masses, giving a bold leadership to their struggles, and finally achieving revolution. In that sense, although the CCP remained a fundamentally Stalinist party, one of the main reasons it triumphed was because it failed to follow the line of Stalinism.

So Maoism and Stalinism are not direct equivalents. The different conditions of time and space in which the Russian and Chinese Revolutions occurred, the different cultural backgrounds and traditions of those who made them, and the different personal qualities of a Stalin and a Mao have led to important differences in both the outlook and the practice of the two men. The elements of identity and difference between them make an interesting and important subject for investigation, from both an historical and a political point of view, to which I shall return in a separate study.[12] But for my present purposes I must insist: checked off against my earlier list of the basic characteristics of Stalinism as a political force and a political system, the CCP is still fundamentally a Stalinist party and Maoism is still fundamentally a variant of Stalinism.

One question that is worth discussing is what will become of the CCP now that Stalin and Stalinism are coming under fire in the Soviet Union and Eastern Europe and the Stalinist camp is beginning to differentiate.

Immediately after the victory of the revolution in China many people were inclined to think that Stalinism in the CCP would be shaken off much earlier and much more easily than in other Stalinised parties, and that in some branches of the new-born state machine Stalinist methods of rule and institutions would never be systematically established. Later developments showed this view to be naive. Judging from its reaction to 'de-Stalinisation' in the CPSU and its hostile attitude to the Hungarian Revolution, the leadership of the CCP sticks faster to Stalinism than many of us thought. It has not actively facilitated the breakdown of Stalinism, and in some ways it has even turned out to be a bulwark of this obnoxious doctrine and its reactionary practice.

But this is hardly surprising, for the CCP set out to construct socialism from a socio-economic level lower even than that of the Soviet Union in the early 1920s and based its policies on the Stalinist principle of nationalist autarchy. So Stalinism will persist and even grow in China, at least in the short term. However, there is an important difference between now and when Stalinism first emerged and consolidated itself as a system. Then the curve of world revolutions was downward, now it is upward. What's more, even though the Chinese Revolution is artificially confined by its leaders to within strict national boundaries, it is impossible to prevent it from coming under the influence of revolutionary movements elsewhere in the world. The most obvious example was the tragicomic 'Hundred Flowers' campaign, unimaginable but for the Hungarian Revolution of 1956. It would be naive to think that campaign was

---

12   San Yuan (Wang Fanxi), *Mao Zedong sixiang yu Zhong-Su guanxi*, and this present volume deal with this question in more detail.

in any way a real attempt to grapple with the actual problems of Stalinism, but even so there was a strong link between it and the events in Hungary.

The 'Hundred Flowers' campaign showed that most top-level intellectuals in China and many students and workers and practically the whole of the peasantry are deeply dissatisfied with the CCP's Stalinist regime. But their demands were ruthlessly suppressed during the subsequent 'anti-rightist' campaign, and those called upon by the party to speak out were mercilessly persecuted. The result of this act of treachery will be (as Mao Zedong himself said in another context) to 'make such a mess of things that it can never be cleaned up.' If through the current anti-rightist campaign the CCP further strengthens the Stalinist system in all its aspects, the anti-Stalinist indignation of China's intellectual youth and of its workers and peasants will explode all the sooner and with all the more serious and wide-ranging consequences. Impelled by events both in China and in the world, a genuine and powerful left wing may come into being within the CCP, perhaps linking up with the forces of Chinese Trotskyism to channel all anti-Stalinist (that is, anti-Maoist) movements in the direction of a new anti-bureaucratic revolution. Such a revolution would aim to establish a real government of workers and peasants and to ally with the world proletariat to speed the advance to socialism.

I believe that history will show that such a prospect, far from being a mere pipedream, is entirely realistic.

APPENDIX 3

On the 'Great Proletarian Cultural Revolution' (1967)

In 1967, Wang Fanxi published a pamphlet in Hong Kong presenting his analysis of the Cultural Revolution. At the time the world was confused by the Red Guards and Maoist ideology. European Maoists and even some Christian groups saw the Cultural Revolution as an expression of the possibility of the transformation of human nature in the direction of greater freedom and collectivity. Western politicians saw it as a call for world revolution, and Soviet leaders too felt threatened. Wang's essay, here edited and condensed, contains a perceptive and prescient analysis that gradually became shared in its essentials by many commentators: that the Cultural Revolution was both a power struggle between leadership factions and an outburst of popular discontent. His prediction of a rapprochement with the United States was also fulfilled after the Nixon visit to Beijing in 1972. Unlike academic commentators, however, Wang believed that the Cultural Revolution could be further deepened and transformed, and might become the starting point for a genuine revolution in China: a dream that failed to materialise. (From a manuscript in the editor's archive.).

The Red Guards are the most perplexing of many perplexing things about the Cultural Revolution. In the CCP, Mao is still the most powerful leader. His control of the party, the administrative apparatus, the army, and the police (open or secret) is no less than Stalin's in the 1930s, and might even be greater. But Stalin used the secret police to eliminate the opposition in the party, the army, and the administration. Why does Mao, who is better respected, more powerful, and more firmly established, not do the same to deal with Liu Shaoqi, Deng Xiaoping, and their followers? Why must he rouse young people and authorise them to rebel, resulting in upheavals throughout the country?

This question puzzles the China watchers, who call the Red Guard movement an enigma wrapped in the mystery of the Cultural Revolution. Unable to solve the mystery, they say Mao is sick and has lost the power of judgment; some even say he is dead and that the person appearing at the Gate of Heavenly Peace is a fake, manipulated by his wife Jiang Qing and Lin Biao,[1] head of

---

1 Jiang Qing (1914–91) was Mao's third wife and a member of the 'Gang of Four.' Lin Biao (1907–71) was a senior military leader in the Chinese Revolution who was instrumental in the 1960s

the army; others, that he is having epileptic fits and trusts only Jiang and Lin. In reality, however, the Red Guards are easy to explain, and quite in accord with Mao thought.

The spiritual life of young people under communist rule is 'frustrating, hopeless, and empty.' This is an inevitable result of the CCP's bureaucratic rule. The Red Guard movement is a manifestation of discontent with this rule and its policy towards young people.

As a young man, Mao led student movements, and he has a deep understanding of young people. He is also a brilliant tactician, good at manipulating opposing forces without regard for principle. Seeing that the party and the administration had been usurped by his opponents, he turned to young people, and directs their discontent against his opponents, the capitalist-roaders. Anger that might have been directed towards him is deflected onto bureaucratism, corruption, and capitalist degeneration, with him as the Great Helmsman. He is able to destroy the Liu-Deng clique[2] and strengthen his own absolute rule. The mass movement he has called into being makes revolution while putting through its paces a new cohort of cadres implicitly loyal to him. With it, he can replace the old corrupt cadres and prevent the next generation from going down the revisionist road.

To achieve his purpose, he denounces the idea that 'heroic fathers have heroic sons and reactionary fathers have idlers' as a 'reactionary theory of lineage' and a means of suppressing young people.[3]

Young people in China fall into three categories: (a) the offspring of workers and peasants, who are the majority; (b) the offspring of 'bad families,'[4] of whom there are fewer; and (c) the offspring of 'heroes and great men and women,' the smallest group. The second group are the least happy and the most discontented. They have nothing to lose and everything to gain. In the past, they despaired, but now Chairman Mao turns out to be on their side. He opposes their repression and blames it on the power holders in the party and the state. He tells them to rebel, seize power, and remove 'the handful.' Their enthusiasm 'reaches the sky.' They pledge to 'defend Chairman Mao to their deaths' and to 'overthrow those who have taken the capitalist road.'

---

in boosting the Mao cult. He was Mao's designated successor from 1969 until his death in a plane crash, following an alleged failed coup attempt against Mao.
2 Liu Shaoqi and Deng Xiaoping were committed to a more orthodox politics and were classed together in the Cultural Revolution as capitalist-roaders.
3 The theory that only children of 'revolutionary heroes' could be revolutionaries, criticised in the Cultural Revolution for allowing cadres' children to enjoy privileges.
4 'Bad families' were the families of landlords, rich peasants, counter-revolutionaries, 'bad elements,' 'rightists,' and 'capitalists.'

Few of those who have had the chance to enter school belong to the second category. Nor are most students and Red Guards the offspring of heroes and great men and women, a group whose members have been advised by the Cultural Revolution Group in the Central Committee not to become leaders of Red Guard organisations. Most Red Guards belong to the first category, the offspring of workers and peasants and ordinary city dwellers. They are unhappy with the status quo; they are opposed to the bureaucracy and they are angry, because of their own experience and that of their parents. They too can also be inflamed and inspired by Mao's slogans.

Many foreign observers liken Mao's Red Guards to Hitler's Youth Corps. There are, of course, fundamental differences between the two, but they have at least one point in common: in both cases, a group of power holders harness youthful discontent to attack the ruling class and the system. By raising the spectre of revolution and mouthing high-sounding slogans, they mobilize young people to attack the opposition within the ruling class as well as true revolutionaries. Hitler seized on young people's dissatisfaction with capitalism to 'make revolution' in order to defend capitalism. Mao has seized on young people's dissatisfaction with the CCP's bureaucratic rule to 'make revolution' in order to defend bureaucratic rule.

The class nature of Hitler's 'revolution' differs from that of Mao's, but both use young people for similar reasons. The profound contradictions between the ruling class and the people, especially young people, are very much the same in both cases.

In 'normal' capitalist countries, crises within the ruling system are dealt with in parliament. However, when capitalism enters an 'abnormal' stage, crises no longer respond to the parliamentary contest, and fascism or some other 'revolutionary' means of preserving the capitalist system emerges. Similarly, when communist rule proceeds normally, problems are solved by means of democratic centralism. This happened constantly in Lenin's day. However, when things become abnormal, i.e., when the party and the state become more and more degenerate, the old ways of solving problems no longer work and 'emergency measures' are employed. In communist systems, two different kinds of emergency measures are used: one is Stalinist – the secret police and the courts are used to kill people on a vast scale: the other is that of Mao, who relies on mass mobilisations supplemented by Stalinist methods. The former is a conspiracy of the few, the latter an open conspiracy of the many.

Stalin and Mao use different methods to solve problems partly because of their different personalities but mainly because they perform different roles and occupy different positions. Mao is confident (perhaps overconfident) of his authority and standing, and seems to believe that it would serve no educational or other purpose to use 'organisational tactics' or other conspiratorial means to eliminate his enemies (who predominate in the party and the administration). So he has decided to mobilise millions of young people to practise 'great democracy' and to 'struggle, criticise, and transform' in order to crush his opponents and train new cadres inoculated against 'revisionism.' He knows that to do so will lead to widespread opposition and disturbances, but he is confident that everything will go according to plan.

Mao's first aim is to deflect popular discontent. Will the Red Guard movement lessen the discontent, especially that of the students? Will the Red Guards attack the 'handful of power holders who have taken the capitalist road' and support Mao?

Perhaps, but only fleetingly. Mao has always been the accuser and never the accused. If he wins, he will heap all manner of accusations on his rivals and scapegoat them. But if 'the people's eyes are bright and clear,' no dictator will ever manage to deceive them. Victories speak volumes, but it is important to ask how they have been achieved and what they actually represent. If they are won merely by lies and force of arms, and if the same methods are used against both enemies and supporters, Mao is unlikely to find scapegoats to sacrifice to the 'God of the People.' Victories of this sort will increase the resentment, and eventually channel it onto Mao himself.

Mao's other aims are to use the mass movement to defeat his opponents in the party, unite the party and the nation around Mao Zedong Thought, and bring everything under his personal control; and to train a new generation of cadres immune to 'revisionism' and bureaucratism.

Can these ends be achieved? CCP ideology over the past twenty years has always taken Mao Zedong Thought as its unifying centre, and Mao has always remained in control of the party. However, Mao was unhappy with the extent of the unity and control, especially in recent years, when they have been open to serious challenge. How absolute must unity and control be before Mao is satisfied? Apparently more so than in Stalinist Russia and even in Hitler's Germany. He wants his every word to be a supreme instruction and absolute truth. He wants his Little Red Book of Quotations to serve as a source of magic incantations and to substitute for the sum total of human knowledge, present and past, as the encyclopaedia of proletarian culture. He calls all other books feudal or capitalist and burns them, and he persecutes anyone versed in literature, history, philosophy, or art.

However, he will never establish the kind of unity and control he craves. Authority and resistance will always jostle with one another to prevail. The new collectivism cannot but include individualism. Chinese people have become been more enlightened in recent times and Chinese intellectuals have embraced science and democracy. Worldwide, despite the adverse current, socialism will replace capitalism and democratic communism will replace policed communism. So Mao's ambition, which surpasses that of Qin Shi Huangdi and Stalin, will be shown to be no more than an illusion and anachronism, even if it succeeds briefly in conveying the appearance of unity and control.

As to whether Mao can use the Red Guards to create a new generation of cadres immune to 'revisionism' and bureaucratism, I would answer as follows. Yes, he can create a new generation, but his cadres will not be immune to 'revisionism' and bureaucratism. I have explained why elsewhere. Here, I will say only this. Unless we opt for permanent revolution, give up the reactionary idea of socialism in one country, and see the Chinese Revolution as the spark for revolutions in other parts of the world, developed and underdeveloped, poor, blank China will never be able to prevent 'revisionism' and bureaucratism.

Under Mao's policy of 'communism in one country,' most of the new cadres selected from among the Red Guards will degenerate faster than the old ones, who at least went through a long period of real struggle rather than a staged performance of revolution. The Red Guards made their Long March by train, using free tickets, and have been artificially raised in the hothouse of Mao's Cultural Revolution.

What class interest does the Cultural Revolution serve? In Stalin's case, it is obvious which interest he served. He represented the interests of conservative centrists in the bureaucratic caste. He attacked first the left, then the right, to protect the interests of the bureaucracy and the social base on which it had fastened – the system of state-owned property.

Mao also represents the interests of the bureaucrats, but his stance is somewhat different from Stalin's. Mao seems at first sight to represent the left wing of the ruling bureaucracy, and the Cultural Revolution to be directed against a Chinese equivalent of the right wing in the CPSU in Stalin's days. Is this really the case? No, for since around 1930, when the CCP expelled its Left Opposition, it has no longer had a true left wing (at least not at the top). Since 1930, all the CCP's internal struggles – between Mao and Wang Ming, Mao and Zhang Guotao, or Mao and Liu Shaoqi – have been about tactics and even personal interests and rarely about revolutionary principles. These struggles have resulted from differences within the Stalinist School, between its right and its left, both of which are centrists, as was Stalin.

The CCP, long dominated by Stalinism, was naturally affected by this constant jumping back and forth. Every jump led to a change in it and a concomitant struggle between supporters of the old line and the new. In these struggles,

Mao has not always been on the left. However, he usually is – for example, he refused to retreat on the question of seizing political power by force or to unite with the bourgeoisie.

So Mao is a successor to the Stalinist left wing. He particularly embraced the Stalinism of the late 1930s, including political and economic adventurism, narrow-minded sectarianism (clothed in ultra-leftist clichés), authoritarian bureaucratism, and Bonapartism. The Stalinist left wing is not, of course, the equivalent of a Marxist left wing.

On many occasions – in 1928, on the question of a Constituent Assembly for China; in 1930, regarding the collectivisation of the Russian countryside; and, in the early 1930s, on the question of whether or not to form a united front in Germany with the Social Democrats – Stalin seemed to be on the 'left' but in reality was on the 'right,' for his policies delayed the revolution.

The same goes for Mao and his clique. Among those who oppose Mao from the 'right' are some (especially those who have consistently backed the Stalinist position) who support a line of prolonged cooperation with the capitalists. However, another group, very large in size, is rooted in the masses (this group includes some in the party top). These people are not associated with Stalinism and might actually be 'left.' Their proposals might well be in the interests of proletarian revolution in China and the world. Mao, a 'leftist' in relation to the first type of anti-Maoist, is a 'rightist' in relation to the second. Like Stalin, he is a 'centrist bureaucrat.' His Cultural Revolution resembles Stalin's 'anti-rightist' struggle in that although it has 'anti-capitalist' connotations, it does not serve the workers' interests. Instead, it serves the interests of the bureaucrats.

Some argue that because the Cultural Revolution is mobilising millions of people to seize power, it amounts to an attack on the bureaucrats. This is true, and it is what makes Mao different from Stalin. However, the difference is not fundamental. The Cultural Revolution differs in form from Stalin's mobilisations, but both are designed, in essence, to protect the interests of the bureaucracy – more obviously so in the case of Stalin than in that of Mao, whose true aim is better concealed by false appearances.

The few small differences that do exist can be explained by the relationship of each leader to the bureaucracy. Stalin represented its more conservative sector. Domestically, its members yield again and again to capitalist pressure, and fight back only as a last resort, in panic. Externally, they yield to imperialist pressure, which is why they have abandoned world revolution. The bureaucrats that Mao represents seem to be more radical. Their internal and external policies appear to be extreme left and uncompromising. Under hostile pressure either at home or abroad, Mao has shown no inclination to back down. On the contrary, he becomes even more militant. Does this mean that the Maoists are a revolutionary sector of the CCP's ruling caste?

I think not. Centrists swing from right to left and back again by definition. From the late 1920s through until his death, Stalin was consistently 'right': he compromised with the imperialists and betrayed the world revolution. Occasionally, however, he turned 'left,' for example during the Third Period (1929–33),[5] when he used terrorist methods to eliminate the rich peasants at home and resolved despite his isolation to fight imperialism abroad. This 'leftist' policy helped bring Hitler to power in Germany and boosted reaction throughout the world, forcing Stalin to swing back dramatically to the right in 1935, when he adopting the Popular Front strategy.

Mao's present policy, at home and abroad, is more or less the equivalent of Stalin's Third Period. It is the polar opposite of the reactionary policy of People's Democracy. It will meet with new, heavier blows, and will probably turn once again to the right and end up submitting to the imperialists, especially the Americans. Today's ultra-left policy is the result of yesterday's ultra-right policy, and can switch back again tomorrow.

There is only one way of breaking this centrist chain of causes and consequences, and that is to use the opportunity created by today's ultra-left line to turn Mao's fake revolution into a real one, so that proletarian democracy prevails in China.

---

5 The Third Period was announced at the Sixth Congress of the Comintern in 1928, to follow the First Period of revolutionary upsurge and defeat of the working class after the First World War and the Second Period of capitalist consolidation in the 1920s. The Third Period was to be one of capitalist collapse and the possibility of proletarian revolution.

APPENDIX 4

The 'Criticize Lin Biao, Criticize Confucius' Campaign (1974)

Mao and his supporters in the leadership (the so-called Gang of Four) launched the 'Criticize Lin Biao, Criticize Confucius' Campaign in 1973. The campaign lasted until shortly after Mao's death in 1976, when the Gang of Four were arrested and the Cultural Revolution was finally wound up. The campaign initially took the form of an interpretation of Chinese history, and extended to an attack on Lin Biao, Mao's previous 'Second-in-Command,' who had been accused of trying to assassinate Mao in 1971. Wang interprets it, in part, as a necessary attack on corruption and other social ills, but strongly doubts its efficacy. (From a manuscript in the editor's possession.)

Why have the movements to criticise Lin Biao and to criticise Confucius been linked? Lin was a soldier. According to recent descriptions of this one-time 'close comrade-in-arms' of Mao, 'he didn't read books or newspapers and was ignorant of Marxism-Leninism and China's ancient culture.' Lin is accused of wanting to oppose Mao's thought with the teachings of Confucius and Mencius as part of a plot to 'restore capitalism,' but this is clearly untrue. The real explanation for the conflation of Lin and Confucius can be found in the Lin faction's anti-Maoist programme, which said that Mao 'is abusing the trust and status given him by the Chinese people to go against the tide of history. He has become a modern Qin Shi Huangdi. He is not a genuine Marxist. He is the biggest tyrant in Chinese history. He follows the teachings of Mencius and Confucius and uses the methods of Qin Shi Huangdi.'

So the Maoists accused the Lin Biao clique of being followers of Confucius and reopened the question of Qin Shi Huangdi to turn the charge back against them. Foreign China-watchers have, as always, got the wrong end of the stick. As soon as they heard the name Confucius, they started thinking of Duke Zhou,[1] (4) whom they associated with Zhou Enlai, thus concluding that the campaign against Confucius was actually aimed at Zhou Enlai – a far-fetched explanation.

---

1 One of Confucius's 'morally superior men' and younger brother of the founder of the Zhou dynasty (1046–256 BC), China's longest-lasting dynasty.

In fact, Mao is far more obviously 'a follower of Mencius[2] and Confucius' than Lin Biao. Confucianism is one of the three main components of his thinking. Lin might have been able to quote a phrase or two from Confucius, but only in the way a parrot might. However, the criticism of Mao in the Lin Clique's programme was an excellent description of Mao's character and behaviour. It was probably written by Chen Boda, who for many decades was Mao's private secretary.

The attack was effective and left Mao quivering with rage. He counter-attacked (1) by declaring that Lin Biao was the real Confucian; (2) by insisting that his Marxism was deep-rooted; and (3) by declaring that Qin Shi Huangdi's activities, including his burning of the books and his burying alive of Confucian scholars, were not reactionary but positively progressive.

This was the immediate cause of the linking of Lin and Confucius. Now, however, the Maoists use the campaign to resume the attack on the Confucian family shop that began during the New Culture Movement of the 1910s. The reasons for this are extremely complex, and here I consider only one aspect: the contradiction between the new system and old thinking. China is a backward country, even though the revolution won power twenty-five years ago and the new political system has made progress along the road to modernisation. Its backwardness is linked in all respects, directly and indirectly, to Confucianism. 'Putting self before the common interest,' 'putting relatives before strangers,' the resort to blood ties, marriage ties, and local ties and the nepotism and corruption they entail have their origin in Confucian clan theory. Any revolutionary government that wants to change society or the economy fundamentally must seek to 'overthrow the Confucian family shop.' Otherwise it will encounter massive difficulties in socialist construction and state modernisation.

China's biggest problem, long a deadly tumour on its body politic, is corruption. One reason the Guomindang collapsed so soon after the end of the Anti-Japanese War was corruption. One of the biggest problems confronting the communists is how to prevent its re-emergence in their new administration. The movements launched since the establishment of the new China – *sanfan, wufan, siqing*,[3] and the Cultural Revolution itself – were not just about

---

2 Mencius (372–289 BCE or 385–303/302 BCE) was a Confucian philosopher, second only to Confucius himself.
3 *Sanfan*: Campaign against corruption, waste, and bureaucracy. *Wufan*: Campaign against bribery, tax-evasion, theft of state property, skimping on work and cheating on materials, and theft of state economic information. *Siqing*: 'Four Cleans,' a campaign in which the masses and low-level cadres were asked to give accounts of their political and ideological stands, family background, and financial situation.

corruption, but corruption was nevertheless their common theme. The roots of Mao's theory of permanent revolution and his insistence on the need for a new Cultural Revolution every few years lie in China's chronic and traditional corruption. Although Mao is acting in his own interests and those of a small clique in the party rather than of the Chinese Revolution, he is still forced again and again to combat corruption in the party and the administration. Otherwise, to judge by what happened to the Guomindang, communist rule could collapse within a decade.

As a result of the Cultural Revolution, some corrupt elements were forced to retreat a little and certain bureaucratic privileges took a tumble, with reductions in wage differentials, etc. Since then, however, the real mass movements that arose during the Cultural Revolution have been suppressed and the so-called ultra-leftists and anarchist elements have suffered a witch-hunt. Domestic and foreign policy has been 'normalised' and there have been two or three years of 'peace.' Corruption, which had been brought temporarily under control but not radically cured, has returned with a vengeance, although its extent is hard to judge. The CCP does not provide reliable data about this sort of thing. However, it is obvious that large numbers of old bureaucrats have been reinstated in party and state organs, along with 'enlightened' bourgeois; that 'going through the back door' is now the best way to get to university; that pay differentials have widened in industry; and that old habits and customs (especially regarding marriage) are re-emerging in the villages.

If only to preserve their own rule, Mao and his clique have had to start up another movement to oppose these tendencies. This need ties in neatly with Mao's eagerness to slap a 'Confucian hat' on Lin Biao's head. The 'criticise Confucius' tag was therefore added to the 'Oppose the Four Olds'[4] movement that developed out of the 'criticise Lin' campaign.

So the 'criticise Confucius' movement is not entirely fake, and is real in the sense that Mao has no choice but to recognise the contradiction between Confucian thought and the needs of modern China and communist revolution. Mao is a revolutionary, and his opposition to Confucianism is sincere. However, it is diminished by two things. (a) Mao's 'first love' as a thinker was Confucianism, which slipped into his subconscious and took root there. Consciously, it was negated and rejected, but it maintained its hold on his thought and continues to play a big role in it. (b) Mao's grasp of Marxism is shallow and tainted by Stalinist revisionism. He rejects the revolutionary spirit of Marxism and workers' democracy and replaces them with a totalitarian and bureaucratic content,

---

4 Old thought, old culture, old customs, and old habits.

which is in some senses counter-revolutionary. So Mao's anti-Confucianism can never be genuine. Mao himself has constantly proposed and enforced a despotic and bureaucratic hierarchy, and he gives expression in his words and actions to one of the most reactionary aspects of Confucian theory.

By extolling the Legalist School[5] and Qin Shi Huangdi at the same time as 'criticising Confucius,' Mao confirms that he is in effect a supporter of Confucianism. The question of the roles played by Confucianism and Legalism in Chinese history is complex, but even if we accept the Maoist view that the former was reactionary and the latter progressive,[6] their distinct origins have meant nothing ever since the reign of Han Wudi (140–86 BC), when the formula 'Confucianism on the outside, Legalism on the inside' came into being.[7] On the surface, Chinese rulers paraded their Confucian 'humanity in government,' but in reality they used the despotic methods of Qin Shi Huangdi. From the people's point of view, the only difference was that one claimed to be benevolent and the other did not, although in reality each was equally despotic. It is true that legalism was open about its nature while Confucianism was hypocritical, but it is still impossible to call one progressive and the other reactionary. The more Mao 'criticises Confucius' in this way, the more credible Lin Biao's charge of 'Confucianism' becomes.

If Mao hopes to destroy the 'Four Olds' and prevent corruption and bureaucratic degeneration by this kind of campaign, he will end up disappointed. In China today, nearly everyone, at all levels of society, is fed up with the continuous churning out of campaign after campaign in the course of Mao's permanent revolution. It is not only 'bad elements' or rightists who tremble when they hear the words 'campaign' and 'struggle.' Even workers and peasants, who are dissatisfied with bureaucratic rule in all its forms, live in fear of them. Everyone now knows, after more than twenty years' experience, that campaigns can never be

---

5 Legalism was an anti-Confucian school of thought that demanded strict state control in all spheres, a uniform system of rewards and punishments, and absolute rule by the supreme leader.
6 The idea of 'support Legalism, oppose Confucianism' is based on two premises: (1) That the passage from the Spring and Autumn period (770–476 BC) to the Warring States period (475–221 BC) represents the passage in Chinese history from slave-owning to feudalism. (2) That the Confucians represented the old slave-owners, while the Legalists represented the newly emerging feudal landowners. But both these presuppositions are, at the very least, debatable. First, one cannot force Chinese history into the same stages of development as Western European history. Marx recognised that Asian states had their own histories. Second, because the autocratic, centralised system of the Qin dynasty was hardly a model feudal state (note by Wang).
7 The actual severity of legalism combined with the apparent leniency of Confucianism.

taken at face value and never live up to their promises. They might swat dead a few house flies or even overthrow one or two small tigers, but in the end the swatters suffer the same fate as the flies or even a worse one. As for beating the small tigers, this invariably turns out to be in the interests of the biggest tigers. The campaigns sometimes benefit the workers and peasants in some ways, but after everything is all over, nothing ever seems to have really changed – people continue to suffer the same hardships. The Cultural Revolution was especially disappointing. It aroused people's hopes, only to dash them to the ground again. It ended up persecuting the true revolutionaries. From now on people will have every reason to suspect Mao's movements and campaigns as potential traps.

To 'Oppose the Four Olds' is doubtless necessary. Any corrupt thinking or habits that hide behind a Confucian screen should be eliminated. But to do so effectively, Mao should at the very least follow his own precepts and be 'open and above board' instead of 'plotting and scheming behind closed doors.' He should certainly stop treating the workers and peasants as simple tools to be wielded by an 'omniscient and omnipotent supreme leader,' as pawns in his power struggles.

If Mao and the CCP really want to cure China of its traditional ills, the first step they should take is transfer political power downwards to the workers and peasants. They should set up a broad-based system of socialist democracy, under popular control and supervision in the towns and villages, a system of workers, peasants, and soldiers' soviets like in the USSR in Lenin's time. They should allow the people to exercise leadership from the bottom up. This would be the best way to sweep aside old thinking and old institutions in every sphere, through the conscious and collective efforts of the people.

Bibliography

A Proposal Concerning the General Line of the International Communist Movement. The Letter of the Central Committee of the Communist Party of China in Reply to the Central Committee of the Communist Party of the Soviet Union of March 30 1963, Beijing: Foreign Languages Press.

Beasley, W.G. and E.G. Pulleyblank (eds.) 1961, *Historians of China and Japan*, London: Oxford University Press.

Benton, Gregor 1996, *Urban Revolutionaries: Explorations in the History of Chinese Trotskyism, 1921–1952*, Atlantic Highlands, NJ: Humanities Press.

Benton, Gregor 2014, *Prophets Unarmed: Chinese Trotskyists in Revolution, War, Jail and the Return from Limbo*, Leiden: Brill.

Bromage, Bernard 1956, *Molotov: The Story of an Era*, London: Peter Owen.

Chen Boda 1953, *Stalin and the Chinese Revolution*, Beijing: Foreign Languages Press.

Fan Wenlan 1944, *Lun Wang Shiwei de sixiang yishi* ('On Wang Shiwei's ideology'), N. p.: Jiluyu shudian.

Huang Changyong 2000, *Wang Shiwei zhuan* ('Autobiography of Wang Shiwei'), Zhengzhou: Henan renmin chuban she.

Ives, Peter 2004, *Gramsci's Politics of Language: Engaging the Bakhtin Circle and the Frankfurt School*, Toronto: University of Toronto Press.

Kemp-Welch, Tony 1991, *Stalin and the Literary Intelligentsia, 1928–39*, New York: St. Martin's Press.

Lenin, V.I., *Collected Works* (CW), Moscow: Progress Publishers.

Lenin, V.I. 1970, *Left-Wing Communism, An Infantile Disorder*, Beijing: Foreign Languages Press.

Lenin, V.I. 1972, *Materialism and Empirio-Criticism*, Beijing: Foreign Languages Press.

Lenin, V.I. 1973, *What Is To Be Done? Burning Questions of Our Movement*, Beijing: Foreign Languages Press.

Li Fu-jen [Frank Glass] and Peng Shu-tse [Peng Shuzhi] 1974, *Revolutionaries in Mao's Prisons: The Case of the Chinese Trotskyists*, New York: Pathfinder Press.

Liu Jialiang 1949, *Zhongguo de xianzhuang yu qiantu* ('China's present and future'), Hong Kong: N. p.

Li Rui 1957, *Mao Zedong tongzhi de chuqi geming huodong* ('Comrade Mao Zedong's early revolutionary activities'), Beijing: Zhongguo qingnian chuban she.

Lu Xun 1956–60, *Selected Works*, translated by Yang Xianyi and Gladys Yang, 4 vols, Bejing: Foreign Languages Press.

Mao Zedong 1961–5, *Selected Works*, Beijing: Foreign Languages Press.

Mao Zedong 1995, *Mao's Road to Power: From the Jinggangshan to the Establishment of the Jiangxi Soviets, July 1927–December 1930*, edited by Stuart Reynolds Schram and Nancy Jane Hodes, Armonk: M.E. Sharpe.

Marx, Karl and Frederick Engels, *Collected Works*, London: Lawrence and Wishart, various dates.

Marx, Karl and Friedrich Engels 1953, *Selected Correspondence*, Moscow: Publisher unknown.

Moloughney, Brian, 'From Biographical History to Historical Biography: A Transformation in Chinese Historical Writing,' *East Asian History*, no. 4, December 1992.

N. a. 1958, *People's Communes in China*, Beijing: Foreign Languages Press.

Nagahori Yūzō 2011, *Ro Jin to Torotsukī: Chugoku ni okeru 'Bungaku to kakumei'* ('Lu Xun and Trotsky: *Literature and Revolution* in China'), Tokyo: Heibonsha.

Pantsov, Alexander V. and Steven I. Levine 2012, *Mao: The Real Story*, New York: Simon and Schuster.

P'eng Shu-tse (Peng Shuzhi) 1980, *The Chinese Communist Party in Power*, New York: Monad.

Peng Shuzhi, *Xuanji* ('Selected works'), Kowloon: Shiyue chuban she, 1982.

Plekhanov G.V. 1961, *On the Role of the Individual in History* [1898], *Selected Works of G.V. Plekhanov*, vol. 2, Lawrence & Wishart.

Plekhanov, G.V. 1976, 'Translator's Preface to the Second Edition of Engels', *Ludwig Feuerbach and the End of Classical German Philosophy*,' in *Selected Philosophical Works*, volume 3, Moscow: Progress Publishers.

Richard L. 2004, *Historical Records of the Five Dynasties*, New York: Columbia University Press.

Rules and Administrative Regulations of the International Workingmen's Association 1964, Moscow: Progress Publishers.

San Yuan (Wang Fanxi) 1972, *Mao Zedong sixiang yu Zhong-Su guanxi* ('Mao Zedong thought and Sino-Soviet Relations'), Hong Kong: Xinda chuban she.

Schram, Stuart R. 1971, 'Mao Tse-tung and the Theory of the Permanent Revolution, 1958–69,' *The China Quarterly*, no. 46.

Serge, Victor 1932, *Littérature et révolution*, Paris: Libraire Valois.

Shuan Shan 1974, *Lun wuchan jieji wenhua da geming* ('On the Great Proletarian Cultural Revolution'), Hong Kong: Xinda chuban she.

Schwartz, Benjamin 1951, *Chinese Communism and the Rise of Mao*, Cambridge: Cambridge University Press.

Snow, Edgar, 1968 [1936] *Red Star Over China*, first revised and enlarged edition, London: Victor Gollancz.

Stalin, Joseph, *Works*, Moscow: Foreign Languages Publishing House, various dates.

The 70s (eds.) 1976, *The Revolution is Dead, Long Live the Revolution*, Hong Kong: The 70s.

Trotsky, Leon 2005 [1925], *Literature and Revolution*, Chicago: Haymarket.

Trotsky, Leon 2012, *My Life: An Attempt at an Autobiography*, Mineola, New York: Dover Publications.

Tumarkin, Nina 1983, *Lenin Lives! The Lenin Cult in Soviet Russia*, Cambridge, MA: Harvard University Press.
Yi De (Wang Fanxi) 1950, *Sulian yanjiu* ('A study on the Soviet Union'), Hong Kong: N. p.
Wang Fan-hsi 1980, *Chinese Revolutionary, Memoirs, 1919–1949*, Oxford: Oxford University Press.
Wang Fanxi 2004, *Wannian zhaji, 1989–1998* (Reading notes in old age, 1989–1998), Hong Kong: Xinmiao chuban she.
Wang Xizhe 1996, *Zou xiang heian* ('Into the darkness'), Hong Kong: Minzhu daxue.
Wu, Guoguang 2015, *China's Party Congress: Power, Legitimacy, and Institutional Manipulation*, Cambridge: Cambridge University Press.
Yap, Joseph P. (ed. and tr.) 2009, *Wars with the Xiongnu: A Translation from Zizhi Tongjian*, Bloomington, in Authorhouse.
Yap, Joseph P. (ed. and tr.) 2016, *Zizhi tongjian: Warring States and Qin*, n. p.: CreateSpace.
Zhdanov, A.A. 1977, *Soviet Literature – The Richest in Ideas, the Most Advanced Literature*, London: Lawrence & Wishart.
Zheng Chaolin 1997, *An Oppositionist for Life: Memoirs of the Chinese Revolutionary Zheng Chaolin*, Atlantic Highlands, NJ: Humanities Press.
Žižek, Slavoj 2014, *The Most Sublime Hysteric: Hegel with Lacan*, Verso: London.

Index

1905 revolution   129
'A Letter from the Front Committee to the Central Committee'   135n
A Proposal Concerning the General Line of the International Communist Movement, March 30, 1963   247, 247n
'A Single Spark Can Start a Prairie Fire'   103n
A Symbol of Depression   214n
ABC of Communism   3, 84
Abstruse   190
Accommodation   192
Accommodationism   89
Action and theory   193
Advanced capitalist countries   143, 250
Adventurism   35, 142, 171
Aesopian language   194
Africa   38
Age of socialist revolution   161
Agrarian revolution   134, 170
Agricultural country   144
Agriculture   250, 251
Ah-Q   277
Ali, Tariq   8, 15n
All-Union Communist Party (Bolsheviks) [AUCP(b)], name of CPSU, 1925–1952   51, 60, 93, 133, 243, 248
Alliance of all revolutionary classes   241
Alliance of the democratic classes   143
Altruism   230
American(s)   69, 76, 115, 124
Amnesty International   10
Analects   32
anarchist(s)   7, 202
Anglo-American   76
Anti-bureaucratic revolution   292
Anti-Dühring   48
Anti-feudalism   143
Anti-imperialist   188
Anti-imperialist, anti-feudal alliance   132
Anti-Japan sentiment   92
Anti-Japanese   84, 142
Anti-Japanese War   14, 95, 172, 216
Anti-militarism   188
Anti-rightist campaign   292
Anti-Stalinist faction   133

Armed counter-revolution   151, 167
Armed peasantry   160
Armed revolution   102, 150, 151, 160, 167, 168, 169
Armed struggle   64, 65, 152, 156, 160, 166, 168, 171, 239
'Arms of criticism'   35
Art of war   152
Art of War   116, 120n, 121
Asia   38
A-type contradiction   185
A-type method   185
Austerlitz   115
Awareness   127

Ba Ren (pseudonym of Wang Renshu)   219, 219n
Bacon, Francis   99
Backward countries   189
Balzac, Honoré de   212, 213, 214
Bancang   69
Bancang Yang   70
Banditry   234
Base areas   102
Bebel, August   57
Beidaihe   228
Beijing   1, 2, 3, 4
Beijing dialect   75
Belles lettres   196
Bengbu   285
Benton, Gregor   20n, 33n, 34n
Berdyaev, Nikolai Alexandrovich   173
berets   9
B-type method   185
Bi   80
Bi Gan   79
Big-bourgeois   241
Big bourgeoisie   135, 189
Blanquism   113
Blanquist   112, 182
Blockade   236, 244
Bo Gu   94, 172n
Body and shadow   166
Bolshevik(s)   12, 35, 51, 58, 104, 126, 163, 181, 183, 196n, 197
Bolshevik Party   165

INDEX 309

Bolshevism   112, 125, 131
Bolshevisation   12, 38
Bonapartist   281
Book of Changes (Yijing)   77, 78, 190
Borchardt, Julian   3, 84
Border Region   244
Bourgeois   209, 281
Bourgeois democracy   59, 62, 105, 111, 136, 139
Bourgeois dictatorship   136, 243
Bourgeois restoration   131
Bourgeois revolution   66, 130
Bourgeois-democratic revolution   131, 133, 134, 146
Bourgeoisie   102, 109, 130, 132, 135, 142, 145, 159, 168, 208, 281
Braun, Otto   172n
Brest-Litovsk   126
Britain   62, 66, 69, 243
British   5, 9, 61, 120n
British Chinese   8
British Communists   283
Bromage, Bernard   194n
Buddha   91
Buddhist   81
Building socialism   168
Bukharin, Nikolai Ivanovich   3, 84, 87, 89, 159, 162, 202
Bureaucracy   166, 167
Bureaucratic   62, 168
Bureaucratic collectivist   281
Bureaucratic degeneration   192
Bureaucratic dictatorship   14, 203
Bureaucratic totalitarianism   219
Bureaucratisation   58, 65, 79, 218
Bureaucratism   59, 128

Cadres   64
Cai Tingkai   126
Cao Cao   97, 115, 226, 226n, 228
Capital and labour, contradiction between   193
Capitalism   112, 148, 149, 188, 230, 240, 242
Capitalist countries   110, 111, 167, 189
Capitalist industry and commerce   251
Capitalist roaders   44
Capitalist world system   161
Capitulation   142

Capri   216n
Cardinal principles of righteousness   78, 79n
Carlyle, Thomas   50, 52, 55, 56
Carthaginians   31, 150
Carr, Edward Hallet   266n
Categorical imperative   151
CCP   12, 14, 21, 33, 35, 36, 38, 46, 59, 60, 61, 63, 64, 74, 80, 84, 88, 89, 91, 92, 98, 103, 104, 107, 109, 114, 117, 120, 121, 122, 133, 142, 184
CCP Propaganda Department   173
Central Area   237
Central Army   108
Central Committee   32, 89, 90, 90n, 94, 102, 103, 134, 169, 170, 233, 251
Central Conservatory of Music   227
Central Powers   125
Changsha   61, 62, 68, 71, 157
Changshao, Battle of   115
Chen Boda   84, 84n, 92, 93, 93n
Chen Duxiu   2, 2n, 3, 5, 6, 8, 12, 20, 23, 27, 31, 32, 32n, 35, 36, 37, 67, 67n, 70, 74, 76, 87, 92, 96, 133, 275, 289
Chen Changhao   88, 88n
Chen Sheng   228, 228n
Chen Wangdao   71
Cheng Hao   72n
Cheng Yi   72n
Chenggao, Battle of   115
Cheng-Zhu school of Confucianism   69, 72, 72n, 74
Chiang Kai-shek (Jiang Jieshi)   2, 4, 9, 13, 35, 47, 80, 88n, 90, 92, 117, 121, 122, 124, 127, 135, 145, 151, 152, 153, 154, 156, 157, 235, 282
Chibi, Battle of (Battle of Red Cliffs)   115
China's independence   171
China's Great Revolution (1926–27)   133
Chinatown   8, 108
Chinese Communist Party (CCP)   1, 3, 7, 46, 94, 116, 137, 147, 149, 150, 151, 152, 153, 156, 160, 161, 169, 175, 188, 192, 206n, 214n, 215, 216, 217, 220, 222n, 223, 234, 239, 240, 243n, 251
'Chinese learning for the foundation, Western learning for application'   62, 63, 76, 118
Chinese Marxist historians   179

Chinese 'people's revolutionary army' 151, 152
Chinese People's Political Consultative Conference 149
Chinese Red Army 27, 84, 88, 90, 91, 92, 94, 102, 103, 110, 117, 121, 122, 137, 142, 143, 155, 169, 231, 232, 234, 237, 238, 243, 282
Chinese revolutionaries 132, 188
Chinese Soviet 117, 231, 237, 238
Chinese Soviet Government 142
Chinese Stalinists 277
Chinese students 243n
Chinese Trotskyists 12, 26, 27, 31, 37, 38, 104, 122n, 275, 277, 281, 282, 292
Christianity 14, 73, 75
Chu (name of state) 115
Churchill, Winston 54
City University of Hong Kong 14n
Civil-service exams 82n
Civil war 103, 105, 108, 111, 115, 121, 121n, 124, 144, 188, 248
Cixuan 157
Class 145
Class consciousness 127, 162, 167
Class contradiction 187, 189
Class culture 200
Class enemy 229
Class hatred 229
Class nature 229
Class relations 210
Class society 229
Class structure 159
Class Struggle 71
Class struggle 109, 112, 138, 147, 159, 164, 187, 188, 189, 229, 230
Classical poetry 225, 226, 227, 228
Classless culture 200
Clausewitz, Carl von 113, 115
Coalition government vs joint action 168
'Cogs-and-screws' metaphor 195, 197, 204, 205, 206n, 209, 217
Collective will 167
Cooperatives 236, 251
Cold War 12
Colonial 143, 188
Comintern (Communist International) 21, 37, 87, 89, 90n, 90, 96, 102, 104, 122, 132, 133, 134, 142n, 152, 154, 155, 156, 159, 241, 249, 285, 289
Comintern, Third Congress 7
Commandism 202
Communism 63, 74, 79n, 98, 99, 132, 167, 223, 242
Communism in one country 237
Communist Manifesto 48, 71, 159
Communist party 159, 166, 180
Communist Parties in capitalist countries 105, 106
Communist Party of China 61, 62
Communist Party of the Soviet Union (CPSU) 51, 60, 93, 133, 243, 290, 291
'Communist Policy Toward Art' 201n
Communist(s) 3, 66, 108, 109, 112, 124, 132, 152, 160, 170, 216
Communist countries 202
Communist sects 164
Communist society 145
Compass, theory as a 177
'Conclusions on the Repulse of the Second Anti-Communist Onslaught' 123n
Confucian(s) 23, 24, 32, 61, 62, 63, 70, 71, 72, 73, 74, 77, 78, 83, 156
Confucian communism 74
Confucian Family Shop 74
Confucian forbearance 94
Confucian socialism 74
Confucian-style 166
Confucianism 2, 22, 23, 63, 72, 73, 74, 75, 77, 84, 179, 180, 216, 227
Confucius 18, 23, 52, 74, 75, 80, 81, 82, 223, 272
Consciousness, determined by being 163
Constituent Assembly 5, 27, 33
Constitutional monarchy 66
Contradiction 166n, 213
Contradiction of our times 190
Contribution to the Critique of Political Economy 210
Cooperative 143, 237, 238
Cooperative tactics 129
Corsican Emperor (Napoleon) 56
Corruption 164, 234
Counter-revolution 65, 127, 134, 135, 136, 137, 152, 155, 156, 157, 169
Countryside 102
Cowhig, David 146n

'Criticism of arms'   35
Cromwell, Oliver   52, 55, 56, 59
Cuba   9
Cult of the individual   64
Cult of the leader   54
Cultural Revolution   7, 18, 44, 84, 97, 219n
Cultural army   207
Cultural troupes   206n
Cyclical   190

Danish   9
Das Kapital   84, 230
Datong (great harmony or unity)   76, 79n, 145
Darwin, Charles   33, 69, 76
Decembrists   273
Deduction from ideas   138
Defeat   135
'Deformed workers' states'   288
Degenerate   163, 288
Degeneration and death   160, 161, 163
Democracy   143, 168
Democracy in the army   234
Democratic contradiction   184
Democratic dictatorship of various classes   141
Democratic dictatorship of workers and peasants   102, 130, 182
Democratic economy   144
Democratic parties   149
Democratic programme   169
Democratic republic   109, 114, 140, 145, 186
Democratic revolution   131, 134, 141, 147, 148, 180, 184, 189
Democratic-revolutionary means   183
Democratic-revolutionary struggle   149
Democratic rights   147
Democratic supervision   167
Democratic tasks   147
Deng Xiaoping   10, 18, 98, 99
'De-Stalinisation'   291
Dewey, John   32
Dialectic   190, 193
Dialectical   181, 205
Dialectical idealism   78
Dialectical materialism   174, 218
Dialectician   78, 179, 190
Dialectics   95, 173, 179, 180, 185

Dialectics of opportunism   179
Dictatorship of the proletariat   131, 132, 143, 145
Difficulties and defeats   160
Ding Ling   219, 219n
Dogmatist(s)   27, 93, 95, 172, 174, 289
Dongshan Higher Primary School   68
Dongxiang   69
Draft National Programme for Agricultural Development   252
Duan Qirui   108
Duke Zhou, see Zhou Gong
Dualism   176, 177

Eastern Europe   287, 291
Eastern Han dynasty   228
Ecclecticism   176, 177, 191
'Economic and Financial Problems in the Anti-Japanese War'   244n
Economic construction   238, 239, 240, 246
Economic foundations for socialism   240
Economic thinking   231, 240
Economic policy   238, 241
Economic work   231, 235, 238, 238n, 240
Economism   161
Eighteen Kinds of Weapons   120, 120n
Eighth Congress of the CCP (1956)   91, 97, 97n, 98, 168
Eighth Route Army   109, 282
Elections   167
Emancipation of the working classes   160, 161
Emergency conference   154
Empirical   242
Empiricism   27, 95, 138, 172, 174, 177, 178, 193, 235
Epistemology   173
Engels, Frederick   48, 48n, 84n, 93, 110, 172, 211, 212, 212n, 213, 213n, 221, 230
English political economy   72
Enlightenment   74, 247
Entente   188
Era of world proletarian revolution   186
Ethical self-reliance   247
Ethics   69
Europe   111, 167
Europe's communists   159
European   76, 111, 115, 129n
Exhortation to Study   62n

External trade   236, 237
External trade bureau   239
Extra-class   198

Fake foreign devils   174, 223
Fake theoreticians   174
Far Eastern Bureau   88
Fascism   64, 112, 122, 167
Fan Wenlan   14
'Farewell Letter to the Swiss Workers'   126
Faulty compass   174
February Revolution   180, 181, 181n, 183
Fei River, Battle of   115
Feng Dao   83, 83n
Feng Xuefeng   217, 217n, 219, 222n
Feudal   227
Feudal exploitation   134
Feudal forces   174
Feudal oppression   106
Feudalism   105, 111, 132
Feuerbach, Ludwig Andreas von   172, 173
Fifth Encirclement and Suppression campaign   117
Fifth Plenum, January 1934   90
Fighting spirit   127
Financial policy   238
First Civil War Period (1924–1927)   87n
First Conference of Proletarian Writers   202
First Congress of Soviet Writers   203
First Five Year Plan   250, 252
First Normal School   69, 70
First Provincial Middle School   68
First United Front [1923–7]   95, 121n
First World War   167
Five Antis (1952)   149, 149n
Five Dynasties   68n, 83
Foreign advisers   120
Flower-vase deputy ministers   149
Form of government   145, 146
Four Books   179n
Four don'ts   78, 79
Four revolutionary classes   134
Fourier, Charles   76
Fourierites   177
Fourth International   8, 37, 287, 288, 290
Fourth Normal School   69
Fragmentation   160
France   7, 33, 35, 62, 66, 69, 243

Franco-Prussian War   120
Frank, Pierre   9
Frankfurt   213
French   61
French Revolution   191
French socialism   72
From Idealism to Materialism   33
Fuchun River   228
Fujian   237
Fujian-Zhejiang-Jiangxi border area   237
Fundamental principles of Marxism   159
Führer   127

Gaixia   224
Ganzhou   236
Gaozu (Emperor)   224, 224n
General Secretary   67n, 88n
Genghis Khan   30, 228, 228n
George, Henry   75
General law of contemporary world revolution   185
Genghis Khan   271
German   72
'German agent'   187
German fascism   188
German militarism   188
German Revolution   94
German Social Democratic movement   87
German-Soviet friendship   127
Germany   62, 122, 126, 188, 243
Gide, André   33
Glass, Cecil Frank   9
Goethe, Johann Wolfgang von   34, 212, 213, 214
Goethe Faction   219
Gongshan Furao   80
Gorky, Maxim (pseudonym of Aleksei Maximovich Peshkov)   196, 196n, 216, 216n, 217
Government bonds   238
Government of workers and peasants   169
Grain regulation bureau   238
Gramsci, Antonio   7
Great Scribe, The, (Confucius)   78
Great Harmony (*Datong*)   145, 248
Great Swords sect   120
Great Leap Forward   18, 98, 98n
Great Purge   87n
Great Proletarian Cultural Revolution   44

INDEX 313

Great Revolution 154, 156
Great-Russian chauvinism 247
Great Swords sect 120, 120n
Great Wall 228
Great War, Europe's 187
Greece 69, 87, 111, 157
Guandu, Battle of 115
Guan Zhong 266, 266n
Guangdong 133
Guangdong Army 151, 152, 153
Guangwu (Emperor) 228
Guangzhou-Hong Kong general strike, 1925–6 3
Guangzhou Uprising (Guangzhou Insurrection) 135, 153, 154, 154n
Guerrilla operations 234
Guevara, Ernesto 'Che' 9
Guilin 108
Gun(s) 159, 168, 174
Guo Jie 83
Guo Moruo 221, 222n, 225, 225n
Guomin (national) 122
Guomindang 26, 35, 38, 47, 64, 80, 80n, 81, 84, 89, 92, 93, 94, 102, 103, 104, 105, 107, 116, 120, 121, 124, 127, 132, 141, 148, 152n, 153, 162, 168, 169, 174, 184, 216, 233, 244, 245, 281, 282, 285
Guomindang-CCP alliance 169

Han (name of state) 115
Han dynasty 30, 81, 224
Han people 30
Han nationalism 30
Han Fei 81
Han Wudi (Emperor Wu of Han) 82, 226, 226n, 228
HanYu (Han Changli) 63
Handicrafts 251
Hangzhou 3
Hangzhou Commercial Middle School 2
Harkness, Margaret 212n, 221
He Zishen 157, 157n, 289
Hegel, Georg Wilhelm Friedrich 172, 190, 191
Hegel's *Science of Logic* 191n
Heraclitus 190
Hereditary Family of Confucius 78
'Hiding the head but showing the tail' (half truths) 178

Highly developed capitalist economy 143
Histoire générale de la Chine, ou Annales de cet Empire 69n
Historical materialism 49, 210
History of Monism 210
History of Socialism 71
Hitler, Adolf 13, 94, 122, 127, 275
Hitler-Stalin Pact (Molotov-Ribbentrop Pact) 36, 127
Hodes, Nancy June 142n
Hong Kong 1, 6, 8, 11, 14
Hong Xiuquan 62, 62n, 75, 76, 157, 226
Hongqi (Red Flag) 146, 222n
Hu Feng (pseudonym of Zhang Guangren) 3, 204, 204n, 217, 218, 219, 221, 222n
Hu Qiaomu 28, 29, 91
Hu Shi 2n, 74
Hu Yepin 219n
Huang Chao 157n
Huang Changyong 14n
Huangpu Military Academy 108, 121, 121n
Huang Lizhou 74, 74n
Hubei 168
Hugo, Victor 49
Hui Qian, pseudonym of Wang Fanxi 8
Humanity and compassion 229, 230
'Humans conquering nature' 240
Hunan 68, 71, 75, 157, 168
Hunan Provincial Committee 157, 232, 233, 289
Hunan-Jiangxi border 88, 88n, 154
'Hundred Flowers' campaign 98, 224, 224n, 292
Hungarian Revolution 291
Hungarian workers' uprising 98
Hungary 287, 288, 292

Idealism 191
Ideological and organisational education 167
Ideological convergence 138
'Infantile leftists' 190
Infantilism 199
Imperialism 64, 106, 109, 112, 117, 132, 133, 134, 139, 151, 152, 174, 188, 193, 240, 243
Impetuosity 142
Independent workers' organisation 167
Inductive reasoning 138

Industrial country   144
Industrial proletariat   160
Industrialisation   251
Inseparability of party and class   166
Instructor Hong   115
Intellectual   160, 161, 164
Intellectuals   168
International aid   246
International capitalism   139
International dimension   168
International proletariat   166, 243
International Settlement, Shanghai   5
International Workers Party of China (IWP)   7
International working class   248
Internationalism   36, 126, 138, 245, 247
Islamic thinking   73
Italy   243
Ivan the Terrible   273
Ives, Peter   7
Izvestia   196

Japan   27, 36, 62, 69, 92, 169, 243
Japanese   27, 35, 109, 115, 122, 244
Japanese Foreign Minister   127
Japanese imperialism   188
Japanese invasion   169
Japanese Trotskyists   15n
Japanese War   12
Jeffersonianism   75
Jensen, Finn   9
Jesuit   68, 125
Ji Xingwen, Commander   5, 38
Jiangsu daxue xuebao (Jiangsu University Journal)   146n
Jiangxi   89, 90n, 117, 121, 122, 157, 168, 236, 237, 243, 247
Jiangxi Soviet   235, 237
Jin dynasty   115
Jinan Massacre   134
Jinggang Mountains   154, 157, 233
Joint dictatorship of various democratic classes   148
Joint dictatorship of the revolutionary classes   139
Joseph-Anna-Marie de Moyriac de Mailla   68
Judas   53
Junzi (ethical person)   52

Kamenev, Lev Borisovich   52, 173, 182
Kang Youwei   62, 62n, 67, 68, 72, 74, 75, 76
Kant, Immanuel   33, 69
Kantian   151
Kardelj, Eduard   287
Karl Beck, *Lieder vom Armen Mann*, Or The Poetry of True Socialism   213
Kautsky, Karl   71
Key provinces formula   142, 142n
Khrushchev, Nikita Sergeyevich   60n, 61, 98, 247, 287
King of Zhou   79
Kirkup, Thomas   71
Knowing and doing   175
'Knowledge, practice, again knowledge, again practice'   178
Kolkhoz   80n
Korea   5
Kremlin   24, 87, 92, 94, 98, 249
Kropotkin, Pyotr Alekseyevich   33
Krupskaya, Nadezhda   266
Kuaiji   229
Kunyang, Battle of   115
Kuriyagawa Hakuson   214n
Kutuzov, Prince Mikhail Illarionovich Golenishchev   273

Labour movement   161, 164, 166
Labour Party   283, 283n
Lam Chi Leung   15n
Land question   148
Land revolution   170
Landlord class   134
Language   199
Laozi   190
Latin America   38
Lau San-ching (Liu Shanqing)   15n
Leader cult   54, 59, 60, 64, 138, 215, 222n
Leading role of the party   162
Leading role of the proletariat   159
'Leaning to one side'   246
Leap from perceptual to rational knowledge   176
Leeds   8
Left Opposition   87
Lenin cult   22
Lenin's 'idle chatter'   177
Lenin-Trotsky era   59
Leningrad   243n

INDEX 315

Leninism   22, 36, 53, 86, 112, 242
'Leo Tolstoy as the Mirror of the Russian Revolution'   212
'Let a hundred flowers bloom'   220n
'Letter to Bezymensky'   199n
'Letter to Margaret Harkness in London'   212
'Letter to Wilhelm Bracke'   176n
'Letters From Afar'   216n
Letters Home   266, 266n
'Letting Be, and Exercising Forbearance'   164
Levine, Steven I.   21n
Levy, Paul   126
Li (profit)   54
Li (rite)   77
Li Dazhao   4, 31, 70
Li Fu-jen, pseudonym of Frank Glass   9n
Li Ji   84
Li Lisan   87, 88, 90, 91, 96, 97
Li Lisan line   87, 87n
Li Rui   68n, 69, 69n, 70n
Li Zicheng   157
Liang Qichao   19, 68, 74
Lianjie zazhi she   14n
Liberal bourgeoisie   130, 140
Liberation   103
Literature   28, 194
Literature and art for the proletariat   200
Liebknecht, Wilhelm   57
Lin Chong   115
Liquidationism   126
Liquidationist   171
Literary censorship   219
Literature and art   28, 199, 210, 222, 222n
Literature and Revolution   199, 202, 221
Liu Bang   224
Liu Bei   97
Liu Jialiang   285
Liu Shaoqi   17, 18, 18n, 31, 99, 99n, 145, 145n, 146, 146n, 149, 167, 167n, 168, 252
Lixian (constituent)   122n
Liying waihe (coordinating from inside and outside)   9
Long March   24, 90, 91, 91n, 117, 122, 169, 172, 236, 237, 243
Logic   185
Lou Guohua   10, 14, 29
Lou Shiyi   15n, 29, 34

Lu (name of state)   115
Ludendorff, Erich   120
Luddites   177
Ludwig Feuerbach and the End of Classical German Philosophy   172, 173
Lu Xun   3, 214n, 215, 215n, 216, 217, 217n, 218, 219, 219n, 220, 277n
Lunacharsky, Anatoly Vasilyevich   196, 196n, 202, 266, 266n
Lungao   14
Luo Fu   94
Luo Guanzhong   63, 63n

Ma Su   120, 120n
Ma Yusheng   11
Macao   1, 7, 8, 11, 16, 275
Machiavellian   179
Machiavellianism   113
Main contradiction   188
Main force   164
Malraux, André   6
Manchu   120
Mandarin   75
Mann, Thomas   33
Mao Zedong Thought   15, 24, 43, 61, 86, 96, 97, 98, 99, 129, 213, 214, 240, 241
Mao Zedong sixiang yu Zhong-Su guanxi   291n
Mao('s) cult   22, 23n, 29, 46, 59, 64, 65, 98n, 98, 215, 225
Mao thought   44, 45, 46, 61, 66, 72, 79, 79n, 86, 91, 96, 97, 100, 118, 222, 237, 241, 242
Mao worship   59
Mao's personality cult   59
Mao's poetry   29, 230
Mao's *Selected Works*   46, 90, 93, 95, 231
Maodun (contradiction)   225, 225n
Maoism   1, 38, 291
Maoist   7, 172, 221, 283
Martial arts   120n
Marx, Karl   3, 7, 30, 31, 48, 49, 50, 81, 84, 86, 93, 101, 147, 172, 176, 183, 210, 211, 230, 248
Marx and co.   60
Marxian   202
Marxism   31, 34, 66, 71, 72, 74, 84, 86, 93, 94, 104, 156, 159, 160, 163, 177, 201, 210, 211, 217, 218, 223, 227

Marxism-Leninism   17, 61, 87, 94, 96, 99, 104, 167, 178, 241
Marxist-Leninist   177, 180
Marxist   1, 34, 66, 72, 77, 103, 109, 112, 159, 163, 165, 166, 172, 175, 201, 202, 210, 211, 212, 216, 223, 239, 250
Marxist aesthetics   205
Marxist theory of knowledge   95
Marxism-Leninism   173, 289
Marxist-Leninist   61, 92, 94, 105, 110, 160, 163, 170, 197, 222
Mass line   59
Mass movement   103
Materialism and Empirio-criticism   172
Materialism   191
Materialist   162, 221
Materialist epistemology   177
Matsuoka Yōsuke   127
May 4th Movement   2, 38, 70, 70n, 74, 106, 216, 217, 222, 222n, 223, 224
May 21st Incident   137
May 30th Movement   2, 3, 106
Mayakovsky, Vladimir Vladimirovich   203
Mechanical   181, 185
Mechanical determinism   210
Mechanical Induction   177
Mechanicalism   181
Mechanistic   183
Medievalism   130
Meditation   70
Meixian   236
Mencian   74
Mencius   74n, 75
Menshevik(s)   86, 130, 131, 140, 143, 182, 202, 241
Menshevism   140
Mercenary army   153
Merezhkovsky, Dmitry Sergeyevich   33
Metaphysical   183
Middle class   179
Middle Way (the Doctrine of the Mean, *zhong yong zhi dao*)   179
Mif, Pavel (pseudonym of Mikhail Alexandrovich Fortus)   87, 87n, 88, 152
Mikhailovsky, Nikolai Konstantinovich   8n
Miliband, Ralph   8
Militarisation   112, 167, 168
Militarism   188
Military control   166

Military dictatorship   169
Mill, John Stewart   69
Milton, John   207n
Mindless activism   132
Minli bao (People's Independent Daily)   71
Ming dynasty   62
Miss Sophie's Diary   219n
Mohammed   53
Mohism (doctrine of Mozi)   82
Mohist (follower of Mozi)   82
Moloughney, Brian   19, 20n
Moltke, Helmuth Karl Bernhard, Graf von   115
Monopoly finance capital   112
Montesquieu, Charles-Louis de Secondat, Baron de La Brède   69
Moral communist   127
'More on the Differences Between Comrade Togliatti and Us'   101n
Moscow   4, 11, 21, 33, 34, 89, 90, 91, 93n, 94, 95, 97, 109, 133, 174, 243, 246, 289
Mount Liang   63, 63n, 154, 234
Multi-class alliance   143
Multi-class dictatorship   136, 145, 148
Municipal tactics   129
Mussolini, Benito   220

Nagahori Yûzô   29n
Nanchang   154, 154n
Nanjing   7
Napoléon Bonaparte   25, 55, 56, 115, 157
Napoléon III (Charles-Louis Napoléon Bonaparte)   49, 51
Narodnik   104
Narodnikism   130
Nation-based socialism vs international socialism   168
National Assembly   122, 135, 136, 137, 138, 138n, 169, 171
National bourgeoisie   135, 144
National capitalism   148
National Conference of the CCP, Yan'an, May 1937   95
National contradiction   187, 189
National characteristics   223
National defence   138, 144
National factors   222
National forms   222, 223

INDEX 317

National People's Congress   20n
National independence   106
National liberation   134, 170
National peculiarities   222
National revolution   134
National traitor   127
Nationalism   128, 245
Nationalists   19, 219
Nationalist-Communist reunion   80
Nature and nurture   175
Nazism   188
Negation   191
Negative   191
Neo-Confucian   63n
Neo-Confucianism (New Confucianism)   61, 62, 63, 69, 72, 72n, 73
Nero Claudius Caesar Augustus Germanicus   14
New Army   68
New culture   200, 207n
New Culture Movement   2, 29, 67n, 70, 74, 222
New Democracy   139, 140, 144, 240, 241, 242
New-democracy   143, 145
New-democratic revolution   130
New-democratic stage   206
New Economic Policy (NEP)   165, 199, 199n
New Fourth Army   24, 95, 95n, 219
New learning   62
New ruling caste   164
Nianpu   20
Ninggang   234
Nihilism   199
Nihilistic   190
Ningdu   89, 235
Ninggang   232
Ninth Congress of the CCP, 1969   98, 98n
Non-capitalist road   132
Non-Chinese   103
Non-class   198
Non-principal contradiction   186, 189
Non-proletarian base   163
Non-proletarian toilers   163
Non-revolutionary   191
Northern Expedition   104, 106, 107, 108, 120, 132, 152, 153, 168
Northern warlords   153
Novaya Zhizn (New Life)   196, 196n

October Revolution   21, 58, 64, 66, 76, 105, 129, 131, 144, 180, 181, 182n, 183, 194, 203, 206n, 240
Old Bolsheviks   64
Old Confucianism   72, 72n, 73
Old learning   62
Old Man from Changle (name for Feng Dao)   83
'Old Man History'   37
'On Authority'   110n
'On Coalition Government'   143n
On Contradiction   27, 28, 95, 173, 174, 178, 180, 185, 187n
'On Investigation Work'   251n
'On New Democracy'   96, 223n, 241, 242, 242n, 243
On Practice   27, 28, 95, 172, 173, 174, 174n, 175n, 176, 176n, 177, 177n, 177, 177n
'On Proletarian Culture'   199
'On Protracted War'   241
'On Proudhon [Letter to J.B. Schweitzer]'   192
On Tactics Against Japanese Imperialism   94, 122, 122n, 126n, 141, 141n
On the Party   99, 167
'On the People's Democratic Dictatorship'   62, 62n, 144, 144n, 146, 246
'On the Question of the National Bourgeoisie and the Enlightened Gentry'   144n
On the Role of the Individual in History   50
'One divides into two'   166, 166n
Opium War   62
Opportunism   92, 104, 154, 159, 171, 179, 180, 181, 190, 191, 193
'Oppose Stereotyped Party Writing'   96
Opposition   32, 152, 323
Organisation   111
Oriental Book Company, Shanghai   33
Origin of Species   69
Original Vows of Bodhisattva Ksitigarbha's Sutra   229n
Other, the   191
'Our Economic Policy'   237n, 239n
Our Study and The Current Situation   123n
Ouyang Xiu   83

Pacific War   6
Pan Huilian   11n
Pantsov, Alexander V.   21n

Paper tigers   101
Paris   9, 69n
Paris Commune   104, 112
Parliamentary tactics   129
Parochialism   160
Party of the working class   160, 163
Party literature   194, 195
'Party Organisation and Party Literature'   194, 195n, 197, 198n, 204, 205
Parvus, Alexander Lvovich (born Israel Lazarovich Gelfand)   196
'Pay Attention To Economic Work'   235n, 238n
Pearl River Delta   7
Peasant armed struggle   155
Peasant armies   103
Peasant base   192
Peasant existence   160
Peasant revolts   170, 171, 228
Peasant wars   159, 282
'Peasant War in China and the Proletariat'   280
Peasantry   102, 144, 159, 160, 161, 168, 239, 281, 282
Peking University   3, 31, 218
Pen and sword   157, 175, 228
Peng Shuzhi [Peng Shu-tse]   6, 7, 9, 12, 16, 18n, 22, 22n, 23, 34, 35, 36, 37, 280, 280n
People, the   144
People's army   144
People's Communes   44, 65
People's Daily   144n
People's democratic dictatorship   145, 146, 147, 148, 184n
People's democratic revolution   144, 184
People's government   148
People's interests   144
People's Liberation Army   6, 121
People's livelihood, democracy and national rights   161
People's police   144
People's Republic   138n, 146, 148
People's Republic of China (PRC)   13, 36, 146, 148, 290
People's state   147
People's state apparatus   144
Perceptual experience   174
Perceptual knowledge   175
Perceptual stage of cognition   174
Permanent revolution   35, 129, 129n, 131, 132, 144, 145, 147, 148, 168, 183, 184, 242
Person of action   175, 178, 186, 193
Personalisation of power   64
Personality cult   51, 52, 53, 56, 58, 59, 60, 63, 64, 65, 97, 98, 99
Peter the Great   273
Petrograd   115
Petrograd Soviet   66
Petrov (pseudonym of Fyodor Fyodorovich Raskol'nikov or Fyodor Ilyin)   152
Petty bourgeois, petty-bourgeois   192, 209, 227, 241
Petty bourgeoisie   170, 191, 281
Philistinism   213
Philosophical basis   185
Philosophical Notebooks   172, 178, 191
Philosophy   172, 185
Pingzhuan   19
Plato   32, 190
Plekhanov, Georgi Valentinovich   33, 50, 51, 51n, 130, 173, 173n
Plenum of the Executive Committee of the Communist International (ECCI)   153
Plutarch   54
Poland   287
Polish Social Democratic movement   87
Politburo   90, 91n
'Political Report of the Central Committee of the Communist Party of China to the Eighth National Congress of the Communist Party of China'   145n, 146n
'Political Report of the Central Committee of the CPSU(B)'   155, 155n
Political Science Group   108
Political tutelage   166
'Poor, blank' country   143, 246
Popular Front   94, 95, 122, 168, 241
Popular rebellions   228
Popularisation   225
Populism   66
Portuguese   8
Positive   191
Poznan workers' uprising   98
Practice   138, 173, 175
'Practice, knowledge, again practice, and again knowledge'   178
Practice as the criterion of truth   174

Pragmatic 242
Pravda 127n, 153, 202
'Preface to *Rural Surveys*' 251n
'Preliminary Draft Theses on the National and Colonial Questions' 248n
Preobrazhensky, Yevgeny Alekseyevich 33, 84
Primitive accumulation 230
Primitive communism 234
Principal and central contradiction 190
Principal aspect of a contradiction 186, 189
Principal contradiction 186, 187, 188
Principle of Democracy 270
Principle of Nationalism 270
Principle of People's Livelihood 76, 270
Prisoner of war (POW) 126
Private capitalism 149
Private ownership 143, 159, 239
'Problems of Strategy in China's Revolutionary War' 64, 93, 94n, 101, 116n, 241
'Problems of Strategy in Guerrilla War against Japan' 241
'Problems of War and Strategy' 107n, 109n, 114n, 151n
Professional revolutionaries 163
Progressive Party 108
Proletarian 103, 167
'Proletarian art' 199
Proletarian art and culture 202
Proletarian dictatorship 131, 142, 146, 147, 148, 148n, 149, 199, 200
Proletarian ideology 96, 217
Proletarian intelligentsia 200
Proletarian leadership 132, 134, 144, 149, 159
Proletarian leadership 239
'Proletarian literature' 200
Proletarian literature and art 199
Proletarian party 281
Proletarian revolution 66, 229
Proletarian self-reliance 243
'Proletarian writers' 202
Proletarian-socialist 133, 139, 146, 148
Proletariat 105, 111, 140, 142, 147, 148, 159, 160, 171, 208, 243
Proletcult 202, 203
Propaganda 88, 103, 111, 221
Proudhon, Pierre-Joseph 50, 191, 192, 192n
Provincial Committees 233

Provisional Goverment 183
Puritan Revolution 207
Puritanism 56
Putschism 154, 159
Putschist 64, 155
Putting Mr Zhang's hat on Mr Li's head (false attribution) 178

Qi (name of state) 115, 266
Qianshao yuekan 11n
Qin dynasty 78n, 81, 115, 228n, 229n
Qin Bangxian 87, 88n, 89, 97
Qin Shi Huangdi (Emperor of Qin) 78, 78n, 226, 228n, 229n
Qing dynasty 10, 62n, 67n, 68n, 72n, 74n, 107n, 108, 120n, 122n, 289
Qu Qiubai 88, 90
Qu Qiubai line 87, 87n
Qu Shengbai 70, 70n
Quixote, Don 190

Radek, Karl Berngardovich 87n
Radical democrat 216
Radishchev, Alexander, Nikolayevich 273, 273n
Rational cognition 174, 191
Rational knowledge 175
Raumer, Friedrich Georg von 192
Reactionary armies 153
Realism 201, 221, 222n
Record of Rites 77
Rectification movement 92n, 96, 97
Red areas 232, 236
Red Army 115
'Red compradors' 93n, 289
Red Guards 233
Red political power 102, 103, 110, 137
Reform Movement of 1898 67n, 72n
'Rectify the Party's Style of Work' 96
'Reform Our Study' 96, 251
'Regional socialism' 237
Relations of production 210
Relationship of knowing to doing 174
Ren (benevolence) 76, 79
Renwu zhuan 20
'Reply to Xu Maoyong on the Question of the United Front' 219n
Representative assemblies 152
Republic of China 2, 62n

Resolution of CC AUCP(b), 'On the *Resolution on Certain Questions in the History of Our Party* (April 1945)' 90, 97, 123n
Restoration 147
'Reunification' 121, 121n
Revolt against The Tang 67
Revolutionary Communist Party of China (RCP) 7
Revolutionary war 64
Revolution 104, 113, 124, 134, 201
'Revolution at gunpoint' theory 153
'Revolution and War in China' 132
Revolution of 1905 130
Revolution of 1911 108
Revolution of 1925–27 132
Revolutionary 65, 124, 147
Revolutionary armed forces 152, 156
Revolutionary army 151, 152, 238
Revolutionary art 201
Revolutionary classes 230
'Revolutionary defeatism' 35
'Revolutionary defencism' 35
Revolutionary censorship 207
Revolutionary dictatorship 64, 148
Revolutionary leaders 230
Revolutionary literature and art 200, 207
Revolutionary methods 185
Revolutionary movement 176, 178
Revolutionary party 111, 160, 189, 190, 207n
Revolutionary practice 114, 176
Revolutionary regime 238
Revolutionary shop sign 153
Revolutionary stages 148
Revolutionary strategist 149
Revolutionary strategy 129, 130, 147, 150
Revolutionary struggle 65, 109, 166
Revolutionary tasks 185
Revolutionary theory 178
Revolutionary tide 103
Revolutionary transition 147
'Revolutionary utilitarianism' 220
'Revolutionary victoryism' 36
Revolutionary war 102, 107, 111, 113, 117
Rich peasants 142
Rich-peasant economy 241
'Rich peasant line' 90
Right opportunism 90, 235
Righteousness, cardinal principles of 78, 79
Rightist 89, 94, 95

Rites 79
Road to socialism 14
Robin Hood 23
Romance of the Three Kingdoms 68
Romanov dynasty 273
Romanticism 221, 222n, 227
Rome 7, 125
Ronglu 120, 120n
Rossiyskaya Gazeta (Russian Gazette) 196
Rousset, Pierre 9
Rousseau, Jean-Jacques 69
Ru (Confucianism; Confucian scholars) 81, 82
Ru general 120
Ruijin 103
Rules and Administrative Regulations of the International Workingmen's Association 160
Ruling class 167
Rural and urban bourgeoisie 136
Russell, Bertrand 32
Russia 23, 58, 66, 69, 104, 105, 110, 111, 115, 123, 125, 126, 130, 132, 141, 147, 165, 176, 194, 203, 206n, 224, 240, 249
Russian 115, 212
Russian bourgeoisie 130
Russian capitalism 130
Russian Civil War 84n
Russian Communist Party 109, 113
Russian economists 163
Russian Marxism 66, 86, 130
Russian proletariat 131
Russian rhetoric 199
Russian Revolution 59, 72, 130, 131, 145, 183, 248, 291
Russian Social Democracy 51, 58
Russian Social Democratic Labour Party 58

San Yuan, pseudonym of Wang Fanxi 21, 291n
Sanguo yanyi (Romance of the Three Kingdoms) 63n, 68, 115
Sansculottism 55, 56
Satan 53
Sceptical 190
Schram, Stuart Reynolds 129n, 142n
Schwartz, Benjamin 16n
Schemer 138
Sealed train 125, 126

INDEX 321

Second International 129, 164, 187
Second Session of the Eighth Congress 252
Second United Front [1937–45] 95, 121n, 123
Second World War 184, 188, 199, 285
Self-reliance 240, 242, 245, 247
Semi-colonial 186, 187
Semi-feudal 62, 111, 187
Separability and inseparability 165
Separating 167
Serge, Victor, (Victor Lvovich Kibalchich) 202
Seven Military Classics 120, 120n
Seventh Congress of the CCP, 1945 61, 89, 94, 97
Semi-colonial 35, 106, 110, 117, 120, 143, 188
Semi-feudal 62, 106, 110, 111, 143
'Send Away the God of Plague' 225
Separability and inseparability 166
Separation 168
Serge, Victor 6
Seventh Congress of CCP, 1945 89
Shaanbei 61
Shaanxi 92, 247, 117, 237, 244
Shaanxi-Gansu (Shensi-Kansu) 94
Shaanxi-Gansu-Ningxia border area 245
Shanghai 1, 5, 6, 7, 88, 90n, 103, 153, 151, 243n
Shanghai International Settlement 33
Shen Yinmou 225, 225n
Shengci (temple to the living) 59
Shi Dakai 226, 226n, 228
Shi Nai'an 63, 63n
Shi Dongxiang 145, 146n, 147, 148, 149
Shuang Shan, pseudonym of Wang Fanxi 17, 18n, 19n, 36n, 43, 43n
Shengshi weiyan (Warnings in the Golden Age) 68
Shi (literati, members of the scholarly elite) 78, 82n
Shuihu zhuan (also known as *The Water Margin*) 63n, 67, 81, 83, 83n, 115, 157
Silone, Ignazio 220
Sima Guang 63, 63n, 68n
Sima Niu 79
Sima Qian 78, 82, 83
Sincere Press (Xinda chuban she) 14, 43
Sino-Japanese War 84, 117, 120, 169, 188
Sino-Soviet relations 21, 247

Sino-Soviet split 22, 30, 43
Six Arts 77
Sixteen-character formula 116, 117
Sixteenth Congress of the All-Union Communist Party (Bolsheviks) (June 1930) 155, 156
Sixth Army (Nationalist) 137
Sixth Congress of the CCP (July 1928) 88, 102, 135
Sixth Plenum of the Sixth Congress of the CCP, 1938 95, 105
Skin-hair metaphor 160, 161, 162
Slavophiles 130
Smith, Adam 69
Snow, Edgar 16, 16n, 32, 67, 68, 69n, 94
Social and economic self-reliance 248
Social-democratic 28, 129, 162, 194, 195, 197
Social-democratic consciousness 162
Social-Democratic Party 195, 204
Social-democratic tactics 129
Social-patriots 188
Social-traitors 187
Social revolution 161
Social system 164
Socialism 79, 109, 141, 147, 160, 239
Socialism in one country 168, 237, 245, 247, 248, 249, 250
Socialist 145, 148, 167
Socialist agenda 136
Socialist agriculture 252
Socialist construction 131, 239, 247, 252
Socialist culture 20
Socialist economy 239
Socialist literature and art 206
Socialist measures 147
Socialist movement 161, 166
Socialist organisation 165
Socialist party 161, 164, 166, 176, 177
Socialist programme 161
Socialist platform 159
Socialist realism 96, 204, 206, 214, 220, 221, 222n
Socialist republic 140
Socialist revolution 130, 135, 136, 142, 143, 147, 149, 180, 229, 239
Socialist society 143, 200
Socialist tasks 146, 147
Socialist theory 162
Socialist thought 164

Soldiers, workers and peasants' soviets   152
Socialist world   248
Song-and-dance ensemble/troupe   207, 225
Song dynasty   62, 63n, 79, 81, 83, 157, 228
Song Jiang   157, 157n
'Song of the Gaixia'   224
'Song of the Great Wind'   224
Song Taizu (Emperor)   228, 228n
Sophistic   190
Sophistry   192, 193
Soviet   21, 22, 34, 89, 98, 115, 120, 121, 121n, 122, 132, 137, 143, 196, 239, 240
Soviet factionalism   5
Soviet literary historians   203
Soviet Opposition   4
Soviet Union   6, 215
'Soviet and Red Army' period   282
Soviet government   206
Soviet slogan   169
Soviets vs national assembly   168
Soviet Communist Party (Communist Party of the Soviet Union)   98
Soviet Congress   89
Soviet dispute on strategy in China   133
Soviet economy   248
Soviet Federative Socialist Republic   248
Soviet government   155
Soviet Opposition   133
Soviet Socialist Republics   248
Soviet Union   21, 24, 31, 36, 58, 89, 91, 115, 192, 202, 206, 206n, 240, 243, 246n, 250, 285
Soviets of workers' and peasants' deputies   154
Soviet Writers' Association   204, 206
Sovkhoz   60
St. Petersburg   196, 197
St. Petersburg Soviet   196, 197
'Speech on Affiliation to the British Labour Party'   283n
Spinoza, Baruch   69
Spiritual civilisation   120
Spring and Autumn Annals   77
Stages   141
Stalin's works   240
Stalinised   218
Stalinism, pp   288, 291
Stalinist   224

'Stalinist Mao'   168
Standing Committee   32, 91n
'State capitalism'   199n, 281
State apparatus   200
State sector   143, 239
State power   146, 147, 148, 149
State and Revolution   58, 172
'Stereotyped party writing'   96
Stockholm   197
Strategic   150, 156
Strategies and tactics   120, 121
Strategist   110, 114, 137, 138, 147, 166, 171, 175, 180, 186, 193, 250
Strategy   140, 156, 166, 168
Struggle   166n
'Struggle in the Jinggang Mountains'   102, 137n, 170n
Struggle for democracy   169
Struggle for socialism   130
'Struggle to Win the Masses in Their Millions for the Anti-Japanese National United Front'   138n, 141, 142n
Student Federation Council   71
Style, behaviour, policies   164
Style, thought, behaviour   165
Su Shi (Su Dongpo)   63, 63n, 224
Subjective idealism   179
Subjective initiative   240, 252
Subjective schemes   239
Subjectivist   96
Sublation [*yangqi*]   191, 191n
Substance and shadow   164
Suichuan   232, 234
Sun Chuanfang   153
Sun Quan   115
Sun Wu (Sunzi)   25, 112, 115, 116, 117, 119, 120, 121, 158
Sun Yat-sen   18, 62, 62n, 67, 67n, 75, 76, 83, 107, 121n, 157, 223, 241
Sun Yat-sen University   87, 87n
Sun Yatsenism   282
Sun Zhongshan (alternative name for Sun Yat-sen)   62
Superstructure and substructure (base)   210
'Supra-class'   193, 198, 229
Suvorov, Alexander Vasilyevich   273
Suzhou   11
Syndicalism   162
System of Logic   69

INDEX 323

Tactics 125, 153, 186
Tactician 110, 114, 150, 175, 179, 186, 189, 193
Tailism 141, 161
Taiping Revolution 10, 226n
Taiwan 8, 11
'Talks at the Yenan Forum on Literature and Art' 204n, 208n, 209, 209n, 218n, 227n
Tan Pingshan 133
Tan Sitong 62, 67, 67n, 69, 70, 72, 72n, 74, 76, 83
Tang dynasty 30, 72n, 81, 228
Tang Taizong (Emperor) 228, 228n
Tang Zong (Emperor Xuanzong) 226, 226n
Tangram 248
Taoism 179
Taoist 81
Temple 158, 158n
Ten Commandments 173
Ten counter-commandments 214
Ten Principles 117
'The Causes of the Victory of the CCP Over Chiang Kai-shek and the CCP's Perspectives' 280n
The Character of the Russian Revolution 130n
The Chinese Revolution and the Communist Party of China 123n, 240
'The Chinese Revolution and the Communist Party of China' 241n
'The Correct Handling of Contradictions Among the People' 98
The Development of the Monist View of History 210, 211n
'The East is Red' 61
The Eighteenth Brumaire of Louis Bonaparte 49
The Husk Wife (*zaokang zhi qi*) 165, 165n
The Lessons of October 130n
The Poverty of Philosophy 192n
'The Present Situation and Our Tasks' 117, 117n, 121n
'The Prospects of the Revolution in China' 151n
'The Question of the Chinese Revolution' 170
'The Role of the Chinese Communist Party in the National War' 223n
'The Romantic and Realism' 222n
The True Story of Ah-Q 277n

'The Situation and Tasks in the Anti-Japanese War After the Fall of Shanghai and Taiyuan' 95
'The Situation and Our Policy After the Victory in the War of Resistance Against Japan' 124
The Socialist Upsurge in China's Countryside 251, 251n
The Spirit of Laws 69
'The Struggle in the Jinggang Mountains' 134, 169, 232, 232n
'The Tasks of Chinese Communist Party of China in the Period of Resistance to Japan' 138n
The Three Sources and Three Component Parts of Marxism 72n
The Wealth of Nations 69
Theorist 175, 180
Theory 138, 175, 177
Theory of contradictions 173
Theory of permanent revolution 147
Theories of the state 172
Theories of transition 142
Thermidor 64, 203
Theses on Feuerbach 172
Third Chinese Revolution 283
Third Civil War 117, 121
Third Encirclement and Suppression campaign (1931) 116
Third International, see under 'Comintern'
Third Period 88, 94, 155, 156, 168, 239
Thirteen Chapters 116, 118, 120
Thirty Years of the Chinese Communist Party 91
'Thinking in Solitude' 17, 277
'This land so rich in beauty' 156
Tiger skin 219, 220
Thought, style and action 167
Three Anti's (1951) 149, 149n
Three antitheses 168
Three Kingdoms period 120, 226
Three People's Principles 127, 132, 241, 270
Three Red Banners 168, 250
Tito, Josip Broz 290
Tongmeng hui (Chinese Revolutionary Alliance) 107, 108
Totalitarian bureaucracy 79
Tolstoy, Lev 205, 211, 213, 214

Town and village, relationship between 157
Trade unions 89, 111, 162
Trade union tactics 129
Traditional culture 222
Transition 143
Transition to socialism 134, 141
Transitional period 200
Treaty of Brest-Litovsk 125
Treaty of Versailles 70
Triple Alliance 188
Trotsky, Lev (Leon) Davidovich 5, 12, 33, 52, 53, 58, 66, 81, 88, 122, 126n, 129, 129n, 130n, 132, 133, 135, 136, 145, 147, 151, 152, 153, 155, 156, 168, 169, 170, 171, 183, 196, 200, 200n, 201n, 202, 202n, 203, 204, 207, 208, 221, 249
Trotskyism 5, 37, 53, 59, 61, 86, 145, 242
'Trotskyist Mao' 168
Tsarism 182
Tsaritsyno 115
Twenty Eight Bolsheviks 87n
Twentieth Congress (of the CPSU) 60, 98, 287
Tu (earth, local) 89, 89n, 91, 97, 180, 222, 224
Tuhao (local tyrants) 233, 234
'Two combine into one' 166
Twitchett, Denis 20n

Unification Conference 5
'Uninterrupted' 129
United Front 95, 95n, 121n, 127
'United Front and Eighth Route Army' period 282
United States 7, 9, 62
United States Military Academy at West Point 120
Universal suffrage 135
Universal truth(s) 222, 223
Urban and rural poor 147
Urban base 163
Urban petty bourgeois 137, 144, 169
Urban revolutionary class 159
Utopian socialists 230

Vanguard 163, 167
Victory 121
Vietnam 7, 7n, 9, 147, 150, 168
Violence 114
Viscount of Ji 79

Viscount of Wei 79
Voroshilov, Kliment Yefremovich 115

Wang Chuanshan 62, 69, 70, 72, 72n, 74
Wang Fanxi 1, 2, 3n, 4, 34, 35, 36n, 37, 37n, 38, 39, 70n, 275
Wang Fenggang 11
Wang Jiaxiang 88, 88n, 94
Wang Jingwei 4, 152, 152n, 154
Wang Mengyou 33
Wang Ming (Chen Shaoyu) 4, 11, 21, 24, 27, 31, 34, 64, 64n, 80, 84, 86, 87, 88, 90, 91, 94, 95, 96, 97, 97n, 98, 104, 117, 122, 138, 142, 172, 172n, 219, 219n, 289
Wang Ming faction 172, 235
Wang Ming line 90, 94, 96
Wang Mingites 283
Wang Wenyuan, original name of Wang Fanxi 2
Wang Shiwei 3, 14, 214, 214n, 215, 218, 220
Wang Yanqi 11
Wang Xizhe 15, 15n
Wang Yuping 11
Wangite(s) 89, 90, 94, 95, 174
Wannan (New Fourth Army Incident) (January 1941) 121, 121n, 219
War communism 199
War of Agrarian Revolution 106
War of Resistance to Japanese Aggression 30, 93, 106, 108, 231
Warlord 120, 134
Warlord taxes 171
Warring States period 68n
Wayaobao 94, 133
Waterloo 115
'We Must Learn To Do Economic Work' 245, 245n
Wei Wu (Emperor Wu of Wei) 226, 226n
Weimar 213
Wen (civility, culture) 83, 83n
Wenshi ziliao 20
Wenxue (literature) 194
West, the 130
West Point, see United States Military Academy
Western Europe 248
Western sages 150
Western European labour movement 104
Western working class 114

Western learning   76, 83
What Is To Be Done?   56, 58, 162, 176
White areas   232, 233, 236
White terror   163
Wholesale westernisation   120, 223
'Why is it That Red Political Power Can Exist in China?'   134, 231, 232n
Words and deeds   193
Workers   145
Workers' consciousness   127
Workers' interests   167
Workers' party   167
Workers, peasants and soldiers   235
Workers' political programme   160
Working class   144, 167, 282
Working-class consciousness   162
Working-class struggle   171
Working people   248
World communist movement   98
World proletarian movement   216n
World proletarian-socialist revolution   139
World revolution   117, 128, 147, 249
World socialist movement   176, 191
Wu (martial)   83, 83n
Wuchang (impermanent)   81
Wu Cheng'en   68n
Wu Guang   228, 228n
Wu Guoguang   97n
Wuhan   4, 94, 154, 157

Xi You Ji (Journey to the West)   68, 68n, 81
Xia (knight, swordsman)   82
Xi'an   80, 92
Xi'an Incident   80n
Xiang Ying   95, 219
Xiang Yu   229, 229n
Xiangxiang   68
Xiangxiang Middle School   68
Xianyang   229
Xiashi, town in Haining county   2
Xin (name of dynasty)   115
Xin Qiji   63, 63n, 224, 224n
Xin Qingnian (New Youth)   70, 71
Xinda chuban she ('Sincere Press')   14
Xinmiao chuban she   14n
Xinmin congbao (New Citizen)   68, 68n
Xinmin Society   70
Xiucai (imperial examination graduate)   83, 83n, 157

Xu Maoyong   219
Xuanzang   68
Xu Zhixing   289
Xue Feng   13n

Yan (name of state)   266, 266n
Yan Fu   62, 62n, 76
Yan Ziling   228
Yan Yuan   79
Yan'an   24, 84, 94, 109, 137, 216, 218, 224, 237n
Yan'an Forum on Literature and Art   206, 214n
Yan'an Talks   207, 215, 225n, 227
Yang (ocean, foreign)   89, 89n, 91, 97, 180
Yang Changji, also known as Bancang or Huaizhong   61, 63, 69, 72, 242
Yang Hucheng   80
Yang, Kevin (Yang Yang)   12n, 15n
Yang Xianzhen   166n
Yangtze River   134, 168
Yao, Shun, Yu, Tang, Wen, Wu   270, 270n
Ye Mingchen   120n
Ye Nairen (Ye Ying)   11
Ye Sen   11
Yellow River   228
Yi (righteousness)   54
Yongxin   232
Youxia (wandering swordsmen, knights errant)   23, 24, 72, 81, 83, 85, 156, 227
Yuan dynasty   228
Yuan Shao   115
Yuan Shikai   108, 266, 266n
Yue Fei zhuan (Biography of Yue Fei)   67
Yue Yi   266, 266n
Yupi zizhi tongjian ('Comprehensive Mirror for Aid in Government')   68, 68n
Yugoslavia   287
Yusi (Threads of Talk) magazine   3

Zang Kejia   225, 225n
Zawen (satirical essay)   218, 218n
Zeng Wenzheng (another name for Zeng Guofan)   266, 266n
Zhang Guotao   19, 20n, 92, 92n, 95, 96, 108
Zhang Xueliang   80n
Zhang Zhidong   62n, 289
Zhang Zuolin   153
Zhdanov, Andrei Aleksandrovich   199, 199n, 203, 203n, 204

Zhejiang   2
Zheng Chaolin   6, 8, 9, 12, 13, 14, 23, 31, 33, 34n, 884, 281, 290
Zheng Guanying   68, 68n
Zhong Gong   79
Zhou Enlai   5, 89, 89n, 90, 94, 243n
Zhou Gong (Duke Zhou)   266, 266n
Zhou Yang   219, 220, 222
Zhou Zuoren   3, 3n, 150, 150n
Zhu De   94, 114
Zhuge Liang   266, 266n
Zhu Jia   83
Zhu Xi   68n, 72, 72n, 79, 242
Zhu Zheng   14n
Zhuangzi   164, 164n
Zizhi tongjian ('Comprehensive Mirror for Aid in Government')   63, 63n, 68n, 69n, 115n
Zinoviev, Grigori Yevseyevich   52, 53, 86, 182
Zola, Émile   212
Zunyi Conference   90, 91, 94, 172, 172n
Zuozhuan ('Zuo's Commentary')   115, 115n

www.ingramcontent.com/pod-product-compliance
Lightning Source LLC
Chambersburg PA
CBHW071332080526
44587CB00017B/2815